BUTCHE

David Loyn has been a foreig
twenty-five years, and was the
Taliban when they took Kabul in 1996. He has covered
conflicts on three continents, and won major awards for both
TV and radio reporting, including 'Journalist of the Year' in
the Royal Television Society Awards in 1999. His first book,
Frontline, was shortlisted for the Orwell Prize.

Praise for *Butcher & Bolt*

'David Loyn is a distinguished foreign correspondent who knows Afghani-
stan intimately. His book offers an admirable historical summary . . .
It would be naïve to suggest that the odds favour success [in Afghanistan].
Loyn's excellent primer explains why, and should be slipped into Barack
Obama's Christmas stocking' Max Hastings, *Sunday Times*

'I could not have enjoyed it more and think it quite excellent. It is a great
pity some of those who involved us in what is going on now did not
understand what we would be up against' General Lord Guthrie, Head of
Britain's armed forces when the Afghan war was launched in 2001

'Excellent' Ben Macintyre, *The Times*

'I would recommend this book to anyone who wants a well-rounded, no-
nonsense overview of Afghanistan. A brilliant read' *Soldier*

'A loving and closely woven account of this troubled country' Jonathan
Steele, *Guardian*

'Brilliant . . . A must-read for every politician who sends our squaddies
into Afghanistan – but one based fairly and squarely on the weight of
history' John Sweeney, *New Statesman*

'David Loyn has offered a salutary overview of blunder and barbarism in
foreign interventions' Kim Sengupta, *Independent*

'This is a terrific reminder of how effective a book can be when the place
it depicts is beyond the average traveller's reach' *Irish Times*

'Splendid . . . A very honest, very balanced and very depressing account of
a series of disastrous entanglements over the past 200 years' Anatol
Lieven, *BBC History Magazine*

Also by David Loyn

*Frontline: The True Story of the British Mavericks
Who Changed the Face of War Reporting*

BUTCHER & BOLT

David Loyn

✤ WINDMILL BOOKS

Published by Windmill Books 2009

4 6 8 10 9 7 5 3

First published in Great Britain in 2008 by Hutchinson

Windmill Books
The Random House Group Limited
20 Vauxhall Bridge Road, London, SW1V 2SA

Addresses for companies within The Random House Group Limited
can be found at: www.randomhouse.co.uk/offices.htm

The Random House Group Limited Reg. No. 954009

www.rbooks.co.uk

A CIP catalogue record for this book
is available from the British Library

ISBN 9780099522638

The Random House Group Limited supports The Forest Stewardship
Council (FSC), the leading international forest certification organisation. All our
titles that are printed on Greenpeace approved FSC certified paper carry the
FSC logo. Our paper procurement policy can be found at:
www.rbooks.co.uk/environment

Typeset by SX Composing DTP, Rayleigh, Essex
Printed and bound in Great Britain by
CPI Bookmarque Ltd, Croydon, CR0 4TD

Dedicated to the memory of H.E. Zahir Shah
the last king of Afghanistan

who ruled a united country
with no conflict for longer than any other leader

Contents

Maps

All maps apart from Lieutenant Macartney's by Alex Maxwell

Illustrations

Section One

17. Maiwand, 1880: *Saving the Guns*, 1882, Richard Caton II Woodville (Walker Art Gallery, National Museums Liverpool/Bridgeman Art Library)
18. Sir Henry Mortimer Durand
19. Abdur Rahman
20. Ghazi warriors
21. Two armed Afghan tribesmen in traditional clothing during the Second Afghan War (Capt. John Burke/Getty Images)

Section Two

22. Bridge of Boats over Indus at Attock, 1863
23. Planes bomb Emir's fort, 1919 (Mary Evans Picture Library)
24. Queen Soraya, 1928
25. Amir Habibullah with his harem, *c.* 1905
26. Soviet army armoured personnel carrier on patrol in Kabul, 1980 (AP-Photo)
27. Afghan students studying computing technology at the Polytechnical Institute in Kabul (AFP/Getty Images)
28. Gulbuddin Hekmatyar, 15th March 1994, in Charasiab, Afghanistan (Robert Nickelsberg/Liaison/Getty Images)
29. Ahmed Shah Massud (Jens Palme)
30. Former Senator Charlie Wilson from Texas (Photo courtesy of Charlie Wilson)
31. Afghan horseman against the blue backdrop of the mountains (Estate of Rory Peck)
32. Afghan guerrillas atop a downed Soviet MI-24 helicopter gunship, 1981 (AP Photo)
33. Soviet troops leaving Afghanistan, 16th May 1988 (AP Photo/Liu Heung Shing)
34. TV grab taken secretly by BBC *Newsnight* shows Taliban's spiritual leader Mullah Mohammed Omar in 1996 (AFP/Getty Images)
35. Taliban fighters in Musa Qala, 2007 (Photo by Aziz Ahmad Tassal, Institute for War & Peace Reporting)
36. US Army soldiers of the 10th Mountain Division and a Canadian Army officer in Afghanistan (Robert Nickelsberg/Getty Images)
37. US President George W. Bush with Afghan President Hamid Karzai, 1st March 2006 (MANDEL NGAN/AFP/Getty Images)
38. Royal Marine Commandos in Helmand Province, Southern Afghanistan, early 2007 (LA(Phot) Gaz Faulkner © Crown Copyright 2007)
39. Prime Minister Tony Blair meets British troops at Camp Bastion in Helmand Province, Afghanistan, 20th November 2006 (Stefan Rousseau/PA)

Characters *in* Butcher and Bolt

Afghans (listed with first names in alphabetical order for clarity)

ABDUL RASHID DOSTAM   Uzbek militia leader who emerged as head of the north of Afghanistan, and remained loyal to communist side until 1992; made and broke many alliances with mujahidin leaders; ousted by Taliban 1997; re-emerged after 2001, but never again in undisputed control of north.

ABDUL RASUL SAYYAF   Cairo-educated Wahhabi fundamentalist; commander of mujahidin group in 1980s financed almost exclusively by Saudi Arabia; prominent member of post-2001 parliament.

ABDUR RAHMAN   'the iron amir'; grandson of Dost Mohammed; Barakzai dynasty; lost five-year civil war after death of Dost in 1863 and fled north to Russian-controlled territory; returned to Kabul and installed as amir by British in July 1880; united Afghanistan for first time in a century; agreed Durand line as border with British India 1893; stirred up frontier tribes to fight jihad against British control; died in 1901.

AHMED SHAH DURRANI   first amir of united Afghanistan, known as 'father of the nation'; founder of Sadozai dynasty; died 1772.

AHMED SHAH MASSUD   mujahidin commander nicknamed 'Lion of Panjshir'; trained as guerrilla by Pakistan, and led first uprising against reformist government in Afghanistan in 1975 (four years before Soviet invasion); successfully blocked seven Soviet attempts to take the Panjshir valley; defence minister in post-Soviet government in 1992; lost

Kabul to the Taliban 1996; killed by bomb in TV camera two days before attacks of 9/11.

AKBAR KHAN   son of Dost Mohammed; Barakzai dynasty; killed Macnaghten in 1841 and presided over slaughter of retreating army; defeated by Sale who broke out of Jalalabad siege in 1842; appointed wazir when Dost returned to power in 1843; died (possibly poisoned) in 1845, aged 29.

AMANULLAH   reformist amir who succeeded his father Habibullah in 1919; lost war against Britain, but succeeded in winning full Afghan independence; embarked on radical programme including rights for women; ousted in violent uprising against reforms in 1929.

BACHA SAQAO   Tajik warlord who seized power in Kabul amid chaos following uprising of 1929; name means son of a water carrier; executed when order restored in same year.

BABRAK KARMAL   communist leader of Afghanistan installed by Soviet invasion in December 1979; ousted when Gorbachev took over in Moscow in 1985.

BORJAN   *nom de guerre* of veteran of mujahidin war against Soviet control who was first military commander of Taliban; died in battle for Kabul September 1996.

BURHANUDDIN RABBANI   Cairo-educated professor who led Islamist underground movement in early '70s; fled to Pakistan when President Daoud moved against fundamentalists; remained on Pakistani side of frontier during war against Soviet invasion as head of Hezb-i-Islami, one of main groups fighting against Soviet forces; was briefly president in post-soviet chaos.

DAOUD   Afghanistan's first president; abolished monarchy in 1973 when he led bloodless coup against his cousin Zahir Shah; attempted reforms, but killed with many of his family members in Saur revolution of 1978.

DOST MOHAMMED   'the great amir'; Barakzai dynasty; took power in 1826 after fighting his way to the top of large family of competing brothers; forced out by British invasion 1839; returned to power in 1843; ruled until death in 1863.

GHULAM HAIDER   commander of Abdur Rahman's army in the 1890s; played key role in fomenting insurrection against Britain on the frontier.

GULBUDDIN HEKMATYAR   mujahidin commander who began as Islamist student leader; fled to Pakistan in early 1970s after crackdown by Afghan government; trained as guerrilla by Pakistan; received largest share of US funding to defeat Soviet invasion of Afghanistan; in 2006 announced he was now fighting US under al-qaeda banner.

HABIBULLAH   amir who succeeded his father Abdur Rahman in 1901; assassinated 1919.

HAFIZULLAH AMIN   briefly leader of Afghanistan after murdering Nur Mohammed Taraki in September 1979 to seize power for his faction of communist party; desire for better relations with Western countries and Pakistan provoked Soviet opposition; killed in Soviet invasion in December 1979.

ISMAIL KHAN   Afghan army captain involved in uprising against communist control in Herat ten months before the Soviet invasion in 1979; became leader of mujahidin in the west; governor of Herat from 1992 until forced out by Taliban attack in 1995; reappointed governor 2001, but removed by President Karzai after fighting in 2004, and appointed minister of energy.

JABAR KHAN   brother of Dost Mohammed; Barakzai dynasty.

KAMRAN SHAH   British-backed ruler of Herat from 1818; Sadozai dynasty; lazy, oppressive and fond of sadistic punishment; killed by his wazir in 1842.

MAHMUD TARZI   intellectual whose magazine inspired Amanullah's radical reforms in 1920s; became foreign minister.

MULLAH MUSHK-I-ALAM   leader of uprising against British control of Kabul in 1879.

MULLAH OF HADDAH   known as 'the Light of Islam'; Afghan mullah who backed 1897 uprising on the frontier against British control.

MULLAH OMAR mujahidin commander who became founding leader of the Taliban in 1994; head of Taliban government 1996–2001; Taliban fighters still said he was leader in 2008, although in hiding.

NADIR SHAH general who took power after chaos of 1929 uprising; heir of Musahiban branch of Barakzai dynasty.

NAJIBULLAH communist leader of Afghanistan installed by Gorbachev in 1985; had been head of Khad secret police; remained in office after Soviet troops withdrew in 1989; forced out by mujahidin in 1992, and held in safe confinement at UN compound; tortured and murdered with his brother in 1996 when Taliban took Kabul.

MULLAH RABBANI founding member of Taliban; governor of Kabul after Taliban seizure of the city in 1996; no relation of the other Rabbani who became President.

MULLAH RAZZAQ founding member of Taliban; governor of Herat after Taliban seizure of the city in 1995.

NUR MOHAMMED TARAKI seized power in communist Saur Revolution in 1978; provoked opposition by introducing radical land reforms and rights for women; murdered in palace September 1979.

SHAH SHUJA the 'unlucky amir'; Sadozai dynasty; ruled in Kabul 1803–9; reinstalled with British support in war of 1839; killed by mob 1842.

SHIR ALI son of Dost Mohammed; Barakzai dynasty; became amir in 1868 after civil war that followed death of Dost Mohammed in 1863; attempted treaty with Russia led to British invasion 1878; fled to north and died soon afterwards.

SHIR ALI no relation of the amir of the same name; Sadozai dynasty; installed as wali of Kandahar in short-lived British attempt to keep some of country out of hands of Abdur Rahman in 1880; fled soon afterwards to British pension in Karachi.

SIBGHATULLAH MUJADDIDI Islamic scholar; leader of one of the smaller mujahidin groups during Soviet war; respected as the only survivor of a clan with role as kingmaker in Afghan history; appointed speaker of the upper house in first elected parliament after the fall of the Taliban.

YAKUB KHAN   amir after his father Shir Ali fled in November 1878; Barakzai dynasty; negotiated Treaty of Gandamack with British, but did nothing to stop slaughter of British mission to Kabul in September 1879; abdicated and went into exile in India.

ZAHIR SHAH   took power in 1933, aged 19, when his father Nadir Shah was shot; heir of Musahiban branch of Barakzai dynasty; ousted by his cousin Daoud in 1973 while in Rome; returned to Afghanistan after fall of Taliban; died in Kabul in 2007.

ZAMAN SHAH   amir who emerged after bloodbath following death of Timur Shah in 1793; Sadozai dynasty; lost power after rivalry with Barakzai clan; blinded and sent into exile in India in 1800.

Non-Afghans

JAMES ABBOTT   political officer whose mission to release slaves in Khiva in 1840 unnerved Russia; one of Henry Lawrence's 'young men'; became administrator of Hazara, large northern frontier region between Kashmir and Indus River; town of Abbottabad named after him.

LORD AUCKLAND   governor-general responsible for ordering British invasion in 1839.

SHEIKH ABDULLAH AZZAM   wrote *In Defence of Muslim Lands*, the book that inspired Osama bin Laden to take up jihad.

BENAZIR BHUTTO   prime minister of Pakistan 1988–1990, 1993–1996; assassinated 27th December 2007 running for office in first Pakistani election to be held since 1999.

GENERAL SIR BINDON BLOOD   commanded Malakand field force that put down 1897 uprising.

DR WILLIAM BRYDON   famous as the 'only survivor' of retreat from Kabul in January 1842; also survived siege of Lucknow during the 1857 Mutiny; died in bed in Scotland in 1873.

SIR ALEXANDER BURNES adventurer who became British envoy to Kabul; first book of travels to Central Asia was best-seller in 1830s; failed in attempt to secure deal with Dost Mohammed in 1837; became deputy head of British mission to Kabul after Shah Shuja was put on the throne in 1839; killed by mob in December 1841.

WILLIAM CASEY director of the CIA during 1980s war against Soviet control of Afghanistan.

LIEUT COL SIR PIERRE LOUIS-NAPOLEON CAVAGNARI frontier political officer who headed mission to Kabul in 1879; killed by mob two months after his arrival.

ROBERT CECIL Tory MP who campaigned for Afghan mujahidin cause in 1980s; managed huge flow of aid funds; became Marquess of Salisbury; descendant of the Marquess of Salisbury, who, as the prime minister in 1899, detected 'an impulse stirring' in the Islamic world to restore a time 'when they were victors in every part of the world'.

BRIGADIER NEVILLE CHAMBERLAIN 'most-wounded' soldier in the British army; part of the Army of Retribution in 1842; commanded force in tough campaign against Hindustani fanatics in 1863 in Ambeyla; attempt to move down Khyber Pass in 1879 would lead to Second Anglo-Afghan War.

ARTHUR CONNOLLY political officer who first coined the term Great Game; made several long trips across the region to gather intelligence; beheaded alongside Stoddart in Bokhara in 1842; brother of John.

JOHN CONNOLLY political officer who remained in Bala Hissar during negotiations in 1841–2; taken prisoner by Afghans; died of fever 1842.

LORD CURZON viceroy 1899–1905; created North-West Frontier Province putting region under direct central control; also partitioned Bengal; won Gold Medal of the Royal Geographical Society for travel to the source of the Oxus.

SIR HAROLD DEANE political officer at Malakand during the uprising of 1897; became first commissioner of North-West Frontier Province when it was established in 1901.

COLONEL (LATER BRIGADIER) WILLIAM DENNIE led 'forlorn hope' under withering gunfire to take Ghazni fort in 1839; died in attempt to break out of Jalalabad siege 1842.

SIR HENRY MORTIMER DURAND foreign secretary of India; negotiated frontier between British India and Afghanistan in 1893 that was named after him; went on to become envoy to Tehran.

LORD ELGIN viceroy at time of 1897 uprising.

LORD ELLENBOROUGH member of Secret Committee of East India Company that drew up frontier policy in late 1820s; became governor-general of India after 1842 Kabul catastrophe; sent in Army of Retribution and took controversial decision to withdraw forces quickly after sacking Kabul; mocked for removing Somnath gates from Afghanistan that he believed to be ancient Hindu artefacts.

MOUNTSTUART ELPHINSTONE first British envoy to Afghanistan in 1808; later governor of Bombay and pioneer of education; founded Elphinstone college.

WILLIAM ELPHINSTONE general who took command in Kabul in 1841; cousin of Mountstuart; veteran of Waterloo, but his inability to make decisions blamed for the Kabul catastrophe; died in Afghan captivity 1842.

ABDUL RASHID GHAZI mullah in charge of Red Mosque in Islamabad; killed when the Pakistani army stormed the mosque in 2007.

PRINCE GORCHAKOV succeeded Count Nesselrode as Russian foreign minister in 1856; promoted to chancellor of Russia 1863–1882, keeping control of foreign affairs; architect of Russian expansion into 'barbarian' territory to south.

SIR LEPEL GRIFFIN political officer who negotiated terms for Britain to allow Abdur Rahman to take power in 1880; after his retirement in 1893, he led campaign against division of frontier that left large part of ancient Kafir tribe under Afghan control.

GENERAL BORIS GROMOV commander of Soviet 40th Army; last Soviet soldier to leave Afghanistan on 15th February 1989.

COLONEL THOMAS HOLDICH geographer who demarcated much of Afghan border; led the British force that came closest to a clash with Russia during all the years of the Great Game at the Panjdeh Oasis in 1885.

SIR HARFORD JONES British envoy to Tehran who negotiated 1808 treaty.

GENERAL KONSTANTIN KAUFMAN commanded Russian frontier region from 1867 until death in 1882; architect of expansion; proposed truce with Britain against what he saw as the common enemy of Islamic fundamentalism.

SIR JOHN (LATER BARON) KEANE commanded British force that invaded Afghanistan in 1839; warned of 'signal catastrophe'.

COLONEL JAMES KELLY led raid across high, snow-covered mountains to relieve siege of Chitral in 1894.

COLONEL ALI KHANOFF Russian frontier commander who seized Panjdeh Oasis in 1885.

MOHAN LAL author, translator and fixer; described himself as a 'gentleman and Kashmirian'; with Burnes on his adventures in early 1830s; attached to the British mission in Kabul 1838–1841, remaining alive and at liberty to negotiate for the lives of British captives.

LORD LANSDOWNE viceroy at time of negotiations over Durand line.

GEORGE LAWRENCE brother of Henry and John; political officer with Macnaghten when he was murdered in December 1841; held in Afghan jail; had subsequent long colonial career, told in his *Forty-three Years in India* (outdoing later forty-one-year literary effort by Field Marshall Roberts).

HENRY LAWRENCE legendary frontier political officer in 1840s; inspired group known as his 'young men' who employed unconventional methods of controlling rebel tribes.

JOHN LAWRENCE opposed to any settlement with Afghanistan; as viceroy was architect of policy of 'masterly inactivity' outlined in famous *memo* of 1867.

GENERAL SIR WILLIAM LOCKHART commanded largest army assembled under one general during years of British rule of India to put down 1897 uprising.

LORD LYTTON viceroy appointed by Disraeli's new Tory administration in 1876; conducted most aggressive Forward policy leading to Second Anglo-Afghan War; lost office when Disraeli replaced by Gladstone in 1880.

LIEUTENANT JOHN MACARTNEY surveyor; member of Elphinstone's 1808 mission who drew highly influential map of Afghanistan.

SIR WILLIAM MACNAGHTEN British Resident in Kabul; headed mission that installed Shah Shuja on the throne in 1839; murdered by Akbar Khan during negotiations December 1841.

JOHN MCNEILL doctor who became political officer; appointed as British envoy to Tehran 1835; followed Persian court into Afghanistan for siege of Herat 1837; wrote influential analysis warning of Russian threat.

SIR JOHN MALCOLM British envoy to Persia; negotiated anti-French treaty in 1800; clashed with Jones mission in 1808.

CHARLES MASSON real name James Lewis; army deserter who fled to Kabul to make a new life in 1820s; gifted archaeologist credited with discovery of remains of city built by Alexander the Great north of Kabul; eccentric scholar who travelled widely disguised as a beggar; worked as British agent in 1830s, but left Afghanistan when not employed by British mission to Kabul in 1839; died in Edmonton in north London in 1853.

WILLIAM MOORCROFT adventurer and horse-breeder; travelled widely across region, including pioneering journey across Himalayas to Mount Kailash and Lake Manasarovar; died of fever near Balkh in 1825.

PRESIDENT PERVEZ MUSHARRAF Pakistani general who led military coup to become president in 1999; before he took control of the country he had master-minded a Pakistani attack on Indian-controlled Kashmir in the Kargil war; received billions of dollars of US funding in return for support against terrorism after 9/11.

COUNT NESSELRODE Russian foreign minister from 1816–1845; disowned Vitkevitch after Britain complained of Russian involvement in Afghanistan in late 1830s.

GENERAL JOHN NICHOLSON maverick frontier political officer; taken prisoner during his first campaign when garrison at Ghazni surrendered to an Afghan force in December 1841; one of Henry Lawrence's 'young men'; famous for no-nonsense tactics in pacifying frontier; object of reverence by religious cult; died in Delhi in 1857 fighting to suppress the Indian Mutiny.

MULLAH POWINDAH fundamentalist leader of insurrection against British control in Waziristan in 1897; continued opposition until death in 1913.

LORD PALMERSTON British foreign secretary at time of First Anglo-Afghan War.

ELDRED POTTINGER British officer who assisted in defence of Herat against Persian siege in 1836; part of British force that took Afghanistan in 1839; took over as senior political officer on death of Macnaghten 1841; taken prisoner by Afghans, and subsequently cleared of blame by Committee of Inquiry for surrender; died of typhoid in Hong Kong 1842.

ROBIN RAPHEL head of south Asia desk at the State department when Taliban emerged in mid 1990s; worked in Iraq reconstruction effort after 2003; currently vice president of the National Defense University in Washington DC.

MULLAH SADULLAH led Swat uprising against British rule of frontier region in 1897; known as the 'mad mullah' or 'mad fakir' by British troops.

SIR THOMAS SALTER PYNE engineer who operated weapons factories for Abdur Rahman in Kabul; left Afghanistan during cholera epidemic in 1900 and opened chemical factory in Britain.

FIELD MARSHALL FREDERICK ROBERTS soldier known as 'Bobs Bahadur' (Bob the brave); won VC on Delhi Ridge in 1857; saw camp of Hindustani fanatics in 1863; commanded force that took Kabul after slaughter of the garrison in 1879; reputation sealed by forced march to Kandahar to avenge defeat at Battle of Maiwand.

RANJIT SINGH   Sikh ruler from 1799; formed one of the most effective armies in Asia; 1809 secured British treaty marking the Sutlej, easternmost of five rivers of Punjab, as his border; died 1839; Sikh alliance with Britain broke down in 1845.

LIEUTENANT HARRY RATTRAY   commander of small force at Chakdara fort who held out against assault in 1897 that Churchill compared with defence of Rorke's Drift.

SIR GEORGE ROOS-KEPPEL   commissioner of the North-West Frontier Province 1908–1919; wrote English/Pashtu dictionary that became the standard reference book.

LADY FLORENTIA SALE   wife of General Sale; survived retreat from Kabul and wrote highly critical diary listing military failings; died in Britain in 1853.

GENERAL SIR ROBERT SALE   known as 'fighting Bob'; led main force into breach of Ghazni fort in 1839; commanded part of army detached from Kabul in October 1841 to give a 'thrashing' to rebel tribes and open pass to east; besieged in Jalalabad fort for winter, surviving a major earthquake; died in Sikh war in 1845.

SIR ROBERT SANDEMAN   British agent in Baluchistan in late 1870s who established system of control giving power to tribal elders to govern in return for British subsidies; popularised term 'hearts and minds'.

COLONEL JOHN SHELTON   unpopular officer commanding 44th Regiment of Foot that was annihilated in 1842 Kabul retreat; blamed for debacle; lost right arm in Peninsular War in 1813.

SHUJA AL-MULK   ruler installed by British in Chitral in 1895 aged 14; knighted and remained loyal to Raj; died in 1936.

COUNT SIMONICH   Russian envoy to Tehran in the 1830s; dismissed after failure of Persia to take Herat.

CAPTAIN THOMAS SOUTER   officer whose decision to wrap himself in the colours saved his life at Gandamack in 1842.

COLONEL CHARLES STODDART   political officer; delivered
   message persuading Persia to withdraw from Herat in 1838;
   taken prisoner on mission to Bokhara and beheaded in 1842.

IVAN VITKEVITCH   Russian envoy to Kabul 1837; committed
   suicide shortly after returning to Russia.

SIR CLAUDE WADE   British political agent in the frontier
   region in 1830s; blocked Burnes's attempt to assist Dost
   Mohammed in negotiations in 1838.

CONGRESSMAN CHARLIE WILSON   masterminded effort to
   raise US funding for mujahidin fight against the Soviet
   occupation in the 1980s.

MOHAMMED YOUSAF   headed Pakistani operation to
   manage the mujahidin during most of the war against the
   Soviet occupation.

GENERAL ZIA UL-HAQ   took power in military coup in
   Pakistan in 1977; hanged the ousted prime minister, Zulfikar
   Ali Bhutto; backed war against Soviet forces in Afghanistan;
   killed in mysterious plane crash in 1988.

Glossary

BALA HISSAR   means high fort; common name in south Asia for fortresses. The Bala Hissars in Kabul and Peshawar are still under military control.

BUZKASHI   horse-riding game where riders compete ferociously to carry the stuffed carcass of a goat or calf to a marked spot.

DURAND LINE   name of Afghanistan's eastern border agreed after negotiations between the Amir Abdur Rahman and Sir Henry Mortimer in 1893.

FERINGHEE   means foreigner in several south Asian languages; origins lie in the word Frank.

FERUNG   woollen floor-length one-piece Kashmiri garment with a hole through the middle for the head; in the winter wearers carry a small fire-pot in their arms under the ferung for heating.

GHAZI   religious warrior.

GHILZAI   sub-tribe of Pashtuns living mostly in eastern border area.

GOVERNOR-GENERAL   head of British imperial administration in India until 1858, replaced by viceroy.

JEZAIL   long matchlock weapon used by Afghan warriors; used mounted on rest; better range and accuracy than British weapons in First Anglo-Afghan war.

JIHAD   means struggle; word used to describe duty of Muslims to wage war.

KILIM JAM   common name for the northern Uzbek militia under General Dostam in the 1980s;

	literally means 'the carpet is gathered up', describing the looting that some experienced when they came to call.
KOTWAL	chief of police.
KHAN	nobleman or lesser king.
LOYA JIRGA	means great gathering; word used in Afghanistan for gathering of elders to discuss issue of national importance.
MALIK	tribal elder.
MEHMANDAR	courier sent by king carrying official permission for a visitor to proceed to court.
MUJAHIDIN	fighters who have taken up requirements of jihad.
PASHTU	majority language in southern Afghanistan and frontier region.
PASHTUN	largest tribe in Afghanistan, based mainly in the south of the country and across the frontier in what became Pakistan in 1947.
PASHTUNWALI	honour code of Pashtun tribe.
QIZALBASH	Persian cavalry who had their own fortress in Kabul in the early part of the nineteenth century.
RISSALDAR MAJOR	most senior officer's rank of locally recruited cavalrymen in British army in India; equivalent to major.
SAUR	month approximating to April in Afghan calendar; name given to 1978 revolution that toppled President Daoud.
SECRET COMMITTEE	body comprising usually only three members of the Board of Directors of the East India Company; able to issue secret orders without reference to other directors.
SEPOY	lowest rank of infantry soldier for the British army recruited in India.
SHARIA	Islamic legal code.
SHURA	Arabic for 'consultation'; used in Afghanistan as word to describe meeting of elders.

SIRDAR	Pashtun nobleman; commander of body of Afghan warriors.
SOWAR	lowest rank of cavalry trooper recruited for the British army in India; means horseman in Persian.
STAN	common name for the states of central Asia that emerged in the early twentieth century under the wing of the Soviet Union.
SUBEDAR	officer's rank for locally recruited soldier in British army in India; equivalent to captain.
WALI	Arabic for 'friend'; formal title for leader of an area in Afghanistan; approximating to 'Lord of the Manor' in earlier times in Britain.
WAZIR	chief minister or adviser to Afghan king (no connection to the frontier province of Waziristan).
YABOO	small stout horse bred in Afghanistan.

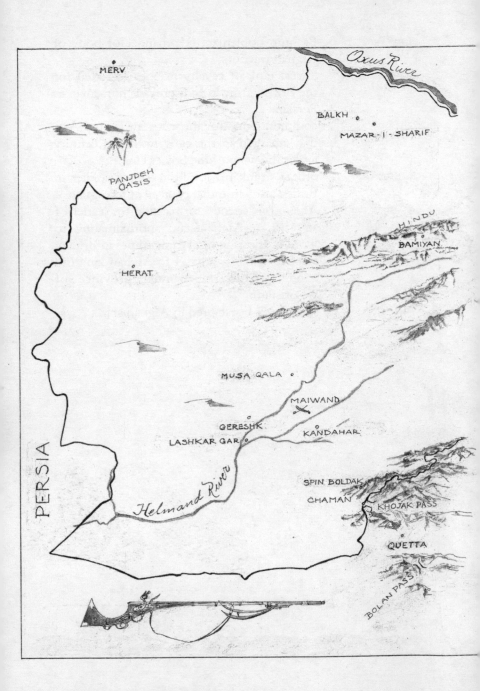

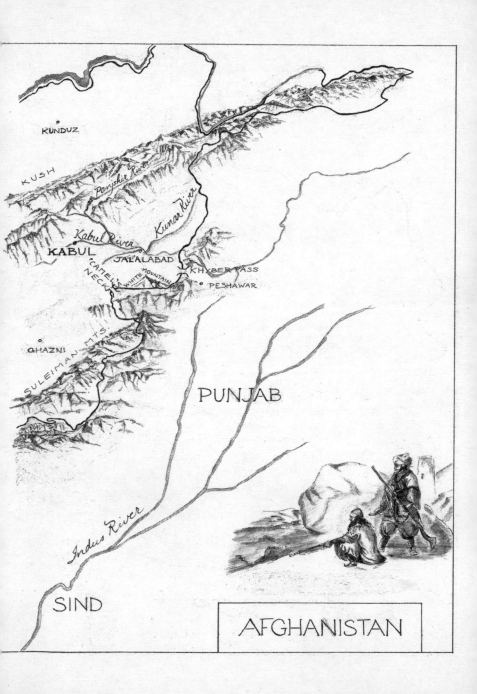

KUNDUZ

KUSH

Panjshir River

Kunar River

Kabul River

KABUL

JALALABAD

CAMEL'S NECK

WHITE MOUNTAIN

KHYBER PASS

PESHAWAR

GHAZNI

SULEIMAN MTS.

PUNJAB

Indus River

SIND

AFGHANISTAN

Introduction

I first heard the word Taliban on a Friday night in September 1994 over a beer in the colonial bungalow that served as the Foreign Correspondents' Club in Delhi. A freelance had just returned from the south of Afghanistan, where he had come across a new group of fighters using the name. 'It might be worth checking them out,' he said. 'The Taliban seem different to other mujahidin, they are some kind of student militia.' The Afghan conflict was then mired in a bloody stalemate 15 years after the Soviet invasion. We did not know that what he had witnessed was the beginning of something that would have implications far beyond Afghanistan.

Two years later, in September 1996, mine was the only TV crew to witness the Taliban takeover of Kabul, driving through the night past the wreckage of a defeated army towards the city. The pace and ruthlessness of the Taliban assault shook Afghanistan, putting more of the country under one administration than at any time since the Soviet invasion in 1979. After only five years in power, in 2001, the Taliban were targeted as the hosts of the 9/11 bombers, and forced out after a war that was a technical triumph, victory without tears – at least for the US, who suffered no combat fatalities. But by 2008 the number of foreign forces in the country had risen to

50,000 for the first time, and a call went out for more, to tackle a worsening insurgency.

What had gone wrong? When the Taliban were ousted, few in Afghanistan appeared to lament the fall of these fundamentalist zealots. But that did not take long to change. The Taliban never went away but instead emerged from underground to win new supporters. The international community had made some basic early mistakes after 2001, as what the World Bank would call an 'aid juggernaut' drove into town, providing funds for itself and living in a parallel world rather than building a new Afghan state. Corruption was allowed to flourish, driven by huge profits from illegal drugs. And a military campaign had focused on arresting terrorists rather than restoring order. But were those failures enough to explain the resurgent Taliban?

Afghanistan had long ago built a reputation of resistance to foreign invaders. As I write, it is exactly 200 years since a Scottish political officer working for the Raj, Mountstuart Elphinstone, set out from Delhi, the first formal envoy sent by any European power to discover who ruled the 'Kingdom of Caubul'. Another 30 years were to pass before Britain would attempt its first military expedition. That first war ended in catastrophe, and in the years that followed, Afghanistan would inflict other defeats on British forces; Persia and Russia made even less headway. None seemed to learn any lessons from history. As a reporter travelling in Afghanistan I wondered if there really was something in the nature of the people and the country itself that made it so hard to conquer?

I had first encountered Afghanistan as a journalist after I went to live in India in 1993 as the first new BBC South Asia Correspondent for almost 30 years, succeeding Mark Tully. Afghanistan was the furthest outpost of the region, and the common complaint at the club bar was that it was then a forgotten war. Editors were not easily persuaded to invest in travel to a country locked in the confusing and bitter conflict that followed the pullout of Soviet troops in 1989. Besides, it was very dangerous, as I was reminded when a local journalist working for the BBC, Mirwais Jalil, was targeted and killed in cold blood in July 1994. Fighting in those years between rival mujahidin did far more damage to Kabul than the preceding decade of guerrilla warfare against the Soviet invasion, but had hardly any coverage worldwide.

Journalists who ventured there told of narrow escapes in a city that crackled with the constant sound of gunfire, their days spent moving riskily through hostile checkpoints, and nights sleeping in basements with a shovel by the bed to dig themselves out if the house above was struck by a rocket. They told tales too of the resilience and hospitality of Afghans despite everything, with an honour code – the *pashtunwali* – that meant that although Afghans were ruthless to their enemies, they would risk their own lives to guarantee safety to their guests.

I saw this in action in October 2006 when I interviewed a senior Taliban commander in Helmand Province, who was leading the renewed campaign against British troops. The invitation came from the Taliban, and my safety depended on his word, a system tested when a group of battle-weary fighters arrived from a gun battle with British soldiers and said they wanted to shoot me. In the subsequent argument for my life, he resisted their demands to hand me over, saying they would have to kill him first.

By then I had amassed a collection of classic books about the country, many of them copies reprinted in dusty back-alleys in Peshawar on the North-West Frontier, and sold in small ramshackle shops squeezed in among the carpet and curio dealers, who were still hoping that one day it would be safe for tourists to return.

Elphinstone's account of his mission was the best, but on the shelf alongside him in Saaed's Book Bank sat Connolly, Vigne, Moorcroft, and others – tales told by horse dealers, spies, thieves and scholars. There was the extraordinary account of survival through the thick of battle by the redoubtable general's wife, Lady Florentia Sale, and Sir George Robertson's story of the relief of Chitral, after Colonel Kelly led troops that fought their way across high mountain passes, forcing mules that ferried their field guns through the snow. Robertson described a world on the frontier where 'even fairy tales had a crimson atmosphere. Sensuality of the grossest kind and murder, abominable cruelty, treachery or violent death, are never long absent from the thoughts of a people than whom none in the world are more delightful companions, or of simpler, gentler appearance.'

The books described an Afghanistan with characteristics that were still recognisable, peopled by men of enormous charm and grace, with elaborate codes of dress and hospitality alongside unspeakable cruelty. One hardly met any women. The *pashtunwali*, the honour code that had saved my life, demanded respect for mullahs and loyalty to commanders, restricted contact between the sexes, turned women into virtual commodities, and ensured revenge would be carried down through generations. This harsh moral code – guaranteeing life to friends, and death to strangers – was carved out of unforgiving mountains and deserts. The Kabul plateau is almost 6000 feet above sea level, surrounded by mountain ranges that go higher – a wild lunar landscape of breathtaking beauty. My screen-saver shows a picture of a man on a horse, alone in a wilderness where little grows, behind him the sheer bare face of a blue mountain. Elsewhere the mountains are grey-green or red, or broken into dust-coloured folds that seem to stride over the horizon; and behind it all, like the icing on a cake, the white peaks of the Hindu Kush cut across the centre of the country, with the Suleiman Mountains to the east.

Apart from the Pashtuns, I had now travelled among the Mongol-looking Hazaras, Turkic-featured Uzbeks and their neighbours the Tajiks, and high in the mountain fastness of Nuristan, tall paler-faced people, often with fair hair, blue eyes and freckles. This tribal diversity told of a complex history lived in a landscape that had been fought over and traded through since the dawn of time.

In the north of Afghanistan lie the ruins of the world's first city, Balkh, and in the same region Avicenna, the founder of modern European medicine, was educated in an Islamic school, a madrassa. What had happened in the thousand years since he went to school, that these madrasas had become internationally notorious, known only for the most restrictive fundamentalist education? In the Bamiyan valley, carved into the wall of the Hindu Kush, had stood two giant Buddhas, until they were blown up by the Taliban. I had lain on the head of the bigger Buddha only a few months before the destruction, gazing at the fragile frescos on the ceiling – visions of the pleasures of the flesh, painted longingly 1500 years ago by monks who had abandoned that life for austerity in a cave. The Buddhas have gone, and the monks' caves are filled with refugees, the smoke from their fires blackening the red rock.

There was another question raised by foreign engagement in Afghanistan during the 200 years since Elphinstone's trip in 1808 – why was holding the country far more difficult than. taking it? Seeking an answer would set me on a trail that would involve deeper reading than the reprints available on the frontier. The extraordinary collection of letters and memoirs in the British Library is a treasure trove. Lady Sale turned out to be a gifted artist, whose exquisite watercolours of details of Indian village life and the Taj Mahal were as much a revelation as her highly critical account of the military failings that led to British defeat in Kabul. She was 50 years old when she moved to Kabul, and cast from an Empire-building mould, having already witnessed an uprising in Gwalior in India. She found things to say in the darkest of moments, retaining her leather-bound notebooks in a bag around her waist when she had lost everything else. The morning after her soldier son-in-law died in her arms, and she and other women were taken away from the ranks of the retreating British army to an uncertain fate by Afghan tribesmen, she still noted, 'I could not but admire the romantic tortuous defile we passed through, being the bed of a mountain torrent, which we exchanged for the terrific pass I have mentioned.' Before the defeat and catastrophic retreat the letters sent by Sir William Macnaghten, the British envoy to Kabul, show with unbearable poignancy his nagging fear of how things might turn out. He wrote, 'we shall be high and dry ere long'.

But the most telling account of Britain's failure in its first attempt to take Afghanistan was left by an Indian, Mohan Lal. He was an unassuming man, virtually ignored by some historians of the period who dismissed his books as the writings of an embittered *munshi* getting above his station as a translator. But Lal showed that he had the better understanding of how hostility grew to British rule. His unthreatening character allowed him to remain at liberty in Kabul, even after his colonial masters were besieged in their garrison. His worth was shown early when he was a member of a British mission to Kabul facing competing claims from Russia. In 1838 Lal found his way in to report back on an Afghan royal new year party at which the Russian envoy was the guest of honour, but the flamboyant British envoy Sir Alexander Burnes had been snubbed.

I recognised Lal because he was the sort of companion I would have chosen if he had been available to work as a fixer for a journalistic assignment. Good locals who can speak the right languages and find their way round obstructions are the key to foreign reporting: people like Rahimullah Yusufzai, who I travelled with frequently during the early days of the Taliban, including the seizure of Kabul, or Najibullah Razaq, gentle, multilingual and cunning. Finding out what is happening under the surface in a complex society, where manners and hospitality remain even in wartime, is the key to success. From men like Rahimullah and Najibullah I learnt to wait and drink the green tea and sugared almonds that lubricate business in Afghanistan, squatting on dusty carpets while lunch was prepared and permissions considered.

Again and again in the past, the local dynamics of Afghanistan were not considered important enough to warrant attention by empire builders. In 1893, half a century after the defeat of the Kabul garrison, Henry Mortimer Durand travelled to Kabul. This was the man who would leave his name on the frontier – still known as the Durand line. Every night of his visit he, or sometimes a secretary, would copy his correspondence into a letter-book, using a pencil. His plans, read alongside the account left by the Afghan amir Abdur Rahman, reveal just how far Durand underestimated his opposite number, whom he regarded 'a brutal savage'.

By the late nineteenth century Russia too was threatening Afghanistan, but made even less progress than Britain. A map from the period shows railway tracks from the west, north and east stopping at the Afghan border. Both Britain and Russia had by then taken vast tracts of Asia, but neither could penetrate Afghanistan. British anxiety over Russia led to them translating many key Russian documents, just as the US translated Soviet and Afghan documents after the 1970s, and for the same reason – to understand a potential foe. Britain's translations were published in Calcutta, while the US translations have been available online since freedom of information laws kicked in. But were these lessons of former conflicts being learnt in the twenty-first century by those nations who had once again gone to war in Afghanistan?

I thought I detected a constant theme running from Britain's first intervention in the early nineteenth century up to the imposition of democracy after 2001: policy was to be shaped from outside whatever the local Afghan circumstances. The most short-sighted example of this was the indiscriminate foreign funding for the mujahidin fighting against Soviet forces in the 1980s, much of the money coming from the US. The fundamentalist Islamic creed professed by rebel leaders like Gulbuddin Hekmatyar and Ahmed Shah Massud was overlooked – they were accorded celebrity status as guerrillas who were on the 'right side'.

But when forces loyal to the two men turned on each other after the defeat of Soviet forces, the Western diplomats who had funded and praised them fell silent. And few appeared to want to understand the Taliban phenomenon when the movement first emerged in the late 1990s, or in its resurgence in 2006. The belief was that since democracy had come to Afghanistan, 'it was not thought necessary for us to understand the tribal system,' in the frank admission in 2007 by the EU representative in Kabul, Francesc Vendrell.

But British forces had seen warriors like these before in their history. In 2006 the British faced their first intense firefights in Helmand province in Sangin, the same town where a British invasion force faced its first major battle in the south in 1878. And then, as now, Afghan defenders were inspired by the demands of jihad, waging holy war against invaders. In the nineteenth century these were known as *ghazis*, religious warriors. The Taliban had clear antecedents in the *ghazis* and Hindustani fanatics of the past, as well as the mujahidin struggle against the Soviet invader – different terms in different times for holy warriors for whom martyrdom is their highest calling.

Jihad was even motivated with exactly the same messages across the centuries. The amir who negotiated the border with Durand in 1893, Abdur Rahman, always protested that he was completely loyal to Britain when uprisings erupted along the frontier, but I had heard that he had written a book about jihad, which had been widely distributed in mosques at the time, although I had never seen a translation. I found a very rare original copy in a Kabul market, and my fixer Najibullah translated it, turning to his father, a retired judge, for some of the more obscure Koranic references. The book was a revelation, and a long way from the consoling messages Britain had heard from Abdur Rahman at the time: it was a ringing call to arms against the British, extolling the virtues of overnight horseback ambushes, and the beauty of paradise for martyrs. Most interestingly, the choice of Koranic extracts was the same as those used both by the Taliban and Osama bin Laden in their appeals for jihad – identical calls to holy war across the same frontier a century apart.

Reporters who spent a lot of time in Afghanistan gathered knowledge about the particular nature of how conflicts work there, and how power changes hands. I learnt a great deal from the veteran cameraman Peter Jouvenal, who has been filming news in Afghanistan since the time of the Soviet invasion, and was with John Simpson when he walked into Kabul after the Taliban fell in 2001. Whether a group of fighters is communist, or mujahidin or Taliban is never important to Peter. Rather it is their constant character as Afghans that he believes determines their behaviour. He could strip conflict down to a few rules. This was a land with strong centrifugal forces, where loyalty was always to individual local commanders and not to the state, although all tended to unite against outsiders. Commanders would change sides often, seemingly without principle, to follow power. He knew too the ferocity that was expected when towns did change hands and were looted as if by locusts. But full combat was to be avoided at all costs. Commanders would do deals rather than fight wars, in a country where, as one observer put it, 'the mere appearance of force is half the battle of ordinary business'. The ties that bound warriors to warlords were stronger than the demands of the state. Elphinstone himself had noticed 200 years ago: 'They are assembled in tribes under powerful chiefs . . . which circumstances have prevented any encroachment by their own sovereign on the rights of the local chiefs.'

So building a central government and national institutions was never going to be easy. The forces pulling the country apart were as strong against the major nineteenth century amirs – Dost Mohammed and Abdur Rahman – as against President Hamid Karzai since he had come to power in 2002. The only period of stability was the long reign of Zahir Shah, from 1933–73, helped for all of the later period of his rule by the frozen balance of the cold war. Afghanistan became a far richer and more developed country by the end of this period – a fact often forgotten by aid workers who came in after 2001 and believed they were starting from scratch – but in the end it was pent-up demands for social and political progress that pushed Zahir Shah out of power, leading to the spiral downwards towards the Soviet invasion in 1979 and the country's long nightmare.

The porous border across the frontier with Pakistan remained an open back door, useful to the US when it sent arms and aid along the mule tracks in the mountains to aid the mujahidin struggle against the Soviet invasion in the 1980s, but 20 years later the boot was on the other foot. Pakistan did nothing effective to combat the safe haven for the Taliban on their side of the frontier, and in April 2008 the outgoing US commander of NATO forces in Afghanistan, General Dan McNeill, said the upsurge in cross-border attacks on his forces inside Afghanistan was 'directly attributable to the lack of pressure on the other side of the border'. Relations worsened as Pakistani troops were killed by US missiles.

This unstable frontier was the one drawn up by Durand in 1893. Its treacherous mountain ranges could not be crossed by an army except in three places – the best-known being the Khyber Pass. The mountains and valleys of the frontier were natural guerrilla territory that define Afghanistan's strategic relationships. Britain never secured full stability and control during the century when this was the western border of British India, despite a policy known at the time as 'butcher and bolt': constant raids to hunt elusive enemies – burning villages in punishment attacks, killing without controlling – directed at men who, in 1897, Churchill called 'northern savages, impelled by fanaticism or allured by plunder'.

The failure of Pakistan to do any better to combat insecurity on the North-West frontier after 2001 meant that NATO armies in Afghanistan were fighting an enemy that could reinforce itself easily, while in front of them corruption, illegal drugs, the failure to build institutions of the state, and lack of development steadily eroded support for their presence among Afghan people. The initial US plan after the fall of the Taliban did not include widespread military operations across the country. Beyond the hunt for Osama bin Laden and others deemed terrorists, always under a separate command structure, there were very few forces sent out beyond Kabul, and their role was very limited. Democracy was seen as a virtue that would spread peace on its own. Comments at the time echoed those made in 1839 by Lieutenant Colonel Dennie, after British forces had installed their choice of amir, 'The war may now be

considered at an end, the King being once again on his throne.'
That first war would go on for another three years, and Dennie
was killed in its closing stages. In June 1879 General Sam
Browne signalled 'the Kabul campaign may now be regarded
as terminated'. After the slaughter of the British mission sent
to Kabul, that war would go on for another two years.

Similarly in early 1980, two months after the Soviet invasion,
there were plans to withdraw troops, since, in the words of an
official report 'having solidified the new Afghan government . . . they have fulfilled their main task'. A month later
these troops were replaced by a larger force sent to combat a
growing mujahidin insurgency in a war that went on for
another nine years.

Similar misunderstanding surrounded Afghanistan in 2001,
when the Taliban were believed to be so unpopular that they
could never rise again. It took several years and the arguments
of commanders such as the British general David Richards to
scale up the counterinsurgency effort. But when the call went
out for more international forces, many countries imposed
such rigid conditions around the use of their troops that they
were contemptuously known as 'pot plants' by NATO
planners, of ornamental use only. With only a small number –
mainly Canada, the Netherlands and France – willing to put
forces in harm's way, the US and Britain shouldered an
increasing burden, and increasing casualties. In a series of
attacks in June 2008 British forces faced their worst death toll
in the war so far.

On 24th June 2008 the Chief of the Defence Staff Sir Jock
Stirrup said Afghanistan would not be 'that long-term an
endeavour for the military'. The aim was to train local forces
to take on the fight for themselves. But British troops had
heard such optimism before, in an operation where the task
seemed to be changing all the time. The first soldiers on the
ground in Helmand when the operation was reconfigured for
the new role in 2006 were told they were there to support aid,
but they found there was no aid to support, and hopes by the
government that they should 'not fire one shot' had to be

rapidly reconsidered as they became enmeshed in the most sustained period of intense fighting the British army had faced for a generation.

In garrisons across the land, which they had left to go and fight in Afghanistan, hung regimental banners with battle honours from Kandahar, Ghazni and Khyber stitched into them, and stirring Victorian paintings depicting defeats of the past – the last stand of the 44th at Gandamack, a horse carrying the sole survivor of the Kabul garrison limping into Jalalabad, and the battle of Maiwand.

Afghanistan had a history of confounding the optimism of invaders.

David Loyn
London, June 2008

Part One

First encounters and the First
Anglo-Afghan War 1808–1842

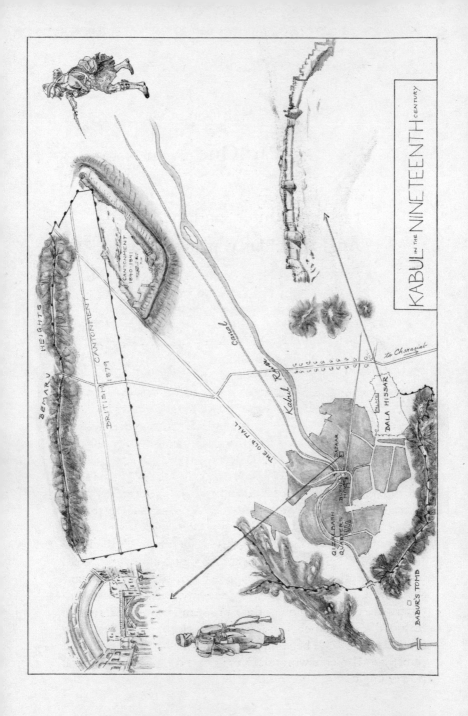

KABUL IN THE NINETEENTH CENTURY

BEMARU HEIGHTS

CANTONMENT 1840-1841

BRITISH CANTONMENT 1879

Canal

Kabul River

THE OLD MALL

to Charasiab

BALA HISSAR

PALACE

BAZAAR

AMIR'S QUARTERS

QIZALBASH QUARTERS

BABUR'S TOMB

1

Wild and Strange

In Afghanistan 'a small army would be annihilated and a large one starved'.

Arthur Wellesley, Duke of Wellington

Elphinstone was dazzled by the jewels. Beneath a crown from which nine-inch-long spikes encrusted with diamonds shone out in all directions, the Afghan amir wore what looked to him like a suit of green armour. On closer inspection, Elphinstone saw that the armour was studded with emeralds. It was the first meeting between an envoy from a European power and an Afghan king, and amid all the finery the Briton at first hardly noticed that Shah Shuja wore a shining rock of a startling size hanging from a bracelet round his wrist – the Koh-i-noor diamond.

When he had left Delhi on 13th October 1808, Mountstuart Elphinstone, a 29-year-old British political officer, had prepared a mission of 'great magnificence', since he had heard that the court at Kabul was 'haughty, and supposed to entertain a mean opinion of the European nations'. His retinue included 600 camels, and a dozen elephants laden with presents. It was the beginning of a relationship that would lead directly to Britain's worst defeats in two centuries of imperial power in Asia.

The background to Elphinstone's mission lay in Britain's realisation of Afghanistan's strategic importance to India. It was only four years since British forces under Arthur Wellesley, later Duke of Wellington, had secured military dominance of India. But this control was threatened when Napoleon set his eyes on Britain's new Empire in the east; and the balance of power in Europe had just shifted decisively in his favour. Napoleon's embrace with Tsar Alexander on a raft in the centre of the river that divided their armies at Tilsit in the north of Europe ended a war that had cost the lives of around 50,000 troops, sealing a new alliance that sent shockwaves not only across Europe but the world.

British spies brought news of a secret clause in the Tilsit treaty creating a joint Russo-French force of 70,000 troops to invade India. Russian territory was far from India, and on the wrong side of the high plateau of the steppes and vast mountain ranges. But what if the invasion came directly from the west, across Persia? Russia had been threatening Persia for years. Now Napoleon sent a mission there, with money, guns and military skills, to train the Persians in the arts of European warfare. If Persia was brought in on the side of the Russo-French alliance, then only Afghanistan would stand in the way of a full-scale assault on India.

John Crokatt, an analyst with the East India Company, which at this time ran India, wrote, 'events seem rapidly approaching which threaten with immediate danger, if not with total subversion, the British government in India'.

Even if France and Russia stayed out, Britain was already fearful of Afghan aggression towards India, and kept forces in the west as a deterrent. Crokatt remembered recent history, when 'Zaman Shah, the brother and immediate predecessor of the reigning monarch, was led by predatory and ambitious motives to meditate acts of hostility against the [East India] company. At this momentous crisis it is of considerable importance to ascertain whether the present King is guided by similar views.' This was the reason for Elphinstone's mission.

Britain knew little about Afghanistan. There had been

travellers' tales from a few individual adventurers, but until Elphinstone set out, no determined attempt to discover the reality of the land beyond the five rivers of the Punjab, at that time the effective western border of British India. Britain did know of Afghanistan's warrior history. It was within living memory that an Afghan amir had ruled in Delhi itself after conquering half the continent. That was Ahmed Shah, founder of a dynasty, and still revered as the father of the Afghan nation, whose dynasty was known as Durrani, meaning 'pearl of pearls'. Shah Shuja, the amir who met Elphinstone, was his grandson.

The Afghans were known for their banditry and lawlessness. An early British traveller to Afghanistan, George Forster, like so many after him, was attacked in 1783, as he went through the Khyber Pass, the long winding pathway through the Suleiman range, the soaring mountain fastness that conceals Afghanistan from the rest of south Asia. Although he had paid a toll to the keepers of the pass, protection money in effect, he was knocked off his mule, and only kept his money because it was wrapped in gaiters round his legs. He saw that the 'freebooting life' was aided by 'a chain of rocky mountains, whose scanty slips of valley afford but the coarsest provision for human wants. This rude race of men have made so slow a progress in civilisation, that the greatest part of them, like the storied Troglodites of old, dwell in caves, or rather in the fissures of rocks.'

Forster grew a beard to blend in. He did not want to admit to being British, and decided against pretending to be French; he thought it too likely that he would encounter a real Frenchman, because of 'the wandering temper of that people, who stray into every corner of the earth'. After 15 months travelling west from India, as he was having his beard shaved on a Russian frigate in the Caspian, he regretted its passing. He reflected on 'the general importance of an Asiatic beard, the essential services which mine had rendered, and our long and intimate association'.

But neither Forster, nor any other of the handful of

Europeans who had been into Afghan lands before 1800, had left maps or detailed guides. Incredible as it may seem, Elphinstone was using accounts left by Alexander the Great, written more than 2000 years before, as he probed the land beyond Britain's known Indian world. He had only Alexander's names for the rivers that crossed the flat country of the Punjab, until he came to the wide barrier of the Indus itself, the defining geographical feature of the region.

Elphinstone was a brilliant classical scholar, and spoke fluent modern Persian as well as Hindi. Personally charismatic, as a teenager he had startled visitors to Edinburgh castle, where his father was governor, by marching around with his long blond hair swept back in the French manner, singing revolutionary songs he had learnt from French prisoners. An uncle in the East India Company in Calcutta then obtained a post for him in India, where he quickly caught the attention of Arthur Wellesley. He was sent as a political officer to secure a peace deal with the Mahrattas, the last major threat to British control of the subcontinent, and when peace talks broke down, he played a crucial role on Wellesley's staff at the battle of Assaye in 1804, when the Mahratta army was defeated once and for all. Wellesley told him he should have become a soldier.

Guided by accounts of ancient battles, but fuelled by apprehension of a French invasion, and the distant threat of Russia, Elphinstone set out from Delhi, heading south-west across modern Rajasthan towards, although he did not know it, one of the largest deserts in the world. The journey took on an epic quality. Soon the camels could go only in single file on shifting tracks through sand hills 'rising one after another like the waves of the sea, and marked on the surface by the wind like drifted snow'. Marching at night, sleeping fitfully through the heat of the day, the two-mile long caravan made slow progress. The heavy sand became too much for the *sepoys*, the Indian soldiers fighting for the British, so they were allowed to ride in turns, two to a camel. Securing water was a constant problem, and even when they found it, the wells were sometimes as deep as 300 feet, emptied in a single night by bullocks turning a winch.

Securing food and water was not made any easier by the decadence of the rulers they encountered, who were constantly drugged by alcohol or opium. Elphinstone found he could conduct business with them only in a brief window of time in the afternoon – 'the interval between sobriety and absolute stupefaction' – after the first fix had eased the pain of the hangover and craving, and before they were too drugged again.

But the difficulties he encountered with minor tribal leaders, who all swore allegiance to Britain – when sober enough – were as nothing compared to the civil war that Elphinstone was nearly drawn into when he came into the region carved up by the five main Rajput rulers. He found the kings of Jodhpur and Jaipur fighting over the hand of the princess of Udaipur, who must have been a beauty, for this south Asian Helen of Troy had little land.

As the desert became more threatening and the war closer, the trickle of desertions from among Elphinstone's camp followers turned into a flood. Any expedition then relied on a village of people moving with it, to keep it on the road. Each horse required its own 'grass-cutter', to gather fodder and water, and a groom to tend it. There were farriers, carpenters and leather-workers for the animals, and cooks, water-gatherers, and laundrymen for the officers. Elphinstone now put the whole expedition onto a military footing, separating out the wives and children and sending them back, and hiring 150 local horsemen to help guard their progress. But the desertions stopped only when they were so far from safety that returning was more dangerous than going on.

Three weeks after leaving Delhi, the British arrived in the city of Bikaner, capital of the richest and largest of the five Rajput kingdoms. It was under attack. The British saw the evidence of the war for the princess's hand in bodies on the ground, and 'disorderly bands of ragged soldiers in all directions'. Elphinstone had to fend off attempts by the warring kings to draw him in. His well-trained and battle-hardened sepoy force, with its British officers, might have been decisive. The Raja of Bikaner exerted pressure by denying his wells to the British force, and sickness and the harsh conditions began to take their toll. From what had not been a large force to start with, forty men died in the first week after they arrived at Bikaner. But the Raja knew about the threat of the French, and once he had demonstrated his power, he relented, gave the British water and promised them his full support, even trying to press the keys of the city onto Elphinstone, who declined since his mission was not to take territory.

When the force moved on from Bikaner they marched by day, since they feared bandits at night, although it meant using more water. The desert sand was firmer now, and they made faster progress, with the camels moving a dozen abreast. Still only just across into modern Pakistan, east of the five rivers, and a long way short of the modern Afghan border on 21st November 1808, British soldiers encountered Afghan troops for the first time.

Elphinstone was impressed. The Afghan force, 150 soldiers on camels, which they managed as if they were light horses, had an appearance that 'was altogether novel and striking'. Two men sat on each camel, each with a long matchlock rifle, highly decorated in black and white chequered wood and mother-of-pearl. This was the weapon the British would later learn to call a *jezail,* and come to respect since it was surprisingly accurate at a distance. The Afghans brought 100 camels carrying skins of fresh water, with four separate jars of water for the British officers, sealed by their leader, the chief of the most southerly of the regions owing allegiance to Kabul.

Elphinstone's trip now took on the appearance of a medieval adventure overlaid by the courtly manners of the rulers he moved among, a long winter where his days were spent hunting, and his nights feasting and watching dancing girls. Two hundred years ago, Afghans had quite different customs to today.

In contrast to the drunken indolence of the Rajput rulers, he was in another world, experiencing the elaborate courtesies of lesser Afghan kings, khans, on his way to meet their overall amir, the ruler of Kabul, whom most of them had never met. They may have been suspicious of Elphinstone's intentions, and feared he wanted to take their land, but they hunted with him and mostly treated him well. Expecting to face incessant demands for gifts, 'as is usual on such occasions in most parts of India', instead he often found it hard to give things away without elaborate negotiation. And in return he found himself the owner of horses, hawks, greyhounds, guns and fine cloths. The khans saw him not as an imperial emissary, but the representative of a power like their own. In those early days of Britain's settlement of the subcontinent, there was far more equality between the two sides than later, at the height of the Victorian empire.

Some of the khans were more graceful than others. Elphinstone was stuck in the ancient capital of lower Punjab, Multan, for three weeks until the arrival of a *mehmandar,* an official courier sent to escort an important visitor to the Afghan court. The khan of Multan was suspicious, speaking quickly and saying often 'you are welcome, you are very welcome', but meaning the opposite. When he finally agreed to visit the British camp, his large armed party marched in at speed, almost sweeping aside Elphinstone's tent and his secretary: 'Mr Strachey's horse was nearly borne to the ground, and only recovered himself by a violent exertion.' But even this khan settled down after this first farcical encounter, and the caravan moved on.

While still east of the Indus, the British caught their first sight of the Suleiman Mountains, the mesmerising and complex wall running from north to south, with only a few navigable passes, the most important being the Khyber, through to the high plains of Afghanistan beyond. These mountains, 400 miles long and 200 miles wide in places, would come to dominate Afghanistan's relationship with the outside world over the next two centuries. 'Their appearance was beautiful; we clearly saw three ranges, the last of which was very high, and we often doubted whether we were deceived by the clouds, or really saw still higher ranges beyond.' The Afghanistan on the other side of the mountains took a powerful hold on Elphinstone's imagination; he knew only that 'beyond the hills was something wild and strange'.

Three months after leaving Delhi, the British crossed the Indus at a point where it was 1000 yards broad, but the flow of the river was weakened as it was broken by islands. The elephants swam across, as those in Alexander the Great's force must have done, while the horses crossed in large flat-bottomed boats, and the camels had their feet tied and 'were thrown into the boats like any other baggage'. By now the British had been in the region long enough for rumours to have spread about them. They were said to carry 'great guns packed up in trunks; and . . . certain small boxes, so contrived as to explode and kill half a dozen men each', without hurting themselves. Another story was a version of an old Asian folk tale, that said the British had made a magic sheep which looked real, but when it was sold was found to be made of wood. Elphinstone's men were among a superstitious and rumour-fuelled people.

There was suspicion everywhere. In a nomad camp Elphinstone was asked why they were there, rather than being 'contented with our own possessions, Cawnpore, Lucknow, and all those fine places?' Two of Elphinstone's officers took a day to try to climb to 'King Solomon's throne', the snow-covered peak that had given the Suleiman mountain range its name. But they found the top of the mountain inaccessible and were robbed on the way back, while in another village a man cocked his matchlock at the two climbers. As the caravan continued north, word arrived with a convoy carrying mule-loads of fruit from Kabul that they would not need to go all the way to the capital; the amir would greet them in Peshawar.

It was the Mughal emperor Akbar who gave Peshawar its name, meaning 'advanced post', in the sixteenth century, designating it as the gateway for the defence of India against Afghanistan. It was a substantial town of mud-walled houses with flat roofs around a teeming bazaar, with a fort, the Bala Hissar, that was 'of no strength' to Elphinstone's eye. From there it was only a morning's ride to the eastern entrance of the Khyber Pass, the narrow pathway through the mountains into Afghanistan. The British party arrived in Peshawar on 25th February 1809 'after some confusion about the mode of our reception'. Armed horsemen had to beat back the huge crowds who came to see them.

More than two weeks later, amid a huge noise 'like a charge of cavalry, which was occasioned by the iron-heeled boots of the guards', Elphinstone was welcomed in to the Afghan court, a complex series of ornate buildings with ponds and fountains, and fine silk carpets hanging from the walls. To the sound of drums and trumpets he was led from person to person through inner courtyards and gardens, and announced with some ceremony outside, before the curiously downbeat moment as he made his way into the presence of the king. As was the custom, in order not to be seen to be making a recommendation, the courtier did not announce him with any formality, but in an offhand aside, as if saying 'Well, here he is, but I don't vouch for him'.

Elphinstone was greeted by the sight of the amir perched on a gold-coloured throne, elevated above the heads of his eunuchs. 'His appearance was magnificent and royal: his crown and all his dress were one blaze of jewels.' But despite the dazzling finery, Shah Shuja was in a weak position. Elphinstone correctly assessed that this 'all bore less the appearance of a state in prosperity than of a splendid monarchy in decay'. He discovered in conversation with one of the amir's key advisers that the man thought Calcutta was in England.

The curse of the Koh-i-noor, which is said to bring bad luck to any male ruler who owns it, may have contributed to Shah Shuja's problems. (This belief appears to continue into the present day. The diamond has been worn by only two rulers since being seized by Britain – Victoria and Elizabeth II. British kings have ordered it to be put into their female consort's crown). But it would have taken a statesman of extraordinary quality to have stabilised Afghanistan in the early nineteenth century, a period of intrigue and royal bloodletting uniquely awful even in a country with such a murderous history.

While the ceremony to welcome Elphinstone was going on, his soldiers and servants were having a hard time trying to hand over the gifts they had brought for the amir. Not only were the camels bearing the gifts taken by force by the amir's men, so were other riding camels that had come in by mistake. British livery was taken off the backs of the elephant-drivers, and there was an attempt to kidnap two servants. It was symbolic of what was taking place across the land. Royal power did not even extend as far as the royal stables. On his way to Peshawar Elphinstone had noticed how even people who worked closely with the amir would speak openly against him, 'I was a good deal surprised at the freedom with which all my visitors spoke of the government, and of the civil wars.'

What was happening was a fight to the death between two rival clans. Both were old Pashtun noble families from the south. When Ahmed Shah Durrani, who came from the Sadozai clan, founded his dynasty in the middle of the eighteenth century, the chief of the other big southern clan, the Barakzais, had stood aside for him, crowning him symbolically with a sheaf of corn (remembered still in a symbol on the national flag). After Ahmed Shah's son Timur died in 1793, the succession was disputed. Initially one of Timur's 23 sons, Zaman Shah, ruled successfully with the assistance of Payendah Khan, the clan leader of the Barakzais, as his wazir or chief minister. This was the king Britain had feared enough to keep troops garrisoned in the west. But voices at court conspired against Payendah Khan, and Zaman Shah had him killed. The power struggle between the two clans would take a further 40 years to resolve, drawing both Persia and Britain into wars in Afghanistan.

Zaman Shah had made too many enemies and lost his throne; he was caught trying to escape, blinded in a savagely symbolic act, and thrown into jail. In the chaos of the following years, he was released and fled to exile as a pensioner of the British in India, beginning the nineteenth-century trail of discontented and dispossessed members of Afghan ruling families who would take rupees from the British while plotting their return to power. Guest houses in Ludhiana and Rawalpindi became royal waiting rooms.

When Shah Shuja, brother of the blinded Zaman Shah, met Elphinstone in Peshawar in 1809, he had just taken Kandahar and Herat, the two principal cities in the south, and the ones Britain had been most concerned about, for this was believed to be Napoleon's likely invasion route. But Shah Shuja's hold on power was precarious. He lost Kashmir to local rivals in the months that Elphinstone was with him, and was not sure it was even safe to return to Kabul. In their discussions Elphinstone did secure a treaty against Napoleon, but he did not demand much, certainly much less than he had sought at first, because the expectation of a French invasion had receded. While Elphinstone had been hunting and hawking on his way to the Indus through that winter of 1808/9, his mentor Arthur Wellesley had proved that he was not just a 'sepoy general'. He was pinning down French forces in the Peninsular war in southern Europe, blocking Napoleon's wider ambitions. This had a profound impact on events in the Indian subcontinent.

Elphinstone's instructions when he first set out from Delhi had been to secure an aggressive pact, binding the Afghans to attack Persia if French forces appeared over the horizon, with promises of troops and substantial military aid. French reverses in the Pensinsular war led to a change of plan. Elphinstone returned to Delhi after agreeing a treaty with Afghanistan that offered far less than had been originally considered – a defensive alliance, with terms that provided for British aid for 'arms, ordnance, and military stores, rather than of troops'. Shah Shuja was the first in a long line of Afghan kings to find himself on the receiving end of a British policy that was determined only by British interests, not helping his hold on power, nor considering wider regional security.

The risk of the French winning the support of the Persian

government had receded despite one of the most ludicrous episodes in the history of British diplomacy. Unlike Afghanistan, not safe enough for another century for permanent embassies from abroad, Persia did admit foreign embassies. Britain had responded to the threat of French influence in the region by sending not one but two missions to Persia, from London and from India, with contradictory orders.

Persia was bemused by the desire of the great powers to court support. When the Persian ambassador in Bombay was killed by chance in a brawl outside his house the British paid lavish recompense, fearing offence. A Persian minister drily commented 'the English might kill ten ambassadors, if they would pay for them at the same rate'. Britain had already concluded a rabidly anti-French treaty with Persia in 1800, amid general European hysteria about the threat of republicanism spreading after the French Revolution. Despite vigorous protests from France, the treaty effectively bound the Persian government to kill French civilians on sight.

With Russia and France now threatening again in 1808, the government in India sent Brigadier John Malcolm, the same man who had secured the original bloody anti-French treaty. But before he set out for Tehran Malcolm heard that the East India Company were planning to send another emissary, under the direct command of London, headed by Sir Harford Jones, newly knighted for the occasion.

Malcolm had fallen out with Jones before, and the row that ensued between London and Calcutta had a personal edge. Malcolm wrote to the governor-general of India, complaining of Sir Harford's 'character and former petty animosities . . . Sir Harford is not in possession of that high local respect and consideration in the countries to which he is deputed that should attach to a national representative.'

But Malcolm's powers of persuasion failed him this time. He arrived in Persia, bearing gold and threats, and was received very coldly. He watched French artillery officers giving the Persians advice, and French surveyors helping them to map their territory, while he had to leave with nothing. His rival Jones was now ready in Bombay, and by the time Malcolm had arrived back and persuaded the government in India to take a tougher line, and threaten military action against Persia, Jones had already set sail. A black comedy followed, with Malcolm securing agreement from the government in India to put together a military force of 2000 men to attack Persian islands in the Gulf, while Jones found his missives ignored by a government that was refusing even to settle his bills, as he continued trying to negotiate peace.

Things became dangerous for Jones when the governor-general, Lord Minto, threatened to damage his reputation in Persia: 'In the event of you not complying, without further reference or delay, with the instruction conveyed in this letter, by closing your mission and retiring from Persia, it has been determined, and measures have been taken accordingly, to disavow your public character in that country.'

Jones was nevertheless able to ignore Calcutta because his orders came directly from London, and he carried on laying the diplomatic groundwork for a treaty that was beginning to look possible. He was lucky as well. He had already proved he was an unconventional diplomat in the way he continued to go forwards despite specific orders. As the treaty came closer to being agreed, the senior Persian negotiator complained about a clause that was unclear and called the British diplomat a very undiplomatic name meaning 'cheat'. Jones pushed him against the wall, told him he was an idiot, kicked over the candles and stormed out. Whatever he did, it worked, although Malcolm fumed away, advocating force and complaining that Jones could never achieve success, which 'every child with him sees is unattainable through the means he uses'.

Jones finally secured his treaty, with a specific clause specifically barring British military assault on Persian islands in the Gulf, inserted by Persia to deal with Malcolm's threat. The turf war meant a loss of face for the government in India so that British relations with Persia were conducted directly from London for most of the rest of the nineteenth century.

Other long-term consequences emerged from this episode of diplomacy. Persia had its own ambitions for Afghanistan then, as in the conflict two centuries later when Persia was called Iran. In the early decades of the nineteenth century, the divisions inside Afghanistan made a Persian advance seem possible. The power struggle between the southern Afghan clan leaders was settling into a pattern that would affect regional balances for generations to come. Kabul became the natural capital of the country, replacing Kandahar, which was now routinely fought over between Kabul and the semi-independent city of Herat, close to the Persian border in the west.

All of this felt remote and distant to the British in India. Even after Elphinstone's first mission, they knew little of what was really going on. Elphinstone had not even crossed the Suleiman Mountains, meeting the amir east of the Khyber Pass. Afghanistan remained a closed book. A surveyor travelling with Elphinstone, Lieutenant Macartney, drew a map of Afghanistan from accounts he was given by travellers, in an effort to understand the country. He had not seen Afghanistan either, but his perspective would come to dominate European thinking, in particular military thinking, about the land across the Indus, for a century. The 'wild and strange' land beyond the mountains was an imaginary country – an Afghanistan of the mind. Inevitably much of the map is inaccurate, but it had a clarity that would come to influence military understanding. Macartney's drawing defines the routes in and out of Afghanistan much more clearly than a modern map, where the sheer complexity of the mountain ranges can conceal understanding.

Guided by the accounts of travellers he met, Macartney's map peers over the mountains, making an educated guess about how Afghanistan looked. The most significant feature beyond the Indus was the Suleiman mountain wall, virtually impassable and, according to Elphinstone, reaching 'up to the sky'. (Modern surveys show the range to have peaks going up to 11,500 feet.) Beyond these mountains on Macartney's map lay uninhabitable wasteland and then another solid wall crossing the centre of the country – the Hindu Kush – a fabled snow-topped mountain range with few known passes through it; its name translates as 'killer of Hindus'.

These two ranges – the Suleiman Mountains running north-south, and the Hindu Kush in an east-west gash across the middle of the country – were the defining features for British strategists. In their mind's eye Afghanistan was huge and treacherous, dominated by these walls set at right angles, and this image informed all of their thinking. They knew very little about the precise topography, but they did know that Alexander the Great had found his way through from the other side and had crossed the Indus. For the defence of India, Britain needed to have a relationship with the people beyond the mountains. Macartney shows too the vital importance of the Helmand River in the south-west, and the impenetrable mountains to the north and west of Helmand. The map demonstrates clearly why the battles of the next 200 years were always fought in the same places. Nowhere does geography more define war than in Afghanistan.

It took until the end of the nineteenth century for Britain to decide which of the two key barriers, the Indus River or the Suleiman Mountains, was the better Afghan border. How far 'Forward' did they need to go to project military power and diplomatic influence in order to defend India? The solution they came to in 1893 was to draw a line down the *middle* of the mountains, a line that became the border between Afghanistan and Pakistan, and has remained a permanent source of instability into the twenty-first century.

The Afghanistan of the mind that developed from Lieutenant Macartney's map was part of a defensive wall on a chessboard. The amir may have dressed as a king, but he was just a pawn, expendable in a bigger game. At the start of the century of British dominance of world events, the Afghan amir was offered neither protection nor support, but instead a demand that he should support British imperial interests. Later in the century Afghan amirs would ask for more protection in return for Britain controlling their foreign policy, but they would not receive it, and this weakened them in their battles to stabilise an unruly country.

Britain offered Afghanistan no permanent guarantees of its own security, but sought temporary defensive deals that lasted only for the reign of the amir who negotiated them. And when the British tried to influence who should be in power in Kabul, during two catastrophic wars in Afghanistan in the nineteenth century, they did so in pursuit of narrow British defensive interests.

So what did the Europeans think of the Afghans they first encountered? Elphinstone, a highly sensitive and articulate man, was the first of a long line of British writers who developed a genuine regard for them. To him, the straight-forwardness, courtesy, and looks of Afghans were appealing compared to the Indians he lived among. They had neat houses 'so unlike those of Hindoostan', and they were more pleasing to his eye: 'their appearance and complexion continued to improve as we got northward'. Afghans tended to be tall, with paler skin than Indians, and Grecian noses. Many had blue eyes, and some from the north had fair hair.

Elphinstone went into admiring detail about the exercise routine of the Afghans, especially their use of Indian clubs, swung around their heads. He was very struck by one exercise in particular: 'the performer places himself on his hands and toes, with his arms stiff, and his body horizontal, at a distance from the ground. He then throws his body forward, and at the same time bends his arms, so that his chest and belly almost sweep the ground. When his body is as far thrown forward as possible, he draws it back to the utmost, straightens his arms, and is prepared to repeat the motion.'

He described approvingly how beneficial this was, saying that one of his officers could soon do 600 of the exercises at a time. The British army had discovered press-ups.

The British force adopted an Afghan giant of a man called Rasool, calling him 'Rasool the Mad', and equipping him with a full British uniform and helmet. He had come to their notice when they first arrived, as he enthusiastically beat back the crowds. Praise for the looks and manly virtue of the Afghans, compared to Hindu plains-Indians, was a constant thread in the writing of male British writers from that first traveller George Forster onwards. It was as if the British recognised something they admired once they came close to the mountains, that was easier to deal with than the dark complexities of India with its many gods.

The Afghans' faith, Islam, was also seen in a more favourable light than Hinduism. One of the early travellers, Alexander Burnes, admired a Hindu on his staff who converted to Islam in the frontier region. Islam would not 'satisfy a Christian' but was still a move in the right direction. 'It is no small step to advance from Hindooism, its superstitions and abominations, to Mohammedanism, even with all its imperfections and absurdities.'

They had no illusions: Afghans were always to be characterised as predatory, murderous and barbarous, with, as Forster put it, a 'fixed contempt for the occupations of civil life'. But they were believed to be honourable, robust and hardy. Victorian British travellers also shared a preoccupation with local sexual practices, culminating in a magisterial collection of stereotypes, laid down by an adventurer who went on to govern India as viceroy at the end of the century, Lord Curzon. 'At Chitral I fraternized with fratricides, parricides, murderers, adulterers and sodomites . . . I start tomorrow for Kabul where a female donkey is the object of favourite solicitude,' he wrote in 1895. The often soft and familiar way that men would walk together, for example holding hands in public, was easily construed as meaning that homosexuality was widespread, although Forster admired what he believed to be a hard line against 'that unnatural passion to which many of the Mohametan sects are addicted; and the perpetrators are punished with severity'.

Elphinstone was told that Afghan men and women could marry for love rather than by arrangement, a situation 'unique for the east' seen from his Indian-trained perspective. Certainly from the way he describes village life, it appears that Pashtun women had far more liberty then than they do today: 'as the women there go unveiled, and there is less restraint . . . between the sexes, the match generally originates in the attachment of the parties, and all the previous negotiations are saved'. If a man were to cut a lock of a girl's hair or take her veil, then that would be enough to win her as a fiancée. With the complicity of the bride's mother, a groom might be allowed to slip in to spend nights with her before the wedding.

If young couples were forced to elope, then he was told that Pashtun hospitality rules would give them sanctuary with another clan or tribe. Elphinstone was an acute observer of both extremes of the *pashtunwali*, their code of honour, that gave protection to guests while guaranteeing death to strangers.

Elphinstone understood aggression towards strangers and travellers as an inevitable and proper part of a system that demanded loyalty. Lone travellers had no relations or tribe so there was no provision for their security, and it was reasonable to rob them. The system was a closed one, depending on a balance of strength. 'To sum up the character of the Afghans in a few words; their vices are revenge, envy, avarice, rapacity, and obstinacy; on the other hand, they are fond of liberty, faithful to their friends, kind to their dependants, hospitable, brave, hardy, frugal, laborious and prudent.'

The strength of their clan and tribal ties gave Afghans the ability to survive without effective central government, and at the same time made it harder for central government to impose its will. The violence and bloodshed caused by continual weakness and war at the centre must have given the country beyond the Suleiman Mountains something of the same feel in 1808 as it had 200 years later, when the US-led invasion had not provided stable government.

But it was better than neighbouring Persia, which did not have the Pashtun honour code. 'We find Persia in a state of decay, after twenty years of entire tranquillity; while Afghanistan continues the progressive improvement which it has kept up during twelve years of civil warfare.' Education was valued, although even then it was too often in the hands of 'half-taught Mullahs, who rather impede than promote the progress of real learning'.

After Elphinstone returned home to Bombay, a young Anglo-Indian called Durie came to his door having travelled across Afghanistan. He had pretended to be a Muslim, and had politely declined an offer of circumcision on the spot when his real identity was discovered. Elphinstone quoted Durie's conclusion that military success in Afghanistan was possible: 'It is evident that a regular courageous army, having provisions, can make them all submit completely.' Military men of more experience than Durie would make the same mistaken prophecy often during the next two centuries.

While Elphinstone had been probing Afghan land west of the Indus, another of Wellesley's young stars, Charles Metcalfe, had been behind him, ensuring that the Sikh army between India and Afghanistan did not stray beyond Punjab, then independent. The Sikh ruler Ranjit Singh, 'the lion of Lahore', was emerging as one of the great south Asian generals of the nineteenth century, and after uniting his nation, he was pushing his elbows into Afghan territory to his north and west, as well as threatening British India to the east. After British forces pushed Sikh cavalry back west of the Sutlej River without a fight, Metcalfe forced a defensive alliance on Ranjit Singh in Lahore in March 1809. Once again the long shadow of Wellesley's success in Spain would help negotiations in India. Ranjit Singh could not count on France, and agreed that British forces could cross his territory if they needed to move west into Afghanistan.

Sikh forces made easy work though of defeating the Afghan Amir Shah Shuja, aided by their European artillery and European, mainly French, soldiers of fortune. Within six months of his meeting with Elphinstone Shuja had lost his throne, fleeing to regroup the remnants of his army just inside British India. He returned to retake Peshawar in 1812 but could offer nothing to the chiefs there, who took a bribe to hand over the ex-amir to the Sikhs. He was held in jail for a year while complex negotiations went on for control of the Koh-i-noor diamond, the symbol of power across the region since the days of the Mughal Empire.

In the end of course it fell into the hands of the new strong man in the region, Ranjit Singh, who signed elaborate promises in return, none of which he fulfilled. Shah Shuja's run of bad luck continued even when he had lost the cursed stone. After escaping from his Sikh jail dressed as a beggar, he bribed a Hindu army with his last money to retake Kashmir, but they were defeated by the snows. He fled in 1816 to join his sightless brother Zaman Shah amid the growing colony of ex-Afghan rulers living on British pensions.

The struggle for control of Afghanistan did not stop with Shuja's flight. When the British horse-breeder, William Moorcroft, visited Peshawar in the early 1820s he found the Bala Hissar, the fort overlooking the city, reduced to a pile of rubble. Sikhs had comprehensively demolished the remaining signs of Mughal and Afghan rule, and even damaged some mosques. The elaborate courtyards where Shah Shuja had ruled from his golden throne were no more.

Moorcroft rejected an offer by four princes from the next generation of the Barakzai dynasty to 'become the channel for negotiation for placing the whole country under British rule'. Afghanistan was for sale to Britain for just 300,000 rupees. As he moved towards the mountains, even the Waziris, the most ferocious, independent and warlike of the Afghan tribes, asked for British protection from the cruelty of their own rulers and the threat of the Sikhs. They were 'torn to pieces by intestine feuds, village being armed against village, and man against man'. But Moorcroft was driven only by the imperative to improve Indian bloodstock. Among the Waziris he noted two horse breeds: one was called *Dagla-gala*, meaning 'thieves' brood'.

The reputation of those who lived hidden in the folds of the remote mountain ranges of Waziristan imprinted itself on generations of travellers. Elphinstone had been told to fear the Waziris – said to be savages who ate human flesh. The region contained no routes into Afghanistan that were useful in military terms, but dozens of mountain tracks that were perfect for thieves, smugglers and, in the wars that broke out after the Soviet invasion in 1979, Islamist insurgents. It was Waziristan that provided the staunchest support for the US-backed war against the Soviet Union, and later the best refuge for Osama bin Laden's foreign fighters after 9/11.

Moorcroft faced the usual threats when negotiating his way through the Khyber Pass into Afghanistan, paying protection money while fearing throughout for his security. He found the Khyberees 'tall for mountaineers, and of a singularly Jewish cast of features'. This referred to an old belief of the Pashtuns that they were the lost tribe of Israel. 'Some of the young women had an arch, lively look, but we saw none that could be described as pretty.' His companion George Trebeck was robbed while they were camping within sight of Kabul.

Moorcroft was the most adventurous of the European travellers who penetrated the further reaches of Asia in the early years of the nineteenth century, even crossing the Himalayas to Lake Manasarovar, at the foot of Mount Kailash, the holiest mountain for both Hindus and Buddhists. He and Trebeck both died of fever in northern Afghanistan in 1825, and were buried at Balkh, a city with claims to be the oldest in the world, where settlements date back to the threshing of the first grain.

But deaths on distant mountainsides did not deter exploration by other British adventurers. Alexander Burnes, a brilliant linguist with a rakish reputation and a flair for self-publicity, first came to Punjab in 1831, bearing the fantastic gift to Ranjit Singh of five British dray horses, four mares and a stallion, the biggest horses in Asia – and a specially built carriage fit for a maharajah. He brought them up the Indus on a flat-bottomed barge. The trip was a hard-headed boast: if Britain could take a carriage and five cart-horses up the river, then why not normal trade?

A few months later Burnes set out west from India again, pretending to be poor, with pots and pans tied to his saddle. This time he led a very small party, including an Indian, Mohan Lal, who was surprised to see his companions sitting on the ground 'which I never saw an Englishman do before'. And they were willing to sleep out without a tent, even when there was frost.

There was a curious link with the 1808 mission in the choice of Mohan Lal, whose father had been Elphinstone's secretary on that journey. He was part of the Indian elite that received a first-class education, and skilfully navigated the cultural minefields between British India and Afghanistan. He was an acute observer of the Afghan temperament: 'The Afghans are bold and careless, with a mixture of rudeness. They are accustomed to shoot on horseback, and a good marksman is always respected, although he may be of low family. They quarrel for an insignificant thing, and kill each other for a trifling offence. They boast of their heroism, and think themselves the most incomparable warriors of the age . . . They cut off a man's head with as much indifference as we cut a radish.'

The most powerful and successful military leader in the region, the Sikh king Ranjit Singh, put on a show for them before they went on their travels. Burnes enjoyed the debauchery of the Sikh court, before disappearing into his not very plausible disguise as a pauper; his confidence in his own abilities reflected in the name he used – Sikander, Alexander in the local language. The only Sikander remembered on the frontier is Alexander the Great. And he chose as his second name Khan – meaning King.

Mohan Lal was unimpressed by Ranjit Singh. The short lecherous Sikh ruler was already showing signs of the skin cancer that would kill him: 'His one eye is ever inflamed, either by the use of opium or wine.' Lal was shocked to find Ranjit

Singh talking familiarly to dancing girls – 'improper in the opinion of the wise'. Worse, he was accompanied by a beautiful boy, whose family he had enriched.

By the 1830s, Russia had replaced France as the country Britain thought most likely to threaten their control of India. A Russian mission was massacred in Tehran, as Lord Ellenborough, a member of the Board of Control that supervised Indian affairs in London, noted in his diary with some satisfaction. 'These accounts only confirm what we had already heard of the arrogance and violence of the Russians. They deserve their fate.' But he was concerned enough to put out a secret order to arrest Russian spies, and recommended that Britain should occupy Kabul if there were any hint of a Russian move south.

Ellenborough, a pompous manipulative man, would be the person called on to clear up after the mess of the disaster of the war in Afghanistan that was to come in 1838. Back in 1829, he laid out a policy that would not change much in its essentials until Britain pulled out of India in 1947. First he wanted information. 'We know nothing of these passes, nothing of the country beyond them, nothing of the course of the Indus.' Preparations were made for 70,000 troops, with as many mounted as possible, and his tactics had an icy cynicism. 'We should have full information so as to be able to crush an advancing enemy, by making the whole country hostile, which money would do.'

The region was to be controlled with cash and cavalry. Britain's long obsession with India's north-west frontier had begun.

2

A War of Robbery

'A war of robbery . . . a new crime in the annals of
nations – a secret war. It has been made by a people
without their knowledge, against another people who
had committed no offence.'

East India Company Select Committee report

The appearance of two dogs, exhausted and thirsty, one
evening at the besieged British garrison in Kabul in December
1841, was the first sign of a missing British force. Lady
Florentia Sale recognised the dogs immediately. They
belonged to officers serving in the occupying force commanded by her husband, General Sir Robert Sale, 'Fighting
Bob', who had set out from Kabul to give rebel tribes a
'thrashing'. But there had been no firm news from the missing
army for several weeks.

As the sun dropped below the hill behind Kabul city to the
south-west, soft remnants of evening light picked out the dark
shapes of Afghan warriors, moving into position among the
scrubby larch and oak trees for another night of firing down
from the Bemaru Hills above the British garrison into the
poorly defended area below. Lady Sale took in the dogs and
ordered servants to feed them, although she knew that the

remaining dogs in the garrison were already eating the corpses of horses and camels that had died of starvation.

Were the officers' dogs harbingers of doom, or messengers coming ahead of the army, on its way back to relieve Kabul, where the British occupation force was now in desperate straits?

For some weeks General Sale's letters to her had somehow got through the chaos. They talked of far fiercer fighting than expected in the passes to the east, with dozens of British dead, until Sale moved in to defend the fort at Jalalabad, and then nothing. Appeals from Kabul for help went unanswered. Colonel John Shelton, who had lost his arm in the Peninsular war, did not endear himself to Lady Sale, saying her husband would not be back, since 'being out of a scrape, keep so'. Shelton promptly moved into the Sales' house in the Kabul cantonment, complaining that it was too cold to sleep outside as winter approached.

Lady Sale was not to see her husband for another nine months. And by the time she did, he had withstood a siege in Jalalabad, during which he saw his defences collapse in an earthquake, and she had emerged from Kabul as one of a handful of survivors of Britain's greatest Asian defeat – a heroine who had taken command of troops when the men around her failed to rise to the challenge. It was her new house guest Shelton, a stiff and unimaginative man, 'a tyrant to his regiment', who was to be responsible for the catastrophe that engulfed the garrison, alongside an old and sick veteran of Waterloo who had not seen action for years, General William Elphinstone (first cousin of Mountstuart Elphinstone). But the military mistakes of Shelton and Elphinstone were just the closing chapter in a story of political miscalculation, hard reality against vain hope, humiliation after hubris – dealt out to another invader by Afghanistan.

It had begun with a note sent to the foreign secretary Lord Palmerston by his ambassador in Tehran in 1836, warning that Russia was urging a Persian advance on Herat in the west of Afghanistan – then not governed from Kandahar or Kabul but an independent city state. Full of mosques, minarets and gardens that told of old wealth gathered from centuries of trade on the crossroads of Asia, Herat was the legacy of one extraordinary woman, Gohar Shad Begum in the fifteenth century, who married the son of the great warlord Tamerlane, and used the wealth of conquest to bring the best artists from around the known world to adorn the city.

The ambassador who had sent the note, John McNeill, was the author of a highly influential analysis of Russia's threat to British control of India, which pointed out how fast the Russians were moving south. 'Russia alone threatens to over-turn thrones, to subvert empires, and subdue nations hitherto independent.' He warned of the knock-on effect if Herat went, weakening Britain's 'moral influence' across Asia.

Britain was backing the ruler of Herat, Kamran Shah, to balance power within Afghanistan, a country that was still divided into several kingdoms. Herat was the only part still in the hands of the Sadozai dynasty, descendants of Ahmed Shah Durrani. An opium addict and wine drinker, Kamran Shah would steal from merchants and the public to pay his troops. 'In lieu of distributing justice, he spends the whole of his life in ornamenting himself with handsome robes, and his abominable conduct . . . has rendered him most obnoxious throughout the whole of Afghanistan.'

Kamran Shah was fond of devising new methods of torture, such as ripping open the bellies of prisoners, and tying them upside down to camels that were driven through the bazaar, colouring the sand red. He wanted better backing against the threat of Persia, telling a British visitor, 'any boy of four years of age in this country knew well that the Persians were the intimate friends, and even the slaves, of Russia'.

What any boy of four knew was certainly believed by Lord Palmerston at the Foreign Office in London: Russia was now the puppet master pulling the strings in Persia, ending decades of British influence. Britain's aim was to avoid military confrontation with Russia, while neutralising its power. It was the same foreign policy thinking that emerged in the days of the cold war in the late twentieth century. And on both occasions it ended up with Afghanistan becoming a battlefield.

For Palmerston, avoiding war with Russia over Turkey, while retaining access through the Dardanelles and influence over Constantinople, was the main objective. Afghanistan was a remote and distant piece on the board, to be shaped and moved into place by the master strategist according to his grand vision, not for its own good, but as a defensive wall against Russia, 'the best rampart India could have'.

The player chosen to fit Afghanistan into Palmerston's design was Alexander Burnes, now the most famous British adventurer of the age. After presenting Ranjit Singh with his carriage and carthorses, he had written an account of his epic trip through Afghanistan and across the Oxus north to the mysterious kingdom of Bokhara in 1831 that became an instant best-seller. Now he was going back to Kabul to try to prevent war on both sides of Afghanistan.

The Afghan capital in the 1830s was a teeming cosmopolitan trading post, with one of Asia's most important bazaars, built in the crook of the Kabul River as it turned a right angle between three high hills that reared up around the centre. On the southern side, set away from the river, lay a fort complex, a military town within a town, known, as was the one in Peshawar, as the Bala Hissar. Overlooked by the ruins of an earlier castle above a large walled area that housed the royal palace and a garrison of troops, it jutted out like an apron into Kabul – its walls and towers grand vestiges of two centuries of Mughal supremacy in Kabul before the eighteenth century.

Kabul seethed with armed men, including thousands of *qizalbashes*, Persian cavalry for hire, who lived in a separate walled compound not far from the Bala Hissar. While nearly all Afghans were Muslim, there was a large Hindu quarter, and also Sikhs, Jews and Christians – a kaleidoscope of Asian humanity as it was before the monochrome of the modern Muslim world. Armenian Christians, valued for their prowess in making guns, had their own church in the Bala Hissar itself. Alcohol was freely available and 'females, both of high and low family, desert the path of virtue and pursue bad principles'. This was so well known that there was an old Pashtun proverb: 'As the flour of Peshawar is always tainted by a little barley, so the women of Kabul are not without lovers.'

Burnes had an appetite for all Kabul had to offer, although he was initially made 'melancholy' by the sight of women in their standard dress, shrouded from head to toe in a burqa with just a lattice window to see and breathe through. He went to the races and recorded that while the first prize was a girl, the second rider took home 50 sheep, while the third won a boy; the prizes then went down through a cow, horse, and camel, until the seventh man won a watermelon, and was the object of 'ridicule and banter for the rest of the meeting'.

Burnes had pretended to be surveying the region for trading opportunities at the beginning of his mission in 1837, although few believed that was his only purpose. And secret orders followed him across Punjab and along the Khyber Pass that would give his negotiations much more urgency. He wrote to a friend that he had been sent 'to see into affairs and judge what was to be done hereafter; but the hereafter has already arrived'.

Persia had carried out its threat to besiege Herat, the Shah himself coming from Tehran and setting up camp on Afghan territory. And on the eastern side of Afghanistan, while waiting to go through the Khyber Pass, Burnes had seen the bodies of men and horses still littering the battlefield at Jamrud, where sizeable Sikh and Afghan armies had fought each other to a standstill some months before – a battle that had taken the life of the Sikh commander-in-chief. Britain wanted to stop another Afghan army roaring through the Khyber Pass to confront the Sikhs, now in control of Peshawar and other former Afghan land west of the Indus. Britain's promotion of the interests of the Sikh leader Ranjit Singh was their first mistake.

On his arrival in Kabul in September 1837, Burnes was greeted warmly as an old friend by the amir's son Akbar Khan, and carried in some ceremony on the back of an elephant through narrow streets where people shouted up at him, 'Do not destroy Kabul.' He was honoured with lodgings in a spacious royal guest house next to the palace itself inside the Bala Hissar complex. The buildings were on a colossal scale. In front of Burnes's window was a formally laid-out square garden 500 feet across, with the clear waters of a stream flowing through elaborately constructed halls of audience at each end.

The day after his arrival, Burnes walked out through the entrance of his grand lodging, and across a square lined with petitioners waiting to see their Amir, Dost Mohammed, who could be seen sitting on a raised dais, in a large audience chamber one floor up. Burnes thought he seemed 'more alert and full of intelligence than when I last saw him'. Later in the day he had the curious honour of being taken to see the brother of the amir, Jabar Khan, in his bath.

Dost Mohammed, who became known as the 'great amir', was one of the two dominating Afghan characters of the nineteenth century. And, like the 'iron amir', Abdur Rahman, at the end of the century, the longest and most successful part of his reign was to follow a failed British military intervention. These two men stood like giants at each end of a period of intense British involvement in the affairs of the country, and a crucial part of the mix that brought success for both was the way they exploited political Islam for their own ends.

Dost's aim was to knit together the frontier tribes in a jihad, a holy war, against the Sikh invader. The willingness to sacrifice everything, for the promise of paradise beyond this life, was a powerful imperative for Islamic holy warriors in Afghanistan, then as later. They responded to kings who would define jihad not as a personal inward struggle, but a call to war.

Dost Mohammed was the first Afghan leader to realise the power of jihad. He was preoccupied with retaking Peshawar and the other former Afghan territory east of the Khyber Pass. He even went as far as to declare himself *Amir al-Mu'minin* – the spiritual leader not just of Afghanistan, but of all Muslims, after a very rare public display of Afghanistan's most precious object, a cloak believed to have belonged to the Prophet Mohammed himself. The next person to take out the cloak and declare himself *Amir al-Mu'minin* was Mullah Omar, the leader of the Taliban, in 1996.

Dost Mohammed, a man of 'tall stature and haughty countenance', had fought his way to the top. He was one of the youngest of 20 half-brothers of Fateh Khan, the main Barakzai claimant to power, but Dost had no status, as his mother was the daughter of a *qizalbash*, a Persian mercenary. He remedied that when, just 14, he killed an enemy of Fateh Khan's with a knife. Dost emerged as amir from a vicious civil war as the most powerful of the Barakzai brothers, after Fateh Khan overreached himself and was literally cut to pieces – first his ears, then his nose, then his hands and feet, before his throat was cut.

Dost had enjoyed wine as a youth, but like Shakespeare's Prince Hal, he turned away from his former self when he assumed power. Some British travellers mocked his conversion. 'Of later years, by all accounts, he has been ambitious of the character of a saint, pretending to have celestial visions.' But Burnes did not mock him; he liked the amir, who had offered him command of the Afghan army when they had last met, believing that much of the strength of the Sikh force lay in its European officers. Burnes wanted Dost Mohammed as a British ally, but he had been given impossible orders.

Britain's alliance with Ranjit Singh's Sikh kingdom dominated the discussions in Kabul, with Burnes being ordered to persuade Dost to make peace at any price. If Dost would apologise for Sikh losses in the battle of Jamrud in 1836 and pay tribute to Ranjit Singh, then there might again be an Afghan prince in Peshawar – but under Sikh domination, and not Dost himself. Instead Britain would install another Barakzai brother in Peshawar – an enemy of Dost, who was discovering how bitter was Britain's game of divide and rule.

But Burnes's ability to negotiate was being undermined. Beneath Palmerston's empire-building map of the world lay layers of British-Indian public officials. The Afghan negotiations were not directly run by the governor-general in India but by a political officer, Sir Claude Wade, who had far more influence in the system than the maverick young adventurer Burnes and put his own spin on the reports as they passed both ways.

Burnes soon realised that Wade had his own agent in Kabul, a man claiming to be called Charles Masson, an American adventurer from Kentucky. He was in reality a deserter from the East India Company's army called James Lewis, pardoned for desertion at the insistence of Burnes himself, who had pressed his case in London after meeting 'Masson' on his first trip to Kabul in 1831.

Masson did not repay the favour. He was the sort of character often washed up on the shores of Afghanistan – independent, resourceful, hugely talented and duplicitous. He had travelled widely across the country in the guise of a beggar, and had an encyclopaedic knowledge of its history and a fine coin collection. Burnes was a threat to his small income as a Company spy, and from his mud house, carved out of the hill in the narrow winding streets of the Armenian quarter below the palace in the Bala Hissar, he conspired against the flamboyant adventurer who had come onto his patch.

Worse than the presence of Masson, who was at least supposed to be on the same side, was the news soon after Burnes arrived that a Russian envoy was also on his way. Dost Mohammed called Burnes in to ask him what he should do, and what Britain would offer if he were to turn away the Russian envoy. Burnes was ready for the question. He had his own spy at court and knew that Dost was planning to see both of them whatever he offered, so he bowed and graciously gave the amir his 'permission' to see the Russian. Messengers were now galloping daily through the Khyber Pass, carrying the assessments of Burnes and Masson in one direction, and orders the other way. The letters often crossed, and Burnes made two offers for which he had no authority, to keep ahead of Persia and Russia. He offered financial help to Dost's brothers in Kandahar to head off a Persian attempt to dominate the town, and then he offered Dost direct help to take Kandahar for himself.

But Britain did not back its own envoy. The British strategy was to keep Kandahar, Herat and Kabul divided, and do nothing to threaten the Sikh leader Ranjit Singh to the east of Afghanistan, as if this could be kept separate from the crisis brewing to the west, where the hawkish envoy McNeill was still writing virulent messages about the Russian threat. 'The evidence of concert between Persia and Russia, for purposes injurious to British interests is unequivocal, and the magnitude of the evil with which we are threatened is, in my estimation, immense.'

McNeill was seeing the threat at first hand. As ambassador he had had to move with the Persian court onto Afghan soil, when the Shah began his siege of Herat, and had seen him take money and artillery advice from the Russian ambassador and shamelessly greet the Russian envoy, on his way to meet Dost Mohammed in Kabul.

In desperation, on 23rd December 1837, Burnes wrote a personal note to the governor-general of India, Lord Auckland, to try to circumvent the Wade loop. The high-handed move was a risk, especially as Wade was already recommending that Burnes should be reprimanded for offering far more than Britain wanted to deliver. In his personal note Burnes put Dost's case against the Sikhs, and said the Afghans had wanted connection with British, but had received 'cold and distant replies to their solicitations'. He said it was impossible to negotiate through Wade, and was a 'matter of great moment that this question should be speedily adjusted'.

While waiting for an answer to his plea, Burnes, with characteristic flair, sent an invitation to the newly arrived Russian agent Ivan Vitkevitch to join him for Christmas dinner. Vitkevitch came to his sumptuous quarters, deep in the Bala Hissar, in the full uniform of a Cossack officer: two of the most gifted mavericks ever drawn to Afghanistan face to face at dinner in the city at the heart of the Great Game – the imperial struggle for influence across Asia.

Vitkevitch had a colourful past. Stripped of his noble title for organising a secret far-right revolutionary society, the Black Brothers, he had escaped execution and was banished instead in what was seen as an almost equivalent punishment – serving as a ordinary soldier on the wildest fringes of Russia in Orenburg, the garrison town facing south to the untamed vastness of Central Asia.

He was a natural spy, resourceful, and with a gift for languages and deception that quickly drew him to the attention of Russian intelligence. In Kabul, he had far more money to offer and more scope to make promises to Dost Mohammed than Burnes had. The Afghan amir had already been in touch with Russia to try to secure their support. The arrival of Vitkevitch meant he was being offered something other than Britain's arid, repetitive humiliating demand that he should pay tribute to the Sikh maharajah Ranjit Singh – an infidel who had taken *Afghan* land.

Dost Mohammed continued to tell Burnes that he would prefer to do a deal with the British, 'I wish no countenance but that of the English, and you refuse all pledges and promises, and mean . . . to do nothing for me.' But Vitkevitch was offering so much more, and it was clear that Burnes's mission was hopeless by the time of the spring equinox in March, when Afghans celebrate the new year. Vitkevitch was Dost's guest of honour, while Burnes was not invited. Mohan Lal, the discreet Indian master-fixer, succeeded in getting an invitation, but only at the last minute, scrabbling together the symbolic gifts of salt, sprouting rice and a purse of money to take with him.

At the party, Vitkevitch took Lal aside and boasted that he would rouse 'all the discontented chiefs of India to rebel'; 50,000 Russian soldiers were on hand. He claimed he had offered Dost enough money to move through the Khyber, retaking Peshawar *and* Kashmir. Vitkevitch sneered, 'The English, who are not soldiers, but merely mercantile adventurers of Europe, would not dare to assist Ranjit Singh, knowing that the Afghans are succoured by the warlike nation of Russia.'

Burnes's position became impossible. His advice to the government in India continued to be distorted by Wade, whose notes condemned the 'extravagant expectations' of Dost. He had to threaten to leave, knowing it would mean war, but still had no response. He had trouble hiring mules to carry his baggage home: Kabul's bankers had lowered Britain's credit rating. When he went to say goodbye to Dost, the amir carried on coldly playing a chess game, neither rising nor turning his face to the British envoy. But as Burnes rode away, two fine horses followed him to the Khyber as a personal gift from the amir.

Burnes was ambitious, but he was also loyal. He could not directly oppose policy, but could perhaps express incredulity at the direction it was heading. In one of his last and most poignant notes before abandoning his mission in Afghanistan, he subtly hinted at what he thought was really behind Britain's increasingly tough line. He wrote that he did not understand apparent non-interference in Afghanistan, unless it was intended to put back in power the 'ex-king at Loodiana, secure through him a footing in these countries, and sweep the present rulers from their authority, which has happily never been contemplated'.

Burnes's worst fear was exactly what was now being contemplated. The ex-king was Shah Shuja, the 'unlucky amir' Elphinstone had met in such finery in Peshawar on the first British mission a generation before. Shuja had never stopped trying to reclaim his throne, taking an army into the field as recently as 1835, with some British financial support, but failing to defeat Dost Mohammed and the other Barakzai 'pretenders' in running battles near Kandahar. Now old and in exile in British India, Shuja pressed his ancestral claim on Wade, the political officer running the negotiations, persuading him he had substantial Afghan support against the usurper Dost.

The Wade/Shuja relationship was a combination that Burnes could never match. The complex reality experienced by the agent on the ground did not count as much as the bureaucratic analysis of the desk officer; it never has.

As Burnes led his small mission out of Kabul, there were celebrations in the large Persian community in the city, who thought Persia would beat the British-backed ruler in Herat too. The loudest roars of delight came from the *qizalbash* cavalry, but the Afghan majority was quieter and more concerned. The British misread this, believing it meant that Dost Mohammed was unpopular; Shuja would be welcomed back. The analysis would have fatal consequences.

Burnes never saw Vitkevitch again. After the new year celebrations, signalling the spring and the start of another fighting season in Afghanistan, the Russian envoy went on to Kandahar, with a treaty from Dost in his pocket, and Russian money to support Dost's brothers and the other sirdars – the tribal chiefs whose support was and is always uncertain, always expensive and always essential for waging war successfully in Afghanistan. With Russian backing, 250 Kandahari horsemen set off to help the Persian army surrounding Herat.

It was the best chance to break a siege that had gone on in a desultory way for more than six months. When the Kandahar sirdars came in on the Persian side, the remaining support in the countryside for those besieged began to ebb away. But in Herat the opium-soaked tyrant Kamran Shah was lucky in having a young British artillery officer on hand. Eldred Pottinger had been travelling in disguise across Afghanistan, first as horse-dealer and then a holy man, with a loose commission from the Intelligence Department in India to report what he found. Pottinger was in Herat when the siege began, promptly dropped his disguise, organised the defences of the city, and trained its troops.

The arrival of Russian support on the Persian side in June 1838 led to the fiercest fighting. The city nearly fell as Pottinger's defences were breached by a determined assault. The defenders fought for their lives, encouraged by the bounty that Kamran Shah offered for the head of an enemy. In one epic day of fighting, 400 enemy heads, including that of a Russian officer, were stuck onto pikes above the city gate.

Enough was enough. Palmerston had been wanting to avoid

military entanglements with Russia, concerned as he was about the possibility of war over Turkey, but he dispatched a fleet to threaten Persia, and called in the Russian ambassador in London to demand that Russia stop its military adventure in Afghanistan. As Herat held out through the relentless heat of a long desert summer, British marines took an island in the Gulf, planted the Union Jack on Persian soil, and threatened to advance onto the mainland.

Britain's ultimatum to the Shah of Persia was couched in diplomatic language, but as it was being read to him by Colonel Charles Stoddart at his camp near Herat, the Shah interrupted and said, 'The fact is that if I don't leave Herat there will be war – is that not it?' Stoddart put down the paper and nodded. A month later, on 9th September 1838, he sent a message that the Persian army had lifted the siege and was heading home.

Palmerston did not stop there: he wanted the Russian ambassador to Tehran, Count Simonich, recalled, and when Simonich returned to St Petersburg he was disowned by those who had sent him to Persia. Russian frontier policy rewarded the success of those willing to take risks, but failure was a chilly place. The Russian government was able to tell London that Simonich had exceeded his instructions. The freeze extended to Vitkevitch too. British intelligence reports from the Russian capital reported that when the envoy returned from Afghanistan he could not get a meeting with the foreign minister Count Nesselrode, who said he knew no one of that name, 'except for an adventurer . . . lately engaged in some unauthorised intrigues in Kabul and Kandahar'.

This was absurd given the lavish funding that the Russian agent had at his disposal in Afghanistan, and the fact that following him on his way home were gifts from Dost Mohammed, including an elephant for the Tsar. But neither side wanted to question the foreign minister's account. Even if Vitkevitch had in fact been warmly greeted and congratulated on his return, if Russia could say the opposite then so much the better, since it would divert awkward questions from London; and Britain did not want to be triumphalist so preferred to believe that the envoy had gone well beyond any orders he might have had. The British game of portraying Russia as 'a riddle, wrapped in a mystery, inside an enigma' has deep origins that on this occasion suited diplomats on both sides.

Vitkevitch would never tell his side of the story. A week or so after arriving in St Petersburg he was seen in high spirits, 'chatting gaily' with friends at the theatre. He then went to his lodgings, and after giving orders that he should be called in the morning, he closed his door, burnt all his Afghan papers and shot himself in the head. He had once told a friend that he would do it, even showing him the pistol.

Shuja agreed to everything that Dost would not; he would do anything to get back into power in Kabul. He even acceded to British demands that he give up all the former Afghan lands east of the Khyber Pass, and pay an annual tribute to the Sikh leader Ranjit Singh, listed in exhaustive detail, beginning with 'fifty-five high-bred horses, of approved colour and pleasant paces, eleven Persian scimitars', going through melons, grapes and pomegranates, and down to 'an abundant supply' of almonds, raisins, pistachios and chestnuts. In return the Sikhs agreed only to send various cloths to Kabul. Britain noticed encouraging signs from inside Afghanistan that Shuja would be welcomed, including the arrival of a note from a chief who supported him against Dost, which said, 'the faggots are all laid, it requires but the torch of the British government to light them'.

Ranjit Singh was delighted with the way things were going. When told of British plans to reinstate Shuja he said, 'That would be adding sugar to milk.' Twenty years before he had humiliated Shuja and held him in prison for a year, wresting the Koh-i-noor diamond from his grasp; he knew how to deal with him. And he was beginning to realise that he could deal with the British by promising them much more than he was ever prepared to deliver. Britain expected significant Sikh military forces to back Shuja in his attempt to retake the country. Ranjit Singh was never going to commit his forces, but he nevertheless signed the treaty.

The summer of 1838 was one of the high peaks of British imperial grandeur. The young Queen Victoria was crowned, and a military parade in Hyde Park displayed the pomp and ceremony of a country that believed its military forces could not be bettered. Before she was queen, when only just a teenager, Victoria had met the glamorous adventurer Burnes after his previous trip across Afghanistan to Bokhara. Now he was knighted and promoted two ranks in the army; the British mission that was to support Shuja in Kabul would include Lieutenant-Colonel Sir Alexander Burnes under the leadership of Sir William Macnaghten. In the afterglow of the coronation, Palmerston approved a 'great operation in Affghanistan; to push on Runjeet Singh, send an English Corps to act with his army . . .'

To Palmerston, the case for war was obvious. Dost Mohammed was troublesome, and a constant threat to Britain's alliance with Ranjit Singh's Sikh kingdom. The solution was on hand: reinstate a king, Shah Shuja, who had a better ancestral claim than Dost Mohammed, and would be loyal to Britain. When the war plans had been first considered, Persia's siege of Britain's other Afghan ally in Herat, was another reason for military action. But Persia's withdrawal did not alter the main reason for the war.

Not taking military action risked leaving Afghanistan in the hands of others. 'If the Governor-General were to leave the chiefs of Kandahar and the Amir of Kabul to pursue their own plans,' wrote Mohan Lal, 'the result would be that Persian agents, superintended and directed by Russian officers, would be placed in the court of the above chieftains; and intrigues would have been conducted and extended by them, even to the very heart of India.' The effective declaration of war in the 'Simla Manifesto' on 1st October 1838 accused Dost Mohammed of unprovoked attacks on the Sikhs, and a 'hostile policy' towards the English.

Old south Asia hands, men of the sort who would later be

Mountstuart Elphinstone:
the first envoy to Afghanistan

British images of frontier tribesmen in the nineteenth century were usually
caricatures of bloodthirsty ruffians.

An inhospitable terrain: in 1838 the Army of the Indus crossed the mountains by the southernmost route – the Bolan Pass.

The continuing complexity of fighting in the frontier mountains is shown vividly in this picture of a US army Chinook in 2007 lowering onto a rooftop to pick up suspects captured in battle.

Sir William Macnaghten, head of
the British mission in Kabul from 1839
until his death in 1841. On the day before
the insurrection broke out he wrote of
'a season of such profound tranquillity'.

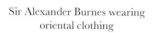

Sir Alexander Burnes wearing
oriental clothing

Contemporary portrayal of the death of Burnes, November 1841. His dying
brother Charley is shown being comforted by a woman at the bottom left.

Dost Mohammed: always depicted as thoughtful and distinguished. He even impressed Macnaghten, who said, 'We ejected the Dost, who never offended us, in support of our policy, of which he was the victim.'

Shah Shuja was brought back to Kabul as amir by the British 30 years after Elphinstone had first met him. He is shown here in the audience room at the Bala Hissar.

The redoubtable Lady Florentia Sale

Mohan Lal – 'gentleman and Kashmirian'

13th January 1842: the last stand of the 44th at Gandamack – note Captain Souter standing towards the right wrapped in the colours.

13th January 1842: *Remnants of an Army* by Lady Elizabeth Butler – one of the iconic images of Victorian Britain – shows Dr William Brydon at the gates of Jalalabad.

The two main architects of international policy towards Afghanistan in the middle years of the nineteenth century – above, Prince Aleksandr Gorchakov, who justified the civilising value of the imperial Russian move southwards, and, right, John Lawrence, proponent of 'masterly inactivity' for Britain

"SAVE ME FROM MY FRIENDS!"

A cartoon from *Punch* in 1878. The amir is Shir Ali, whose desire for an alliance with Russia coincided with the most Forward period in British policy – leading to the Second Anglo-Afghan War.

Saving the Guns – the moment when the Battle of Maiwand was lost in 1880, as the British artillery was withdrawn after arriving with hardly any ammunition

Sir Henry Mortimer Durand, who left his name indelibly on the frontier

Abdur Rahman, the 'iron amir'

1897. *Ghazis* going into battle, inspired by flags and drums, and firing into the air rather than at the enemy, guaranteeing death as a martyr

Frontier tribesmen demonstrate the *jezail* to an early photographer.

called armchair generals, warned of the dangers of the war, and worried about Britain's preoccupation with that 'super-annuated puppet' Shuja. Thirty years after his first mission, Mountstuart Elphinstone urged caution, with a prescient analysis of Afghanistan, that still has echoes for the war that followed the defeat of the Taliban in 2001. Holding Afghanistan was harder than taking it. 'I have no doubt you will take Candahar and Caubul and set up Shuja; but for maintaining him in a poor, cold, strong and remote country, among a turbulent people like the Afghans, I own it seems to me to be hopeless . . . I never knew a close alliance between a civilised and an uncivilised state that did not end in mutual hatred in three years.'

The armchair generals opposing the campaign included the conqueror of India and victor at Waterloo, the Duke of Wellington. But as would happen often when Britain threatened Afghanistan, the press swung in on the side of the most hawkish policy. 'The Russian fiend has been haunting and troubling the human race' thundered *The Times* in 1838, building popular support for the war. Politicians faced competing pressures, with military men and officials in India urging caution, while the press thought war easy.

The 'glorious news from Herat' – the lifting of the siege and withdrawal of the Persian force – did not cause the British 'Army of the Indus', to break step for an instant, as it marched towards Afghanistan. The initial mobilisation included around 15,000 troops, including one detachment under the 'ex-king at Loodiana', the unlucky Shah Shuja, and some 40,000 camp followers. One regiment brought its pack of foxhounds, and others took fine linen, furniture and large tents. A brigadier had sixty camels for his personal use.

Few were to survive. Of the 5000 camels in the advance column to Kabul, only 500 made it all the way. Captain Thomas Seaton wrote, 'The whole system of loading is bad: the saddles are very rude, clumsy, and difficult to pack, and are perfect instruments of torture to the poor ill-treated animals.' Seaton discovered that a measure of whisky would revive his animals when they fell, so they would not be abandoned with the rest.

But such problems were in the future as the Army of the Indus marched west to glory. The Governor-General Lord Auckland reflected on the sheer scale of what he was undertaking as he was borne in his carriage towards a ceremonial meeting with his ally Ranjit Singh: 'The magnitude of the measures in which I am embarking is alarming even to myself, and it will be for others to pronounce whether I am attempting at too great a hazard and at too great expense to establish and to maintain a British influence throughout the nations of Central Asia . . . I have looked upon my course to be strictly one of self-defence. I embarked on it most painfully and unwillingly.'

Auckland was an unlikely war leader, a competent administrator who had been a stopgap appointment at a time when Britain needed consolidation in India not foreign conquest. He had come a long way since the first letter he wrote to Dost Mohammed on his appointment two years before the war: 'My friend, you are aware that it is not the practice of the British government to interfere with the affairs of other independent states.'

Ranjit Singh greeted the force in a ceremony on the banks of the Sutlej, the effective eastern border of Sikh territory – the frontier of British India. The 'distant clangor of a band of indescribable musicians' announced his approach, which was signalled by salutes fired from small guns mounted on the backs of squatting camels, and witnessed by around 300 British officers, in dress uniform and full regalia, 'a picture of military splendor rarely exhibited in India'. The empire felt unstoppable.

Ranjit Singh arrived on an elephant, and put on a performance of the kind that Burnes had enjoyed on his previous trips, but which another officer thought 'an unseemly display of dancing girls', with evening entertainment that was 'still less decorous', washed down with fierce locally distilled alcohol that the Sikh king pressed on his guests.

The following day the Sikh force put on an impressive military display for the British. They were unnervingly good: better dressed and as well drilled as British troops; a 'sad blow to our vanities', said Auckland's sister, Emily Eden. Led by foreign experts, notably the US adventurer Josiah Harlan, the Italian Avitabile, and several experienced French officers, with a number of British deserters as sergeants, and the Sikh warrior tradition behind it, Ranjit Singh's army was a formidable force. But he would not commit it beyond the Khyber Pass. By now that did not matter. The Army of the Indus was so big, and its confidence so high, the Afghan campaign was as good as over. And the invasion went ahead even when Ranjit Singh reneged on another agreement, refusing to let such a large British force cross his territory, and forcing it to go south and take Kandahar first, rather than follow the more direct route up the Khyber.

The Indus was overcome with a bridge of planks on top of 74 boats lashed together to make a road that would carry wheeled traffic including artillery. 'Hurrah for the Bolan Pass and Affghanistan,' said the commander of the leading column General Sir William Nott, 'for poverty, a fine climate, and a gallant race of people.'

The hurrahs were short-lived. The engineers took time to build a military road to allow them passage through the Bolan Pass, the gateway through the southern range; winter and lack of food took their toll of the camels. One of the two columns trying to find a way through ran out of beef cattle to eat as they took so long to move. The second column passed the sombre sight of the bodies of animals and men left to rot in the Pass.

They arrived in Quetta, at the western end of the Bolan, on half rations, having suffered murder and plunder along the way. Thieves even managed to take two elephants belonging to Macnaghten, and a local ruler, the khan of Khelat, asked 'You have brought an army into the country, but how do you propose to take it out again?' He went on to betray the British, who were forced into a battle that cost them 100 lives.

Once the British force had fought its way clear of the

frontier, Kandahar itself fell without a fight. Authority shifted in the Afghan way, as the Barakzai sirdars fled across the Helmand River to the west, and local chiefs came across to the new power in the land. But before the British moved forward, they had to wait for Shah Shuja to catch up. 'Can this be done in the vain hope of giving plausibility to the fiction, of the "Shah entering his dominions surrounded by his own troops",' said Colonel William Dennie impatiently, 'when the fact is too notorious to escape detection and exposure, that he has not a single subject of Affghan among them?' Shuja's high-handed manner with British officers had not made him any friends. He would shout and keep them waiting, standing for hours.

The day after Kandahar fell, Shuja appeared under a canopy in front of 7500 British troops to display his pomp, but hardly any Afghans saw the parade, and the British force was sowing the seeds of its later destruction by not playing the local power game with the tact or subtlety required. Mohan Lal, the Indian master-fixer, understood this well, complaining later that Afghan local leaders 'were forgotten through our vain pride of power'. At the time, he kept this analysis to himself, loyal to the Raj to the end, but bitter at how bad his masters appeared to be on this expedition at anything beyond the exercise of raw military power.

Mohan Lal seemed too gentle to be a threat to anyone; hiding a calculating mind beneath a veneer of subservience and courtly manners, he went under the surface to discover the cultural and political levers that mattered.

When a local chief, at some personal risk, came over to the British with stolen secret documents, the promised reward was not paid. Lal saw the effect on other powerful tribal elders: 'instead of joining us, and facilitating our march towards Ghazni, they moved their families with their valuables into the interior, and continued annoying and plundering us all the way on our flanks'.

Ghazni is the southern point of the triangle of relatively level land in the centre of the country, with Kabul its northern point, and Jalalabad its eastern, that any conqueror of

Afghanistan needs to take. Beyond this triangle to the east lies the Suleiman range and the frontier; to the north the Hindu Kush; to the west the sprawling, deceptive mountain ranges that stretch out like the fingers of a hand clutching the ground, at the end of an arm that rises across Afghanistan to the uninhabitable wastes of the Himalayas; and to the south the flat desert that rolls out to Herat and beyond to Persia.

The Army of the Indus set out north from Kandahar towards Ghazni at the end of June 1839, leaving a detachment behind to control the south. Burnes was offered the senior political role in Kandahar by Auckland, but turned it down. He was only 34, and he had his eye on the bigger prize of deputising for Macnaghten in Kabul, and then succeeding him.

As they marched in the sapping heat of high summer, news came that Ranjit Singh had died. War had been planned when there was a Persian threat to the west, and a powerful Sikh force to the east of Afghanistan – now there was neither.

Even Wade, the administrator whose analysis had made Burnes's negotiations with Dost Mohammed in Kabul so difficult, was now having second thoughts. He changed his advice with the shameless silken ease of a natural civil servant who could argue that black was white. He proposed that Dost should be left in power, since the defensive priority was to ensure a Sikh succession in Britain's favour. But in the Punjab, there was a black farce as Karrack Singh, Ranjit's Singh's successor, died soon after taking power, then the next in line was crushed to death by an arch falling on him at Karrack Singh's funeral.

Despite this chaos in Punjab, far from retreating from Afghanistan, Auckland was planning to leave a large occupation force there after dislodging Dost Mohammed. 'The only objection is that of expense,' he wrote. 'But it would be an act of extravagance to leave our work incomplete, and our strength should not be recalled to this distance until Afghanistan is settled, and the integrity of Herat well assured.'

When the main army arrived outside Ghazni, the city's defenders were well dug in behind sheer walls of a tall solidly built fortress, standing four-square above the river. The British had left their heavy siege guns behind in Kandahar, but took the fortress in a daring operation. The assault was made possible by good intelligence from a spy who told of one gate on the northern side that was not barricaded and bricked up like the rest. At dead of night a small group of volunteers made their way to the gate carrying simple mines made from leather bags packed with gunpowder. It was an act of extraordinary bravery: the way to the gate was up a steep narrow track winding through the outer defences of the castle.

After the charges successfully blew open the gate, 200 men, the 'forlorn hope', dashed through the breach in the dark, and fought their way along an L-shaped entrance way while missiles and bullets poured down on them from above. They were followed by the main assault force led by 'Fighting Bob' Sale, wounded in the face during the fighting. Seventeen British soldiers died for 600 of the defenders. Ghazni woke to see the flag of Sale's 13th Light Infantry flying from the fort. The assault was one of the British military landmarks in Asia in the nineteenth century. It sent a signal across the country about British military ability, and shook Dost Mohammed out of power in Kabul.

Dost Mohammed's son, Afzul Khan, rode fast to Kabul with the news, abandoning elephants, baggage and guns in his camp near Ghazni. Dost immediately sent his brother Jabar Khan to the British camp as a mediator, who was well known to Burnes. He brought a proposal that Dost should stand aside and act as wazir to Shah Shuja, resuming the ancient relationship of the Barakzais to the ruling Sadozai amirs. Britain turned him down, not wanting Dost to retain any power, but none could give a good response to Jabar Khan when he said 'If Shah Shuja is really a king . . . leave him now with us Afghans, and let him rule if he can.' Afghans would make similar challenges often in the wars that followed, up to and including the appointment of President Karzai by the US.

There was another curious incident in the battle for Ghazni with twenty-first century resonance. Among the prisoners were

50 black-shirted warriors fighting under a green banner, most of them not Afghans but Indians. During an assault the day before the fort fell, they had fought with an almost suicidal intensity that British forces would come to know well in Afghanistan and on the frontier. They were *ghazis*, Islamist fundamentalists, who had answered Dost Mohammed's call to fight a jihad, a holy war, against the alien invader. Later in the century they would become known as Hindustani fanatics, men prepared to die for a cause bigger than Afghan nationalism, and the forerunners of al-Qaeda. Taken into Shuja's presence, they were all immediately executed on his orders – a policy of zero tolerance for fundamentalism. The butchery took place behind his tent, and was chanced on by a British officer, who was appalled as much by the casual approach of the executioners as the killing itself: 'They were laughing and joking, and seemed to look upon the work as good fun.'

Dost's son Akbar Khan continued to sound the bell for jihad, especially where he had the most eager listeners, on the frontier itself. But by April 1839, six months after British forces first entered Afghan territory, a new force of 11,000 men, half British and half Sikh, was now heading down the Khyber Pass. Ranjit Singh's death had made it possible for Britain to insist on Sikh support. As the Army of the Indus moved north from Ghazni, Dost Mohammed knew his time had come, and in the first week of August he fled north-west to the Bamiyan Valley, at the western end of the Hindu Kush.

A chief who had come across to the British side in Kandahar, Haji Khan Kakur, was put in charge of 2000 of Shah Shuja's Afghan troops to go in pursuit. But in Afghanistan, issuing orders did not mean they were carried out – there were other loyalties beneath the surface not recognised by Britain. At the time appointed to set out by Major James Outram, the British officer commanding the operation to capture Dost, 'not more than three hundred effective men could be mustered, the residue of those present consisting of from four to five hundred Affghan rabble, mounted upon yaboos, and starved ponies'.

They were only a day behind the fleeing Amir Dost Mohammed, whose progress was slow as his son was ill and needed to be carried, but they never caught up. Kakur had fierce daily arguments with Outram, insisting that they wait for reinforcements, at one point actually grabbing the British officer's reins and trying to pull him from his horse. When they tried to set out at night, Kakur took away his guides so the British were marching blind. Outram heard rumours of significant support for Dost among his supposed allies: 'many of our own Afghans were traitors upon whom in the hour of need no dependence could be placed'.

In the end Outram planned a virtual suicide mission: to ride fast into Dost's escort force with the aim of killing him, deploying only his 13 British officers, and not relying on their Indian sepoys nor Afghans. As he slept in the snow, on the high pass heading into Bamiyan, Outram was 'no more happy than on this night, under the exciting expectation of so glorious a struggle in the morning. All prospect of danger on such occasions as these is met by the soldier with the gratifying conviction that should he fall, he will have earned an enviable place in the recollection of those loved.'

But Outram's sacrifice would have to be postponed. He arrived in Bamiyan to find that Dost Mohammed had fled north of the Hindu Kush the day before – out of reach. The British force had failed to catch him because of betrayal by a tribal leader who had pledged allegiance to them, and disloyalty by troops in the pay of the king they had installed. It was not an auspicious start to the occupation. But the warning signs were ignored.

With Dost Mohammed out of the way, there was to be no battle for Kabul itself. Shah Shuja moved into the city in August 1839, crossing the bridge over the moat into the Bala Hissar fort complex, through the narrow dog-leg entrance onto the main street, with low mud shops of its bazaar on either side, to a 'respectful, decorous, even cold reception'. Some 5000 people lived inside the fort, but there was little sign of emotion at the return of a king who had last ruled 30 years before. He dismounted from his elephant in the palace court-yard, to occupy the palace that had been built by his father Timur, giving Macnaghten the large guest house overlooking a garden on the other side that Dost had given to Burnes on his failed peace mission two years previously.

The buildings were in a 'ruinous state'; the splendour of the Afghan court that Shah Shuja remembered was no more. The ancient Mughal fort above would remain in ruins. A British proposal to restore it and station troops there was rejected by Shah Shuja, because it looked over his quarters. He felt it would draw attention to his alliance with the British and 'the feelings of the inhabitants would be hurt'.

In October 1839, most of the invasion force was withdrawn, with its commander General Sir John Keane giving advice to a young officer as they went: 'I cannot but congratulate you on quitting this country; for, mark my words, it will not be long before there is here some signal catastrophe.' The young officer was Lieutenant Henry Durand, who had lit the fuse on the mine at Ghazni, an act of unusual bravery, and whose family would play a central role in the affairs of Afghanistan and the frontier.

By the spring of 1840, Kabul had become a fashionable destination for the more adventurous sort of British travellers from India, and for the next two summers, there was horse racing, boating on the Wazirabad Lake and hunting in the hills. Amid relative peace, at least in the capital, Sir William Macnaghten set up home in some style. His wife arrived with a group of other garrison wives, and a line of elephants and baggage animals behind them carried rugs, chandeliers, fine china and cases of wine. The high dry mountain air of Kabul was a relief from the sapping heat of the Indian plains.

Lady Sale, a woman whose nature was quarried from empire-building granite, planted a fine kitchen garden, growing peas, potatoes, artichokes, turnip and radishes, all from seeds brought from India, and melons from local seed – topped with colour from sweet peas and geraniums, as if she was in

England. She found the 'Cabul lettuces hairy and inferior to ours, but the cabbages superior and milder'. Her daughter, married to a lieutenant in the engineers posted to Kabul, came to live with her.

Sir Alexander Burnes created a job for his brother Charley, who came out to live with him in a fine house in town, outside the garrison walls. He bought Russian mirrors in the market, and scraped the quicksilver off the back to fit Kabul's first windows into his house. He and his brother entertained lavishly, and with other officers enthusiastically tested what he had heard about the morals of Kabul women – a pursuit that would contribute directly to Burnes's death.

But while foreigners lived in complacent splendour, the Afghanistan beyond the racetrack and boating lake was in ferment. From exile north of the Oxus, Dost Mohammed was writing inflammatory letters all over the country: 'Religion is his watchword, and he hopes to raise the whole country against us . . . I hope we are to be really well prepared for the worst that may happen,' wrote Macnaghten, who saw the threat too of instability spilling over from the frontier region.

Dost Mohammed's son Akbar Khan began recruiting in the Khyber region for jihad: 'I have today left Jalalabad with a view to commence a religious war against the detested infidels.'

The appearance of two Islamist spies in August 1840, 'carrying money and a Koran in an amulet', who were handed over to Burnes by a tribal elder friendly to Britain, was a rare piece of hard evidence amid rumours of fundamentalist plots being stirred up against the British presence in Afghanistan. The older one, whose name was Khodameer, was identified from the style of his cap as coming from the Khyber. The other, Khodadad, 'had a ruddy complexion with a few marks of small-pox'. They said they were on their way to see Dost Mohammed in the mountains, and to try to recruit men to join Dost's allies, who were now conspiring with the Sikhs in Peshawar against British control.

Against British wishes and despite Macnaghten's warnings, Sikh armies were pushing further north and west into the mountains adjoining Afghanistan. 'The cession by the Sikhs of all the countries west of the Indus is what I should think the chief object; next a subsidiary force in the Punjab.' But when Macnaghten wrote with this intelligence in November 1840, it was ignored along with his other warnings, although he thought he had enough against Dost Mohammed's brother in Peshawar to 'hang him ten times over'. The Sikhs were supposed to be British allies, but were acting against British interests everywhere Macnaghten looked. He wrote warning letters constantly, until 'the stumps of my fingers are nearly worn out', but he found himself ignored. The government preferred to think the Sikhs honest, 'most firm friends and most steadfast allies', believing the assurances of Wade.

Events in 1840/41 unfolded in a way that was replayed after the invasion and occupation by international forces after 2001: a growing Islamist insurgency, supported by a power on the eastern side of the Khyber Pass that claimed to be backing the occupation force at the same time as conspiring against it; overstretched foreign troops unable to quell a widening and worsening conflict; a cultural clash in Kabul as the occupiers behaved in a way that offended local sensibilities; an amir who could not rule without foreign support; increasing tension between the occupying power and the amir; and growing anger among tribal elders about foreign promises of financial support that they believed were not honoured. In the First Anglo-Afghan War this set of circumstances would lead to the worst disaster suffered by the British during the whole period of the Empire in Asia.

Britain's biggest concern was always the threat to their own security by a Russian move towards Afghan territory. They knew very little of the land north of the Hindu Kush mountains, or the power of the rulers of Samarkand, Bokhara and Khiva. One of the most adventurous British Afghan travellers, Arthur Connolly, had been up to the remote slave-owning kingdom of Khiva and won a treaty of friendship with its khan, but Russia now sent a deputation there, 'the most unhappy step taken during the campaign' for Burnes, who said the Russian moves 'torture all my thoughts and opinions'.

But such setbacks were ignored in India, where the governor-general, Lord Auckland, saw Afghanistan as settled, and considered pushing further north. 'I am far from able to decide where occupation should end, and the exercise of peaceful influence begin.'

In the summer of 1840 Dost reappeared in Afghanistan, after escaping from virtual house arrest, 'silver handcuffs' that had held him for almost a year as a guest at the court in Bokhara, north of the Oxus. He rode his first horse so hard during his getaway that it died under him, and he continued his escape in a basket on a camel, his beard dyed black. But he failed to make any serious military headway against British forces, despite some advances, including at one point encircling Burnes and a number of other senior British officers in Charikar. Colonel Dennie, the hero of Ghazni, defeated Dost's forces at the beginning of October, leaving 600 Afghan dead and almost capturing Dost and his son Akbar Khan.

A month later, there was a fierce exchange at Parwan, where Britain's locally hired cavalry hung back, with the excuse that 'they did not like the English swords they had been given', and Dost's force nearly won the day. Dost himself was seen on the field, dressed all in white under a blue banner, urging his men to 'drive these Ferengee Kafirs out of the country or I am a gone man'. He took off his white turban and waved it in the breeze. The Afghan cavalry rode into British troops that were 'cut like a flock of sheep'. Among the officers lost on the British side was Dr Lord, who had travelled with Burnes on a former trip and was a leading expert on Afghanistan.

Yet the very next day, Macnaghten was out riding in Kabul when a single horseman came up to check who he was, before Dost Mohammed himself appeared, and dismounted, surrendering personally to the startled British envoy. Macnaghten courteously told him to mount his horse again, and they rode on. When they arrived in the Bala Hissar, Dost handed over his sword, but Macnaghten said he should keep it: 'he seemed gratified for this mark of confidence'. His manner and bearing impressed Macnaghten. 'We ejected the Dost, who never offended us, in support of our policy, of which he was the victim.'

Dost Mohammed went into exile in India in November 1840 on a British pension. And the British government took the opportunity to carry out a reshuffle of its own commanders and forces: 'Major General Elphinstone succeeded Sir Willoughby Cotton in the Affghanistan command, and HM 44th Regiment under Colonel Shelton, replaced the Bengal Europeans.'

The 44th marched into Afghanistan, but only a handful would make it out alive. On Christmas Day 1840, Macnaghten wrote to the government in India, 'I am greatly apprehensive that we shall be high and dry ere long.' He would not live to see another Christmas.

Dost Mohammed's departure did not make security any easier; Macnaghten wrote, 'this country is one mass of loose gunpowder'. As the insurgency spread, the hardest fights faced by the British were in Helmand in the south-west, where there was almost continual campaigning, even during the winter months of 1840/41. With Britain distracted, Persia saw the opportunity to move again on Herat, where Shah Shuja's cousin Kamran Shah was still in power. Britain's influence in Herat was, if anything, weaker now they held Kabul than before. Attempts to introduce tougher laws, turning it into a 'Utopia of justice' by Pottinger and Stoddart, the two political officers in charge, had led to their expulsion. 'Why is it that Englishmen everywhere are rough, overbearing, without tact, and address, and more disliked by foreigners than any other people?' asked John Colvin, Auckland's private secretary.

Kamran Shah now changed sides and conspired with Persia against Britain. Palmerston saw this as cause for war on Herat. 'The Iron is hot; let us strike it; if we let it grow cold it will be too hard for our blows.' But the day the order to attack was agreed in London, 4th June 1841, was the day the government lost a no-confidence motion to Robert Peel's Tories by one vote. Amid the political confusion, a letter from Auckland arrived warning of the huge cost of an assault on Herat, requiring 12,000 men. Diplomacy in Tehran was tried instead, and although British influence there was much reduced as Russia became more dominant, Persia did not move on Herat again.

Shah Shuja was now openly conspiring against Britain. He sent letters to a number of chiefs complaining about his lack of authority, maintaining that the British were governing Afghanistan as they pleased. When a tribal elder friendly to Britain went to Charikar, north of Kabul, to resolve an issue, Shuja's agents went ahead to spread the word that he was 'an infidel, and acting for the ruin of the Shah, and of the faithful of the country'. Shuja become even more difficult to manage when the probability emerged of Burnes taking over when Macnaghten left. He knew that Burnes had tried to keep him out of power.

But it was financial issues that led to the biggest crisis. The cost of grain was going up because of the requirements of the large garrison, and when Shuja ordered prices to be fixed, the British vetoed this in the interests of free trade. (The amir's thugs imposed their will in their way, nailing the ear of a trader to a block in his shop for a day when he raised his prices.) At the same time the British cut the wages of the builders employed in the new cantonment area set apart from Kabul, because they needed to keep them in line with what Shuja was paying. High food prices and low wages were a recipe for disaster, and both could be blamed on British policy.

Just as the financial consequences of all this began to bite, the government in India cut the amount they had been paying loyal tribal elders to maintain forces. It seemed prudent housekeeping now the war was over, and the amount went down from 80,000 to 40,000 Rupees.

This last measure was the prime cause of the rebellion that General Sale was sent to quell in the provinces to the east in the autumn of 1841. The campaign was not expected to be extensive – just a skirmish to open the passes to the east.

Macnaghten sighed at the amount of thrashing that was needed: 'I fear these fellows will require many a hiding yet before they settle down into peaceable citizens.' Securing the route east was important as Britain wanted to reduce its forces in Afghanistan, and Macnaghten was preparing to leave with the departing troops, on his way to a new job in India, handing over to Burnes. When Sale set out to quell the uprising, his wife was confident that she would be joining him in three days.

As Sale's men set up camp on their first night in the passes to the east, they heard the unearthly clang of the loading of *jezails* echoing through the darkness around the bare crags, 'a loud ringing noise, that can be heard at a considerable distance, so unmistakeable in its character that it can never be forgotten by those whose ears have once been startled by the unfamiliar sound'.

The sound was of balls, each about one ounce in weight, being rammed down barrels with an iron ramrod. Hundreds would be fired at the British before the night was out.

3

Retreat

'When Burnes came into this country, was not your
father entreated by us to kill him; or he would at some
future day bring an army and take our country from us?'

Afghan tribal chief talking to
Akbar Khan, son of Dost Mohammed

The event that sparked the uprising that drove the British out
of Kabul was an argument over a woman.

The second of November 1841 was the third Tuesday of
Ramadan, the period when good Muslims are expected to fast
for the hours of daylight. The ageing and ineffectual British
commanding officer, General Elphinstone, was recovering in
bed after a heavy fall from his horse the day before. Apart
from Burnes and some other officers who still lived in the city
itself, the British force was now based mainly in a poorly
defended cantonment area about a mile north of Kabul. Its
'serious defects' were obvious even to Colonel Shelton, who
said it had 'a rampart and ditch an Afghan could run over with
the facility of a cat'.

At first light dawn watchers in this poorly located
cantonment saw smoke rising from the city, and shortly
before 8 a.m., a report arrived that Sir Alexander Burnes had

been injured, followed soon afterwards by news that he was dead.

The storm clouds had been gathering for weeks. Shah Shuja's failings had become apparent to some British officers: 'as great a scoundrel as ever lived' said one general, observing shrewdly, 'We are becoming hated by the people.' But Macnaghten had not seen the final storm coming, talking of 'a season of such profound tranquillity', when he had gone to say goodbye to Burnes, the afternoon before the uprising. He did not appear to be concerned about the continued lack of firm news from the troops led by General Sale that had set off to secure the passes to the East, nor the general unrest provoked by the economic situation.

But there were other signs too of an impending emergency if only he had known where to look. Mohan Lal reported perhaps the most important – although its significance was not recognised at the time by the British – mosques in Kabul stopped praying for Shah Shuja. Forged letters had also appeared in the bazaar claiming strong support from the Sikh government across the frontier for Dost Mohammed – to encourage the idea that he was on his way back. There were rumours too that Macnaghten was planning to round up all the troublesome tribal elders and cart them off to prison in India.

Burnes had made himself unpopular over high-handed demands to tribal elders allied to Britain. At the same time as cutting the subsidies given to them to raise troops, he expected them to provide actual troops for the money for the first time. He attempted to regularise their forces with professional ranks that took no account of tribal structures. One astute officer, Captain Seaton, complained of inconsistency in the British approach, 'a mixture of iron and clay . . . utterly unsuited to the fierce tribes of the country, who soon detected the weakness of their rulers'. A similar result followed the swift introduction of democracy and a Western system of government after 2001 – a violent reaction to the threat to traditional power.

The drama that played out on the night of 1st/2nd

November started when the favourite mistress of a powerful Afghan leader, Abdullah Khan, was taken into the house of a British officer. Abdullah sent his nephew to investigate, who was kept at the front door, from where he heard the rustling of skirts and caught a glimpse of the girl he sought being pushed into a back room. The British officer had attempted to hold the door shut, denying she was there. Abdullah complained to Burnes, who did nothing.

Burnes had already made an enemy by sacking the *kotwal* of Kabul, the police chief, to block an investigation into a claim by another Afghan that his mistress had been spirited away across the roof of his house by a British officer. And Burnes and his brother had tested Afghan moral patience by having Kashmiri women living with them.

On 1st November Mohan Lal warned Burnes of a plot to get rid of him, seeing him just after Macnaghten had visited with his talk of 'profound tranquillity'. When Burnes saw the specific death threat contained in an anonymous letter, he told Lal, 'the time is arrived that we must leave the country'. But he did not act, wanting not to show fear. 'The Affghans never received any injury from him . . . he was quite sure they would never injure him.'

At 3 a.m. on 2nd November, one of Burnes's servants, Bow Singh, received word that merchants all around were removing valuables from their shelves and sealing up their shops. He was afraid that Burnes would reprimand him if he woke him but found the wazir, Nuzamat Dowlah, who came to rouse Burnes. When a message arrived from the Bala Hissar calling the wazir to Shah Shuja's side, Burnes refused to go with him.

The deposed police chief began the insurrection, setting fire to the gates of Burnes's house, the cue for a mob attack. A detachment of Shah Shuja's troops led by a British officer set out from the Bala Hissar nearby to try to restore order, but was quickly cut to pieces, losing two field guns. One British officer was killed as the fire took hold of Burnes's house. Burnes ran upstairs and shouted down from a balcony, offering a reward to any who would save his life. But the city he had tried to make his own deceived him in the end. In the mêlée, a Kashmiri came and offered to take Burnes and his brother out by a safe route, in disguise, then betrayed them, calling out, 'Here he is. Here is Sikander Burnes.'

Burnes's brother Charley ran into the garden with his sword, killing six before he was cut down. But when Sir Alexander knew his own end was unavoidable, he walked out with a black scarf tied round his eyes so he would not see who killed him. Three men were at the front of the crowd and struck the first blows – all connected with the disputes over women – the police chief sacked by Burnes, the man whose complaint against the British he had not investigated, and Abdullah Khan himself.

The next few hours were a critical test for British resolve, and General Elphinstone failed to respond effectively. Lady Sale's son-in-law Lieutenant Sturt was horribly injured with a wound in the throat, and staggered, covered in blood, through the entrance of Shah Shuja's audience chamber. Shuja made threats to put down the insurgency but did not act. His soldiers were considered almost useless, 'the worst set up and most disorderly body of troops calling themselves a regiment that can be imagined', said Lady Sale. 'We seem to sit quietly with our hands folded and look on.'

Within days, the British force had lost nearly all of its supplies, stored in a fort inexcusably located outside the main cantonment, and a general uprising involving tens of thousands of Afghans threatened every British soldier in the country. British officers were killed by their men in Kandahar and Ghazni. A Gurkha regiment in Charikar was encircled and defeated, its survivors taken into slavery – although one of its two British officers made it to Kabul, riding in agony after having his hand cut off. There was widespread desertion by Indian and Afghan soldiers in the British forces, some of whom joined the enemy. The British fired artillery shells into the city of Kabul without much effect, and worst of all, the indecision of officers led to a catastrophic collapse in morale. Lady Sale complained that any story was believed by the 'panic-stricken garrison. It is more than shocking, it is shameful, to hear the way that officers go on croaking before their men.'

Elphinstone and Shelton could not decide whether to prepare for retreat, move into the Bala Hissar, or try to defend the position they were in. When Macnaghten proposed a raid on the nearby Bemaru Hills, because of constant firing down from them, the orders did not go out until the afternoon after fierce arguments by Shelton, who would only agree to fight if Macnaghten signed a form taking responsibility.

Lady Sale stood on the roof of her house watching the fighting, ducking behind the chimney as rounds flew by. A cannonball embedded itself in the wall of the room where her pregnant daughter was sleeping. She developed respect for the military ability of the enemy: 'my very heart felt as if it leapt to my teeth when I saw the Affghans ride clean through . . . The onset was dreadful. They looked like a great cluster of bees.' She noticed how their cavalry could fire while riding, and carry an infantryman with them to the scene of the action 'where he is dropped without the fatigue of walking to his post'. Two Kabul snipers, said to be a blacksmith and a barber, were able to pick off people in the cantonment from 300 yards.

The fighting went on without a pause for several weeks, as autumn turned to winter, and British stocks of food, ammunition and willpower fell daily. The death of the main rebel leader Abdullah Khan at the end of November was one piece of good news, but it was a rare glimmer of light. It emerged that the conspiracy had been months in the planning, backed by a secret pact against the British by tribal leaders signed on the Koran. Dost Mohammed's son, Akbar Khan, powerful among the eastern Ghilzai chiefs, arrived in Kabul with 6000 men, raising Afghan morale. In the middle of December Shah Shuja abandoned the British, setting his seal on a proclamation urging all good Muslims to kill the *feringhees*. It was only 'two days since the king was to have come into the cantonments, in rather light marching order, to accompany us to the provinces', Lady Sale remarked dryly, as Shuja issued his anti-British proclamation and gave the insurgent force access to firing positions in the ruins of the upper fortress of the Bala Hissar.

Macnaghten, whose departure from Afghanistan had been delayed by the uprising, was still hoping for an honourable way out, but had less and less to negotiate with. Through Mohan Lal, still living discreetly in Kabul, he sent messages to Akbar Khan, and other chieftans, while separately trying to secure support from the *qizalbash* mercenaries, and Afghans loyal to the British, including a chief who offered sanctuary in the hills. Macnaghten had turned down an offer to surrender British weapons, and hand over women and children as hostages, saying he preferred 'death to dishonour'. But he was forced into a series of deals, handing over outlying forts in exchange for food. His room for manoeuvre diminished daily, as he fell into the maw of a disparate and complex rebellion.

Afghan spies found they could penetrate inside the British cantonment easily; a British soldier spying for Russia was found and arrested while removing barricades; and when Sturt was standing at the front gate an Afghan came up to ask if he was an officer. When asked why he wanted to know, the Afghan drew his sword and said 'to fight'. Horses in the cantonment were reduced to chewing on tent pegs: there was nothing else to eat.

On 23rd December Macnaghten rode out of the fort for his last fateful meeting with Akbar Khan. The young Afghan commander had laid out a large rug in a cleared patch in the snow, on a rise just 300 yards from the cantonment. Macnaghten had requested that two British regiments should be made ready to arrest Aminullah Khan, a key rebel leader, since he believed that he could secure Akbar Khan's support, and divide the enemy. Akbar Khan wanted to become wazir, while offering to let Shah Shuja remain on the throne, but Macnaghten did not really know what shifting alliances he faced in the snow.

Shelton failed to have the force Macnaghten had requested ready in time, and made an excuse not to join him for the meeting at the last minute. Just before he left, Macnaghten went white as he read a message from Mohan Lal warning of a plot to kill him. He tried to seem scornful: 'A plot! Let me alone for that – trust me for that!' He was carrying as presents a pair of fine pistols and an Arab mare admired by Akbar Khan in the past. In his last recorded words he said, 'Dangerous it is, but if it succeeds, it is worth all risks; the rebels have not fulfilled one article of the treaty, and I have no confidence in them, and if by it we can only save our honour, all will be well; at any rate, I would rather suffer a hundred deaths than live the last six weeks over again.'

The manner of his killing must have felt like a hundred deaths. With three British officers he sat cross-legged on the rug opposite the Afghan leaders they knew so well. One of the officers, George Lawrence, crouched warily, believing they were not safe, as a large number of Afghans mounted on horses, identified as religious warriors, *ghazis*, moved in closer to the group. Akbar Khan told Lawrence to relax, but in almost the same breath he cried out, 'Seize them!' Lawrence found his hands pinioned behind him so he could not reach his weapons, and he and the other two officers were thrown roughly behind riders on the backs of horses and taken into captivity. The last they saw of Macnaghten, he was being dragged head first, screaming, down the bank away from them. A shot rang out from one of the pistols he had just given to Akbar Khan, but only wounded him. Macnaghten was cut to pieces, and his hands, feet and trunk paraded through the streets of Kabul, the head displayed in a horse nosebag in the bazaar.

The humiliation for Britain continued as Macnaghten's carcass was displayed contemptuously in front of the cantonment, his fine uniform cut from it. Lady Sale fumed, 'strange to say no endeavour was made to recover it, which might easily have been done by sending out the cavalry'. One of the three officers who had been with Macnaghten was also killed, but the other two were held for several days, taunted by one of Macnaghten's bloody hands waved on a stick outside the bars of their jail. Akbar Khan paraded through Kabul with a bloodstained sword boasting that it was he who had killed the envoy, but to the British he claimed it was the *ghazis* who had done it, showing his good faith by returning the two captives safely.

The options available to the garrison were now 'a disgraceful treaty or a disastrous retreat', according to Lady Sale. The decision was made to negotiate; the terms agreed involved the British force giving up almost all its artillery pieces, handing over hostages to the Afghan side, and paying a large sum. Major Pottinger, the hero of Herat, had taken over from Macnaghten, and signed the treaty quickly along with the senior military commanders.

Lady Sale now heard a rumour that was to be a ghastly prophecy. 'We are informed that the chiefs do not mean to keep faith; and that it is their intention to get all our women into their possession; and to kill every man except one, who is to have his hands and legs cut off, and is to be placed with a letter *in terrorem* at the entrance of the Khyber Passes, to deter all *feringhees* from entering the country again.'

The British retreat from Kabul began on 6th January 1842. 'All was confusion from before daylight. The day was clear and frosty; the snow nearly a foot deep on the ground; the thermometer considerably below freezing point.' Sturt had been out all night building a bridge of gun carriages across the Kabul River at Shelton's insistence, although Sturt said it was easily forded, and the soldiers' feet would be wet anyway in the snow. The camp followers lined up to cross it, and progress was slow. Shelton had ordered that they bring dozens of planks, dragged by bullocks, in case they needed to cross other rivers en route, which also hampered the retreat. By the evening they had gone only six miles, despite the urging of friendly Afghans that they should push onto the gorge at Khurd Kabul – a name that would etch itself into the collective memory of Victorian Britain. They made camp in the open.

The remnants of the rearguard did not arrive until 2 a.m.,

with stories of terrible slaughter that had begun before they had even left the cantonment. The Afghans began by firing *jezails*, before men and boys darted in with knives. Fifty of the cavalry had not made it out of the cantonment, and a trail of dead soldiers and camp followers marked the way to the river.

All discipline was at an end. The following morning the advance guard set off at first light although 'no order was given, no bugle was sounded'. Camp followers and pack animals pressed ahead, making a disciplined march impossible. Incredibly, the column stopped again at 1 p.m., giving the tribes in the passes plenty of time to organise an ambush for the following day. The only rationale for stopping was to keep the force together. But the delay depleted stores further as Afghan cavalry took what they wanted, and they lost three of their precious field guns to marauding tribesmen, who pressed down from the hills on all sides.

On 8th January, crossing the narrow five-mile defile of Khurd Kabul, the British put up their only determined fight, fortified by the contents of a cask of spirits broached early in the day. Effective deployment was impossible because of the confusion of thousands of camp followers, but both the infantry and cavalry fought off several assaults as the column made its slow progress.

Lieutenant Sturt had to prevent drunken cavalrymen undertaking a suicidal charge into the massed ranks of Afghans. Lady Sale sat on her horse observing events as if she might have been out on a hunt in England, stirrup cup in hand. 'I felt very grateful for a tumbler of sherry, which at any other time would have made me very unlady-like, but now merely warmed me.' At the narrowest part of the gorge Afghan warriors poured withering fire down from behind low stone walls. As Lady Sale rode through, she was wounded in the elbow, and three other balls went through her sheepskin jacket.

More than 2000 camp followers were now dead, as well as hundreds of soldiers. Many of the surviving *sepoys* burnt their clothes to keep themselves warm, leading to instant death the next night, as only four tents had survived. 'An immense number of poor wounded wretches wandered about the camp destitute of shelter, and perished during the night. Groans of misery and distress assailed the ear from all quarters.' Akbar Khan appeared, demanding more hostages, more money and the withdrawal of Sale's force from Jalalabad – all conditions that were immediately agreed to, but the killing still did not stop. Sturt died of his wounds that night, tended by his wife and his mother-in-law Lady Sale, and was buried in a shallow grave scraped out of the frozen mud.

But most of the dead remained unburied, 'the sight was dreadful; the smell of the blood sickening; and the corpses lay so thick it was impossible to look from them, as it required care to guide my horse so as not to tread upon the bodies'. Lady Sale and the other women and more of the senior officers fell into Akbar Khan's hands, and the first thing they saw in his camp was a force of 500 of their sepoys who had deserted to the Afghan side. Lady Sale retained her notebook in a bag round her waist and continued to chronicle the loss of an army. By 9th January, the fourth day out, 'there was not a single sepoy left of the whole Kabul force'.

East India Company coins, looted from the retreating army, have been handed down from generation to generation in the pass since then, and an argument still runs in one Afghan family as to whether their ancestor killed 13 or 14 in the mêlée. Tombs of martyrs from that period are revered, and there is a persistent Afghan legend that a company of British soldiers could not cut down an oak tree when they tried to destroy a holy site, the Seh Baba tomb, in retribution, when their army returned in 1842, despite pulling it with elephants and horses and chopping with axes and sabres.

Woven into local folk memory are frequent accounts of British women taking Afghan warriors as husbands to save their lives, and a story of a boy, John Campbell, brought up in an Afghan house before running away after 15 years. The truth is more prosaic. The British women and children taken into Afghan captivity were gathered together and mostly well treated, and one English girl sold as a slave reunited with her family several months later. However women taken alive from among the Indian camp followers faced rape and forced marriage.

At last Elphinstone took decisive action, ordering a march through a 'fine and moonlit' night, reaching the shrine at Seh Baba by midnight, and turning sharp right towards Jagdallak, the last major pass before the plains of Jalalabad. The column regrouped at daylight, eating raw meat from a bullock to keep alive, before marching on until the mid-afternoon, 30 hours after setting out from their last desperate snatched sleep in the snow. Of the 16,000 who had set out, the survivors consisted of 150 men of the 44th Regiment, 16 dismounted horse artillery men and 25 from the 5th Cavalry. Each had only a handful of ammunition. Several hundred camp followers were still with them. They stopped behind some walls to rest, and Akbar Khan sent a message saying he wanted to see their senior officers.

Elphinstone, Shelton and another officer left the force, and became engaged in a macabre negotiation for the lives of the British soldiers, with Akbar Khan still pretending to be brokering peace, and lying when he said food and water had been sent over to this pathetic remnant of an army. The mountain chieftains insisted they could not let them through unharmed, and Elphinstone offered further cash. They swore to kill the *feringhees*, until Akbar Khan hinted they should switch to speaking Pashtu, which the British could not understand. Then he disappeared, after giving orders that the officers should not be allowed to rejoin their men. When he returned at sunset there was the sound of shooting across the wastes, and Elphinstone and Shelton were still prevented from going back.

Elphinstone had managed to get a note to the force: 'March at once; there is treachery!' That night, 11th January, they set out into hell. As the British climbed to the top of the Jagdallak Pass, they found the way blocked by a double barrier of thorn branches, laced together six feet high. Dr William Brydon was mounted: 'The confusion became terrible, all discipline was at an end, and the shouts of "Halt, halt. Keep Back the Cavalry" were incessant. I made my way with great difficulty, to the front.' As the infantry tore a gap through the branches with their bare hands, under continual attack from all sides, the cavalry forced their way through and the infantry believed they were being abandoned. A survivor, Sergeant Major Lissant, wrote, 'The men in front then said the officers seemed to care for themselves.' Some accounts say the infantry shot at their own officers.

It was now every man for himself. A dozen or so mounted men rode on towards Jalalabad while those on foot made their way to a hill at Gandamack. There was another attempt to negotiate safe passage with a local chief, but when the British soldiers resisted being disarmed, the whole force was cut down. Captain Souter, who had wrapped the regimental colours round his body and must have looked a grander figure than the rest and so worth a ransom, was among the few survivors from the 44th to be taken prisoner.

On 13th January, a week after the retreat from Kabul began, a sharp-eyed sentry on the ramparts at Jalalabad saw the exhausted figure of Dr Brydon, crossing the plain on a pony given him by a wounded Indian cavalryman after his own died under him. He was bleeding from one hand, and had a bad head wound, surviving a blow from a sword only because he had had a copy of *Blackwood's Magazine* under his cap. As soon as his pony was taken into a stable it lay down and died.

Brydon told a tale of treachery. Those on horseback had been offered food and shelter in an Afghan village once they were clear of the mountain passes, only to be set on as soon as they dismounted. Half of the party were killed there, the others cut down by pursuing Afghan horsemen. He was attacked by three more groups of Afghans, riding through the first with his reins in his teeth, 'cutting right and left with my sword as I went through them'. Soon afterwards he encountered another group, and had to jab at his pony with his sword to make it gallop. A round fired from a *jezail* at close range broke his sword and wounded his pony.

Seeing a third party on horseback with the British fort now in sight, he rode towards them believing them to be British, only turning away when he realised his mistake. One of the Afghans rode after him, and slashed at him, but was put off at the last instant as Brydon threw the broken hilt of his sword at the man's head. Still the blow cut into his hand. Unaccountably the man rode off, and Dr Brydon went on, unarmed and badly wounded, into safety.

General Sale ordered a fire to be lit at the Kabul gate of the Jalalabad fort and lights maintained all night, with buglers playing every quarter hour to guide in stragglers who might be trying to cross the plain under cover of darkness. But none came. 'The sound of those bugles I shall never forget,' wrote Captain Seaton. 'It was a dirge for our slaughtered soldiers, and heard through all the night, it had an inexpressibly mournful and depressing effect.'

The massacre of the Kabul garrison sent shockwaves across the region that still reverberated into the twenty-first century, as a lesson was learnt that would always boost Afghan morale in a battle – the British could be beaten. The Amir of Bokhara now had the confidence he needed to execute two British captives, Colonel Charles Stoddart and Captain Arthur Connolly, without fear of retribution, and Britain's sometime ally in Herat, the tyrant Zaman Shah, was murdered in time-honoured royal style, smothered with a pillow by his wazir, Yar Mohammed. Shah Shuja was betrayed after trying to negotiate his way out of the Bala Hissar, and cut to pieces by a mob. The king who had once worn the Koh-i-noor, and a nine-inch-high diamond crown, had his last bag of jewels cut from round his waist and tossed into a field. The man who picked them up assumed them to be worthless coloured rocks but had them torn off him in the bazaar by someone who knew better.

Retribution from British forces in India would surely follow, but first the Jalalabad garrison had to face an assault of unprecedented ferocity by tens of thousands of Afghans whose blood was up. When he had set out to 'thrash' the rebel tribes in October, Sale had led his force through the same passes that later filled with British dead. He sustained 40 dead the first night, and lost some stores, but this force was much better led than Elphinstone's army. Sale fought off successive assaults by the ruse of keeping his men quite still in the dark, even taking casualties from rounds fired blind from *jezails*, until Afghan raiders were within bayonet distance, when he ordered his men to open up with sustained volleys of fire.

Pressure on Sale's force did not stop after they moved into the Jalalabad fort, and the attackers were driven by the compulsion of jihad – novel to British troops then, it would become more familiar in wars in the region later. Dost Mohammed had 'persuaded the Moolahs to preach a religious war against us . . . this had raised the whole country, and roused their fanaticism'. A mullah living inside the fort was ejected after his house was found to be mined.

The fort was very large, and Sale's force worked hard to improve its defences, but a month after the massacre in the Khurd Kabul pass, a sound rolled across the Jalalabad plain like thunder, 'as if a thousand heavy wagons were driven at speed over a rough pavement . . . the ground heaved and set like the sea, and the whole plain appeared rolling in waves towards us'. A severe earthquake destroyed every building. 'It seemed as if some gigantic hand had taken up the houses, and thrown them down into the fort in one confused heap of rubbish . . . worse than the effects of a month's cannonading with heavy artillery.'

The British officers exchanged their uniforms for clothing woven from camel hair – the first combat fatigues, several decades before they were routine wear. They slept where they worked, joining gangs with their men, working in the 'toughness of digging, felling, moisture, dirt and mud' around the clock to rebuild the defences. Captain Seaton earned the undying gratitude of the officers in his mess by setting up a still to give them a glass of spirits each a day.

They rebuilt the defences just in time as Akbar Khan arrived in strength only a week after the earthquake. The British force ran very short of both food and ammunition. To replenish their supply of musket balls, they set a figure on a short pole dressed up in a 'cocked hat, red coat, painted face, not unlike a better sort of "guy"'. When it was hoisted up, Afghan snipers fired at it, and a ready harvest of thousands of rounds of lead was reaped by the garrison.

Keeping their horses alive was more difficult. The gangs of grass-cutters sent out to forage were sustaining heavy casualties every day, despite heavy protection. Akbar Khan tried to press home his advantage by finding flocks of sheep to graze all the grass within a day's ride of Jalalabad, but when one of these flocks came within sight of the fort, Sale sent out cavalry to shepherd it in, supported by lines of infantry in a brilliant pincer movement. Alongside the value in food, the operation raised morale. This garrison was behaving very differently to the one in Kabul.

When news came through that the first attempt to send a relief force through the Khyber Pass had been repulsed, Sale took things into his own hands, mounting an all-out assault, and destroying Akbar Khan's camp itself. One casualty was Dennie, the hero of Ghazni in 1839, dying three years after he had written when Kabul was taken: 'The war may now be considered at an end.'

The attack had the desired effect of weakening the support of the tribes in the Khyber Pass for Akbar Khan: the swirling weathervane that detected which way the wind blew in Afghanistan was swinging back to the east. The next attempt to force the Khyber by what the British called the Army of Retribution did succeed in getting through. But it was not until September that its commander General Pollock could issue orders that the Union flag should fly over the Bala Hissar in Kabul, in a spot where it was 'most conspicuous from the city'. General Nott, who had succeeded in holding Kandahar, marched north, retaking Ghazni on the way to join Pollock's army.

The force was in Kabul for only two weeks. Thousands of

civilians – men, women and children – were killed in an orgy of destruction, and the Kabul bazaar, where Macnaghten and Burnes's dismembered bodies had been put on public display, was blown up and burnt to the ground. Many people had fled the city, but the sword of retribution fell indiscriminately on all those who remained, including some who had previously given protection and help to the British, to Mohan Lal's horror: 'all their families, which had once given our people shelter, were pillaged of all their property, and driven from their houses'.

The bazaar, perhaps the finest in Asia, had been built around four tall arched spaces gazed on in wonder by Lal when he had first arrived in the city ten years before. 'The parts of the bazaar which are arched over exceed any thing the imagination can picture. The shops rise over each other, in steps glittering in tinsel splendour, till, from the effect of elevation, the whole fades into a confused and twinkling mass, like stars shining through clouds, and the people themselves, not so big as beetles, seem as if a pigmy race.' Its destruction would slow the recovery of the Afghan economy.

The slaughter and rape was not confined to the capital. The town of Istalif north of Kabul was destroyed and everything of value pillaged. An officer, Neville Chamberlain, who later played a crucial role in the frontier story, wrote that men under his command had become 'licensed assassins'. Returning to Istalif the morning after its sack, he recorded what he saw with some shame. 'Furniture of all description, wearing apparel, provisions, books, arms, everything made by the hand of man and for his use, lay scattered and destroyed, trampled into the mud, soiled and broken. Here and there the crackling of fire was to be heard.' A wounded Afghan woman, crawling towards a stream with a water pot in her hand, refused Chamberlain's offer of help with a curse. He was left 'disgusted with myself, the world, and above all, with my cruel profession'.

General Sale was put in charge of an altogether different mission – releasing the British captives, including his wife, whom he had left nine months before, expecting to be reunited 'after three days'. He took his force north towards Bamiyan, where the captives were gathered together – about 70 men, 12 women and more than 20 children, some born since the flight from Kabul. Elphinstone had died in captivity, but the other man most to blame for the Kabul catastrophe, Shelton, had survived. His pompous and insufferable character survived even the February earthquake. After escaping from a collapsing building, he turned to a junior officer in captivity with him to complain, with great sternness, that the man had gone down the stairs ahead of him, to receive the cheery response 'I'm sorry; it's the fashion in earthquakes.'

The captives had been able to receive mail and some newspapers, and the key intelligence of the arrival of the Army of Retribution had been transmitted to them by a simple code, picking out letters from random news articles. As news of the British relief force filtered through to Afghan chiefs, power subtly shifted. When the captives offered pensions to local Afghan chiefs, most accepted, giving them an incentive to keep the remnant of the Kabul garrison alive as an insurance policy.

Leadership to the end came from Lady Sale. When Afghan weapons became available, not a single British soldier agreed to carry one, fearing the worst if they were seen armed. Morale had been crushed. Lady Sale sealed her formidable reputation when she said, 'You had better give me one, and I will lead the party.'

She did not record her reunion with her husband – such things were simply not for public consumption – and when it was alluded to by another officer, General Sale 'tried to answer, but his feelings were too strong; he made a hideous series of grimaces, dug his spurs into his horse and galloped off as hard as he could'.

The retreat from Kabul, with Lady Sale waving a sword as she led the fightback, became a popular theme for military displays in rural England. One told of how 'the heart of the Briton, even amidst the snows of India's icy clime, still beats warmly for his native home upon the sea-bound isle'. A country able to weave heroic myth from the worst disaster, Britain turned the last stand of the 44th, and Captain Souter's protection of the regimental colours into icons of fortitude. Meanwhile, the British in India could console themselves with the success of the reprisal campaign. A bullish military analyst said after Kabul was retaken, 'It is a comfort to be able to look at a native in the face again with confidence. Now all is right. How easily achieved!'

But the Select Committee of the East India Company, which ran India, was more concerned. It questioned the whole legal basis of the war. Apart from the loss of life and sheer cost, its angry report listed other consequences: 'chilling the affections of the native army, and the disposition to enlist; loss of England's character for fair-dealing; loss of her character of success; the Mussalman population is rendered hostile; causes of rebellion developed by the pressure of taxes and the withdrawal of troops'.

As the blame game began, claims were made that the record of the negotiations in Kabul carried out by Burnes had been doctored. Leading the attack in Parliament was a bright young Tory MP, Benjamin Disraeli, trying to make his name, and backed by the public outcry over the calamity and the death of the hero Burnes. In contrast to the situation after the attacks on Afghanistan in 2001 and Iraq in 2003, Parliament debated the war fully in 1842, before the Army of Retribution had even reached Kabul, and MPs wanted to see all the papers. The defence of the 'Secret Committee' was that they had altered Burnes's papers only to keep their real intentions secret from Russia – the Afghan war was always about the wider picture, never about Afghanistan itself.

The Tory government, responsible for sending in the Army of Retribution, had not started the war, and its leader Robert Peel could rail about the 'presumptuous and reckless folly of others', in launching it. His choice for governor-general of India was Lord Ellenborough, who had been involved in Britain's frontier policy since the 1820s. However, against the wishes of both government and opposition in London, who wanted to keep troops in Afghanistan until a deal was done guaranteeing India's security, Ellenborough ordered a withdrawal two weeks after Pollock took Kabul and destroyed much of the city.

On 1st October 1842 Afghanistan was abandoned with a proclamation issued by Ellenborough in the same room as the Simla Manifesto that had begun the war exactly three years earlier. Ellenborough talked smugly of how revenge had 'again attached the opinion of invincibility to the British arms'. Cannons were fired at the Tower of London and in Hyde Park, and Queen Victoria was told that the campaign had 'established the supremacy of British power'.

In London the head of the Secret Committee, Hobhouse, complained 'Ellenborough seems positively to have ordered the retreat from Afghanistan, and he is . . . justly abused for that dastardly policy.' In Calcutta, the other members of the Indian government said they had not been told of the decision and lodged a complaint against Ellenborough.

The row over the withdrawal weakened the case being made by Tories in Parliament against the decision to go to war in the first place. Palmerston defended himself against the Tories with sarcasm, saying that perhaps now Britain would need protection: 'We could prevail upon our dear Friend the Czar to take us under his wing.'

Ellenborough further damaged his reputation by ordering the removal from Afghanistan of some gates supposedly seized from a temple at Somnath in India 800 years previously by Sultan Mahmud of Ghazni. Ellenborough wanted to send them on a triumphal tour to demonstrate how much Britain had done for India, and to show 'the happy union of our two countries'. The gates he ordered to be seized were, however, later copies, not the real thing, and the decision offended just about everyone. Christian ministers opposed it; Muslims saw it as encouraging Hindu triumphalism; and Hindus could not see what good it would do, since Indian history had changed and the 'crumbling edifice at Somnath' had long been in the hands of Muslims.

The first account of the war, written by a journalist J.H. Stocqueler in 1843, called the action a 'monstrous piece of folly', and said the decision to remove the gates was 'ridiculed by the press of India and of England; laughed at by the people of his own party in parliament'. The gates were left to rot in Agra, and the triumphal tour abandoned.

As for Afghanistan, Ellenborough's proclamation of 1842 declared, 'The Governor General will leave it to the Affghans themselves to create a government amidst the anarchy which is the consequence of their crimes.' Dost Mohammed, the man the war had been launched to remove, was allowed to make his way back to reclaim the throne he had lost.

This disastrous war set the tone for the British approach to Afghanistan for decades to come. A generation of empire-building Indian civil servants and soldiers believed it was not ready for civilisation, and could not be treated in the same way as other places. 'The people of these countries are far from ripe for the introduction of our highly refined system of government or of society,' wrote Sir Claude Wade, whose prescient analysis could have informed any of the subsequent foreign interventions in Afghanistan. 'There is nothing more to be dreaded or guarded against . . . than the overweening confidence with which Europeans are too often accustomed to regard the excellence of their own institutions and the anxiety that they display to introduce them in new and untried soils.'

British India retreated behind the Indus to lick its wounds, placing 'the barbarous tribes of Affghanistan . . . between the British army and an enemy approaching from the West'.

That enemy was coming uncomfortably close.

Part Two

Russian moves and the Second Anglo-Afghan War 1842–1880

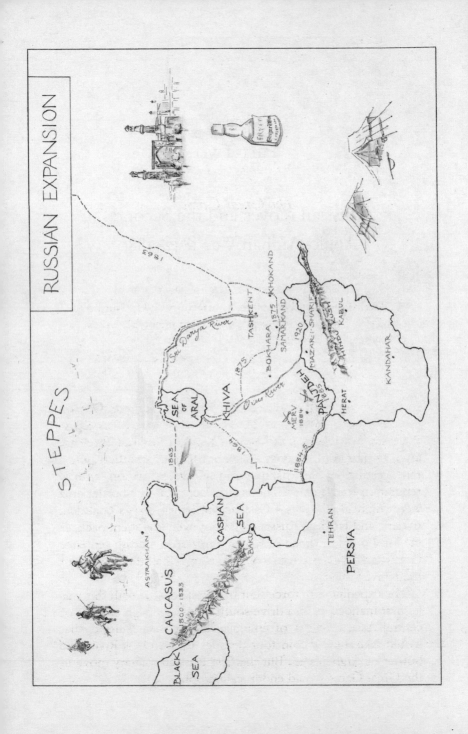

RUSSIAN EXPANSION

STEPPES

BLACK SEA

CAUCASUS 1800-1835

CASPIAN SEA

ASTRAKHAN

BAKU

SEA of ARAL

1863

1864-5

KHIVA

Sir Darya River

Oxus River

TASHKENT 1865

BOKHARA 1875

SAMARKAND

KHOKAND

1920

PANJDEH 1885

MERV 1884

1884-5

TEHRAN

PERSIA

MAZAR-I-SHARIF

KUSH

HINDU

KABUL

HERAT

KANDAHAR

1883

4

The Great Game

'The Afghan will bear poverty, insecurity of life; but he will not tolerate foreign rule. The moment he has a chance, he will rebel.'

'The Lawrence Memo' 1867

In 1836 an old man arrived in the Russian southern garrison town of Orenburg at the end of a journey of 1000 miles across the empty wasteland of the steppes south of Russia. His release after *55 years* in captivity as a slave, with 20 or so others, was a rare gesture of friendship from Khiva, a nation with a reputation for banditry. Thousands from Russia's border area were still held as slaves – Caspian fishermen, Volga boatmen, traders, and farmers. Russia could not even buy them back, as the local ruler, the khan of Khiva, threatened a death sentence to anyone selling a slave to Russia: slavery had the backing of the Khivan State.

The expeditionary force sent by Russia to deal with this was its first manoeuvre in a drive south across the high steppes of central Asia, a region of epic size bigger than Europe, that would take them within four decades to the Oxus River, the border of Afghanistan. But the first Russian military move in the Great Game would end in catastrophe.

In the years before the retreat from Kabul of 1842, the activities of British spies, horse-dealers and adventurers, probing into the region north of Afghanistan, were already causing 'serious alarm to the Russian government'. They turned up in Bokhara, Samarkand and even the savage bandit territory of Khiva, although a Russian official report worried nervously that it never quite knew what they were doing because its own spies were 'unreliable Asiatics'.

After Moorcroft's epic journeys in pursuit of new blood-stock, Burnes went north twice. Even while Russia was planning the expedition to deal with the slavers, another Briton, James Abbott, turned up in Khiva – a reminder that it was relatively easy for the British to reach the region from India compared to the obstacles facing Russia. The Russians did not believe Abbott's assurances that he had gone to Khiva to free slaves; they thought his real aim was to win a treaty in Britain's favour. But still they waited. Russia's military move against Khiva was put on hold until the British army had become more deeply involved in Afghanistan in 1840, so that Britain would have less excuse to complain about Russia's aggressive intentions. Delay into that summer proved fatal to the success of the mission.

Crossing the steppes with an army required first setting up caches of food along the route. The Russians requisitioned every camel they could find, more than 10,000 in all, but the attempt to take Khiva was doomed from the beginning. The advance party set out in the heat of July, when there was not even a thorn to eat along the way, and one third of the horses died. The steppes were not a level plain, but rough ground with treacherous gullies, deceptive pits of deep soft sand and dried salt flats.

By the time the main expedition began, it was winter, and they quickly lost dozens of horses, killed as they tried to eat frozen weeds. After three months it was clear they would run out of food if they went on, so the force turned back without reaching Khiva. Amid the chaos, hungry camels gnawed at bark boxes and sacks, spilling precious rations onto the ground. Eight hundred men, and most of the camels and horses died. The Russians realised too late that they should have learnt the lessons of the ancient conquerors Genghis Khan and Tamerlane, who both crossed the steppes with faster, more mobile forces, travelling only in the late winter and early spring, after the ground thawed, but before it became murderously hot.

Russia concluded that it should advance its border permanently to the other side of the treacherous and inhospitable steppes, to secure access to the Aral Sea, the east shore of the Caspian, and the rivers, Sri Darya and Amu Darya – the Oxus itself. The rivers were lifelines that would take Russia south across the wasteland of central Asia. Russia's long-serving foreign minister, Prince Aleksandr Gorchakov, justified the expansion as similar to the move by the United States across America, Britain in India, or France in Algiers – the search for a border with another settled state because nomads did not make good neighbours. 'The position of Russia in central Asia is that of all civilised states which find themselves in contact with half-savage, nomadic tribes . . . it always happens that interests of security of borders and of commercial relations demand of the more civilised state that it asserts a certain dominion over others.'

By 1864, when Gorchakov made his statement, the Russian border was where they wanted it, on the southern side of the steppes, having taken an area the size of western Europe. But Russian troops still faced unsettled and unruly tribes, and threatened to stride on – Gorchakov's logic would take them to the Hindu Kush and beyond. Russia had big elbows, stretching out at the same time to grab vast areas of northern Asia all the way to the port of Vladivostok, taking advantage of China's defeat by Britain in the Opium Wars.

At the heart of the Great Game was trade. Russia's commerce had advanced across the region ahead of its armies and diplomats. Other than trying to secure the release of slaves, the crucial factor for Russia in launching its first failed assault across the steppes had been the decision by the khan of

Khiva to tax merchants from Russia at a far higher rate than those from other Asian countries.

In Kabul before the British occupation, Mohan Lal had calculated that Russian goods were worth 200,000 rupees a year to 300,000 for British goods. And north of the Oxus, in the old Silk Road town of Bokhara, he saw Russian merchants trading in its bustling market alongside thousands of Jews and Indians. 'Every article neatly laid in the shops of Bokhara had a beautiful appearance, and gave an idea of the influence of trade which is gaining ground in Central Asia.' Guns, knives, sugar, paper, lace and horses came from Russia; cotton cloth, silk, spices, and tea went the other way from India and Kashmir; and European goods, especially French, china and glassware, were just beginning to make an appearance.

On his way north to Bokhara, Lal tested a report that the men of the region would share their wives and sisters with travellers. 'To ascertain the existence of so peculiar a fashion, I exerted my curiosity as far as decency permitted, but did not quite succeed.' He rather ungallantly concluded that he had not missed much. 'The females possess no attractive features.'

At the same time as Gorchakov was justifying imperial expansion as the sensible good housekeeping of civilisation, the thinking of British India was moving in the opposite direction. The losses in the first Anglo-Afghan War led to a strong desire to have nothing to do with Afghanistan at all – a policy defined as 'masterly inactivity' by the viceroy of India in the late 1860s, John Lawrence.

Lawrence remembered watching the Army of the Indus set out with high hopes in 1838, the hubris of every army that has ever tried to take Afghanistan: 'I never heard a word uttered of doubt as to our success, or of anxiety as to the movements of Russia.' The Lawrence family were to have a more decisive impact on British frontier affairs than any other in the middle years of the nineteenth century. John Lawrence's brother George had been Macnaghten's military secretary in Kabul, with him when he was killed at the meeting on a rug in the snow, and one of the handful of survivors held prisoner for months after the debacle. George Lawrence remembered an Afghan coming to their camp and predicting they would lose, saying, 'Yours is an army of tents and camels; ours is one of men and horses.'

John Lawrence believed the biggest mistake had 'consisted in occupying Afghanistan at all. There was no escaping the evils which flowed from that policy . . . To endeavour to hold such a country firmly, to try to control such a people, is to court misfortune and calamity. The Afghan will bear poverty, insecurity of life; but he will not tolerate foreign rule. The moment he has a chance, he will rebel.'

Lawrence believed that if Russia did send a force into Afghanistan then Britain might do better as a liberator, since the Afghans would see Russia as the aggressor. 'The shoe pinches the wearer only. The side which held Afghanistan is the one against whom that people would probably join.' He would have pulled Britain's main defences back east of the Indus if he could, with a large army threatening the frontier region from the plains.

But by now this was no longer an option. Britain had taken over Punjab after two sharp wars with the Sikhs following the death of Ranjit Singh, and these had brought land west of the Indus up to the foot of the Suleiman Mountains, including the former Pashtun 'capital' Peshawar, under British control for the first time. Britain now occupied the line of the whole of the Afghan frontier from the Indian Ocean to the Himalayas, completing the process by annexing Sind in the south almost by accident – 'a good, honest, useful piece of rascality', in the terms of the time. As confirmation of Britain's south Asian supremacy, the Koh-i-noor diamond fell into the hands of the Raj.

It was an attack by Persia on Herat in 1856 that led Britain to make its first overture to Afghanistan since the withdrawal of the Army of Retribution in 1842. Persia had watched Britain and Russia clash in the Crimea, and took advantage of a power vacuum in Herat to carry out its long-standing threat to seize the city. Britain declared war immediately, not risking another army in Afghanistan, but attacking Persia with a ship-borne invasion force. In a tangled tale of love, intrigue and war, a fleet was already in the area to back up diplomatic efforts to release a woman, whose name had been romantically linked with that of the British ambassador. She was the sister of the shah's principal wife, and Britain had threatened to break off diplomatic relations and take military action after she was imprisoned.

The war was a success, and Persia withdrew from Herat, but as so often, Afghanistan was just another piece on the board – there was no need or desire to engage with it on its own terms. Britain's sole aim in talking to Dost Mohammed after the war with Persia was to secure assurances that he would not assist Russia in an invasion of India.

Lawrence was then the senior British official on the frontier, and sent a clear and emphatic recommendation about the proposed talks to the government in India, with two brief points: '(1) you will never be able to get the Afghans to make a treaty, and (2) if they make it, they will not keep it.' But he lost the argument, and had to sign two treaties against his own judgement, first with Dost Mohammed's son and then a year later with Dost himself, who came through the Khyber Pass to Peshawar, a city he believed was his, but was now held by Britain, to sign an agreement, pledging to be 'the friend of the friends and enemy of the enemies of the Honourable East India Company'.

Britain wanted to open an embassy in Kabul, but Dost turned this down, allowing a mission to Kandahar instead – a disaster from start to finish. The British were surrounded by spies, making it impossible to gather information. At last matters got so bad they were glad to leave, concluding that any British mission was likely to be insulted or murdered, an episode that confirmed the view of opponents of a Forward policy like Lawrence, that Britain should have nothing to do with Afghanistan.

The Kandahar mission had other lessons for future deployments in Afghanistan. It had set out with 1500 cavalry, but only 500 were any good when they arrived because of the heat and the difficulties of the journey. And the British assessment of Kandahar in 1857 contained descriptions that would have been familiar to Russian invaders in the 1980s, or indeed British, Canadian and US forces in the region after 2001: 'Quiet and industrious communities are ground to the dust, and their rich and once cultivated lands fast turning to wilderness, while more turbulent races hold their own by sheer force . . . Add to this the fact of all classes being blindly priest-ridden by crafty, bigoted and supercilious ecclesiastics, and a true picture is drawn.'

The treaty with Dost may not have given Britain a foothold in Afghanistan, but it was tested sooner than anyone had expected. It was the last international agreement to be signed by the East India Company, whose long control of Britain's Indian empire was to be replaced by a far more formal system of imperial government in the wake of the biggest challenge to British authority in India, beginning with the mutiny of much of its army.

If tribal warriors from the frontier, or an Afghan army, had intervened against Britain in the desperate days of 1857 that might have been the deciding factor in what was a very close-run thing. But Dost honourably kept his forces out, not knowing that Lawrence was ready to offer Peshawar and the west bank of the Indus to him to do so. Faced with the threat of losing India, Lawrence was prepared to hand over the land despite a single-line telegram from the governor-general, Lord Canning, 'Hold on to Peshawar to the last.'

The frontier region was to play a further pivotal role in 1857. In the long hot months when the future of India hung in the balance, most of the troops who fought for Britain on the Delhi Ridge, and won the final battle for the city itself, assaulting a much larger insurgent force dug in behind well-defended positions, were Sikhs from Punjab and Pashtuns from the frontier. They had been recruited by a group of maverick soldiers and political officers under the leadership of another of the Lawrence brothers, Henry.

The generation on the frontier that became known as 'Henry Lawrence's young men' were encouraged to create their own militias, and train and fight like guerrillas. The names are evocative – Hodson's Horse, Daly's Horse, Coke's Rifles, and Lumsden's Corps of Guides – and all are still remembered officially in the regiments that succeeded these and became part of the armies of India or Pakistan after partition.

This was a unique group forged in the fire of the First Anglo-Afghan War. The best known, John Nicholson, was killed, leading from the front, in the battle to retake Delhi. He was not yet 35 years old and had been appointed a general in the irregular army of the frontier, although he was still down as a captain in the Indian army list. His career exactly bracketed the pioneer days on the frontier, beginning with the war in Afghanistan, and ending on the Delhi ridge. Fifteen years previously, in his first campaign, he had been held for months in filthy conditions in an Afghan jail, after the garrison at Ghazni had accepted Afghan assurances and surrendered following the massacre in the Khurd Kabul pass. Nicholson had looked on helpless as his Indian troops immediately were set upon, stripped and butchered by the Afghans against the terms of the surrender.

As he was making his way out through the Khyber Pass after his release from captivity by the Army of Retribution, a macabre coincidence led to Nicholson himself being the first to discover the body of his younger brother, naked and mutilated. Alexander Nicholson had been killed as the Khyber Pass closed behind the Army of Retribution, the last soldier to die in the First Anglo-Afghan War.

Years later, Nicholson still called Afghans 'the enemy', and refused to attend the treaty-signing ceremony with Dost in Peshawar, although he was by then the deputy commissioner there. He said he could not trust himself if he met them 'and might even be tempted to shoot one'. But he distinguished between the Afghans on the other side of the mountains and the Pashtun tribes of the frontier that he had come to know. To Nicholson, even the Waziris were better than the Afghans.

'I have always hopes of a people, however barbarous in their hospitality, who appreciate and practise good faith among themselves – the Waziris, for instance – but in Afghanistan, son betrays father, and brother brother, without remorse.'

Generations of Britons recognised something that appealed to them when they crossed the Indus. Ahead lay Afghanistan, with its theft, horror and deceit; behind them, India's blood-red sky, sapping summer heat and complex faith with its myriad Gods.

And in between were the Pathans, later more usually known as Pashtuns, who had a character the British thought they could deal with. The Sikhs may have been respected, admired even, as warriors, but they were not liked – their faith was not far removed from what were generally seen by the British as the absurdities of Hinduism. The frontier Pashtun, though, was different. 'There is an air of masculine independence about him which is refreshing in a country like India.' The British could look a Pashtun 'between the eyes, and there they found – a man. Sometimes the pledge they made was broken; there were wild men and fanatics, and on one side the assassin struck, on the other the avenger. But the pledge held, the respect, the affection, survived.'

The landscape had chiselled the contours of the Pashtun character, as Burnes acutely observed when he first encountered them. 'It is . . . the strength of their country, and not their military power, which enables them to cope with the Sikhs.' The Sikhs had sensibly left the frontier tribes to themselves, but British forces tried to settle and pacify the tribes from 1849, when they took over the lands west of the Indus.

Henry Lawrence's young men, licensed to do things not by the book, set off into this hinterland to make it their own in a singular way. Nicholson ordered the body of a well-known robber to be nailed to a door in the market of a village so people would know that the British had killed him, and he cut off the head of a rebel, and placed it on a table in his office, calling in tribal elders one by one to see if they had anything to say. He ruthlessly put down any stirrings of mutiny, hanging suspects without trial, and ordered the beard of an Islamic cleric to be shaved after he thought the man had insulted him. Nicholson's fame was such that a religious cult grew up around him, whose devotees pursued him to his intense and growing annoyance.

There were significant successes. Bandits were turned into British officers. When he was recruiting for his Corps of Guides, Joe Lumsden deliberately sought mountain men who could look after themselves, including those 'notorious for desperate deeds . . . who had defied all authority, and had never been seen in the plains but for murder and plunder'.

Another of the young men, James Abbott, who had first come to prominence when he alarmed the Russians by turning up in Khiva in 1840, became the administrator of Hazara, a vast area to the north on the east bank of the Indus. He made himself popular with Pashtun elders by his simple decision to allow the *azan*, the Muslim call to prayer, to be heard – it had been banned by the Sikhs. When Herbert Edwardes took over in Bannu, west of the Indus, he publicly flogged Sikh soldiers for looting from the locals, and then spent months persuading tribal elders that paying tribute to Britain was both fair and sensible.

This combination of diplomacy and determination – improvising when they could and killing when they thought they needed to – was buttressed by a Christian certainty that the British were doing God's work. It worked, up to a point, in the plains and even the hills of Abbot's Hazara region to the north, but as Britain came up against the reality of the mountain barrier that had dominated its military imagination for almost half a century, since Lieutenant Macartney's map, it faced its own version of the 'Gorchakov dilemma'.

Civilisation demanded that fines were paid and criminals brought to justice. But when revenue officers tried to collect fines, and troops pursued bandits, their way was blocked by Pashtun mountain tribes whose honour code guaranteed hospitality to guests, including criminals. The historian Charles Allen put the problem simply: 'Virtually every one of the scores of confrontations between Government and tribe, that escalated into conflict in the course of the next century can be traced back to this single issue of principle versus honour.' Britain's answer, involving frequent raids into frontier villages, was the policy later to be characterised as 'butcher and bolt'.

The Pashtun honour code protected guests, guaranteed hostility to strangers, and led to feuds between families being carried on through generations – the language even needing a specific word to define revenge between cousins. When Pashtuns were recruited as British soldiers their officers tried not to send them on leave at the same time as each other, since they tended to pursue ancient blood feuds and not return alive.

Hardly a year passed between 1849, when the Sikhs were defeated, and Britain's departure in 1947, when there was not some military engagement to try to subdue the frontier tribes. This was *the* dominant security concern for British India, but under-reported even at the time. A dispatch after one of these bruising encounters said, 'the hardships of the campaign told so severely on the British troops engaged that it hardly deserved to sink into the complete official oblivion which has shrouded it'. In the half-century before 1900 there were around 60 separate military operations in this mountain range, and a general uprising in 1897 – an intensity of conflict unique in the world. In contrast, the Indian Army was deployed just 23 times to other parts of India during this period – nearly all small-scale skirmishes in Assam – and mobilised to fight only 15 times in other theatres of war, including Egypt, Sudan and twice in China.

The campaigns on the frontier required considerable use of force. Reports to Parliament used words like thrashing, crushing and punishing. Force was always the first thing tried, the only language understood. Punishment meant the destruction of walls, particularly defensive towers, as well as the confiscation of livestock and the burning of crops.

Taking reports from just the first four years: in 1849, 2300 troops were involved in collecting unpaid fines. In 1850, after some sappers were killed by the Afridi tribe, who were paid for access through the Khyber Pass, 3200 'troops traversed the country, and the Afridis were punished'. In 1851, after Afghans entered villages in an area Britain thought was theirs, 2050 troops re-established order and took hostages 'for the good behaviour of the tribe'. The same year in the Mohmand country further north several villages were destroyed after a series of raids; the operation involved 1597 troops. In 1851, 600 troops went back into the same area, and forced 'submission'. In 1852, 3270 troops had to restore order in one part of the frontier while 2200 troops destroyed all villages in another. After all that a summary to Parliament claimed, 'Their punishment had a wholesome effect for many years.' But the soldiers were back in the same hills traversing, forcing submission and punishing the following year, and it did not stop.

And now something else was stirring on the frontier, as impervious to the unconventional warfare practised by Lawrence's young men as it was to the thrashing and punishing of Britain's conventional forces. Holy warriors, mujahidin, had emerged, with a social and religious agenda that would have been recognised by the Taliban 150 years later. These were directly related to the fundamentalists swiftly put to death by Shah Shuja in Ghazni on the way to reclaim his throne in Kabul in 1839, when he realised who they were. From the 1830s onwards British intelligence uncovered a trail of Islamist conspiracies across India. Silk letters were found sewn into the lining of clothing worn by messengers apprehended at night; instructions were discovered rolled up and hidden in bamboo canes; and Islamist songs were learnt in secret and passed from Muslim to Muslim. A prophecy told how British rule would end in 1857, but the Islamist rebels did not fade away after the mutiny was defeated.

The most audacious attack was the assassination of the viceroy, Lord Mayo, by a Wahhabi-inspired 'fanatic' while he was visiting a British penal colony in 1872. On his appointment Mayo had expressed his determination to act against the Wahhabi sect. A year earlier in Calcutta the acting chief justice had been murdered on his way to preside over a Wahhabi trial, as Islamic fundamentalism continued to stamp its mark on the story of south Asia.

The trail always led back to the frontier region, where as early as the 1830s the Sikhs had faced a determined assault by mujahidin from the hills, that threatened their control of Peshawar itself. The Islamists were forced back only when they overreached themselves by demanding that their Pashtun allies hand over their daughters to them in marriage. The tribes broke the alliance, turning on the alien 'Hindustani fanatics' and killing many of them including their leader, letting the Sikhs off the hook. Then, as later, the attitude of Islamist warriors to women would dominate their relationship to the outside world.

The 'fanatics' regrouped in the rugged and remote spot of Sittana, concealed in the folds of the mountains among the pine forests at the eastern end of Swat. These were the *ghazis* that Dost Mohammed had encouraged on the frontier against British forces. The willingness of Pashtuns to follow extremist religious leaders had been noticed by travellers for many years. Elphinstone himself said they were 'remarkable for their religious zeal and intolerance, for their attention to all forms of devotion, and for the profound respect which they bear for Moolahs. The tyranny of these priests is there carried to an intolerable pitch.' And Dr Henry Bellew, a surgeon with the Corps of Guides, said that the tribe he worked among in Swat, were 'entirely controlled by their priests, and are at all times ready for a jihad'.

The austere lifestyle of the *ghazis* drew its inspiration from the singular strain of Islam founded by Mohammed ibn Abd al-Wahhab, who was born in Arabia at the beginning of the eighteenth century. The sect that bore his name, Wahhabism, sought to strip Islam back to its fundamentals, the basic texts from the seventh century. Wahhabi leaders rejected the view of many Muslims that jihad was just about inner spiritual struggle: instead jihad was understood as imposing the duty of fighting a holy war against unbelievers. From the early

nineteenth century, Wahhabism spread across India, leading to
the foundation of the Deobandi school of Islamic thought.

Wahhabis did not just oppose British rule but their way of
life. A remarkable insight into the mind of those drawn to this
exclusive and austere cult came in the autobiography of a man
jailed for being part of a network that linked the fanatics on the
frontier with insurrection elsewhere in India. Mohammed Jafar
believed that his contact not just with English people, but with
their *language*, had threatened his soul, since English 'is so
closely connected with materialistic life that it is not only
harmful but dangerous for the spiritual life. If a young man,
before learning Quran and traditions of the holy Prophet in
detail, learns English and reads English books of various types
and different disciplines as I used to do, he will become an
unreligious, uncultured person with excessively free ideas . . .
Such knowledge will certainly make a person unreligious and
atheist.'

This made it essential for the fanatics to found their own
schools and follow a separate way of life. Any contact with
non-Wahhabi culture, including some Islamic culture, could be
damaging to the purity of the faith. The most radical fringes of
the Deobandi tradition taught that there could be no
compromise at all with non-Islamic culture.

By 1849, the year that Britain began its attempts to control
the frontier region, Wahhabi fanatics had secured enough
support among the disparate tribes scattered in the hills to the
north of the Vale of Peshawar for their leader to be named the
padshah, or king of Swat, where 'the inhabitants, a semi-
civilised race, are fanatical Mahometans'.

The Sikh forces that Britain had defeated to take the frontier
region knew what the British were taking on. The American
adventurer General Josiah Harlan, who had led part of the
Sikh army, said he had faced 'Savages from the remotest
recesses of the mountain districts . . . who were dignified with
the profession of the Mahomedan faith, many of them giants
in form and strength, . . . [they] concentrated themselves
around the standard of religion, and were prepared to slay,

plunder, and destroy, for the sake of God and the Prophet, the unenlightened infidels of the Punjab.'

One of the most serious attempts to take on the fanatics, the Ambeyla campaign of 1863, almost ended in disaster for British forces, as the Pashtun tribes came out in force against them, mobilised by the akhund of Swat, a revered figure with both political and religious influence, whose loyalties were never clear nor consistent. The British advance was slow with a long line of elephants and bullock carts, carrying carpets, furniture and crockery, and after a week of fierce fighting, the force was pinned down. Tribal fighters, including among their ranks many ex-British soldiers who had fled to the region after the 1857 Mutiny, continued to pour in to reinforce the rebel forces. The British commander, Brigadier Neville Chamberlain, who owed his advance to Henry Lawrence, was no longer a young man, but a highly respected leader, and reputed to have been injured more than any other man in the British army. He wrote an urgent dispatch in which he stated that even tribes that had been opposed to the fanatics previously were now allying with them against Britain: 'Old animosities are, for the time being, in abeyance; and under the influence of fanaticism, tribes usually hostile to each other are hastening to join the Akhoond's standard.'

Many of the British regiments in the field had been locally recruited and were fighting against their own tribes, one soldier recognising his father among the dead in front of his position after an engagement. After suffering large losses, 36 officers and 800 men, Britain sent reinforcements in enough strength to persuade the fighters to disperse to their homes. The Bunerwal tribe offered to destroy the fanatics' camp themselves, providing the British forces then withdrew from the area. A small detachment of British soldiers accompanied them and found the Islamists' hideout to be far larger than had been anticipated, 'containing several large edifices amongst which were the Moulvie's hall of audience, barracks for the soldiers, stabling and a powder manufactory'. It was an exact forerunner of camps for international al-Qaeda fighters set up in a similar area in the 1990s, inspired by the same Wahhabi vision.

The destruction of the camp was resented by some local people who now crowded round the small British force, threatening to kill them. But one of their hosts said that the British had been invited in by the Bunerwals, and would be escorted out by them – the honour code of the Pashtuns in action. A young officer, Frederick Roberts, already a holder of the VC for his exploits on the Delhi Ridge in 1857, and later to achieve fame in Afghanistan, said it was a 'plucky speech' by their Bunerwal host, who was no friend of Britain.

The British believed that 700 fanatics had died, but body counts, then as in the war against the Taliban in Afghanistan after 9/11, were useless in judging the success of an operation against Wahhabi warriors. Jihad was in the mind, and could not be snuffed out in combat. Only five years later, in the next major attempt to put them down, 12,500 British troops were needed for an assault on tribes who supported fanatics living in the Black Mountain area further east of Sittana – more troops than had been sent from India to China to take Peking in 1860.

Russia's commander on their southern frontier, General Kauffman, appealed to Britain to make common cause with Russia against Islamism, since this was 'the only danger to British rule in India, the others being merely imaginary'. This was typical shadow-boxing, with Russia denying its own aggressive intentions. But Russia did face its own problems with Islamic fundamentalism. In Bokhara mullahs tried to stop foreign trade, and there were religious police similar to those imposed by the modern Wahhabis in Saudi Arabia, and in Afghanistan under the Taliban. 'The men are stopped in the midst of their work by officers to see whether they can repeat their prayers: ignorance is followed by a whipping.'

Bokhara came under the tsar's control in 1869, bringing Russian soldiers onto the Oxus River facing Afghanistan for the first time, and in the 1870s they consolidated their position as the great trading towns of the Silk Road – Tashkent,

Samarkand, and Khokand – came into their hands, as well as Khiva.

Russia had fulfilled the prophesy of that earliest British Forward policy advocate, John McNeill, with a relentless move that had been going on for a century, 'varying the means, but never relinquishing the purpose'. Back in 1836 he had asked why Russia would expend so much 'blood and treasure' to take the south bank of the Caspian Sea. 'These acquisitions can be valued or valuable only in as much as they afford facilities for arriving at some great end which would, in her estimation, remunerate her for all that might have been expended in attaining it.'

The Russian advance was not only south-east towards the Afghan border, but directly south towards Persia, across the giant barrier of the mountains of the Caucasus to the west of the Caspian Sea, where the bright uniforms and set-piece manoeuvres of European warfare were no use in the treacherous forests, mountains and deserts. A Muslim guerrilla leader, Shamil, was as famous an enemy in Russia in the middle of the nineteenth century as Osama bin Laden was to become for the US at the start of the twenty-first century.

Decades of warfare, particularly in Chechnya, informed the generation of writers who came to define Russia's soul, after travelling or fighting in the Caucasus, as Russia imposed its will on people who Lermontov wrote, had 'thieving in their blood'. Pushkin wrote of 'the splendid chain of these mountains; their icy summits, which from afar, on a clear dawn, seem like strange clouds, many-coloured and motionless'.

Tolstoy may be best remembered for his vast novels about Europe during conventional conflicts, but the wild otherness of the Caucasus, beyond civilisation, obsessed him and inspired *Hadji Murat*, the book he was working on in the last years of his life. He compared a guerrilla leader to a thistle with a beautiful and strange flower. Anyone who tried to pick it would be hurt – but the plant would be damaged beyond repair too, since it could not be picked cleanly.

And the way Tolstoy described how the Chechens felt about Russian invaders has a clear parallel with the strength of Afghan feeling against foreign invaders: 'It was not hatred, but the refusal to recognise these Russian dogs as people, and such revulsion, disgust and bewilderment before the ridiculous cruelty of these beings, that the desire for their destruction, like the desire for the destruction of rats, poisonous spiders and wolves, was just as natural a feeling as the feeling of self-preservation.'

The hold of this region on the imagination of Russia has continued. Nearly all of the areas in central Asia taken at such cost by Russia in the nineteenth century achieved independence during the collapse of the Soviet Union in the early 1990s. But Chechnya had been given a different legal status, annexed as part of Russia itself, and has been held by force by Moscow in two of the most ruthless wars seen anywhere in recent years; Hadji Murat's descendants were ground under tank tracks.

Back in 1873, Britain and Russia signed their first agreement over Afghanistan. After dancing round each other for 40 years, both agreed to remain out of the boxing ring – it was to be a buffer state between them. The Oxus was defined as Afghanistan's northern border, while the western desert was to be mapped and surveyed before being carved up. Britain agreed that the mountains at the northern end of India's North-West Frontier were Afghan, particularly a long finger of land running up to China, as they sought to keep Afghan land between them and Russia. As usual Afghanistan was not consulted about its fate.

The death of the 'great amir', Dost Mohammed, in 1863, had coincided with the promotion of John Lawrence to the post of viceroy in India. Britain's policy of 'masterly inactivity' turned into studied indifference as the routine bloody power play between princes began in Kabul to choose a successor, each knowing that British recognition would bring guns and money.

Five years after Dost's death, and following fighting across the country that cost thousands of lives, one of his sons, Shir Ali, emerged from the bloodbath as the next amir. He owed the British nothing, and blamed them in part for the intensity of the struggle for succession, since they did not reply to his first demand for recognition when he took over a mostly united country as Dost's anointed successor. Britain had also recognised the claim of his half-brother, Afzul Khan, after Afzul had swept from the north to take Kabul.

Armies led by Yakub Khan and Abdur Rahman, the sons of the two claimants, had played key roles in a swirling conflict marked by epic violence. After one battle Abdur Rahman claimed to have cut off the heads of 3000 enemy dead and made a tower from them to discourage others, and he blew 50 bandits from the mouths of cannons to try to control the north. But he lost the fight, fleeing north across the Oxus to take refuge.

Even after Shir Ali took power, he complained of the duplicity of the British, believing that they were promoting the interests of one of his sons over another as heir apparent. This unique relationship, in which Britain sought to exert authority over Afghan external affairs by remote control, led to constant friction and misunderstanding. British Forward policy hawks did not believe they got much for their gifts of guns and money, since they could not send even a single squadron of cavalry into Afghanistan to scout the frontier. On the other side it was the constant complaint of succeeding Afghan amirs that they had to renegotiate terms every time; the deal was with an individual, not with the country.

So when Shir Ali emerged victorious and came down to the plains of India to claim his prize from the viceroy, he was not surprised that he was not offered the treaty terms he sought. He was left instead with vague offers of friendship and the standard gift of guns. His diplomatic reserve cracked when he saw the honour guard of Indian sepoys, who did not look like warriors to his Afghan eyes. He laughed openly at them, and said they were fit only to 'feed the kites and enrich the earth as they were unsuited to the purposes of war'.

BUTCHER & BOLT

In London the Liberal party still tended towards the
Lawrence view, restricting engagement, while the Tories urged
the more aggressive Forward policy. The approach see-sawed
as power changed hands, with British officials in India forced
to steer a consistent course between these opposing positions
as orders from London changed. In 1876 Lord Lytton was
appointed viceroy by the Tories, with a far more aggressive
mandate than any before him. He believed Amir Shir Ali to be
a 'savage with a touch of insanity'. Lytton's provocations
would lead to war.

5

'Afghanistan as a whole could no longer exist'

'A non-recognition of their failures and a considerable
and often ridiculous exaggeration of their successes con-
stitute the characteristics of Englishmen. They like to
exaggerate the scale of the enemy, the low casualties, and
the hardship: "The affair was brilliant, obstinately
contested and bloody" is the usual description which
they give to their engagements.'

Major General L.N. Soboleff – former chief of the Asiatic
Department of the Russian General staff, 1885

Russia and Britain ground against each other, like forces of
nature, two huge tectonic plates moving under the surface of
the late nineteenth-century world. Sometimes the surface
above was calm, sometimes it burst open, as in the Crimea. In
Asia the movement felt as if it would erupt into an earthquake
and British officials cynically prepared to let Afghanistan fall
through the resulting fissure in the earth. 'Afghanistan as a
whole could no longer exist', was the stated policy of the
secretary of state in London in a letter to the new viceroy Lord
Lytton.

More than half a century after Lieutenant Macartney first
drew the attention of empire-builders in India to the various

options for defence, the political generation whose caution was based on the catastrophe of the First Anglo-Afghan War had moved on. The Forward policy's time had come.

Disraeli's government had no regard for the details of a pass here or there in the Suleiman Mountains. Their mental map, on which Afghanistan 'would no longer exist', turned India's defensive wall through 90 degrees. Control of the passes through the Hindu Kush, not the Suleiman range, motivated their policy. They saw British forward positions bristling with guns, facing Russian forces over the Oxus, not waiting for them on the Indus. Political memories in London were short, and belief in the power of British arms to prevail was spurred on by the newspapers, who could not understand why Afghanistan was so hard to conquer. Those in Simla and Calcutta who still whispered caution were sidelined, as the laying of a cable under the Red Sea in 1870 brought the government of India under more direct control from London.

An outbreak of war between Russia and Turkey in 1877 took a British fleet to the eastern Mediterranean; the tectonic plates overlapped and crashed under the waves as warships brought troops from India. Tension rose for six months in the Dardanelles, as Britain and Russia glowered at each other across Constantinople, but a year later the European powers agreed to step back from war at the Congress of Berlin.

Afghanistan was a crucial part of this jigsaw. Russia had moved further south, taking a belt of land north of the Oxus, from Khokand in the east, and threatening the oasis at Merv in the west, and there was no certainty as to where the Afghan border lay. Russia could now sweep down to the Hindu Kush at any time, certainly more quickly than Britain could mobilise from India.

Even while British politicians were returning from Berlin with a treaty that they could call 'Peace with Honour', Russia raised the stakes with their most audacious move yet in Afghanistan, sending a diplomatic mission to Kabul, against the terms of the 1873 agreement with Britain that the country was to be a buffer between them. Russia wanted control of all of the land down to the Hindu Kush, and in return offered to help Shir Ali secure Peshawar and the former Afghan territories on the other side of the Suleiman Mountains. The dream of reuniting the Pashtun lands – Pashtunistan – lured him to the Russian side.

Shir Ali had no affection for the British. He thought them duplicitous, and resented what he saw as his one-sided relationship with them in which they made demands and gave little concrete in return. The death of the son he had chosen to succeed him, Abdullah Jan, in August, closed Kabul for a brief period, but only delayed the inevitable – the arrival of a letter from Britain announcing that they too would send a mission to Kabul. On 21st September 1878, a British military force accompanying an envoy attempted to march through the Khyber Pass – a formal charade, the equivalent of a duellist dropping his gauntlet at the gates of a rival. They were refused entry, as they knew they would be, and war was declared on Afghanistan.

The mission turned back at the Khyber was led by General Sir Neville Chamberlain, now almost 60 years old, who remembered coming the other way out through the pass 36 years before, when it was still 'strewn with skeletons of men and animals . . . our gun-wheels ground to dust the bones of the dead. In some places the Affghans . . . had placed the skeletons one in the arms of the other, or sometimes sitting or standing against the rocks as if they were holding a consultation.'

Disraeli's viceroy Lord Lytton had never seen the Khyber Pass, but he viewed war with Russia as inevitable, and wanted it on ground chosen by Britain. He wrote of the

immense importance to us of the triangle formed by Kabul, Ghazni and Jalalabad, with the possession of the passes over the Hindu Kush. Defensively this position, behind a rampart of mountains, and with its communications unassailable directly commands the central group of roads, while directly threatening both the eastern and western group. Offensively it gives the power of debouching at will on the plains of the Oxus, and threatens every point of Russia's extended frontier. It is difficult to imagine a more strategical position; and whenever the moment of collision with Russia arrives, it must find us in possession of it, as friends and allies of the Afghans if possible, but firmly established there in any case.

British politicians anticipated victory, quoting military intelligence reports predicting that 'in case of war with the English, most of the troops at each action will either come over to us or else disperse', while the most significant opposition to moving Forward came from senior army officers, who knew the hazards and the costs. But a rumbling of consensus for war began to roll through the clubs and drawing rooms of the rulers of India, as well as among Tories in London. A member of the Council of India, Sir Henry Rawlinson, argued that Afghanistan had no right to independent existence at all: it was geographically and politically a part of India, so that dealt with 'abstract questions' about the legitimacy of interference. Furthermore, it was 'affectation to apply the nice distinctions of European diplomacy to a barbarian chief like Shir Ali Khan'.

The British mission to Kabul was headed by a frontier political officer with an exotic background and name – Lieutenant Colonel Sir Pierre Louis-Napoleon Cavagnari – born in Parma in Italy to an Irish mother. He looked out the accounts from the First Anglo-Afghan War to find out the going rate to be paid as the toll for an invasion force through the Khyber Pass, and offered the same as before, 87,000 rupees, to the Afridi tribe, who had run the protection racket in the Khyber for centuries. To his surprise there had been no inflation in invasion tolls – his offer was accepted. But despite the payment, British soldiers had to fight their way through from the beginning, in a complex and deceptive war where nothing, even victory, was as it seemed, and the geography and people of the frontier and Afghanistan once again confounded the optimistic expectations of the invader.

The first shots in the Second Anglo-Afghan War were fired on the afternoon of 21st November 1878 during a skirmish in the Khyber between Afghan cavalry and Britain's frontier specialists, the Corps of Guides. The Guides had been marching all night with only one day's cooked rations in their haversacks. 'The night was dark, the road tortuous, rocky and broken, passing for a considerable distance through heavy grass and jungle up the bed of the Lashora stream.' The Guides took casualties and were pinned down without supplies for another day, but first light on the morning of the 23rd revealed that a defensive fort and its surrounding positions had been abandoned, and they moved through the Khyber to Jalalabad. It was a pattern repeated throughout the war – a tough fight, then an absent enemy and an easy march forward – violence, deception, feint. Everything was an illusion.

Two other columns in an invasion army of 45,000 moved into Afghanistan at the same time. The central column moved towards the high pass in the Camel's Neck, while in the south a force moved through mountain passes towards Quetta on military roads built by the British invasion force in 1839. As in that earlier campaign, the lack of food and water on the route took an enormous toll of animals. Almost 12,000 camels died in the first move on Kandahar, and by the end of the war, a third of the camels available in the whole of Punjab had died in Afghanistan. But on the southern front the journey was harder than the fighting. In their only battle in the flat plain before Kandahar, Britain suffered a handful of wounded for about 100 dead of the enemy. And after the battle, some Afghan cavalry asked to join the British force – just as the intelligence assessment had predicted. It was beginning to look easy.

The governor of Kandahar fled, and as the British took the town, most shops remained open, and large numbers of people came out to see their arrival. 'Their attitude was perfectly impassive,' in the words of the official army account of the war, 'showing neither fear, hostility, nor pleasure.' There were some subsequent isolated attacks on British officers in Kandahar, but the first serious military engagement in the south was at the town of Sangin, one of the most hotly contested towns when British forces returned to the area in 2006. In the cavalry battle that followed the first contact with the enemy at Sangin, the British calculated that one third of the 1500 men opposing them were *ghazis*, or 'fanatics'.

Shir Ali failed to retain the support of tribal elders and fled north with the Russian delegation he had welcomed to Kabul. However Russia did not deliver the alliance he thought he had been promised, and he died a disappointed man in Mazar in February. His son Yakub Khan claimed the throne, and although his hold was precarious, Britain agreed to deal with him, demanding considerable involvement in Afghanistan's internal affairs. Yakub Khan's reply said that Britain's emissary to him had 'strung one by one on the thread of description the pearls of your friendly hints', although spies intercepted a quite different message from Yakub to tribal elders, inciting rebellion and the murder of British soldiers.

The meeting took place at Gandamack in May, scene of the disastrous last stand of the 44th in 1842 — transformed into heroic legend by Britain. The reddish stones near the bare summit were said to be stained with the 'blood of the English'. The hill is still called *'Feringhee Ghunadi'* — the mountain of the foreigners.

A British account described Yakub Khan as 'peevishly' refusing everything at first, before changing his mind and agreeing to everything. A crucial element of the deal was that for the first time an Afghan ruler accepted British control of all of the main passes through the Suleiman Mountains, including the Khyber, 'and of all relations with the independent tribes of the territory directly connected with these passes'. The new amir also agreed to conduct relations with foreign states only in accordance with the 'advice and wishes' of the British government. Britain agreed to support the amir against any foreign aggression and pay him 600,000 rupees annually.

There was a vote of thanks in both Houses of Parliament to all involved, and even congratulations in the Russian press for Disraeli: 'By a bold stroke, for which thousands of Indian militiamen have paid with their lives, he obtained for his country a commanding position in Central Asia – a position we have strived to secure for fifteen years.'

By now the expeditionary force had been in the field for longer than planned, and as the summer of 1879 reached its hottest months, cholera broke out in the Khyber Pass. 'In this particular year and at this particular time, the choice is a choice of evils,' wrote the surgeon general with the British force. 'If the troops marched into India, they marched into cholera; if they remained, it advanced on them.' The decision was taken to move, but dozens died, the worst hit being medical staff. There may not have been much fighting, but the war was taking its toll:

> Their clothes were stiff and dirty from the profuse perspiration and dust; their countenances betokened great nervous exhaustion, combined with a wild expression, difficult to describe; the eyes infected and even sunken, a burning skin, black with the effects of sun and dirt; dry tongue; a weak voice; and a thirst which no amount of fluids seemed to relieve.

Heading in the other direction with a small escort force, Sir Louis Cavagnari was the first British emissary to Kabul since Macnaghten. He was given a substantial house behind the defensive walls of the Bala Hissar itself, close to Yakub Khan's palace. But as soon as he arrived in Kabul Cavagnari's position looked precarious. The official British military assessment of what happened next was similar to what was commonly said in Kabul about Hamid Karzai, the leader installed by the US-led invasion force in 2001. 'Yakub Khan's authority was small beyond the walls of his capital, while the Mullahs and the anti-

British party lost no opportunity of exciting the people towards the British alliance.'

In the same way as Macnaghten had missed the warning signs before he was butchered, Cavagnari believed everything was fine until the end. On 30th August he wrote, 'I personally believe that Yakub Khan will turn out to be a very good ally, and that we shall be able to keep him to his engagements.' But a Pashtun officer in his escort, Rissaldar-Major Nakhshband Khan of the Guides Cavalry, thought they were never safe. He saw Afghan soldiers from the south arriving in town, abusing British soldiers as they passed. His debrief by British intelligence after he fled was full of rumour: 'I heard shortly afterwards from a friend of mine that he heard from a friend of his, who was present at the time . . .'

Cavagnari died after the old game of playing different forces off against each other. He paid money directly to a number of Afghan leaders, angering the amir, who had not disbursed the money he had received from Britain. When he was asked why he had not fulfilled his Gandamack pledge to pay the sirdars, the amir answered, 'This is Afghanistan. We cannot get on here without practising deceit.' According to Khan, another tribal leader present said that if that was the case then 'we may look upon Afghanistan as on the way to ruin; it will go out of our hands'.

So the soldiers from the irregular militias who now filled the streets had not been paid, and although it was the amir and their own chiefs who owed them the money, they blamed the British embassy. And there was a rumour that Bibles printed in Arabic to evangelise the country, along with Korans, had been seen in the baggage of one of the members of the British party. According to the source of this story, the Koran in Afghanistan was only ever printed on expensive paper from plants grown in Kashmir. It was sacrilege to print it on European paper. 'The Kabul Mullahs, who are renowned for their fanaticism, were in a state of frenzy when they saw the obnoxious books . . . The regiment, excited by the Mullahs, was of course soon brought into a state of mutiny.'

Early in the morning of 3rd September, Rissaldar Major Khan was recognised and almost pulled from his horse as he rode from his lodgings towards the British residency. He managed to get away, and concealed his horse in the stables at the house of an Afghan friend. From an upstairs window he saw a crowd heading up the hill to the Bala Hissar from the town. They were repulsed when they tried to rob the British-Indian cavalrymen, but an hour later they returned armed, and fighting began.

This did not look like a mindless mob; it appeared to Khan that officers in the Afghan army were directing events. The rebels looted the magazine in the fortress, although they did not try to take the treasury, where 500 of the amir's men remained at their posts. At one point he ordered his horse to be saddled, but he never mounted it, and never intervened, as the events unfolded in front of him.

At around 9 a.m., Cavagnari and the other British officers led 25 of their men out of the residency, charging the rioters on the rough ground in front. 'When charged, the Afghan soldiers ran like sheep before a wolf.' But the position was hopeless, and despite three other sallies, the residency was on fire by mid-morning. There was little shooting heard from it after 3 p.m. Cavagnari's body was never identified. The only survivor of the mission, Rissaldar Major Khan, fled Kabul on a borrowed pony at night, disguised as a grass-cutter, the lowliest of camp followers, and made his way south-east towards the pass out of Afghanistan at the Camel's Neck.

General Roberts, who had commanded the central column in the invasion, was with the viceroy in Simla when news of the slaughter came through, and headed back towards Afghanistan straightaway. This was to be the campaign that would make his name – literally, as Lord Roberts of Kandahar. Yakub Khan knew what was coming, and sent a pleading letter:

Some of the cavalry I have dismissed, and night and day am considering how to put matters straight. Please God the mutineers will soon meet the punishment they deserve, and my affairs will be arranged to the satisfaction of the British government. Certain persons of high position in these provinces have become rebellious; but I am watching carefully and closely every quarter.

The viceroy replied that the British army was coming to support him – a response similar to Moscow's justification for the Soviet invasion in 1979.

Roberts calculated that the pass at the Camel's Neck was the best hope to re-enter Afghanistan, since the tribes at the Khyber Pass were known for their treachery, and managed to get his force over the pass before it was closed by snow, despite transport difficulties that were 'greater than I ever remember'. Every surviving camel and horse available in the region was pressed into service. Roberts sent a blunt message to Kabul:

> Be it known that the British army is advancing on Kabul to take possession of the city . . . all persons found armed in or about Kabul will be treated as enemies of the British government; and further, it must be clearly understood that if the entry of the British force is resisted, I cannot hold myself responsible for any accidental mischief which may be done to persons and property, even of well-disposed people, who may have neglected this warning.

But intelligence, that most basic need for any military campaign, was lacking. What Roberts did not know was that the leaders of several tribes thought his force could be beaten, and had formed an alliance. By October, less than a month after the deaths of Cavagnari and his party, as British troops approached Kabul from the south, a large Afghan force was coming together on the slopes of Charasiab ahead, across a three-mile front. At the same time Roberts learnt that his supplies were under attack back at the high pass in the mountains, where British agents had tried to play brother against brother in the family that controlled the pass.

Roberts could not retreat, and needed to advance to Kabul quickly. But with just 2500 men, he was outnumbered perhaps five to one by an enemy who had the advantage of high ground. After a feint attack at the end of the ridge at Charasiab nearest the road, the most direct route to Kabul, a joint force of Highlanders and Gurkhas assaulted the other end, storming the high ground before the Afghans could reinforce it in time. Most of the Afghan force retreated, leaving hundreds dead.

This decisive victory in the biggest set-piece battle of the war left Britain with 20 pieces of Afghan artillery, including one identified as a recent British gift, and opened the gateway to the capital. The speed of the advance and the ferocity of the fighting – the British force fired 40,000 rounds in the battle for Charasiab – left Kabul defenceless.

Yakub Khan abdicated, telling Roberts he would 'rather be a grass-cutter in the English camp than ruler of Afghanistan'. He went under armed guard into exile and a British pension in India. The acknowledgement on 19th November that he had abdicated was the first dispatch on a new telegraph line completed to Kabul from India, almost a year to the day since the first shots had been fired in the war. Shortly afterwards, it was unclear whether by accident or design, the magazine exploded in the Bala Hissar, causing huge destruction, killing more than 20 people and forcing the British out of their temporary quarters. The Gurkhas were dispersed around other camps, some clad in greatcoats given them by grateful Highlanders for their support in the battle for the Charasiab Ridge, a gesture of comradeship that could be understood 'only by those who know the coldness of the nights here'.

After swift trials, 49 Afghans were executed on a gallows set up in the ruins of residency for their role in the uprising. Roberts also ordered that the remaining buildings in the Bala Hissar should be pulled down as an 'act of retributive justice', and the material used to build barracks in the cantonment at Sherpur, outside Kabul, taken over by the British force.

For a period there was a strange atmosphere in Kabul: it was under martial law; and the residency building was still a charred shell with human bones lying in the ruins; but British soldiers seemed to be able to move about freely, and organised cricket, horseracing and boating on Wazirabad Lake. 'Towards the afternoons the main bazaars present a most lively and animated appearance, and are densely and incongruously crowded: camels, elephants, mules, horsemen, Afghans and Englishmen all jostling along in a busy stream.'

But every morning, posters would appear in Kabul urging jihad against the British occupation. Dissent began in the mosques. A mullah with the unlikely name of Mushk-i-Alam (fragrance of all the world) led the opposition. He signed his letters as *Imam-ul-Mujahidin-i-wal Muslimin* – leader of the mujahidin [holy warriors] – the sort of title that would become much better known in Afghanistan in later conflicts. He was financed by the women of Yakub Khan's family, who literally gave away the family jewels to try to turn the tide against Britain.

The fate of the British occupation force depended, as always in Afghanistan, on whether the tribal chiefs – the sirdars – would mobilise against them. Strength tended to go with strength, while any show of weakness could be fatal. Roberts had been decisive, beating a large Afghan army on the field at Charasiab, to give him a breathing space. The sirdars acquiesced to British rule, even if they did not support it. And they owed nothing to Yakub Khan's son, who was just five years old; they were happy to take his family's money while they waited.

Roberts knew his intelligence was weak, so he did not know the strength of any forces against him, nor who would lead them. The winter came early that year, in the middle of November. Roberts kept his inkstand under his pillow so the ink did not freeze, and three elephants died of cold on a hill east of the city, where they lay stinking for months as the ground was too hard to bury them and there was not enough wood to burn them.

Despite the apparent lull and Britain's military success, General Roberts himself made a list of what the Afghans might be able to complain about:

The prolonged occupation by foreign troops of the fortified cantonment which had been prepared by the late Amir Shir Ali for his own army; the capture of the large park of artillery, and of the vast munitions of war, which had raised the military strength of the Afghans to a standard unequalled among Asiatic nations; the destruction of their historic fortress, the residence of their kings; and, lastly, the imprisonment and deportation to India of their Amir and his principal ministers.

All of these concerns might be exploited to 'excite into vivid fanaticism the religious sentiment, which had ever formed a prominent trait in the Afghan character'.

On 8th December Roberts ordered a parade to be held as a show of force at Sherpur, the fortified cantonment taken by Britain. This was an enormous site with low walls around a four-and-a-half-mile long perimeter, flanked by the Bemaru Hills. One corner covered the ground where General Elphinstone's cantonment had been before the destruction of his force in its retreat to the east in the winter of 1841. But the parade had to be abandoned as Roberts heard of large Afghan forces coming from the south and the west, and quickly sent troops out to engage them. British forces took heavy casualties in a series of running battles.

The hostile force quickly numbered about 100,000 men. A correspondent for the *Daily News* reported, 'The enemy fought desperately, and many of the inhabitants of the city joined his ranks; the villagers too, cut up any soldier who got separated from his comrades, even though he happened to be under the very entrenchments of our camp.'

One of the main leaders of the uprising was Mohammed Jan, written off in a British intelligence assessment as a 'drunkard and smoker of hemp'. He turned out to be a good commander and an impressive artillery officer. One cavalry engagement cost 27 British dead, about one sixth of those engaged, and more than 50 horses. Roberts ordered a retreat into Sherpur and prepared its defences for a siege.

The first snow of winter had fallen, and Roberts paid exorbitant prices for sheepskin coats brought in from Persia to protect his force from the cold. For almost two weeks the British came under intense attack. As in 1841, the Afghans made good use of the high ground to fire into Sherpur, and were now equipped with British-supplied Snider rifles as well as *jezails*. British attempts to break out were repulsed. On 23rd December the Afghans made their most concerted assault. General Hugh Gough was hit by a bullet, but saved by the suit of chain mail he had thought to bring from home – in what must surely have been the final use of medieval armour on a British battlefield. The following day the assault was abandoned and 'The city lay before them undefended', in the words of the Kabul historian, Nancy Dupree. 'The British emerged from behind the walls of Sherpur to find the mountains and the plains which had bristled with thousands of hostile tribesmen now quiet and serene.'

The disappearance of the enemy was as sudden as their appearance. They melted away just as they had in the Khyber Pass in the first engagement of the war more than a year before – violence, deception, feint. Everything was an illusion. Reports that a British relief column was on its way played some part in the abrupt ending of the second siege of Sherpur, but there was another process at work, which the British army at the time missed altogether.

Afghanistan was refusing to be dismembered, dropped down a fissure through the ground as if a casualty of an earthquake. For a century Britain had fought across the subcontinent, beating the great powers of the time – Tipu Sultan's southern forces, the Mahrattas, the Sikhs. They did not see that the Pashtuns, and the other tribes quarried from the landscape of Afghanistan, were different. They would not be annexed, in a 'piece of rascality' like Sind. Even Russia had paused at the Oxus, after buying or beating, cajoling, but ultimately conquering all of the peoples they saw as barbarians in Central Asia along the way.

In the twenty-first century, as military strategists again tried to grapple with Afghanistan, the slaughter of the First Anglo-Afghan War was often quoted as a lesson in the consequences of failure. An analysis of the events of December 1879 in the second war would be far more instructive. Roberts and his staff may have waged a successful military campaign, but they did not understand how power worked. They saw the amir's family as savages, the sirdars as duplicitous, the mullah with the fragrant name as a joke, and the rebel leader as just a hemp smoker; they went sailing while a rebellion swirled around them, missing the signals that a storm was about to break over their heads; and they missed the significance of the sudden peace.

The Afghan leaders, 'warlords' in modern terminology, were using the ancient tactics of mobile indigenous forces, inflicting harm where they could but avoiding confrontation, wearing down their opponents – tactics noted by the historian Herodotus as long as 2500 years ago to explain how the Scythian nomads of central Asia beat King Darius, whose belief in the power of his military forces matched that of Britain in the nineteenth century, or of the US in the twenty-first. Darius's conventional army set off into Scythian territory but never saw their enemy, who constantly retreated into land they knew well, harrying where they could, until Darius gave up, suffering heavy losses as he retreated.

In the same way, the Taliban changed their tactics after suffering heavy casualties in set-piece engagements in 2006, when British troops first mobilised in force in Helmand Province. They moved to classic small-scale guerrilla raids, and asymmetric techniques such as suicide attacks in a shifting alliance with other factions and interests, including the opium trade. They would take ground if it was offered to them, as in the town of Musa Qala, which they held for a year, but they never needed to win engagements on the ground, as long as they kept up the pressure. Winning was not about tactical military advances, but support in the villages and, always the most important thing in Afghanistan, the *perception* of victory – which way the wind of war was blowing. Force was threatened much more than it was used.

Victory on the battlefield was not the point. The Afghans in 1879 learnt in the one set-piece confrontation on the Charasiab Ridge that they would not defeat the British army in open warfare. So they avoided it. They were quarrelsome and confrontational with each other – weaknesses in conventional war, but qualities that gave them flexibility and unbeatable power in an insurgency. Their disunity generated centrifugal forces that made the country ungovernable, as well as giving them a sinuous strength when they came together.

Of all of the foreign attempts to control Afghanistan in the two centuries after Elphinstone's first meeting in 1808, the Soviet invasion in 1979 was the one that came closest to success. And when the Soviet-backed government finally crumbled, the disunity of the forces that had ousted it flared into open civil war. Power had spun out of Kabul, and could not be drawn back. In Afghanistan imposing power from the centre has always been temporary – like gathering together sand or water – since local loyalty outweighs any other. However strong the weapons of foreign forces, they have always achieved less than local forces, which can gather and disperse at will, as General Roberts experienced in the siege of December 1879.

A Russian analysis of British problems in the Second Anglo-Afghan War assessed this well: 'English commanders understood that they had not gained possession of all of those strips of country over which the troops had passed, but only of the actual ground on which their forces were encamped.'

General Roberts took over in Kabul again, but the insurgency had done its job, sending a signal well beyond Sherpur. In India and London Forward policy hawks were now rethinking their options. The length of the military operation, the savagery of the death of Cavagnari and his escort, the cost of occupation and the sudden twists and turns of the war led to new instructions going out to an experienced frontier officer, Sir Lepel Griffin. The British no longer wanted to dismember or annex Afghanistan; they wanted to hand it over.

*

In March 1880, with the country still leaderless, Abdur Rahman made his move, crossing the Oxus River after 11 years in exile in Russian territory, initially supported by only a small force. As he moved south gathering strength, Britain corresponded with him, probing what he could deliver as amir. By the time he was strong enough to cross the Hindu Kush and camp in Charikar, north of Kabul, the government had changed in London, and with it British policy over Afghanistan. The Forward policy, already facing searching questions because of the failure of the war, went into sharp reverse.

The replacement of Disraeli by Gladstone in April 1880 had brought a new moral tone to Britain's handling of international affairs, of the sort that would not re-emerge until the election of Tony Blair's New Labour government in 1997. Gladstone took the high moral ground over Afghanistan in particular. During his Midlothian campaign in December 1879 he high-lighted military atrocities allegedly carried out by the column commanded by General Roberts during the first phase of the war a year earlier.

Several dozen villages had been burnt in retribution for an attack on British forces in Khost in the east – not far from where the Tora Bora cave complex would later be located – and 130 prisoners killed. A locally recruited Pashtun officer had been cleared by an inquiry, but the incident was witnessed by a reporter for the *Evening Standard,* travelling with the army, and led to questions in Parliament. Gladstone used the incident to talk of the 'rights of the savage', recounting the slaughter in the snow in as emotional a way he could, since his audience included women who, he claimed, had little taste for 'the harder, sterner and drier lessons of politics'.

Now in government he wanted a radical new approach, and the first dispatch from Lord Hartington, Gladstone's new secretary of state for India, to his new viceroy was scathing of a Tory policy that had led to 'the assumption of fresh and unwelcome liabilities' for Britain, 'and a condition of anarchy' throughout Afghanistan. Some British soldiers had now been in Afghanistan for two years, and General Roberts himself wanted withdrawal as soon as practicable: 'I feel sure I am right when I say that the less the Afghans see of us the less they will dislike us.'

Sir Lepel Griffin continued to correspond with Abdur Rahman, even after letters were found to be passing between him and the rebel mullah Mushk-i-Alam, but contingency plans were also drawn up to put Yakub Khan back in power instead, as if the British had learnt nothing from the first war – that an amir imposed by Britain was bound to be mistrusted. Abdur Rahman understood this very well: 'If I showed any inclination towards the English, my people would call me an infidel for joining hands with infidels, and they would proclaim a religious holy war against me.' He added that it was hard for an Afghan leader to alter 50 years of mistrust when each side had called the other 'treacherous, unreliable, and breakers of oaths'.

By the late spring of 1880, as the snows melted, and the water flowed off the Hindu Kush to turn the valleys to the south green on either side of the flat gravel-covered moonscape of the plain north of Charikar, Afghan power flowed to four small tents pitched close together in the centre of a military camp. Abdur Rahman sat, in one of the four identical tents, waiting and planning, 'an extremely able man, the like of him has never been seen in this country' in the words of a British visitor. Knowing that Britain had no other realistic choice for amir, he delayed agreement with them. He wanted to know what terms they were offering, whether he held Kandahar, and 'what enemy of the British government am I expected to repel'.

Abdur Rahman had been taught his military skills as a child by a British officer called Campbell, who had commanded the army of his father. It was a tough upbringing. He had been imprisoned for a year after falling out with a powerful figure in court. When he was released, his father's British-born commander was dead, and he took control of the army himself, winning his first major battle aged only 20. In the 1860s, in the murderous tussle for power after the death of Amir Dost

Mohammed, his armies took land as far south as Kandahar, before being flung back to the north.

Defeated, Abdur Rahman had turned down the standard British offer of a pension and a bungalow in Rawalpindi. 'I had never seen the benefit of English friendship. They were the enemies of my friends, whose enemies were my enemies.' It was a specific rejection of the terms of the treaty signed by Dost Mohammed in 1857.

When he later made his only trip to India in 1885, Abdur Rahman was confirmed in his decision not to accept the invitation. He found himself queuing among other petitioning princes from different parts of India:

> the poor things were all dressed like women, wearing diamond pins in their hair, earrings, bracelets, necklaces, and other pieces of jewellery usually worn by women. The straps of their trousers were jewelled, and little bells were hanging in front of their trousers as low as their feet. They were sunk in ignorance, laziness, and indulgence. They did not know what was going on in the world nor what was in it . . . they spend their time in drinking and smoking opium.

Instead, after his defeat as a young man, Abdur Rahman had travelled around Afghanistan, and his account of his journey during a long winter reads like a dream, half seen, half remembered, filled with myth, mysticism and visions of lost kings.

When he lost his last battle and fled, all his cavalry dispersed, except for 40 men, who remained with him all his life and became his most senior military leaders. While he was sitting at the campfire one night, cooking a piece of meat in a blackened and beaten saucepan, a dog tipped it over and grabbed the meat, running off into the snow. It was his lowest moment, defeated by a stray dog, when only days earlier he had been able to command a kitchen that could feed an army. A friend sent 200 gold coins, but they could not be exchanged, so he and his men remained poor and hungry.

In the frontier region a figure dressed in men's clothing ran up, who turned out to be a woman taken by Waziris when she was 12 years old. Abdur Rahman pulled her up on his horse and took her away to freedom. In another village there was a surreal fight over a sheep that they had bought, killed and were preparing to cook. The man who had sold it wanted them to bring it back to life. While they were arguing, a 'king' appeared – a tattered character with bells on his bridle, who called himself Shah Jahan, one of the early Mughal emperors, and led them past an abandoned village where he said 'Dost Mohammed' lived, making a half-hearted attempt to rob them along the way. They headed on through heavy rain to a village where two small dancing boys greeted them. And then they plunged into a long journey across a desert where the 'horses' tongues were as if they were made of wood'.

North of his former kingdom, he met the khan of Khiva whose 60 gunners were 'all negroes'. Then after trekking up the Silk Road, he arrived in Samarkand and lived under Russia's wing for 11 years, developing respect for them. His first son was born there. From Samarkand he had watched perplexed as Shir Ali tried to court Russian support, abandoning his alliance with Britain, and falling into the Second Anglo-Afghan War. 'He had not sufficient sense to understand that property which is not saleable in one market was of no value in the other.' On his return to Afghanistan, Abdur Rahman knew that gaining power required a deal with Britain, but he wanted it on his terms.

As the summer drew on the precarious position of British forces across the country became increasingly obvious. Griffin feared severe trouble after harvest time in July. 'In a country like Afghanistan . . . where the people are ignorant, and where popular opinion is formed and directed by the Mulla class, the most fanatical and inimical to the English – it is impossible to predict with any certainty in what direction the next outbreak may occur.'

Elements of the Forward policy ambition for Afghanistan had lingered, with a call from the army that had taken

Kandahar that the south at least should remain under British control, as had been the plan when they took it. But plans changed as a huge Afghan force was said to be mobilising nearby, and rumours of war spread panic in Kandahar: 'The rich citizens have quietly fled from the place with their families and property. The people are burying their money and ornaments. The Hindu merchants are so alarmed that they have closed their shops. The panic is still stronger in the Fort.'

In late July, ignoring Abdur Rahman's lack of agreement over terms, Griffin held a durbar, a grand meeting for tribal leaders, in Kabul, and proclaimed him amir in his absence. Abdur Rahman pointedly had not even yet arrived in the capital. But Britain's war was not over just because they had found someone to run the country. A week after the durbar news arrived in Kabul of the catastrophic defeat of British forces at Maiwand, near Kandahar, by an Afghan army from Herat.

Britain had never tried to garrison Herat. In the general disorder of 1879 after the British invasion Ayub Khan, another of Dost's grandsons, had made the short journey from exile in Persia and seized the city. He had as good a claim to be amir as Abdur Rahman, and in the summer of 1880, he raised a large army and marched on Kandahar, gathering tribal support as he went.

In a doomed remnant of the policy of dividing Afghanistan envisaged in the Forward policy, Britain had handed Kandahar over to the next generation of the alternative Sadozai royal line, Shir Ali – no relation of the amir of the same name. The aim was to keep Kandahar out of the deal being offered to Abdur Rahman.

It was the last attempt by Britain to install a ruler in Afghanistan until 2001, and indeed the last moment of power for the Sadozais – descendants of the great amir, Ahmed Shah Durrani. With a British sword of honour buckled round his waist, Shir Ali was anointed *wali* of Kandahar, and said he hoped he might have 'an opportunity of showing his readiness to draw it in the cause of the British government'. But when they heard of the size of the army coming from the west, his forces promptly abandoned the British side, whereupon the wali unbuckled his sword of honour and fled to retirement and a British pension in Karachi.

The pace of the advance from the west was not expected by the British defenders of Kandahar, who sent out a slow-moving column led by General Burrows. The attacking force led by Ayub Khan had considerable support from *qizalbashes,* Persian cavalry, and was travelling over terrain they knew. Far more lightly equipped than British troops, the Afghans crossed the Helmand river and advanced on Kandahar. The British force arrived on the flat plain near the little mud fort at Maiwand to find a huge Afghan army in battle formation, with cavalry and artillery ahead of them, and thousands of white-shirted *ghazis,* flags billowing in the wind, to their right.

Poor logistics had caused the British to dump much of their ammunition into a river for lack of transport, and they ran out of artillery shells after the first exchange of fire at Maiwand. Much of the British artillery then withdrew, with consequent loss of morale. The British were then squeezed by the Afghans moving forward in a crescent-shaped formation. Retreat became rout. The message flashed to the viceroy read, 'Total defeat and dispersion of General Burrows's force'. Almost a thousand men died, more than a third of the force, the worst British defeat on the battlefield in Asia.

The battle of Maiwand gave Afghans a legend: they remember how a heroine, Malalai, urged on the troops, waving her veil as a standard before she was killed. She was still used into the twenty-first century in battle by the Taliban with poetry telling of love or martyrdom. 'My lover if you are martyred in the battle of Maiwand, I will make a coffin for you from the tresses of my hair.'

Two days after news of the battle reached Kabul, Abdur Rahman agreed to become amir on British terms, although they still would not put the assurances he wanted in writing. Once again, an Afghan amir would depend on goodwill, while even after the scale of the defeat in the south Britain made demands on him. Clever at constructing a narrative of heroic victory in the aftermath of defeat, Victorian England thrilled to the account of the relief column put together by General Roberts, which marched 334 miles in 23 days, and defeated Ayub Khan the day after its arrival in the south.

What the British narrative of Roberts's march south did not highlight were the orders given by the new amir Abdur Rahman that the column should be given safe passage and Afghan cavalry escorts. He was now in control of Afghanistan. By the spring of 1881, Abdur Rahman had taken Kandahar and Herat, defeating his cousin Ayub Khan and leaving Britain with not much to show for the war.

In the meeting with Griffin at which he finally accepted British terms to become amir, Abdur Rahman described the Afghanistan he inherited from them in terms that could have been written after the conflict in 2001. 'The country is in a deplorable condition. Everything which belonged to the state is ruined and requires renewal. The people are, as you can see, most turbulent and untractable, and devour all they can.'

There is a postscript to the Second Anglo-Afghan War with contemporary resonance. On Saturday 17th January 1880, a religious student, a talib, made history.

In the words of an anonymous diary: 'This morning a man who had been allowed to enter the outer gate of the citadel with a load of wood, threw it down and attacked Sergeant Miller, of the Engineers, with a knife. A Havildar of Sappers standing by hit him with a pickaxe before he had time to strike. The *ghazi* was not well known here, but his dress showed him to be a *talib-ul-ulm* of the country beyond Kelat-i-Ghilzai. He was of extremely small frame and very much emaciated.'

It was the first recorded suicide attack in Kandahar.

Part Three

Making the frontier, the Third
Anglo-Afghan War and Afghan reform
1880–1933

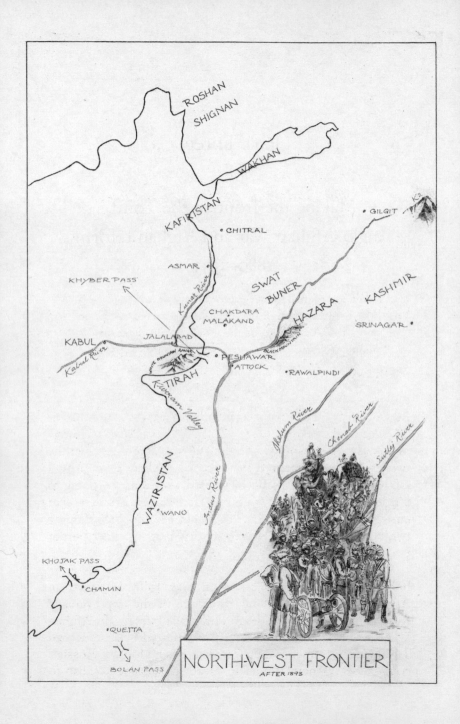

ROSHAN

SHIGNAN

WAKHAN

KAFIRISTAN

• CHITRAL

• GILGIT

K2

ASMAR

KHYBER PASS

SWAT

BUNER

KASHMIR

CHAKDARA

MALAKAND

HAZARA

SRINAGAR •

Kunar River

KABUL •

JALALABAD

WHITE MOUNTAIN RANGE

PESHAWAR

• ATTOCK

BLACK MOUNTAIN

• RAWALPINDI

Kabul River

TIRAH

Kurram Valley

Jhelum River

Chenab River

Sutlej River

Indus River

WAZIRISTAN

• WANO

KHOJAK PASS

• CHAMAN

• QUETTA

BOLAN PASS

NORTH-WEST FRONTIER

AFTER 1893

6

The Oasis War and the Durand line

'How can a small Power like Afghanistan, which is like a goat between these lions, or a grain of wheat between two strong millstones of the grinding mill, stand in the midway of the stones without being ground to dust.'

Abdur Rahman (Amir of Afghanistan 1880–1901)

In 1885, Russia and Britain came closer to war than at any other time during the years of the Great Game, in a battle for control of an oasis on a disputed border. This was at a time when the two great powers realised they needed to draw a line round Afghanistan, and mark out the ground, if neither was going to put troops inside the country. The eastern frontier that emerged – the Durand Line – would see more continuing conflict across it over the next century than any other border in the world.

Russia had seen its chance to grab more territory six years before, while Britain's attention was fully occupied in Afghanistan. In a repeat of the failure of the opportunistic Russian move across the desert during the First Anglo-Afghan War, the initial Russian advance was defeated by agile nomad Turkmen horsemen, and suffered heavy losses. Russia's commander General Lomakin faced a problem familiar to

British armies on the other side of Afghanistan: the death of 12,000 camels in three weeks left him unable to move.

It was the most audacious Russian attempt to take land after years of gradual advance across the desert towards the west of Afghanistan. Fine sand like powder, whipped by hot winds in the summer and the savage cold of fierce winter nights, made this one of the most unforgiving terrains in the world. Two years after Lomakin's defeat, in January 1881, a much larger Russian force returned to defeat the Turkmen and threaten the substantial prize of Merv, with its oasis. This was one of the ancient cities of the world, the capital of Khorassan – an old term for Afghanistan. Russia wanted to ensure that Merv would not be part of the modern Afghanistan. The city controlled a large area of desert north-west of the Hindu Kush, a busy trading area in the ancient world, but now an empty quarter, where the winds blew sand onto the ruins.

By the nineteenth century, Merv did not naturally fit any-where. When Burnes had travelled to the region in 1832, it was held by Khiva. Fifty years later, Britain did not appreciate Russia's ambition, nor its ability to move that far that fast. In 1882, when Russia offered a meeting to draw up a border, the offer was ignored in London, and the chance to negotiate its future was lost.

In 1884 Russia made its inevitable move, annexing Merv and biting a slice from what Abdur Rahman called 'Afghanistan's North-West Frontier'. His warnings had been ignored. London knew a response was essential – politicians were hit by what one observer called 'Mervousness'. It had been three quarters of a century since the East India Company analyst John Crokatt first noticed a 'threat of immediate danger' to British control of India from Russia. None could now deny the immediacy of the threat. The seizure of Merv brought Russian forces and a railway line to within 200 miles of Herat, with no natural obstacles in between.

Russia procrastinated as Britain sought to negotiate. Both sides set off to map the desert, the British force led by the geographer Colonel Thomas Holdich, a laconic adventurer who was to play a crucial role in drawing the border of Afghanistan.

As he headed west towards Persia, Holdich believed that no Englishman had been even as far as Herat since Pottinger had helped to defend it against the Persians 50 years before. The whole of the ground west of Kandahar was unmapped – Helmand just an 'open field'. The account left by Alexander the Great was still the most recent guide available to him. Twenty-three centuries earlier the Greeks had brought their elephants down to southern Helmand in the winter, where it was warmer than on the high mountain plateau further north. The place they had camped became known as Lashkar Gar – literally 'the place of the warriors'. It was the main head-quarters of British forces in 2006.

Holdich led his force beyond Herat through the winter of 1884, drawing and surveying as they went. 'Pheasant shooting and camel fights were our relaxation from the monotony of mapping.' But there was urgency in the task. He knew that Russian officers in the field had much more independence than their British counterparts: seizing ground made careers on the Russian frontier.

The British force numbered 3000 in all, including camp followers. New, more compact horse-feed made it easier to travel without the old armies of grass-cutters. The expedition had been equipped not to fight, but to impress the Russians, with 'tents such as have never before been seen in Turkestan, mess equipment and mess tents, stores of wine and delicacies such as might serve the purpose of a royal banquet'. The Russians preferred their own sweet sparkling wine to the French champagne carted across the desert by the British force, but did develop a taste for English ginger wine when the two sides met, circling around the subject of the frontier as they each sought out the other's true intentions.

Directly south of Merv, halfway to Herat, lay the next strategic oasis, Panjdeh. The first attempt by Russia to move in had led to strong protests from local Afghan leaders, and the Russian force withdrew. But there was silence from the

Gladstone government, which was opposed to any further military adventures in Afghanistan. In India, Forward policy veterans muttered that the lack of a robust response would have consequences.

The Russians were led by a locally recruited officer, Ali Khan, his name Russified to Ali Khanoff. While his surveyors were enjoying English ginger wine, Khanoff probed again and again towards Panjdeh, knowing that control would give Russia another huge triangle of desert, access to water at a vital rail bridgehead, and make his name. When Khanoff pounced, Holdich himself was at Panjdeh, and believed the British should have gone forward to support Afghan defences. But he was ordered to withdraw, and complained that he was put in a 'false position . . . the sort of position that only an irresolute government could be responsible for producing'.

Holdich concluded his last local negotiations with Khanoff at 3 a.m., and 'the morning broke gloomily over the damp plains of Panjdeh'. Clouds and drizzle concealed the Russian advance in the dawn. Outnumbered and outgunned, the Afghans were easily defeated, and slaughtered in their trenches. As British troops withdrew, they tried to offer medical assistance to the wounded, but a local chief sent them a pair of dilapidated boots as an insult – a signal they should leave.

Khanoff now offered 400 rupees for the head of any British officer, and the British force tried to disentangle themselves from the Afghan withdrawal, losing all their camels and dogs as they went. Holdich noted, 'A rabble of beaten soldiery is not a nice rabble at any time, and it became a dangerous rabble when composed of Afghans all more or less prepared to lay their disasters at our door.'

It was a bitter day, made worse by a freezing wind. The next morning the horses were covered in ice, 'as if clad in iron'. Holdich withdrew his force to assist in the defence of Herat, now a rich target of opportunity for an ascendant Russian commander already thought to have exceeded his orders from St Petersburg. The British force assisted in the destruction of several blue-tiled minarets and a medieval mosque in order to give a clear line of sight against the Russian threat: 'The most glorious productions of Mohammedan architecture in the fifteenth century, having survived the barbarism of four centuries, were now razed to the ground under the eyes, and with the approval, of the English,' wrote the travel writer Robert Byron, as he later surveyed the curious scene – a field of scattered minarets left isolated in a landscape where all the other buildings had been flattened.

If Khanoff's advance had failed, his actions would have likely been disowned by Russia. But Russia admired bold moves that were successful, and its newspapers took it for granted that Russian forces would continue forward and take Herat.

News of the fall of Panjdeh was broken to Abdur Rahman by the Indian foreign secretary Sir Henry Mortimer Durand. The amir was making his only visit to India, to meet a new viceroy in 1885, when the disaster happened. He had a right to be disappointed, as his understanding of the terms he had been offered when he came to power compelled Britain to come to his aid. He later wrote contemptuously 'The English army and officials were so frightened and nervous, that they fled in wild confusion, not knowing friends from foes, and owing to the intense cold, several of their poor native followers lost their lives in falling from their ponies as they rode along.'

But Abdur Rahman continued to seek protection from Britain, believing that ultimately Afghanistan faced a greater threat from Russia, whose border continued to move remorse-lessly south 'like an elephant', crushing everything in its way – 'The Russian policy of aggression is slow and steady, but firm and unchangeable.' Besides, he preferred British civilisation. He had an English governess for his children, an English tailor, an Irish dentist, and an irrepressible cockney engineer, Thomas Salter Pyne, whose whisky glass he personally filled, and whom he confided in, as long as Pyne continued to turn out high-quality copies of European guns in his Kabul factory.

Success in warfare was becoming dependent on engineers.

Better guns, and railways to carry troops, had changed the strategic map of Asia. Russian railways were being hammered into the sands in territory that had traditionally been subject to Afghan influence to the north and west, while British railway tracks continued to spin their spider's web across the map to the east.

Abdur Rahman had never accepted British influence in the Suleiman Mountains. To him the frontier region was 'the hereditary property of Afghan kings, being part of their country' all the way to the Indus River. A railway line to Quetta, the route into Kandahar and the south of Afghanistan was just like 'pushing a knife into my vitals', he wrote in a letter Durand called 'embarrassing, stubborn and impertinent'. And Abdur Rahman knew Britain had plans to go further. His spies brought news of a shed full of railway tracks marked 'For the line to Kandahar'. He proposed instead that the frontier mountains should remain under Afghan control. If Russia attacked, then he, the amir, would be able to recruit the frontier tribes to fight for Britain and not against. Prophetically he wrote, 'If you should cut them out of my dominions, they will neither be of any use to you nor to me; you will always be engaged in fighting and troubles with them, and they will always go on plundering.'

Durand wanted a firmer line to be taken, fearing the government in India was too inclined 'to see the Amir as a poor injured orphan, and declare that we have done nothing right'. To Durand's eyes it all looked easy – if only the others could see what he could. Britain sought control of all of the land around the strategic passes into Afghanistan. Durand approached the negotiations with the instincts of a bureaucrat, as if tidying up a few final details. But he felt there were so few men in India now who really *understood* the frontier. As Abdur Rahman pushed across the mountains into areas close to British forces, the British response – holding back and trying to talk – would make another war with Afghanistan inevitable. Why could they not see it? But India was run by men who did not know a 'Pathan from a Poobah'.

Durand, a stiff, unimaginative, unclubbable man, saw Abdur Rahman as a 'brutal savage', and thought he had the measure of him. 'The Amir is not the Emperor of Germany, and to treat Afghan filibusters with diplomatic tenderness is pure folly. What they understand and expect is action, not talk.' This was the man chosen by Britain to negotiate India's western border.

He had turned down a job in Burma because he wanted to remain and sort out the frontier question once and for all. But he felt himself surrounded by men who had never 'seen an Afghani or given study to frontier questions. Their arguments fill one with despair.' He was short of money and could not afford to go to England for a break. 'As for me, I can do no good now, and I am afraid that the present state of things must end in a smash, while my own position is most unpleasant.'

Durand had other personal preoccupations as well. His father had been criticised in a new book for abandoning his post during the Indian Mutiny, and while trying to clear his father's name, he was also writing to everyone he knew to help his son get into officer training at Sandhurst. He feared the boy would not pass the exams and might need a helping hand. Durand could feel the sands of time shifting under his feet. The India he knew of adventurers and empire-builders was changing. In a private letter he wrote, 'Englishmen are being excluded in favour of natives in all directions.'

Durand 'made a promising start at 0600' from Peshawar on 19th September 1893 in warm autumn weather, charmed, like every British visitor since Elphinstone, by the gentle, familiar-looking landscape with its hint of Surrey, that they never wanted to give up. As he wrote that night to the viceroy, Lord Lansdowne, from Landi Kotal, 'I never saw the Pesh. Valley looking so green and prosperous, and the climate just now is quite delightful, almost as cool as Simla, with a soft easterly breeze.' There was a threatening storm to the west. 'It was a fine sight, some masses of black cloud lay on the hills to the north and south of the Khyber. The mouth of the pass itself and Jamrud fort lying in sunshine under a patch of blue sky.' When the storm broke, 'dust devils began to spin out across the plain to right and left of us, and curved streaks of rain broke across the blue patch in front'.

It was a small party that made camp that night. Apart from Durand, there were only four British officers, and a detachment of Bengal Cavalry. The amir had sent his most senior commander, Ghulam Haider, who stayed with them throughout, and to Durand his Afghan soldiers looked like 'a set of ragamuffins'. Durand warned all his men about 'any dealings with Afghan women, and I think they understand clearly that they are no longer in a land of law courts, and that any misconduct will be summarily and severely punished'.

Durand settled quickly to the rigours of camp life. He had been a political officer in the army of 1879 that had taken Kabul and was besieged in the cantonment at Sherpur, and was philosophical about the discomforts. 'It was not altogether agreeable to see the General's dirty attendant putting lumps of frozen snow into the long blue and gold glasses with his unwashed fingers.' But he consoled himself with a memory: 'I have known a Cornish parlour maid bring me a piece of bread in her hand from the side-board.' The camp followers took to smoking opium and marijuana, now readily available, and Durand mildly noted his opposition, but did not put a stop to it. On the journey he came across pomegranates for the first time. He sent some to Lansdowne, 'I think they are horrid things myself but you may like to see them.'

They were soon in Jalalabad, where he airily second-guessed the options available to General Sale, besieged there in 1842. Half a century later, Durand had contempt for Sale's inability to mount a counter-attack. 'How Sale ever allowed himself to be shut up with a whole brigade in this place, with beautiful flat fighting ground all around passes my comprehension.' With this observation neatly recorded and another military record condemned, the foreign secretary who had never actually fought as a soldier himself swept on to his destiny in Kabul. He had a naïve belief in the indomitable power of British military might in all circumstances. He admitted that he had once been a 'Lawrence man', wary of entanglement beyond the Indus, but by now he was a committed believer in going Forward. Ignoring the evidence of decades of military intervention with no victory, he believed that once the frontier tribes were under the British, they would soon fall into line. 'I am quite sure that these tribes are very much overrated, and that we have shown an unnecessary and unwise timidity in shrinking from the task of controlling them.'

Among his papers Durand carried a copy of the last messages of Macnaghten from Kabul in 1840, to remind him of the dangers of getting it wrong. Britain now had its own history in Afghanistan – memories that did not rely on the campaigns of Alexander the Great. The military geography of Afghanistan had not changed since it was laid out so clearly in Lieutenant Macartney's map, but the Russian border was much closer to India than it had been then.

Durand also carried an intelligence overview of the whole border question, by Major Robert Warburton. 'The Russian Warning' was a Forward policy manifesto of the most extreme sort – a rabid call to arms, frothing and foaming with warnings of how 'socialism' was being given a foothold now that Indians were being educated. Warburton had learnt none of the lessons of the Second Anglo-Afghan War. After securing control of the passes across the Suleiman Mountains, he wondered if Britain should take Kabul and hold the triangle from Jalalabad to Kabul and south to Ghazni in order to command access to the Hindu Kush. Britain's policy should be based on one principle: 'Never to give the Russians an entry into the plains of Hindustan. Every endeavour should be made to fight them in Afghan soil and outside British possessions.'

Durand used Warburton's analysis of the 108 passes across the Suleiman Mountains. Only a handful of these passes had any military use, but Warburton believed it essential to own them all to guarantee control. The key ones were the Khyber Pass, the 20-mile avenue controlling the main access to Kabul in the north; the Bolan Pass to Quetta in the south; and the

Shutar Gardan, the back door to Kabul in the crook of the Camel's Neck halfway between. Durand knew that his most difficult negotiations would centre on Waziristan; control of the Waziris was crucial to Britain's security. But despite Durand's huge confidence in the ability of the British imperial will to prevail, the Waziris would never be controlled.

In Kabul Abdur Rahman, who now held more Afghan territory than any amir for a century, was making elaborate preparations for the visit. A house in its own grounds was made ready for the party, away from the centre of the city, since he wanted to reduce contact between his people and the British delegation. In his palace he prepared a room for the meetings with a curtain concealing a secret scribe who spoke both English and Dari to keep minutes for him, and he wanted all of the meetings to be held openly with witnesses present. There was to be no backstairs twisting of arms.

The Russians were not idle. Another of their frontier young bucks, Colonel Vannovsky, had taken his troops into Roshan, a tiny kingdom in the north-east of Afghanistan that Abdur Rahman had seized a decade before, along with the neighbouring area, Shignan. Vannovsky was no maverick border adventurer; this was a calculated move by St Petersburg to put pressure on the talks in Kabul. The two mountain statelets straddled the upper reaches of the Oxus River. Just in case no one had noticed, Vannovsky sent a messenger to Abdur Rahman to say he was there.

The amir sent the Russian letter on to Durand, who read it in Jalalabad. It seemed 'civil enough' and he sent a 'colourless answer' back to the amir, trying not to stoke up the fire. He was certainly not going to send troops to protect Afghan land, as the amir wanted. In fact the Russian move may have played directly into British hands. Durand wanted permanently to secure a sliver of Afghan land pointing like a finger directly up to the northeast to the Chinese border. The Wakhan Corridor, 218 miles long but only 11 miles wide at its narrowest point, was a natural geographical barrier of high mountains with few passes. He wanted it to be a political barrier too – keeping

Russia out of the vast, almost uninhabited wastes above British India.

The disputed kingdoms, Roshan and Shignan, were north of the Wakhan corridor, and in order to be able to sell the deal to Russia – in the spirit of creating an Afghanistan that was a true buffer zone – Durand needed Russia to have a stable border too. Across most of northern Afghanistan, Britain believed the best border was the Oxus River, which flows from the Wakhan region westwards in a great arch forming the northeast tip of Afghanistan, and then cuts directly west, wide and deep, gathering strength as one of the world's great rivers, before ceasing to be the Afghan border and sheering off to the north to drain into the Aral Sea. Where it runs through Roshan and Shignan the Oxus is just a narrow stream, but it was still a much better border than any other.

South of the Wakhan Corridor lie the huge snow-covered wastes of the western Himalayas, including the world's second highest mountain, K2. This was the land immortalised in Kipling's Great Game novel *Kim,* concerning a conspiracy of 'five confederated Kings, who had no business to confederate', in Chitral, Gilgit, Hunza, Nagar, and Dir. British policy towards this trackless region was still evolving in 1893, and Durand's brother was one of the officers who moved between the 'Kings', so he would have known the problems as well as anyone. In his letter to the amir, Durand made it clear that Britain would not deploy forces against Russia. He feared that the letter would upset him, and he warned Lansdowne, 'You must not be astonished if, to use Rudyard Kipling's elegant expression, "the hand begins to play".'

A week after the British delegation arrived on Afghan soil, Abdur Rahman sent Pyne to join them on the last leg of the journey to Kabul. He would prove to be an invaluable intermediary between the stiff-collared Durand and the suspicious amir. He had a natural charm. While mocking his cockney accent in asides, Durand thought Pyne a 'genial wine-bibber, with a real fund of anecdote and an acute sense of the ridiculous . . . real common sense in certain ways and self-restraint. There is no doubt that he is a man of unusual character.' Pyne woke up the whole camp one evening by shooting a hole in the roof of his tent with his revolver.

Pyne's key message on his arrival in the British camp was the amir's concern about the Russian incursion. He said that Abdur Rahman was 'sick with anxiety' and not happy with the British advice to let the Russians pass through without incident. Pyne told Durand that he should give Abdur Rahman guns or the 'promise of guns thereafter' to show they trusted him and to provide him with the ability to parade his strength. Durand replied, 'I don't carry guns about in my waistcoat pockets, but I suppose we should be ready to give him a few hereafter.'

All the ingredients for the summit were now in place, with the parties displaying their opening hands while keeping their aces concealed. Britain had been harassing Abdur Rahman's officials in the frontier regions for the last couple of years, and the viceroy had choked off his gun supply, so Durand would have something to give in return for the amir agreeing to the new border. Russia was at the table – in spirit if not in fact – exerting pressure short of conflict. And Abdur Rahman had something to complain about, loudly – the Russian incursion – while saying nothing about the much bigger border questions in the south.

On 1st October 1893, with the weather still warm, Durand caught his first glimpse of the Bala Hissar across the Kabul plain. It was 'intensely interesting to see all the old places again'. A message arrived from the amir to say he was pleased that they had travelled without a big military escort. They made camp ahead of a formal arrival in the city the following day close to a 'rather ghastly illustration' of the amir's methods. An iron cage by the roadside contained some human bones, 'the remains of a noted highwayman who was caught and left in the cage to die'. He had survived for 16 days.

Four days later they held their first meeting with Abdur Rahman, and already he had flexed his muscles. On their first morning they had tried to go out for a ride, but General Ghulam Haider said there were orders that they should not, 'for their own protection'. Now the amir was able to be generous and allow them to ride. Unlike Russia and Britain he may not have had much to bargain with, caught as he felt he was, 'like a grain of wheat between two grindstones', but he was going to use everything he had.

It was the first time Durand had seen Abdur Rahman since 1885, and the Englishman was struck by the changes. The man he remembered as a burly figure with a poker face like Henry VIII was now 'with his new white teeth from O'Meara, and his ready smile and joke, quite different from the Afghan wild boar of '85 with his scowl and his tusks'. He could hardly believe this gentleman was the same man. Abdur Rahman was very short, but had a large head and penetrating eyes. He succeeded in embarrassing his Victorian guest: Durand confessed that the amir 'held my hand so long and was very affectionate that I began to feel quite uncomfortable'.

For all the good humour and gentlemanly manners, it was clear that Abdur Rahman was in no hurry to get down to business. For several days Durand paced the veranda of his house, or went out riding with an escort, feeling as if he were a convict. One day he went down to Charasiab, remembering Roberts's victory in 1879. And while there was no news from the amir, a constant stream of gifts and visitors arrived – cucumbers, apricots, a squirrel-skin blanket, and a barber, 'an awful old ruffian, who looked as if he would cut one's throat for sixpence'. Durand tried not to show his anxiety for progress as Pyne kept him entertained and showed him his gun factory. He told Durand that Abdur Rahman thought of nothing else. When someone gave him a telescope he said, 'Oh, blow the moon. What's the use of the moon to me? Can't you make a gun of it?'

Five days after their arrival, Abdur Rahman sent across a map. It was a bold opening gambit, conceding nothing, and handing the Wakhan Corridor to Russia. Durand was relaxed about it, although he confided his fears to Lansdowne that perhaps the amir had done a deal with Russia, dropping his claim to Wakhan in return for retaining all of Roshan and Shignan, including the areas east of the Oxus. None of this mattered compared to Britain's territorial ambitions in the main Pashtun areas further south – they were shadow-boxing ahead of the main fight. Messages passed in both directions about the format for the talks, and the size of the British delegation, with the amir wanting all of the British officers present. Durand insisted on bringing who he liked, and Pyne smoothed the way, to Durand's amazement. 'He is a very useful man. It is amusing to feel that the mission is being personally conducted by a little cockney trader.'

At last, more than a week after they had reached Kabul, they held their first proper meeting. It was the first really cold day since they had arrived, and a reminder in the high mountain capital that winter was on its way. Durand did most of the talking, raising the Roshan and Shignan issue, and giving Abdur Rahman a chance to get his resentment off his chest, that Britain had not protected 'his territory' in the Panjdeh Oasis incident. But each knew that this was not the real negotiation.

The atmosphere was good-humoured. Abdur Rahman said he had a cold and, miming the pouring of a bottle, he said he could not warm himself as they could, since he was a Muslim. Durand told him that the British demand to delimit the border relied on the 1873 agreement which made Afghanistan a buffer zone between Britain and Russia – an agreement that Shir Ali had come to Simla to sign. Abdur Rahman sighed and said that Shir Ali had been a fool, and during the days that passed with no more meetings, he asked for the British copy of the agreement. Durand sent it across with the treaties signed by the Afghans in 1884. This 'leaves him not a leg to stand on. But he may elect to stand on his head.'

More days passed, with more requests for letters and maps coming from Abdur Rahman, while cold winds blew the fine Afghan dust into everything, bending double the forest of poplars outside Durand's house. Indian camp followers were now visiting the Kabul bazaars every day, and Durand was afraid of an incident if the talks went on too long. He discovered that a draftsman working for the British side had been leaking details of their position to the amir, and feared that further delay could wreck the process. He began to dangle an offer of guns in front of the amir, at Pyne's suggestion, and realised how valuable it had been that Lansdowne had cut off the supply before the talks.

The amir appeared to accept the loss of those parts of Roshan and Shignan that lay to the east of the Oxus. But when they did meet now, which was rare, it was only to chat, not to talk substantively. Abdur Rahman told tales of the 'air freezing at Samarkand so you could hear the ice particles tinkling against each other'. In his formal correspondence he seemed to be going backwards, writing now to request an answer to a letter he had sent the viceroy before the talks began, then laying out his reasons for wanting to hold on to different parts of the frontier – retaining Chaman in the south, Asmar and the Kafir region in the north, and not dividing Waziristan.

Another letter was so 'full of generalities and impossible claims', that it was hard not to answer unpleasantly. Durand wrote to Lansdowne, 'I cannot help a sort of feeling of pity for him – standing there fighting his game out against Russia and England – absolutely alone. There is something rather touching about it.' Durand was frustrated by the formality of the process and the snail's pace. 'Alone with him I am sure I could convince him.' Abdur Rahman's negotiating strategy was vindicated in this one sentence. He was never going to sit alone with Durand to 'have things explained to him'.

While he was waiting, Durand would pace about the house, listening to bagpipers practise outside and Pyne at the piano inside. 'Pyne, who is a universal genius, has just been murdering the Lost Chord in the next room. I have my fill of harmony . . . There is something strangely exhilarating to me in getting across the Indus. The dry clear climate, and the men one has to deal with, and the freedom from office work, and other things are all a pleasant change.'

Finally, in the last few days of October, almost a month after their arrival, Durand began to get indications that a deal would emerge. The amir sent across a map. Outside there was intense activity in the fields, with ploughs out now that the rains had come, men bent against the strong winds, urging their oxen on to break the ground. As Durand rode towards a meeting with the amir, he saw the bodies of four people who had been executed 'insufficiently buried' by the roadside, and further on, the naked head and torso of a general, sticking out of the ground, still alive in the perishing wind, half buried as a punishment.

Now the negotiations became crude – one disputed frontier region, Chageh, was bought for 100,000 rupees. But the amir still resisted handing over Chaman, where Britain wanted to build its railway in the south, Asmar, in the north, and Waziristan itself. He warned again and again of the perils of partitioning Waziristan. Who would deal with the divided tribes, or those who moved in summer and winter between what was now going to be British and Afghan territory? For Durand none of this was of any concern. His map was not about the people who lived in these areas, but the military geography. As long as Britain controlled access to the Shutar Gardan Pass, the Camel's Neck, then the question of summer and winter pastures was of no interest. His overwhelming belief in the civilising power of the empire blinded him to the trouble he was inviting. 'After all', he said to the amir, 'you will only be losing a little population and a little wealth.'

Abdur Rahman held Durand's gaze for a long time in response, and then answered with just one word – *Nam* – Honour.

The next day came a request for a large sum of money in return for the partition of Waziristan. Durand derided it as a 'rather stupid letter', but if all they were haggling over was the price, he knew that the negotiations had effectively ended. The maps passed to and fro during the next two weeks until, on 12th November, almost six weeks after the talks began, they had a deal. Durand had secured the Wakhan Corridor as an

Afghan buffer zone sheltering the roof of the British Indian world, control of all the passes across the Suleiman Mountains, and had conceded only an area north of the Khyber Pass that Britain believed to be of little strategic significance – the Asmar valley, and the area of Kafiristan that went with it. In return, Britain agreed to raise its subsidy to the amir by 50 per cent to 1.8 million rupees, and as for trade, all that Abdur Rahman asked for was the right to sell Afghan brandy and opium in India. As Durand took the quick way home, a raft down the Kabul River, he heard intelligence reports that the amir was already writing 'fiercely' to people, 'informing them that we have now given him a clear line round his country, which neither the Russians nor we will overstep'.

Durand could never see why the amir had made such a fuss about it all. 'We ought now to have . . . a contented Amir, though we shall never have in him an unsuspicious and perfectly satisfactory ally. It is not in his nature. His jealousy as to our interference in his internal affairs amounts to insanity, and makes him extraordinarily difficult to deal with.' Nor did he ever appreciate what he had done in dividing Pashtun territory. He thought it meant Britain now had 'our hands free on the frontier'. Rather than freeing them, however, it tied British hands in the North-West Frontier region in ways that he could not have dreamed of. When the Sikhs controlled the land west of the Indus, they had stopped short of going into the mountains with good reason. By insisting on control of the passes, and pushing the border into the pashtun mountain fastness of Waziristan, Britain ensured permanent instability in the frontier region, with consequences lasting until today.

The one concession Durand made to Abdur Rahman – ceding the Asmar valley and dividing Kafiristan – caused a storm of protest in Britain. The Kafirs were a strange mystical tribe, with their own religion that had enough similarity to Greek mythology to lend credence to the legend that they were left over from the days of Alexander the Great. Kafirs had traditionally been taken in the region as slaves, and as soon as the border was drawn Afghan forces moved in, looting and murdering as they went. The British anti-slavery campaign went into top gear, protesting and petitioning parliament. Sir Lepel Griffin, the official who had first offered Abdur Rahman the throne, was now retired and led the campaign. He wrote in the *Saturday Review*, 'A tragedy is now impending, for which, if consummated, England will be directly responsible, and of which no time will ever suffice to efface the stain. The country of a lion-hearted race, which for 1000 years has successfully resisted Muhammedan conquest, is about to be invaded by the trained army of the Amir of Afghanistan. This will be done with the sanction and in the name of England.'

A new viceroy, Lord Elgin, was contemptuous. He saw no virtue in the Kafirs and no merit to the notion that they were related to the Greeks (whose treasures from the Parthenon his own ancestor had so enthusiastically taken to London). 'They appear . . . to be an ignorant, idolatrous, and slave-dealing race . . . with no national sentiment, and always feuding with one another.'

The viceroy was already facing problems of his own in the areas that Durand had put on the British side of the contentious new border.

7

'Tribes generally are rising'

'The next expedition to the Black Mountain will I hope
be a very long time hence, and Bajaur and Bunar will
cease to have any terrors . . . I trust that we shall now
take annual revenue from the Waziris.'

Sir Henry Mortimer Durand, architect of the agreement
defining the Afghan border, writing in 1895. Within months
the whole frontier – including these regions – was in flames.

From the 'Throne of Solomon', that gave the Suleiman
Mountain range its name, Colonel Holdich could see 40,000
square miles in front of him. The curtain of ice and snow that
he had climbed was only one of a complex array of similar
peaks above 15,000 feet, not aligned in three distinct ranges as
in the imagination of Lieutenant Macartney, but pitching and
tossing against each other like a frozen sea above the world, a
backdrop hanging from an impossibly blue sky.

It was 1894. The British now had many years experience of
dealing with Afghanistan, but Holdich mused that they still did
not know much about the terrain. It was all very well for
Durand and the amir to draw a line on a map; the line on the
ground was harder to find. He had a ringside seat as the
frontier emerged, and as the commander of troops ordered to

withdraw from a fight at the Panjdeh Oasis, he knew the cost of failure. He had been in the siege at Sherpur too, and had camped in the Bolan Pass amid a scene of desolation after that war. 'Carcasses of bullocks, dogs and camels were the decorative features of the landscape. The rest was a wild-weird waste of snow.'

High as he was on the Throne of Solomon, a snow-covered saddle amid the peaks, nothing grew, but lower down, looking across into Afghanistan, he could see small firs dotted across the hilltops, sparsely as no rivers rose in the limestone range, and further still the brown of the lower hills like dust cloths dropped from the peaks, folding one over another to the horizon. Any one of a thousand valleys could conceal an army.

The Suleiman range spread north of where he stood until it pointed west into Afghanistan, curving round the Kurram valley up to the bend in the mountains they called the Camel's Neck, the high pass that was still the British army's preferred route into Kabul. Beyond the Camel's Neck, the mountains bent back round to the straight line of peaks running east-west that formed the horizon – the Safed Koh or White Mountains – the defining heights of the whole frontier region, flanking the range that was cut through by the Khyber Pass to the north. And the Khyber was the last useful gap before the mountains curled east around the top of India, higher and higher, beyond endurance, into the Himalayas.

In the creases and folds of the earth in front of the White Mountains lay the hidden villages of Tirah – remote, forbidding and hostile to outsiders – whose boast was that they had never been penetrated by a foreign army. He knew the true heart of the frontier lay directly to the south-east in Waziristan. And he knew why the Waziris were restless about Durand's border. The boundary had been drawn 'between them and some of their pleasantest summer resorts'. There were no passes of any value to an army across the whole of the Waziri range, but dozens of tracks known by a nomadic people who considered the mountains their own, and had no concept of a frontier.

His generation on the frontier knew only too well how hard it was to impose order from outside. The land west of the Indus on the plains, including the Vale of Peshawar, was 'settled' and taxed and policed like anywhere else in British India. But since the early 1870s Britain had not tried to impose its law beyond where the first shadow of the hills fell. The mountain tribes were left to administer themselves, and British officials called on *maliks*, local elders, to arbitrate if they had a problem. Some places, in particular Waziristan, were beyond even this rough and ready law. The tribal leaders here were too weak or unwilling to play Britain's game, and even the usual remedy of force did not work.

Holdich noted 'the extreme difficulty of administering a satisfactory thrashing to a mountain-bred people who have ever an open door behind them'. US forces might have used other language but undoubtedly recognised the truth of this observation as they tried to control the Afghan side of the frontier in the war that began after 9/11, when Taliban and al-Qaeda fighters could cross to and from the Pakistani side of the frontier with ease. Marking Durand's line in the mountains did not close the back door.

There was a singular harshness in the land and the people, and a complex faith of ritual and magic bubbled beneath the surface. On their way down from the peak, Holdich's local guide suddenly stopped the party and spoke to the mountain. He addressed the rocks in ringing tones, saying that they meant no harm and asking that they should be allowed to travel unmolested. It was an arresting moment, dramatic, weird and other-worldly. No one laughed.

But beneath the local accretions, the loyalty of the Waziris to Islam and to their mullahs was unquestioned. On 3rd November 1895, before first light, an attack on the first major party sent from the British side to demarcate the frontier at Wano in Waziristan led to the deaths of four officers and 17 men. The raiders stole 23 Martini rifles and 15 horses. The ferocious attack had been led by a mullah, and it demanded retribution. British officers asked tribal elders to deal with it themselves, but they replied honestly that they would not be able to impose any sanctions, since they had no power over the mullah.

The leader of the Wano raid was Mullah Powindah, one of a network of fundamentalist mystics who by the summer of 1897 had incited tens of thousands of Pashtun tribesmen to believe that Britain could be beaten. This movement rippling up the frontier from the south-west headed towards another wave led by Wahhabi-inspired Hindustani fanatics moving down from the north-east. Where the two forces met, in Swat in 1897, the frontier ignited, leading to the most serious challenge during all the years of British rule of the region.

In Kabul, Abdur Rahman gave the rebellion significant backing. He was careful to conceal this in public, since he did not want to provoke another British attack on Afghanistan, and Britain preferred to give him the benefit of the doubt, believing his assurances, even when intelligence reports suggested that he was inciting mullahs on the frontier. Rahman had always skilfully used political Islam to his advantage.

Before he became amir, as he crossed Afghanistan during the fighting in 1880, he had left letters in mosques saying that he had come to 'liberate Afghanistan for Islam from the English', and he declared himself *imam* as well as *amir* – priest as well as king – claiming spiritual as well as political leadership.

This gave Abdur Rahman the authority to declare that if attacked by the British Afghans should take up a jihad to repel them. His book on jihad, passed from hand to hand on the frontier, was as bloodthirsty as anything later written by Osama bin Laden, and even quoted from the same passage of the Koran always used by bin Laden in his statements, which instructed Muslims to put the demands of jihad over their family, tribe or property. This was a particularly significant call for Pashtuns, who put their loyalty to family and tribe above all else.

Abdur Rahman's book specifically mentioned the effectiveness of night raids, like the Wano ambush, where horses would 'generate fire when their horseshoes touch the flint of the rock, lighting up the night'. And he defined in poetic terms the glory of eternal life promised to those killed fighting jihad, whose souls would be 'placed in the throat of green-winged birds who circle in the air, and make their nests in the branches of the most blessed tree in paradise'. Such images were an inspiration to poor and dispossessed frontier people, and stirred them to revolution.

Abdur Rahman was not a Wahhabi, nor were the mullahs he inspired, Mullah Powindah in Waziristan and the Mullah of Haddah – 'the Light of Islam'. But although they did not share precisely the same Wahhabi Islamist outlook as Mullah Sadullah in Swat – known as the 'Mad Mullah' or 'Mad Fakir' by British troops – yet they could all agree on the need for jihad against British rule.

The ability of Muslims with different views of jihad and various political ends to join against a common enemy would have profound importance when the frontier again became the front line, a crucible of violence, in the conflict that began in the late twentieth century. The frontier villages in Waziristan and Tirah that gave the best support to the Taliban and the foreign fighters in al-Qaeda were the same ones that had supported the mujahidin a decade before in the US-backed fight against the Soviet Union, and had been quickest to rise against Britain in the nineteenth century – finding common cause against a common enemy – first Britain, later the USSR, then the US-led invasion.

There is another sinister similarity between the conflicts of the nineteenth century and later. Just as Amir Abdur Rahman incited jihad while claiming the opposite, receiving British guns and a salary all the while, so President Musharraf of Pakistan signed up enthusiastically for the 'war on terror', receiving billions of dollars in military and other aid, while his intelligence forces continued to play a double game, supporting jihad in Afghanistan. These two Muslim leaders were playing the same game in conflicts more than a century apart, as if on opposite sides of a mirror, promoting jihad across the same frontier, while denying it.

Something bigger was always at stake than power or land in conflicts across this frontier. For many in the field this was a duel between different world views – a clash of civilisations. British observers in the 1890s may have characterised the mullahs as mad fanatics, preying on a credulous and superstitious people. But to the mountain tribes who followed them into war they were a powerful political force that might rid them of the threat of alien rule.

Exactly the same process happened at the end of the twentieth century when the mujahidin emerged against the Soviet occupation. A nationalist struggle took on the cloak of a holy war (assisted by billions of US dollars), radicalising a new generation, leading directly to the rise of the Taliban, and turning Afghanistan and the frontier into a safe haven for those who wanted a global jihad.

At the end of the nineteenth century on the frontier the enemy was not just British rule, but British ideas, and progress. 'The priesthood, knowing that their authority would be weakened by civilisation, have used their religious influence on the people to foment a general rising,' wrote Winston Churchill, who had taken leave of absence from the Indian Army to work as a war correspondent for the *Daily Telegraph* during the 1897 uprising. 'Embedding' as a correspondent then was a far more engaged business than in later conflicts – Churchill found himself drafted in as an officer to make up the numbers for one battle, and Lord Fincastle, correspondent for *The Times,* actually won a VC for attempting to rescue a wounded officer. The man who died in the attempted rescue was another journalist, reporting for the *Times of India,* who had also taken leave of absence from his regiment.

With an extravagant disregard for what would later be called political correctness, Churchill noted a bloodthirsty impulse in Islam: 'That religion, which above all others was founded and propagated by the sword – the tenets and principles of which are instinct with incentives to slaughter and which in three continents has produced fighting breeds of men – stimulates a wild and merciless fanaticism.' On the frontier with its history of warfare, this became an explosive mixture:

the Mahommedan religion increases, instead of lessening, the fury of intolerance. It was originally propagated by the sword, and ever since, its votaries have been subject, above the people of all other creeds, to this form of madness. In a moment the fruits of patient toil, the prospects of material prosperity, the fear of death itself, are flung aside. The more emotional Pathans are powerless to resist. All rational considerations are forgotten. Seizing their weapons, they become *ghazis* – as dangerous and as sensible as mad dogs: fit only to be treated as such.

Churchill reserved special venom for talibs, religious students: 'a host of wandering Talib-ul-ulms, who correspond with the theological students in Turkey, and live free at the expense of the people'. The way Churchill told it, the sexual morality of these *taliban* was rather different to the reputation of those who took over the government of Afghanistan exactly a century later: 'they enjoy a sort of "droit du seigneur," and no man's wife or daughter is safe from them. Of some of their manners and morals it is impossible to write.'

As Britain tried to manage the upsurge in violence in Waziristan after Durand drew the border with the amir in Kabul, there was an argument over the right approach to take. Some proposed full annexation, since merely sending troops to garrison the region would antagonise other tribes. 'Any attempt to subjugate the Waziris and hold their country by military force is eminently calculated to set the whole frontier in a blaze.'

But the senior British official in the region, Sir Denis Fitzpatrick, opposed annexation. To him the border of British India should not go beyond the foot of the mountains. Britain should build forts only along the roads they needed, and leave it at that. He was opposed to any attempt 'to undertake so formidable a task as that of establishing the pax Britannica generally throughout the Waziri country'. The government in London agreed with Sir Denis and in response to the attack on the camp at Wano, tribal elders were told that Britain 'had no wish to conquer or dominate the country', leaving the elders to wonder what conquest would have meant, as 10,983 troops arrived and destroyed hundreds of villages in a three-month winter campaign of retribution instead.

The attempted demarcation of the border that had provoked the uprising in the first place went on, and Britain established several permanent garrisons across Waziristan. There was further unrest in March 1897, at the time of the Islamic festival of Eid, and British reports identified 'religious students' among the ringleaders, under the overall leadership of Mullah Powindah.

In June, near a new British post at Tochi in Waziristan, on a perfect frontier summer afternoon, a British force some 300 strong was attacked without warning during negotiations. The calm was such before the attack that a Scottish piper was playing, during a break in the talks, at the request of tribal elders. Four British officers were killed before they could defend themselves, while around 100 locals were killed once British artillery had been set up on a ridge. A telegram described this as another 'fanatical' outbreak. The attack happened during the festival of Moharram when the Viceroy was warned 'Waziris kill sheep, distribute food and hold meetings, and consider the period as most auspicious for martyrdom.' Punishment raids continued throughout the summer of 1897, confiscating livestock and burning crops, but by now, the problems were not limited to Waziristan. A brief telegram was received by the viceroy from Swat in the north: 'Tribes generally are rising.'

The problems in Swat went back to the building of a road. Roads brought progress and trade; to Churchill the Swat road represented the best hope of spreading the values of the empire. 'As the sun of civilisation rose above the hills, the fair flowers of commerce unfolded, and the streams of supply and demand, hitherto congealed by the frost of barbarism, were thawed.'

The road had been built to ensure stability in Chitral, the northernmost town of any size before the uninhabited high Himalayas. For 20 years the ruler of Chitral had been a quiescent British ally, but he died in 1892 leaving too many sons and an ambitious brother. With Abdur Rahman in Kabul playing off one pretender against another, and an anti-British tribal leader, Umra Khan, plotting from the east, sometimes in league with the Afghan amir and sometimes against him, the next three years were unstable and bloody for Chitral. As brother murdered brother in a Shakespearean orgy of violence, Britain found it hard to realise its three ambitions – influence Chitral, keep Russia at arm's length, and demarcate a stable border with Afghanistan. In the winter of 1894, a small British force was besieged in Chitral fort, and Britain went to war to get its men out.

The ever-present Holdich had by then been assigned to draw the border north of the Khyber Pass, a three-cornered region abutting Russia and Afghanistan. Some places were so inaccessible that all sides agreed to leave them as just a line on a map, not marked on the ground with stones as had been done elsewhere. The first thing Holdich knew of the siege was when a group of Chitralis came across the mountains to his camp on the Afghan side, demanding protection. They were 'idle, good for nothing, and happy-hearted people, who have a deadly propensity for wholesale murder and family butchery . . . not a fighting people, but in a country such as theirs . . . a race of monkeys could make themselves respected as foes if they took to defensive tactics'.

Holdich witnessed Afghan government support for the anti-British forces in Chitral. Abdur Rahman's commander-in-chief, Ghulam Haider, a close ally of one of the most political mullahs, was running guns through the camp, and an Afghan unit that Holdich had inspected as a formality on his arrival suddenly disappeared, he thought across the border in the direction of the conflict.

He also heard that the Afghan government was encouraging the frontier chiefs, *maliks,* to attack the British. They were 'promised ammunition as well as compensation in kind for any loss of grain . . . special concessions have been promised the leading maliks who have property on both sides of the border'. The camp became increasingly dangerous: as well as the Chitrali refugees there were hostages taken by the Afghans from villages on the other side during the border demarcation, and forces loyal to the rebel leader Umra Khan appeared. When Holdich tried to send a Chitrali messenger across the mountains to the besieged British garrison in the fort, the messenger was shot before he had even left the Afghan camp.

The fort at Chitral was relieved before the arrival of the main British force after an epic march across the snow-covered passes from Gilgit in the east by a small force under Colonel Kelly, a manoeuvre of extraordinary bravura, pushing mules laden with guns up mountains, across rivers and fighting all the way. A British officer in the fort, Sir George Robertson, said that when the relief force arrived, 'All seemed to think, from Kelly downwards, that their march was a mere trifle, their hardships undeserving of reference.' Meanwhile 16,399 British troops were sent through the Swat valley to subdue the tribes all the way up the road to Chitral – a massive movement of men – and this was before the general uprising along the frontier broke out.

Britain installed a 14-year-old prince, Shuja al-Mulk as leader in Chitral. But there were the same arguments as in Waziristan over how deeply they should become involved in the mountains. The engineers wanted to build a road to guarantee swift movement of reinforcements, but pushing a road into tribal territory made it look as if it was being colonised, and incorporated into the settled areas of British India. The engineers had their way, and the controversial road was pushed across difficult terrain up to Chitral. Sir Lepel Griffin wrote to *The Times,* 'This policy consists in spending a quarter of a million annually on a post of defence and observation which defends and observes nothing, and on the maintenance of a road which leads nowhere.'

The expense was not only in building the road and defending it; tribes along the route needed to be compensated for not collecting tolls – Britain was buying peace. Troops in the Malakand garrison on the new road also paid for the fodder and grain they obtained from local people, rather than seizing it, while their doctor treated 7000 people, many from 'the fanatical priestly classes'.

The priestly classes had their own plans. The British force may have paid for rice, the fanatics could make it appear at will in a bowl to feed a crowd; the British military road carried ammunition to Chitral, the fanatics could make the bullets turn to water; and to match the British queen-empress, the fanatics produced a boy they claimed was the last survivor of the Mughal line, the Muslim emperors of India. Their leader, Mullah Sadullah, was not afraid. He could conjure up flags to appear with his forces in the field; and make them immune to gunfire. It was a win/win proposition: if his protection did not work, then as martyrs in jihad against Britain, his warriors had a special place in paradise, and he issued elaborate scrolls to say so.

The two British garrisons on the road from the plains, at Malakand, and the more remote fort of Chakdara guarding a bridge across the Swat River, were further fortified. But plans to send reinforcements up from the plains were put on hold, in case they only aggravated the situation. The scale and the ferocity of what happened next was beyond such rational military thinking.

The cry of jihad had been raised often before on the frontier since the Hindustani fanatics had first mobilised the Swat tribes against the Sikhs 60 years before, but Mullah Sadullah, the 'Mad Fakir' now led the most determined campaign for deliverance from the British. On 21st July 1897, he prophesied that by the rising of the next full moon, the British soldiers would have been driven back to the plains.

The way Churchill told it, Swati tribesmen watching polo

were sporting enough to wait until the game had finished before leaving to arm themselves for the fight that they knew would start that night, even whispering a warning into the ears of locally hired grooms as they left. 'They knew, these Pathans, what was coming. The wave of fanaticism was sweeping down the valley. It would carry them away. They were powerless to resist. Like one who feels a fit coming on, they waited. Nor did they care very much. When the Mad Fakir arrived, they would fight and kill the infidels. In the meantime there was no necessity to deprive them of their ponies.'

Lieutenant Harry Rattray, the commander of the detachment at the small Chakdara fort, left the polo ground to return to his post when an urgent message arrived to say that tribesmen were massing around his fort. He rode back to take command before it was dark, straight through a group of local tribesmen who did not try to stop him. He managed to send a message to Malakand to warn them before the line was cut and every telegraph pole along the new British road burnt to the ground.

The defence of Chakdara was compared to Rorke's Drift by Churchill. The fort was surrounded by high ground, and the enemy could fire into it day and night, joined by the irregular forces that Britain had paid to protect the road using their British-supplied rifles. A small relief detachment of cavalry arrived the day after the siege began, after a desperate ride from Malakand, fording a river and crossing paddy fields, where the horses sank deep in the mud while, 'the bullets of the enemy made watery flashes on all sides', then five days in, Rattray sent a simple message by heliograph, the letters flashing from his signal tower: 'HELP US'. The signal tower was 200 yards from the main fort, and it was now hard to supply the men there with water. He had also lost his hospital building to the enemy, who were now using it as another firing position. But after a week of firing a Maxim gun from behind solid walls, of the 14,000 tribesmen who had surrounded the fort, 2000 were dead, for the loss of seven British dead.

The relief of Chakdara was carried out by a column from

Malakand, where both the fighting and the weather had exacted their toll on the British forces. Twenty-one men in a detachment died of heat exhaustion after a forced march to relieve Malakand. There had been desperate hand-to-hand fighting as waves of tribesmen poured into the fort. A Sergeant Harrington saved his life by remaining motionless after dozens of Swatis broke into the hut he had been defending. They killed an officer, but although they felt along the walls, never found him in the dark.

The political officer at Malakand, Major Harold Deane, saw the 'Mad Fakir' advance towards British troops with crowds of unarmed teenage boys pushed ahead of him, among them 'a boy aged thirteen or fourteen on whose head he bound a turban'. Deane believed this to be the mysterious last of the Mughal line. He was killed instantly. Some of the fanatics marched on British positions firing their rifles straight up into the air, believing they were invulnerable. Among the white cotton clothing of the Swat warriors, increasing numbers of black and blue-clad warriors could be seen – men of the Bunerwal, Wahhabi Hindustani fanatics.

A British infantry officer wrote, 'Bands of *ghazis*, worked up by their religious enthusiasm into a frenzy of fanatical excitement, would charge our breastworks again and again, leaving their dead in scores after each repulse, while the standard bearers would encourage their efforts by shouting, with much beating of tom-toms, and other musical instruments.'

As Britain regained control of the Chitral road and the two forts, with a force of more than 11,000 men under the command of General Sir Bindon Blood, word came that the 'Mad Fakir', Mullah Sadullah, had survived, although injured, and had fled to the west to join forces with another fundamentalist mystic, the Mullah of Haddah – the man anointed by Abdur Rahman as 'the Light of Islam'.

The tribal chiefs of Swat were now handing in a few weapons, and swearing obedience to Britain again. Beaten in a fair fight, they could not understand why retribution should inevitably follow. 'No black looks, no sullen reserve, marred the geniality of their welcome,' wrote Churchill. 'As we approached the first fortified village the sovereign and his army rode out to meet us, and with many protestations of fidelity, expressed his joy at our safe arrival.'

The local slang term for British officers was *shikar*, hunter, since that was how they had first encountered them, coming up into the mountains to shoot game. It led to a Pashtun saying: 'You should always kill an Englishman. First comes one as a *shikar*, then two to make a map, and then an army to take the country, so better to kill the first one.' But in the battles for the Chitral road, the *shikari* had won. Should that not be an end to it?

'It was not, however, possible to accept this sportsmanlike view of the situation,' wrote Churchill.

They were asked where were the rifles they had been ordered to surrender. At this they looked blank. There were no rifles. There never had been any rifles. Let the soldiers search the fort and see for themselves. The order was given; three or four *sowars* drew their carbines, dismounted and entered the great and heavy gate, which had been suspiciously opened a little way.

The gate gave access to a small courtyard, commanded on every side by an interior defence. In front was a large low room of uncertain dimensions: a kind of guard-house. It simply hummed with men. The outer walls were nearly five feet thick and would have resisted the fire of mountain guns. It was a strong place. The Lancers, accustomed to the operation of hunting for arms, hurriedly searched the likely and usual places, but without success. One thing, however, they noticed, which they immediately reported.

There were no women and children in the fort. This had a sinister aspect. Our visit was unexpected and had taken them by surprise, but they were prepared for all emergencies. They had hidden their rifles and cleared for action. The two chiefs smiled in superior virtue. Of course there were no rifles. But matters took, for them, an unexpected turn. They had no rifles – said Major Deane – very well, they should come themselves. He turned to an officer of the Lancers; a section rode forward and surrounded both men. Resistance was useless. Flight was impossible. They were prisoners. Yet they behaved with Oriental composure and calmly accepted the inevitable. They ordered their ponies and, mounting, rode behind us under escort.

The British force moved up the Swat valley in the later months of 1897, destroying defences, burning crops and negotiating with tribal elders, but to Churchill's dismay they remained in Swat, rather than heading east to the lair of the Hindustani fanatics. General Blood was keen to press home the advantage, but with memories of the difficulties of the Ambeyla campaign in 1863, and a reluctance to push deep into the mountains, the government held back. Building the Chitral road had been controversial enough; now it had been retaken there was no reason to go further.

The paradox at the heart of frontier policy was exposed: Britain could not successfully annex it, nor leave it alone. The mountains and the men who fought in them had lost a battle – they always would in a straight contest against a large and technically superior force – but they were still free, and always would be. Fields could be replanted, walls rebuilt, tribes rearmed. Churchill expressed the frustration of the military men in the field, who felt they had done only half a job, and that their failure to finish it would have consequences. 'The news . . . spread like wild fire along the frontier, and revived the spirits of the tribes. They fancied they detected a sign of weakness. Nor were they altogether wrong. But the weakness was moral rather than physical.'

In late August, a month after the Mullah Sadullah had first gathered his banners, there was a raid by warriors from Mohmand at the west of the frontier on a Hindu village within sight of a British fort near Peshawar. This was seen as a far more serious incident than the uprisings in Waziristan or Swat because it was an incursion from the mountains into the 'settled areas' – British India itself. The telegraph crackled to Simla with a report to the government of India that called the raid the 'most open and audacious violation of British territory which has occurred in the Peshawar District, or indeed in any Frontier district for many years'.

Half of General Blood's Malakand force was sent west to Mohmand to 'inflict severe punishment'. They found themselves facing a far more competent enemy than the hordes of *ghazis* that had offered themselves for slaughter in front of their guns in Swat. The Mohmand tribesmen deployed classic guerrilla tactics: avoiding set-piece battles, withdrawing and then ambushing the better-equipped British force. In one engagement Churchill nearly lost his life and wrote that 'the actual casualties were, in proportion to the numbers engaged, greater than in any action of the British army in India for many years. Out of a force which at no time exceeded 1000 men, nine British officers, four native officers, and 136 soldiers were either killed or wounded.'

The Mohmands were defeated, and among the rifles handed in was one identified as having come from the British army defeated at Maiwand. The uprising was now causing profound concern, and questions were asked about the wisdom of the past policy of paying subsidies to the mountain tribes and letting them govern themselves. When the revolt then spread to the Orakzai and Afridi tribes, it shook at the foundations of frontier policy. They were not only loyal, and the main source of Pashtun recruits to the British frontier regiments; the Afridis were also the guardians of the Khyber Pass.

The viceroy Lord Elgin wrote to London, demanding the right to inflict severe punishment: 'the unprovoked aggression on Khyber pass gravely affects our position on the frontier, and is calculated seriously to weaken us in relation to tribes generally'. The fall of the Khyber was the worst British miscalculation of the summer. Reports that the Afridis and Orakzais were rising were initially discounted because of their loyalty, so preparations to deal with the outbreak were slow and late. And even when there was no doubt that 10,000 Afridis were moving towards the pass, the British still hoped that the Khyber Rifles would stick to their treaty obligations, so did not reinforce them with regular troops. Many Afridi British soldiers remained loyal, but they were rapidly out-numbered by those who changed sides. As the rebels swept down the pass, they burnt British border posts behind them.

The British defence at Landi Kotal, the gateway to the Khyber Pass, was under Subedar Mursil Khan, an Afridi who had one son under his command and two in the attacking force. He led a small defence detachment of just 374 men, many of whom fled at the start of the fighting. The battle for the fortress went on for a day and a night, until the gates were treacherously opened from the inside. During the negotiations that followed, Mursil Khan was killed, and the fort and 50,000 rounds of ammunition fell into rebel hands. An afternoon's ride away, a relief column in Peshawar waited for orders. But no orders came. Churchill called it the 'shocking and disgrace-ful desertion of the forts'. At an angry public meeting in Simla, a civilian received considerable applause when he said 'the 23rd of August was a day of pain and humiliation for every Englishman in India. We had 12,000 troops at the mouth of the pass . . . marking time . . . and we allowed those forts to fall one after the other.'

By October, General Sir William Lockhart had assembled a force of 43,703 troops to save the frontier. And this army, then the largest put together in Asia under a single general, was still heavily outnumbered. The fall of the Khyber Pass had led to a general mobilisation of tribal warriors in Tirah, the mysterious and enclosed region beneath the shelf of the Safed Koh. Lockhart inserted his force here to split the rebellion and prevent the union of forces from Waziristan and Tirah.

The battle at the start of the Tirah campaign in October was one of the most controversial of the war. Gordon Highlanders, with Gurkha assistance, and against little opposition, took a lofty ridge, the Dargai Heights. It was a commanding position,

5000 feet up, and looked down from a series of ledges over open ground. But Lockhart abandoned the ridge, because he could not easily supply those who held it. When the British force next looked up there were 12,000 well-armed tribal warriors on top of the Dargai Heights, who had no concern about supplying themselves. After a day in which every effort to retake the heights was beaten back, the same two regiments, Gordon Highlanders and Gurkhas, fought their way up again, taking 200 casualties, including 39 dead. It was a reverse of the usual frontier battles in which British defenders would inflict heavy casualties on a tribal assault.

General Lockhart then fought his way into Tirah, proud to have broken the 'boast of the tribes' that it was impregnable. And after his force had spent months burning villages, and destroying livelihoods, they withdrew.

Experienced military voices were now asking whether all the punishing and crushing, pulling down towers and trampling crops under the feet of elephants, had done any good at all. Half a century of 'butcher and bolt' had not brought peace. Lord Roberts, who left India as a field marshall in 1893 after 41 years, had seen much of this at first hand. He wrote, 'Burning houses and destroying crops unless followed up by some sort of authority and jurisdiction, mean . . . for us a rich harvest of hatred and revenge.'

Retribution had been a central policy for Britain in controlling its Asian empire. Anyone who killed a British soldier had to know there would be a heavy price to pay. One of Kipling's darkest poems, 'The Grave of the Hundred Dead', tells of how all must know that a 'a white man's head must be paid with heads five-score'. A locally recruited platoon count up the heads of rebels killed in revenge for one English officer: 'Each man bearing a basket / Red as his palms that day . . . And the drip-drip-drip from the baskets / Reddened the grass by the way'.

But after the 1897 uprising there was a growing realisation that 'blockades and small punitive expeditions' might not work any more; the frontier tribes were flexing a new kind of strength, and among the rebels were men who had learnt modern ways to fight as British soldiers. Reasons given for the revolt included concern over the Durand line and an increased salt tax. But Britain understood the insurgency to stem mainly from the ability of the mullahs to gain a hold over 'these ignorant, fanatical, bigoted, priest-ridden people, who absolutely believed that we should be driven out of the country'. The power of a virulent strain of political Islam to mobilise revolution had been learnt by Britain at the end of the nineteenth century – a lesson forgotten until it had to be relearnt at the end of the twentieth century.

After the uprising, the black-coated Wahhabi fighters, Churchill's 'sombre-clad warriors of Ambeyla', were forced to move further north, to an even more remote camp. But they were more than a camp, a base – they were an ideology, a mission, a mindset – not to be defeated by force of arms. They continued to put out a newspaper, called the *Mujaheed*, which preached that it was the religious duty of all Muslims to wage jihad against the British.

The genie could not be put back in the bottle; something else needed to be tried. But the British did not know what that something should be. The decision to withdraw after taking the previously unconquered hills of Tirah led to another argument. The viceroy wrote, 'We do not contemplate as the basis of settlement with Afridis . . . the annexation or permanent occupation of Tirah,' adding, as if in an aside, 'The Commander-in-Chief dissents.'

Most were agreed that no 'new responsibility should be undertaken, unless absolutely required by actual strategical necessities and the protection of the Indian border'. But fierce political debates went on in London and India even over whether to continue to garrison the Swat road, let alone move further into the frontier region.

There were calls for a more enlightened frontier policy, employing officers who spoke local languages, and could avert the constant conflicts. By the turn of the century Britain could look back at two golden ages on the frontier – the time of

Henry Lawrence's young men in the 1840s and 50s, and Sir Robert Sandeman's control of the southern frontier area of Baluchistan, pushing forward to Quetta in 1879. Sandeman had stressed the need to 'deal with the hearts and minds of the people' – an early use of the phrase that would come to define enlightened counterinsurgency strategy a century later. But some still wanted Britain to play no further role west of the Indus. In a debate in the Commons, one opposition MP said that Britain had 'no more right to be in Chitral than . . . in Timbuctoo'.

Wars in Afghanistan and on the frontier bookended Victoria's long reign. The First Anglo-Afghan War, within months of her coronation, scarred the reputation of the army in India for a generation; the Second put an end to any thoughts of a garrison on the Hindu Kush; the 1897 uprising would pull British imperial ambition even further back – to the eastern foot of the mountains, where the Sikh warrior-king Ranjit Singh had stopped in the 1830s.

The Marquess of Salisbury, prime minister when the queen-empress finally died, was confident that ultimately Britain would prevail: control of 'these splendid tribes' was an 'inevitable conquest'. But he was concerned about what might have been unleashed: 'I do not underestimate the difficulty which all over the world we are feeling with the Mahomedan population wherever we come across them. There is an impulse stirring in them. A slight victory, an exaggerated victory, has recalled to them their past of a thousand years ago, when they were victors in every part of the world, and they cannot but believe that that glorious period of their history is to be repeated.'

8

Bolt from the Blue

'Considering how overtaken by surprise we were by what you rightly describe as a bolt from the blue I think that everything has gone off better than we had any right to hope it would.'

Sir George Roos-Keppel, British Commissioner in the North-West Frontier Province, writing in 1919 as an Afghan force attacked through the Khyber Pass and Waziristan.

'His Highness asked me about his marital duties.'

Times were changing. The sex life of the new amir was not what Major Robert Bird of the Indian Medical Service expected to be dealing with, but this was the twentieth century, and an Indian Army doctor felt able to offer advice. Whatever he said, Freud would probably have approved. Two days later Amir Habibullah did not call Bird in until the afternoon, after spending the whole day in his harem, and said he felt 'much better'.

Habibullah had taken over as amir without opposition, on the death of his father Abdur Rahman in 1901. Afghanistan was entering a new century in which its ability to negotiate its way in the modern world – on sexuality and on so much else – would be tested, quite literally, to destruction. A century that would end in mutual incomprehension between the Taliban and the West, began with the Afghan king consulting a British doctor about his sex life.

Habibullah was a short, hugely fat man, who enjoyed going slowly round his estate on a tricycle. He was moderate in sexual matters, since 'his appearance gives no evidence of excess', whatever Bird meant by that as he obsessively recorded the sexual appetites of people he met. When the amir's senior adviser came in with a headache, Bird learnt from an interpreter that his tastes were 'far too connubial'.

Bird had been initially called to Kabul in an emergency to save the amir's arm, injured when his gun burst while he was out hunting. In his diary the doctor was an unsympathetic observer of Habibullah's court. The palace was grimy and poorly maintained, and the water supply contaminated as the seals on the filters were broken. The cavalry drilled in a sloppy way, their uniform sashes worn the wrong way round; even on the amir's own carriage 'the horses were unkempt, the harness dirty'. Although the palace was beautifully furnished in an English style, with pure gold ornaments and fine carpets, there were inferior prints on the walls and, horror of horrors, 'a Cadbury's advertisement book lying on the centre table. I told him this was hardly appropriate.'

More seriously, Bird heard there had been food shortages for two years and an outbreak of cholera. Stocks of grain in the caves at the foot of the Buddhas at Bamiyan and elsewhere were low. There was hunger in the land, but Habibullah did not seem to notice. Like his father, he was preoccupied with guns, and strengthening Afghanistan against the inevitable Russian invasion. He thought Britain was ignoring the threat. 'Afghanistan is the first step of the ladder,' the amir told Bird. 'The man who wants to strike must put his foot on something firm before he reaches over to strike with his sword.' A Russian shadow was ever present. During the doctor's visit, three men who were believed to be Russian spies were discovered in Kabul – one was shot, one imprisoned, and the third turned to work for Afghanistan.

When he came to power, Habibullah made the same complaint as every Afghan amir for half a century. Although Britain expected them to keep to their side of existing agreements, they had to renegotiate protection as a personal deal. It was a one-sided contract. Britain relied on the deal imposed on Shir Ali in 1873, which defined Afghanistan as a buffer state where Russia had no rights, and on the terms of the Gandamack Treaty, signed by Yakub Khan in the Second Anglo-Afghan War in 1879, handing over the right to manage Afghanistan's foreign policy to Britain, confirmed by Abdur Rahman before he became amir in a letter given to Sir Lepel Griffin in the tent at Charikar. One treaty imposed over the head of an amir, another extracted under the duress of war, and a signature on a letter by a man not even in power – these were the documents relied on by Britain to control the foreign policy of Afghanistan. But the terms Britain would offer in return depended on the nature of the external threat, and needed constant renegotiation by succeeding amirs.

Afghanistan was paid handsomely for the relationship, and given weapons, but its unwillingness to open up further, allow foreign troops on its soil, or even a permanent embassy, was a source of constant frustration, especially as the amir was 'unable to check the fanaticism' of his subjects, in the words of a new secretary of state for India, Lord Morley, in 1906.

It was hard to take this amir seriously. An invitation to India turned into high farce. The initial aim had been for Habibullah to spend a few days in Calcutta then join a shooting party in central India. But he was mesmerised by the nightlife and two English women in particular, ignoring the fact that one was married. At parties he was followed around by a servant carrying a velvet bag of gemstones, which he would hand out to women he fancied. He overstayed in Calcutta by weeks and missed the shoot, the main reason for the invitation.

His Afghan escort became restive, and after he visited a Masonic lodge, the decision was taken that he must leave following a rumour that he had become a Christian. Lord Kitchener, conqueror of Khartoum and commander-in-chief of the Indian Army, was recruited to bundle him onto a train late at night, threatening him with an uncomfortable boat trip instead if he did not do as he was told. Rumours of the amir's deviation from the Afghan norm in sex and religion led to a failed assassination attempt on the road back to Kabul.

By now the frontier region had been brought under the direct control of the viceroy, rather than the neighbouring Indian province of Punjab. But whatever political system was tried, Britain still felt the need to conduct frequent raids into the frontier region, particularly Waziristan. Lord Curzon, the most political of viceroys in this period, had long been opposed to the 'infatuated nonsense' of the Forward policy. He wanted to put local forces in forward positions, with British troops in reserve to strike hard if needed – remarkably similar thinking to what was developed by British and Canadian forces in southern Afghanistan during the worsening insurgency in the war that followed 9/11. Afghan forces were to take the lead role in operations against the Taliban as far as possible, with the foreign troops and their heavy weapons in reserve.

Back at the beginning of the twentieth century on the frontier, whatever the policy was called – 'close border', 'modified forward' – for British soldiers, it was business as usual: 'The sudden alarm, the long dust-choked ride through the stifling heat of a July night, clattering out to the stony glacis of the frontier hills, and away forty miles before dawn only to find as often as not that the birds had flown, leaving a trail of death and destruction behind them.' Young officers on the ground became contemptuous of the military value of such missions, known to them as General Willcocks's Weekend Wars, 'after General Sir James Willcocks, who waged them to the satisfaction of himself and of the government of India'.

Curzon was brilliant, opinionated and impatient. By bringing the Frontier under his direct control he thought he could shape a more consistent policy, less vulnerable to mood swings at Westminster. The region was divided between the settled area, the mostly level ground west of the Indus, and the mountainous tribal areas beyond, which now came under central government influence but had more autonomy. The change emerged from Curzon's impatience that responsibility for what he saw as the 'most important sphere of activity' in Indian foreign policy was delegated to a regional government in Punjab, and not controlled centrally. When he first became viceroy in 1900, he wrote a long memo, framed in the most undiplomatic terms, outlining the weaknesses of those who had run the Punjab government over the previous quarter of a century. 'None had any substantial experience of the frontier.'

Curzon liked to paint a sentimental picture of the frontier, where 'young British officers have gone in and out among the tribes, lived with them, hunted with them . . . played polo with them'. But the old arguments about the depth of engagement still went on. Moreover, direct rule did not persuade Kabul that the frontier area was permanently British, and the Durand line remained an open wound. Whether for the vanity of individual commanders like General Willcocks, or for any wider military purpose, constant skirmishing engaged another generation of British soldiers on the frontier.

At the most robust end of the spectrum sat Sir George Roos-Keppel, commissioner in the North-West Frontier Province, writing in 1916 after a quarter of a century on the frontier. There should be no more 'butcher and bolt'. The old policy of short expeditions 'has had its day': what was needed was for the whole of the region to be crushed. Not taking control decisively when the Durand line was drawn had been a mistake; the tribes needed to be militarily defeated *for their own good*. The frontier was seen almost an unruly boy in a public school – in need of a good thrashing to bring him into line.

'I do not advocate the crushing and disarming of the tribes and the occupation of their country in any spirit of revenge – far from it – I look upon it . . . mainly in the interest of the tribes themselves – in fact as a scheme for the reclamation of a fine, manly and courageous people capable of great development and of becoming a source of strength instead of weakness to the Empire.'

This scheme would be especially effective in Waziristan, 'the plague spot of the whole frontier', and would end a situation where there were 'hostile savages from one end of our border to the other . . . I would begin with the Mahsuds and Wazirs . . . I would go on to the Mohmands, Bajaur, Swat and Buner. There is not much fight in these people if they are attacked by a sufficient force and I do not think that these operations would prove very costly either in lives or money.'

Whatever happened on the frontier, Roos-Keppel believed that war with Afghanistan was inevitable. As early as March 1916 he wrote 'the belief is universal that we shall find ourselves at war with the Amir during the course of this summer'. In the event it would be another three years before a joint force of Afghans and irregular tribal levies would pour down the Khyber Pass, crying, 'Death or freedom'.

Although Habibullah was still taking a British subsidy, he had allowed a German mission to open in Kabul during the First World War, and even allowed Indian insurgents to set up a German-backed 'Provisional Government of India'. Germany has the distinction of being the first foreign country to exploit jihad for its own ends in south Asia. Its agents spread an extraordinary rumour that the kaiser had secretly become a Muslim, so joining Germany's war against Britain was now an act of jihad. One German spy held meetings in villages, claiming to have the kaiser on the other end of an open two-way radio circuit while he negotiated with tribal elders, offering them extravagant gifts for support.

Germany's alliance with Turkey, home of the caliph, the historical leader of the world's Muslims, was central to this new alignment. Habibullah became increasingly concerned as several members of his family, and other leading Afghans, joined a 'War Party' opposed to the continued connection with Britain. He had allowed the German delegation in for a while, and the Indian rebels to set up their provisional government, but he had gone no further than that and did not want to provoke Britain.

Habibullah's brother Nasrullah was a constant threat during his reign. Operating on the amir in 1904, the Indian Army doctor, Major Bird, thought that Nasrullah's face expressed anything but brotherly concern. 'I read it as expressing a fervent hope that something would go wrong. The moment I turned and caught his eye he squeezed out one tear, rather crocodilian.'

But when an assassin finally did get Habibullah, while he was out hunting near Jalalabad in 1919, it was the amir's third son Amanullah, then governor of Kabul, who seized his chance, took power and threw Nasrullah into jail where he died soon afterwards. War with Britain followed, partly to divert the attention of the tribes in case they blamed Amanullah for the death of his father. Amanullah's ally, the commander-in-chief of the armed forces, Nadir Shah, had already moved out of Kabul. He was to play a crucial role in the war, leading his forces through the Camel's Neck into the Kurram valley, and encouraging a general tribal uprising in Waziristan on the British side of the Durand line.

The war started with the distribution of a proclamation from Amanullah in Peshawar, appealing for a jihad against Britain, and Afghan forces moved down the Khyber Pass, gathering tribal support along the way.

Exhausted by the First World War, Britain found it hard to mobilise the forces it needed. Thousands refused the order to move up to the Khyber and remained under canvas in a mass protest that was not reported at the time. Those who would fight were often young and inexperienced, but within a week they had reversed Afghan gains in the Khyber Pass, and pushed forward onto the plain towards Jalalabad where British soldiers had been before. On 9th May 1919, south Asia saw its first air raid, as two war-worn Sopwith Camels dropped bombs on Afghan forces at Dakka. They did not have enough power to clear the surrounding mountains, so had the disconcerting experience of being fired down on as they flew along the Khyber Pass.

The planes had some psychological value, since tribesmen

would flee from them, but the conditions were very tough. One plane mistook a dust storm for the ground, and landed on top of a tent; nobody was hurt but the plane was destroyed. The only larger bomber available, a Handley-Page, bombed Kabul once. A convenient east wind blew it over the Khyber Mountains, and by good fortune changed course to blow it home again after the raid.

There was mass desertion from British forces by frontier-recruited troops, but Roos-Keppel was surprised that there was not a more widespread revolt on the frontier. Other than 'about a thousand scallywags' most remained calm. He wanted to go all the way to Kabul – another generation believing it could be done, brushing aside the lessons of history. 'In the last forty years which have elapsed myths have grown up about the Afghan fighting strength and these are firmly believed by the people of India.'

But the government in Delhi was resolutely opposed to such an entanglement, believing it would take more troops than were in the whole of India to occupy Afghanistan effectively. They ordered the main force not to push forward even as far as Jalalabad. Towards the end of May, less than a month after beginning the war, the amir sent envoys pleading for peace, but there were three more months of fighting before the tribal regions were pacified again. Reinforcements of planes were sent from Mesopotamia, and by the end Britain had lost two shot down.

Over several rounds of peace talks Amanullah won the freedom he wanted. Britain's long and costly control of the foreign policy of a country where it could not even send its troops came to an end. The talks were prolonged while Britain sought a treaty to prevent Afghanistan falling straight into the hands of the new Soviet Union. Twice the British delegation set off homeward from Kabul following 'absolutely final' treaty terms from Amanullah that were unacceptable, but each time they came back, while Turkey trained Afghan forces, and Soviet-backed Indian revolutionaries set up an office. The prospect of communist influence in a resurgent Islamic

Afghanistan was potentially as bad as anything Britain had feared during the century-long Great Game.

The Russian Revolution had changed the dynamic in central Asia. Roos-Keppel saw it as a direct factor in the 1919 war: 'I cannot help feeling that there is a great deal of Bolshevik influence in the Afghan lunacy.' T.E. Lawrence, Lawrence of Arabia, while working in the region as a humble aircraft mechanic in the 1920s, thought that war between Britain and the Soviet Union over Afghanistan looked likely. 'It's quite on the cards Russia may have her go in our time.' But ultimately the Soviet Union needed better relations with Britain more than it needed Afghanistan. A Soviet delegation in Kabul in 1921 began by offering Afghanistan the return of the Panjdeh oasis and the slice of land taken with it, as well as a large subsidy. But as the talks went on, the offer was withdrawn; relations with Britain mattered more.

As his Turkish-trained armed forces took shape, Amanullah was far more interested in an alliance with other Islamic powers, and sent troops north across the Oxus to assist a Muslim revolt against Soviet control. But the rebellion fizzled out when its leader died, and Amanullah's dreams of expansion were further crushed when the Soviet Union seized control of Bokhara, pushing out its Khan. Stalin had begun by sending pacifying messages to the Muslim majority regions of central Asia that Russia had gobbled up in its century-long push south, but then seized power by force where he could not foment revolution. They emerged as the '-stans': Tajikistan, Uzbekistan, Kazakhstan, Kyrghystan and Turkmenistan. Relations between Afghanistan and the Soviet Union became even more strained after Amanullah gave asylum to tens of thousands of Muslim rebels who had streamed south into Afghanistan across the Oxus.

The new amir had also been forced to give refuge to thousands of Indian Muslims who flooded along the Khyber into Afghanistan to live in protest at Britain's war on the Turkish caliphate. The Khilafat movement was designed to weaken British rule by draining India of people, but the rug was pulled from under this bizarre protest when Ataturk and his Young Turks founded the secular nationalist Turkish state that emerged from the rubble of the First World War, and terminated the caliphate. Shah Reza was reforming Persia along similar lines.

Amanullah was impatient for reform in Afghanistan too. Since 1911 a highly influential fortnightly magazine, published in Kabul, had been bringing Afghanistan into contact with the secular Islamic reform movement spreading worldwide. Founded by Mahmud Tarzi, who went on to become Afghan foreign minister, the magazine bound nationalism, religion and modern technological progress together in a way they had not been linked before, at least not in Afghanistan. The magazine extolled the benefits of schools, road building, chemists' shops and equality for women, alongside pieces about the need to reform Islam to take its place in the modern world. It was the earliest stirrings of a global Islamic movement – against imperialism and strongly anti-British.

The long years of plotting and reading Tarzi's reformist magazine could be put into effect once Amanullah was in government. Clothing took centre stage in what became a battle over more than politics – it was a fight for the Afghan soul. Amanullah followed the lead of the reformers in Turkey and Persia to demand the opposite to what the Taliban would later try to impose – *Western* clothing should be worn as often as possible. To appear at court and in some other parts of Kabul men had to wear Western suits; turbans and lambskin hats were banned and replaced by bowlers and homburgs; women were encouraged to appear in public unveiled.

In a poor country it was not as easy to impose this strictly as it had been in Persia and Turkey, and visiting tribal leaders from outside Kabul were given Western suits when they arrived for meetings, which were solemnly reclaimed from them and folded up as they left town, to be given to the next visitor.

Amanullah was prone to walking about with a pair of shears to cut the clothes off anyone who did not follow his rules, but behind this clownish behaviour was serious intent. In an effort to reform Islamic practice and reduce the influence of the mosques, he introduced education for mullahs, and cut their government subsidies; a secular school of law was set up to replace Islamic judges; and in a direct assault on the Wahhabi tradition any mullah trained in an Indian Deobandi college was disqualified from preaching.

Women were given freedom of choice in marriage, and there was support for women's associations. Extravagant spending on weddings was discouraged, and a minimum marriage age of 18 was stipulated for girls to get married. There was education for girls, and primary school classes became mixed up to age 11. Plans for hospitals, clean water, adult literacy classes, foreign language teaching, and new newspapers poured forth. Slavery was banned and commerce encouraged. Whole factories were bought abroad and reassembled in Afghanistan. Amanullah looked beyond Afghanistan's Islamic allies, Turkey and Persia, who had inspired his reforms, for new links. Britain was kept at arm's length, but other European countries, in particular Germany and France, were encouraged to send engineers and archaeologists, as a museum was opened and Afghanistan's extraordinary past began to be unearthed.

But Amanullah's dreams were wrecked by the obdurate conservative tribal reality of Afghanistan. Only a few years later in 1933 the travel writer Robert Byron would visit the shell of Amanullah's half-finished and now deserted grandiose new town at Paghman, in the hills near Kabul. He saw

a French municipal office, surrounded by a French municipal garden and entirely deserted. While below it, occupying the centre of the whole four mile vista, stands a German match factory in the ferro-concrete-farmhouse style . . . In each glade stands a house or office or theatre of such appalling aspect . . . that it is impossible to imagine where Amanullah could have found the architects to design them, even as a joke. But no, they are not a joke. Untenanted, shoddy and obscene, they defile the woods and streams and the view of the plain beneath.

The first uprising against Amanullah, in 1924, was led by mullahs from Khost in the east, who stirred people up holding a Koran in one hand and a copy of Amanullah's legal code in the other, and proclaiming that the country could not have both. The rising was crushed with the help of two planes bought from Britain and flown by German pilots, and the mullah seen as the main instigator was hanged. But at a national *loya jirga* Amanullah was forced to compromise on some of his reforms, in particular over women's rights.

His reform programme regained impetus after a seven-month tour in 1927/28. By the time Amanullah drove himself in a new Rolls-Royce back across the border from Persia into Herat, he had bought several more factories, and had a clear plan for his country. He now called himself the king, not amir, of Afghanistan, and spoke for four days to a *loya jirga,* where he insisted on Western dress. A British observer thought the tribal chiefs 'were an unhappy and pathetic sight. Clad in black morning coats and trousers, with white shirts, black ties, and soft hats, they looked very much more like caricatures of Nonconformist clergy than Ghilzai, Mangal, and other tribesmen.'

Amanullah outlined a far more radical programme than before, including the complete emancipation of women, monogamy and education for all. Just as the Taliban would later use the police to force women to cover up, so Amanullah employed them to persuade women to reveal more. Women in rural areas routinely went without a head covering for practical reasons, so they could work, and would put on a burqa to come to town. Under the new rules, in the new town of Paghman, women wearing any covering except for a specially designed flimsy veil would have it removed. The king's appeal to women to go bare-headed was answered by his queen dramatically removing her veil in public.

When the uprising that brought Amanullah down began

months later, it was pictures of Queen Soraya in an evening gown taken on her trip to Europe, bare-armed and with a plunging neckline, that the mullahs showed to demonstrate how far things had gone. The spark for the revolt was the arrest and execution of five mullahs. As unrest spread, Amanullah desperately tried to rescind much of the reform programme, and closed girls' schools. But it was too late, and he was forced to flee Kabul only six months after his bold schemes were outlined at Paghman. He rallied some support in Kandahar, and in a desperate last move went to the shrine where the cloak of the Prophet was kept, and declared he was a good Muslim. Made by another man, the gesture might have seemed bold, but he was no Dost Mohammed, and his reign ended in bathos.

The throne was held for a while by a man known as Bacha Saqao, meaning son of a water carrier, a Tajik bandit who had rallied enough force to take power. Afghanistan could never be ruled by a Tajik, but the real power-brokers, the Pashtun tribal leaders, delayed giving their support to Amanullah's commander-in-chief, Nadir Shah, as he tried to restore order. It was only after Britain signalled quietly that 'their' tribes would not be stopped if they wanted to cross the frontier to fight for Nadir Shah that the balance of power shifted decisively in his favour.

Bacha Saqao's forces were defeated on the ridge at Charasiab where British forces had won the decisive battle for Kabul in 1879. He barricaded himself into the palace, where his hostages included two members of Nadir's family, but the general did not flinch and ordered a bombing raid. Bacha Saqao's brief reign was over and he was hanged.

They were perilous times. Nadir Shah knew the price he had to pay and allowed the tribes who had supported him to loot the capital, including the palace. Their loyalty was not to him, but to themselves and their clans. And then, like the hordes that had appeared and disappeared, making and unmaking kings during Britain's attempts to take Afghanistan in the nineteenth century, they were gone. Nadir Shah, who was descended from another branch of the ruling Barakzai clan, took power for himself, rather than trying to reinstall Amanullah, whose grandiose schemes had emptied the treasury.

Afghanistan's conservative tribal culture had defeated an invasion from abroad – not an invasion by foreign armies this time, but foreign ideas, particularly about the treatment of women. Of the Islamic countries that modernised in that unique window of opportunity after the First World War, Turkey's secular path was the most robust, Persia looked determinedly westward for decades, but Afghanistan quickly turned back to what it knew. Amanullah's Western suits were put away – his new town abandoned. The boldest attempt to modernise Afghanistan had been made too quickly and chaotically to succeed, and without any attempt to build support outside a tiny Kabul elite.

Only four years later Nadir Shah was assassinated, but his brothers were now firmly in control. Afghanistan had peered over the precipice in the disorder that followed the death of Amanullah and backed the new dynasty. Nadir Shah's son Zahir, aged just 19, was put on the throne in 1933 and was to rule for 40 years of peace and relative prosperity.

Part Four

Revolution and the Soviet invasion
1973–1994

9

'Muslim Reactionaries'

'When the highest political leaders of the USSR sent its forces into this war, they did not consider the historic, religious, and national particularities of Afghanistan.'
Post-war assessment of the Afghan War by the
Russian General Staff

Congressman Charlie Wilson from Texas opened the door of his room in the Pearl Continental Hotel in Peshawar in January 1984 to greet one of the richest, and certainly the most influential of Afghan leaders. Almost two centuries had passed since the first encounter between a Western emissary and an Afghan leader, but this meeting would have a more immediate impact on Afghanistan than when Elphinstone met Shah Shuja in the same town. Behind Wilson, climbing off the bed to greet the Afghan guest, was a former Miss Northern Hemisphere no less, known as Snowflake. Not wanting to expose too much flesh in this conservative Muslim town, Snowflake was covered up. Her version of modest was a pink nylon jumpsuit with a zip that ran from neck to navel, and the footwear she thought would put the Afghan visitor Gulbuddin Hekmatyar at his ease were combat boots, chosen because he was a warrior – the most prominent leader of the mujahidin, holy warriors, fighting the US-financed war against Russia's invasion of Afghanistan.

Hekmatyar's dark expressionless eyes and thickset face, framed by the standard ragged Pashtun beard, showed no reaction, although he preferred his girls covered from head to toe by a burqa. As a student leader in Kabul in the late 1960s he had achieved notoriety by encouraging his followers to throw acid in the faces of girls whose heads were not completely covered. He was opposed to the drinking of alcohol too, but he would forgive Wilson anything because the congressman was bankrolling the war. Hekmatyar had become used to the whisky-drinking Texan having a different girl with him every time he came to town, and he was not going to complain.

Afghanistan's fate hung in the hands of a fun-loving buffoon and a psychopathic Islamo-Fascist. And now the money was really beginning to make a difference. Only two years after this meeting, in 1986, a new leader in the Kremlin, Mikhail Gorbachev, would signal his desire to end the war, calling Afghanistan Russia's 'bleeding wound'.

Hekmatyar's progress, from acid-throwing student thug to someone the US government would trust with billions of dollars had begun in the early 1970s as Afghanistan's longest period of stability under a single monarch began to unravel. Zahir Shah had been on the throne for 40 years when his cousin Daoud dislodged him in a palace coup in 1973, while Zahir was on a trip to Rome.

Afghanistan's long peace had brought some prosperity. During the cold war it was a member of the non-aligned group of nations, competed over by each side of the divided world. In Victorian times Britain had used guns and pensions; Afghanistan now found itself bribed by roads and power-plants.

Development meant that in the 1970s Afghanistan exported more raisins than California, mostly from Helmand in the south-west, after the US built a huge irrigation system – this was to come in useful later when opium poppies emerged as the staple crop in the region. Power for the capital came from a hydroelectric plant built by Germany, harnessing the force of the Kabul River as it plunged off the high central Asian plain and down towards the Indo-Gangetic lowlands to the east, while China put in the irrigation system that carried the melting snows of the Hindu Kush into the canals of the flat Shomali plain north of Kabul. Less than 5 per cent of a country of deserts and mountains was irrigable agricultural land, so anything that carried water further made a big difference.

But pressure for political and social reform had come with economic progress, and Daoud was impatient for radical change, wanting Afghanistan to join the modern world. He was from the tiny lucky elite that had received education abroad during the brief reform years under Amanullah in the 1920s and would govern as a president not an amir.

Around 15,000 foreigners lived in Kabul, mostly young people who had been in the vanguard of the social revolution of the 1960s, another tribe to add to Afghanistan's rich tapestry. In those far-off more innocent days before Iraq's collapse and the Ayatollah's revolution in Iran, it was possible to take a bus from London to Delhi across virtually open borders. Hippies brought in their lifestyle, and took back rugs and shawls and embroidered sheepskin jackets. (The travel writer Bruce Chatwin blamed them for introducing Marxist ideas – the first cause of the Afghan descent into chaos.) The influence of the modern world may not have made much of a difference to life out in the provinces, but it did in cities like Kabul, Herat in the west and Mazar in the north. Afghan women sought education and jobs. There was even a Miss Kabul competition – hardly the cutting edge of feminism, but a sign of change nonetheless in this traditional Islamic culture.

As part of his reform package, one of the first things Daoud did when he seized power from his cousin was to launch a crackdown on Islamic fundamentalism, then competing as one of several political ideologies. In the Kabul student elections in 1970 Islamist activists had won a majority. Daoud rejected offers from the Saudi government to pump some of its colossal new oil wealth, gained in the price hike of 1973, into Kabul University. He knew it would come with Wahhabi strings attached, and wanted no part of it. The Saudis took their oil money to Pakistan instead, providing a fresh injection of cash to the fundamentalist system of education in Wahhabi madrassas, where boys learn the Koran by heart to the exclusion of almost all other teaching. After spending a year in jail for his role in planning the murder of a Maoist university student, Hekmatyar followed the money, and ran away from progress in Afghanistan – one of the first in a wave of Afghan fundamentalists who fled across the border.

Pakistan quickly recognised the potential of the disaffected Islamists, recruiting and training them to fight against Daoud when he played the Pashtun nationalist card. Daoud was trying to gain domestic support by reigniting the old dream of Pashtunistan, which pushed the Afghan border east across the mountains as far as the Indus. The issue of the frontier still lay like rough sandpaper between the two sides – as much a cause of friction at the end of the twentieth century as it had been 200 years before. The mountain tribes remained desperately poor with a reputation for banditry, while Pakistan had inherited Britain's problems on the frontier, along with its system of government, leaving the elders to run things as far as possible. There was also a new legal argument now the Durand line was almost 100 years old. Afghan Pashtun nationalists interpreted clauses in the 1893 deal to mean that it was good for only a century. It was now close to its expiry date.

The Afghan Islamist exiles were open to recruitment on Pakistan's side against the narrow nationalism of Pashtunistan: their ideology ignored borders in favour of a wider global Islamic view. Afghanistan's long unfinished nightmare began here, five years before the Soviet invasion, as the men the US ultimately backed against the Soviet Union took up arms to oppose the mild social reforms of the Daoud government. Alongside Hekmatyar in the first Pakistani-financed three month training course as guerrillas in 1974 was another Islamist student leader – Ahmed Shah Massud.

Massud was not a Pashtun like Hekmatyar, but a Tajik from Panjshir, a long oval-shaped valley not far north-east of Kabul. Panjshir means 'five lions'. Surrounded on all sides by high ridges, and accessed only by a narrow choked canyon where the river bursts out between winding cliffs to the south, and a high pass in the north, Panjshir is a natural fortress concealed among the deceptive mountains of the Hindu Kush, as Massud was to discover in the war that was to come.

Within a year of his training and still four years before the Russian invasion, Massud had led an uprising in the Panjshir, exploiting rumblings of discontent against the president's reforms, particularly in relation to women. It was a disaster, failing to attract popular support. More than 100 of Massud's followers were arrested, and many executed. The plan had called for simultaneous uprisings in several provinces. But none of the other Islamist student revolutionaries did what they had said they would, although there were several suicidal attacks on police stations across the country.

It is said that Massud never spoke to Hekmatyar again, blaming him for the failure of the uprising. The deep divisions between the mujahidin that were later to cause so many Afghan deaths began then. Hekmatyar formed his own party, Hezb-i-Islami, the party of Islam, and a year later had Massud arrested in Peshawar on charges of spying. Massud was released, but a close friend was tortured and killed. The Panjshir uprising gave Daoud the excuse he needed for a much wider crackdown on Islamism. A radical mullah was executed, and Professor Burhanuddin Rabbani, the leader of the secret underground Islamist network, fled to join his ex-students in Pakistan. He would not return to Kabul until the chaotic post-communist days of 1992, when he emerged as president of Afghanistan.

The Soviet Union looked on with increasing concern. There had been Soviet military advisers in Afghanistan since 1954, even during the long reign of Zahir Shah. The Afghan officer corps, pilots and tank drivers all trained in the USSR, the technical language of the military was Russian, and when Daoud had ousted the last king of Afghanistan, he had had Soviet help. But as the British empire had found, buying guns for Afghanistan did not buy absolute loyalty. When Daoud sought better links with Western countries, the Soviet leader Leonid Brezhnev called him to Moscow for a personal warning. His approach to this troublesome client state was similar to that adopted by some Victorian viceroy.

In response Daoud told Brezhnev that his demand that Afghanistan break ties with other countries was an unacceptable intervention in Afghan internal affairs. 'We will never allow you to dictate to us how to run our country and whom to employ in Afghanistan.' His face was 'hard and dark' according to a Soviet witness, and he had to be reminded to shake Brezhnev's hand on his departure. A year later he was dead, overthrown and murdered along with many of his family in the Saur (April) Revolution in the spring of 1978. Pressure for more radical political reforms had been growing for several years, and the revolution succeeded with the backing of a significant part of the officer corps of the army.

Daoud was replaced by a communist regime that became more hard line as each day passed. The communists changed the national flag, painted schools red, encouraged education for girls and rights for women, cancelled all rural debt and started to impose land redistribution measures that upset the clan and tribal system of the Afghan countryside. Much of this, in particular rights for women and rural land reform, would have been seen as progress in any other country, but the chaotic cancellation of debt backed by the use of force provoked an insurgency led by rural landlords that spread across the countryside. The repressive response of the government sparked a worsening cycle of violence.

Some estimates put the number of Afghans who were killed in fighting in the year *before* the Soviet invasion as high as 50,000. These reports may have been exaggerated by Moscow to justify its intervention; in the chaos nobody was keeping a tally as hundreds of thousands of technocrats, intellectuals and political moderates, as well as Islamists fled the country.

Ninety per cent of university teachers joined the exodus. A Soviet witness spoke of 'mass arrests, shooting of undesirables, and the shooting of Muslim clergy'. Hundreds of men in Kunar in the east were killed in one massacre, while others were thrown into the Oxus and drowned in reprisal for an uprising in a village. The revolution had split the army, where loyalties were severely challenged as the violence worsened. There was a mutiny at the Bala Hissar fortress itself in Kabul, still a key strategic location as it had always been, while outside Kabul some military units were down to one third of their normal strength.

The Islamist guerrilla forces trained by Pakistan now had a clear target and a simple message. To them, both Daoud's gradualist approach to democracy and the shock tactics of the communists came to the same thing – a threat to their way of life. They went to war to defend traditional Afghan rural conservative values against democracy, progress, the education of girls and godless communism.

Hekmatyar led the first successful raid by the new mujahidin in January 1979, almost a year before the Soviet invasion, attacking the fortress at Asadabad, north of the Khyber Pass. A force of around 5000 men under Hekmatyar's command left Pakistan via the pass and penetrated the Kunar valley, the route used by Alexander the Great. There was no battle. In a pattern repeated often during the long war that was to come, the commander of the fort came over to the side of the mujahidin.

As events spiralled towards the Soviet invasion and a wider war in 1979, the most serious single uprising, in Herat, began with the deaths of several Soviet advisers and their families, killed when a group of army officers took control, dividing the government forces. Several thousand people were killed during the ground and air assault on the city to retake control for the government. One of the rebel army officers who fled when order was restored was Captain Ismail Khan, who later emerged as the key mujahidin leader in the west of the country in the fight against the Soviet occupation.

Following the Herat uprising, the new Afghan leader Nur Mohammed Taraki made the first of 20 Afghan requests to the Soviet Union to send troops. He suggested that they be disguised as Afghan soldiers, so would appear as troops from neighbouring Soviet republics, ethnically similar to Afghans from the north. He said this was the only way to 'save the revolution'. The Soviet prime minister Alexei Kosygin declined, although he was shocked by the violent death of the Soviet advisers and their families, since he had believed that the communist regime in Kabul was popular. When Kosygin and Taraki spoke on the phone the Soviet leader asked what had happened to the thousands of Afghan soldiers trained in Moscow. Taraki said that most had become 'Muslim reactionaries', and he could now rely only on 'older secondary school pupils, other students and a few workers'.

The conversation is a window into another world, the banal rhetoric of Marxist analysis, in which a large and complex country urgently needing development was not seen as ready for the historical processes required by a real communist revolution because it did not yet have a proletariat. Taraki admitted that 'the working class in Afghanistan is very small, and it is a long affair to train them'. Once again, as so often in the past, Afghanistan found that foreign involvement in its affairs was shaped to fit a pre-determined picture drawn abroad. But direct Soviet military intervention was ruled out for now. The Afghan leader flew to Moscow to be told to his face by Kosygin: 'If our troops were introduced, the situation in your country would get worse.' Soviet deployment 'would immediately arouse the international community, and would invite sharply unfavourable many-faceted consequences'.

Nine months later Soviet forces crossed the Oxus River. What changed was a rapidly deteriorating situation. A power struggle within the Afghan government ended in a shoot-out in the presidential palace between Taraki and his prime minister, Hafizullah Amin. Taraki's retirement 'on health grounds' was then announced on Kabul radio. The truth is that he was killed, smothered by a pillow at Amin's orders. The

Soviet leader Brezhnev, now old, decrepit and apparently understanding little of what went on around him, wept when he heard the news. In Afghanistan, the new leader Amin tried to change tack, admitting government mistakes and blaming the country's problems on Taraki. In November he arranged a public reading of the names of those who had died in prison in the 18 months since the Saur revolution that had ousted Daoud. There were 12,000 names recorded, but the reading had to be halted soon after it began amid scenes of chaos and public hysteria.

Soviet suspicions that Amin wanted a 'more balanced' foreign policy – one less dependent on Moscow – were confirmed by the Pakistani president, General Zia, who later said that Amin constantly appealed to him for support; by December the appeals were 'frantic'. Amin was right to be concerned: the Soviet Union had given up on him, a politburo report describing the Afghan leader as 'an ambitious, cruel, treacherous person . . . insincere and two-faced'. Amin had spent some time in the West, and Soviet intelligence reports suggested he was a CIA stooge. The suspicion alone was a death sentence.

The Soviet Union turned instead to Babrak Karmal, one of the founders of Afghan communism in the 1960s, but now sidelined as an ambassador abroad after long-standing doctrinal and personal disagreements with the Afghan leadership. In the middle of December he flew in a Soviet plane into Bagram airbase, not far north of Kabul, expecting to mount a coup against Amin, but it did not happen, and he returned to Moscow. Karmal's non coup epitomises the confusion of the period, as the Soviet Union moved like a sleepwalker into its longest and costliest military engagement since the Second World War. No one will admit to taking the decision to invade, and in the rewriting of history that subsequently happened, those alive afterwards found it easy to blame those who were dead.

By the beginning of December the Soviet Union already had the equivalent of two battalions in Afghanistan. The largest concentration of troops was a battalion of central Asian reservists who had been moved into position to hold Bagram airbase, north of Kabul. Elite Spetznaz troops guarded key Soviet positions in Kabul itself, but they were deployed only in a defensive capacity. It is clear that the Soviet military was opposed to a larger intervention. In an eerie repeat of the suicide of the Soviet envoy Vitkevitch soon after meeting Burnes in Kabul for Christmas dinner in 1837, a key Soviet military adviser shot himself when he returned from Kabul to Moscow and realised that his political masters had now changed their minds and were intent on a major military deployment.

The Soviet military was not even consulted about the operational implications of what was being planned. On 10th December, only two weeks before the invasion, the chief of the general staff Nikolai Ogarkov was summoned by the Defence Minister Dmitri Ustinov and ordered to prepare a force up to 80,000 strong for 'a temporary introduction of Soviet troops into Afghanistan'. Ogarkov called the decision 'reckless', saying that the force would not be large enough to take the country, if that was what was wanted. He was interrupted by the defence minister: 'Are you going to teach the Politburo? Your only duty is to carry out the orders.' That evening he was summoned to Brezhnev's inner office, to meet the so-called little politburo – Defence Minister Ustinov, the long-standing foreign minister Andrei Gromyko, and the head of the KGB, Yuri Andropov.

The fingerprints of these three men are on the decision to invade, although Gromyko, who survived long enough to be able to spin his version of history, always pointed to Andropov as the key figure: he said it was Andropov's KGB reports that tipped the balance. But even Andropov did not envisage a full-scale invasion. In mid-December he sent a memo to Brezhnev saying that he thought the two battalions already there should be 'entirely sufficient for a successful operation' to install Karmal as leader.

It is certain that the whole politburo did not pre-approve the invasion. A remarkable handwritten document survives showing that there was no widespread consultation at this level. The final decision to invade was taken on 12th December, but some of the Soviet ruling body did not sign the 'order' to invade Afghanistan until the 26th, once the country had fallen. The first that Brezhnev's foreign policy adviser heard about it was on the BBC after it happened.

The main invasion began on 22nd December with the first of more than 350 flights by heavy Illyushin and Antonov transport planes, carrying paratroopers into Kabul and Bagram. Some of the troops took over the capital, while others went directly north to secure the Salang tunnel, the route through the Hindu Kush from the north for the armoured brigades that were now pouring across the Oxus River on makeshift pontoon bridges. There was little Afghan resistance amid contradictory orders as some officers believed the Russians had come to keep Amin in power. Soviet advisers had taken the precaution of removing the firing pins from the guns of as many Afghan tanks as they could get their hands on, making the excuse that they were to be replaced by 'winterised' versions. President Amin's palace guard did put up a fight but they were overwhelmed and he was shot dead by Soviet soldiers.

There was from the start a lack of clarity about the motives and aims of the military intervention, further muddied by deliberate propaganda. Broadcasts claiming to be from Kabul Radio, actually beamed from across the Soviet border while the invasion was taking place, denounced Amin as a tool of US imperialism and reported that Karmal had taken over, as if this was all an internal matter. By the time the real Kabul Radio had fallen into Karmal's hands on 27th December and broadcast a request from Afghanistan to the USSR to send 'political, moral, and economic assistance, including military aid', the invasion was over.

Karmal would later promote various versions of how he came to power. He hinted that he had been running an underground resistance movement for months, or alternatively he would say that he had been invited to take over by the Afghan politburo, who had told him that Amin was planning to flee abroad with money 'savagely plundered from our toiling people'. He began to drink heavily, was seen to shake in public, and tried unsuccessfully to resign. It was not an auspicious start to his rule.

One key reason for the invasion, in a formal statement from the Soviet defence ministry, was concern that instability would spread north across the Oxus to the predominantly Muslim republics that were then part of the Soviet Union. Apart from giving 'internationalist assistance to the friendly Afghan people', the intervention was designed 'to prevent possible anti-Afghan actions on the part of the bordering states'. There was no evidence though that the invasion was seen as having any historical inevitability. None saw it as unfinished business from the long nineteenth-century Russian push across central Asia and the Caucasus. Prince Gorchakov, the architect of Russian expansionism then, would not have understood the limited aims of the Soviet Union now. This was not an imperial grab, the long-feared move to allow Russian soldiers to 'dip their boots in the warm waters of the Arabian Gulf', rather it was portrayed as assistance to friends, as Soviet troops had deployed for example to Ethiopia and Angola.

The Soviet defence minister did not expect to have troops in Afghanistan by the following winter, believing that the mujahidin would throw down their weapons when faced by the Soviet army, although he was warned by the Soviet general staff that it was more likely that the rebellion would worsen. The troops were ordered to remain in their garrisons as much as possible, and not become involved in combat. Their stated aim was to help the local population with aid.

Decision-making machinery in the West was closed for Christmas when the invasion happened, and the US had any-way taken its eye off Afghanistan that year, even after the murder of its ambassador, who had been caught up in the political intrigue in Kabul in February. The Soviet invasion came out of the blue for Washington, and did not fit the pattern of behaviour they had come to expect from Moscow. Spy planes had seen the troops gathering on the border, but the force was clearly not big enough for a full-scale invasion. Vice-President Walter Mondale said 'What unnerved everyone was the suspicion that Brezhnev's inner circle might not be rational.'

US military and diplomatic attention had been focused instead on Afghanistan's western neighbour Iran, after the US-backed regime there had been ousted by the Ayatollah Khomeini's Islamic revolution. In November 1979 warships were sent to the Gulf as the long ordeal began for US diplomats besieged in their Tehran embassy by student zealots. And although President Carter did speak out against the Afghan invasion – in a protest that he called the strongest of his presidency – promising to 'make Soviet involvement as costly as possible', early measures fell short of arming the mujahidin. There was to be a boycott of the 1980 Moscow Olympics, a cut in grain sales to the USSR and some delay in signing a nuclear arms reduction deal.

Carter did not like secret wars, and had tried to bring the CIA into line over the funding of guerrillas in Central America. In early 1980, however, he changed his mind and allowed covert operations to be funded for Afghanistan, to be launched from Pakistan, and even though they were at a very low level at first, this was a significant policy reversal.

The other main backers of the mujahidin made uncomfortable bedfellows for the US. China had long had a strategic alliance with Pakistan, and the countries shared significant defence technology, naturally moving into joint support of the mujahidin. The new Islamic government in Iran opposed the Soviet invasion too. Afghanistan had traditionally been seen as Persia's backyard. It was no coincidence that the first major uprising against the communists, in the spring of 1979, well before the full-scale Soviet invasion, broke out in Herat, very close to the Iranian border. About a quarter of the refugees that had fled from Afghanistan went west to Iran, and Tehran allied itself particularly with guerrilla groups based in Afghanistan's Shia minority.

In Kabul, Karmal's new government tried to win back support with a number of radical shifts in policy: scrapping the red flag and restoring the three-coloured Afghan flag, funding the building of 2000 mosques, and granting state salaries to 16,000 Muslim leaders. The measures resembled the desperate attempts by Amanullah to save his reform programme in the 1920s, faced by an Islamist backlash, and they were as useless.

The 'official mullahs' were targeted by the mujahidin, and by the end of February there were mass uprisings in Kabul, initially led by students but then spreading city-wide. Civil servants defected en masse and normal government ceased to function, as the regime gave up any pretence of being part of an idealistic revolutionary movement. Remaining discipline in the ruling elite was undermined by Soviet aid and the easy availability of consumer goods. In April 1980 President Karmal complained of 'lawlessness, disobedience, embezzlement, bureaucracy, pilferage of public property, chauvinism and so forth', but given that his mistress was the education minister, and his half-brother also had a post in the administration, he was hardly practising what he preached.

The communist reign of terror against dissidents continued. A Soviet observer said Kabul justice reminded him of Stalinist excesses: it 'practically repeated ours, point by point, of the 1937-38 years'. A Kabul academic, Mohammed Hassan Kakar, who was held in Pul-e-Charki jail for five years, calculated that 150,000 people were arrested, and 50,000 of them executed there.

But nobody, least of all Russia, really expected the ragtag, pyjama-clad mujahidin to pose much of a threat. Violence between different communist factions killed more people than the mujahidin at the beginning, and for some years most of the rebels were equipped only with copies of British-era Lee Enfield rifles, not the AK-47 assault weapons that were later supplied in huge numbers. Funding included collections in the Gulf States, but it was still small, and US support in the first two years totalled less than ten million dollars.

The mujahidin nevertheless made progress as initially Soviet forces rejected Karmal's appeals to take them on; that was not their mission, despite extreme provocation, including a revolt in January 1980 in Kandahar, the main city in the southern Pashtun heartland, when Soviet citizens and troops were literally hacked to pieces. But at the beginning of March, as disorder spread, new orders arrived from Moscow: 'Begin active operations for destruction of the formations of the armed opposition.' The Soviet military had been drawn against its better judgement into an Afghan civil war.

Once it became clear that the mujahidin were not going to throw down their weapons, there was a fundamental shift in Soviet military policy. Far from being able to begin a withdrawal, the Soviet Union changed the make-up of its forces in Afghanistan, replacing reservists with regular troops, and dug in for the long haul. The Limited Contingent, as the invasion force had been called, had no training for counter-insurgency warfare, and was equipped with heavy armoured vehicles designed for a different task.

The Soviet army began operations against Hekmatyar's forces in the east in March, just as the melting snows of the Suleiman Mountains opened the mule tracks for the mujahidin.

10

Charlie Horse

'Well if that's your only problem, I can have my Israeli
friends put Swastikas on the guns.'
Congressman Charlie Wilson's response when the CIA told
him they could not be seen openly to source weapons for
Afghanistan from Israel

If it was an unpromising start for the Soviet side, in contrast
the situation could not have been more favourable for the
mujahidin. They had textbook conditions to mount an
insurgency: support in the Afghan villages, a safe haven across
the mountains with access by narrow tracks that suited them
but were impassable for the Soviet forces, and a ready supply
of young men willing to die. Death in this holy cause was
considered an honour, followed by swift burial in the soil of
Afghanistan and a short cut to paradise as a *shaheed,* a martyr –
a narrowly focused aspiration for a generation, with an
inevitably degrading impact on other cultural values.

The mujahidin had a unique, mad courage: some were able
to travel wounded for days without complaint, and a reporter
saw a man put his hand into a fire when his honour was
challenged, and not withdraw it until the fat from his flesh was
dripping into the flames. Best of all for their cause, Afghans,

and Pashtuns in particular, never forgot an insult, but would seek *badal*, revenge, through the generations.

In a system of recruitment based on patronage that would have been recognised by the Durrani nobles of the eighteenth century, clans would provide men for the war effort. The fighters were not paid, but would spend up to four months in the field, before being replaced by a brother or cousin and returning to melt into the civilian population until called on again. In the beginning there were dozens of different mujahidin groups, although the most successful leaders were the ones who knew how to attract funding, and those like Hekmatyar who were most ruthless.

From the start he imposed on the refugee camps in the frontier region the kind of Afghan society he wanted to see. Intellectuals, progressive reformers and women's leaders were murdered or jailed, and survival was impossible outside the mujahidin cause. To concentrate the military effort, Pakistan limited the number of insurgent groups to seven, and ration cards were issued only to those who belonged to one of the seven, so the refugees were radicalised and recruited for the war whether they liked it or not.

There was no room for free thought in this wartime economy. Many children, particularly orphans, went to the Saudi-financed madrassas, now well established in the frontier region as well as elsewhere in Pakistan, which preached an unreconstructed Wahhabi view of Islam similar to that of the Hindustani Fanatics at the centre of Britain's frontier war in 1897, and provided the ideological bedrock for those who would ultimately create the Taliban.

Hekmatyar continued to polarise opinion. His mujahidin comrades were suspicious of the personality cult that surrounded him, believing that his desire to control the camps took his focus off the fighting in Afghanistan, but he saw the big picture, encouraging the belief that Soviet forces could be beaten in Afghanistan. This was a hard argument to win as the CIA then thought that the key battleground where they could destroy communism was in central America, the backyard of the US and a region they thought they understood. CIA Director William Casey said, 'If America challenges the Soviets at every turn and ultimately defeats them in one place, that will shatter the mythology. Nicaragua is that place.' No CIA operatives spoke Pashtu; the conflict in the Hindu Kush seemed remote.

It was not until 1982 that Congressman Charlie Wilson made his first trip to the region, intrigued by reports he heard of the mountain warfare against a communist invader. Moved by the conditions he saw in a hospital for wounded fighters on the frontier, he immediately donated a pint of blood and always did the same when he visited afterwards. The trip changed Wilson's life and would transform the war. Until then the CIA had been cautious, following the advice of one of its officers who had spent three years in Kabul before the war: 'Don't put white men in charge. Don't give the Afghans a lot of money. Don't trust them. It would be like throwing money into a cesspool. All they need is a little help and the Russians will be sorry they ever went into that country.' No one in the CIA thought that the mujahidin could ever defeat the Soviet army; all they hoped for was containment.

Wilson believed the mujahidin could do much more than be 'a burr under the saddle, an extreme nuisance'. Fresh from the frontier, he met the CIA station chief in Pakistan, Howard Hart, at an absurd meeting in an inner room at the US embassy, with the *1812 Overture* playing loudly to mask their conversation from spies. Wilson came away unimpressed by Hart's lack of ambition: 'He never envisioned killing the beast.'

An instinctive cold warrior, six feet seven inches tall, and with ambitions as lofty, Wilson went back home to try and change things, playing the one game he knew really well, the political game on Capitol Hill. The mujahidin were heroes he could understand, from the same stock as the defenders of the Alamo. At last he had a cause, something to echo the work of his childhood hero Winston Churchill, who had saved *his* country from a threat others had ignored and, like Wilson, was fond of a drink. Wilson was on the defense appropriations subcommittee, responsible for funding CIA operations. When he returned from that first trip to the frontier he called to ask how much was allocated for Afghanistan. When he heard it was five million dollars, he said 'Double it'. There was no executive order, no debate in Congress. Nobody noticed.

He was on the right committees and called in favours across the Hill, securing first millions and then billions of dollars from the federal budget for the mujahidin. The humiliation of Vietnam was still fresh, and he knew the names of every one of the 167 men from his congressional district who had died there. This was payback. 'I love sticking it to the Russians. And I think most Americans do. They need to get it back, and they're getting it back.'

The aid all went through Pakistan, where the US now backed the military dictator General Zia, who liked to say that they needed to 'keep the pot boiling' in Afghanistan but not let it boil over and spread the war back into Pakistan. Zia was already hosting more than three million Afghans, the world's largest refugee population. Like the British during their century and a half of domination in this region, he did not want the Russian army on his side of the Suleiman Mountains, and they were closer now than they had ever come during the British period.

Zia did a deal with his secret service, the ISI, one of the key power-brokers in Pakistan, giving them carte blanche to run the war in Afghanistan providing they did nothing to upset his authority at home. Wilson was clever at finding new sources of non-US manufactured weapons: military aid to Afghanistan had to be deniable, so as not to provoke Moscow to retaliate elsewhere. Arms were bought with funds mainly from the US and Saudi Arabia, shipped to Karachi and driven in trucks to a nondescript unmarked distribution site amid the sprawling encampments near Rawalpindi, originally built as the main British garrison town in north-west India and now the head-quarters of the Pakistani army. The ISI insisted from the start on direct control of the weapons supply.

The system could not have been better designed to

encourage corruption: the CIA later calculated that 20 per cent of the arms and funds destined for Afghanistan went astray. And apart from the leaks in Pakistan, the need for US deniability led to shady deals with suppliers. On his trip to Peshawar with Snowflake in 1984, Wilson was testing the ground for a promising new source of weapons – guns seized by Israel from the Palestinians. The guns were of Soviet origin or design, and so not traceable to the US or Israel. Wilson was one of Israel's strongest advocates in the US, and he knew that on the face of it taking arms from the Israelis to fight an Islamic jihad in Afghanistan was unthinkable.

He wanted to short-circuit objections from both the CIA and Pakistan by asking Hekmatyar directly if he should buy them. The reply came swiftly back, delivered without expression: 'We take Russian weapons from dead Russians to use against them – I don't see why we can't take them from the Israelis. Allah has many mysterious ways of providing for his faithful.' That evening Wilson and Snowflake hosted all seven leaders of the different mujahidin groups, and late that night one of them returned to present him with a captured Russian AK-47. He was their man.

Britain's answer to the hard-drinking, womanising Texan Charlie Wilson came from a rather different background. Robert Cecil, Viscount Cranborne, from one of the country's grandest families, had recently been elected a Tory MP. Like Wilson he believed that Afghanistan represented a unique opportunity to challenge communism, against the prevailing wisdom at the time across the British political establishment. After Cranborne spoke out strongly against the invasion at a meeting in London, the Soviet ambassador grabbed him by the arm on the way out, and said, 'Why not let us do it? We will win and then you will look silly.' At an Oxford seminar in early 1980 Cranborne urged the strongest possible response to the Soviet invasion and was ignored for the rest of the day.

But he had seen CIA intelligence demonstrating the weakness of the Soviet economy, and became part of a drive to shift domestic opinion, turning the Afghan struggle into a fashionable cause, aided by the visceral anti-communist instincts of the then newly elected prime minister Margaret Thatcher. Tory ministers began to idealise the mujahidin as noble warriors – not terrorists but freedom fighters – their struggle was favourably compared to that of the French resistance in the Second World War. Neither US nor British backers of the mujahidin knew what problems they were storing up when they funded Islamic fundamentalism.

Although Britain could never match US funding, it punched above its weight in other ways. British soldiers and spies were not prohibited from entering Afghanistan, as US citizens were, and they collected intelligence as well as supplying high-technology equipment. They would also take direct action. The CIA operative who ran the war, Gust Avrakotos, said the Brits had 'a willingness to do jobs that I could not touch. They basically took care of the "How to Kill People Department".' At a time when the CIA was facing strong criticism for providing an 'assassination manual' to gangs in Nicaragua, this British support filled a useful gap.

Cranborne provided another key component in the war effort, by focusing on humanitarian aid. He had read his Chairman Mao. The Chinese leader had compared the civilian population around insurgents with the water that fish need to swim in. The refugee outflow to Pakistan was draining the pond, so if Cranborne could get food and money in, Afghans would be more likely to stay in their villages, providing the support the mujahidin needed to operate.

Soviet military planners had read Mao too, and from early on in the war the most intense application of military violence was applied to a wide strip of territory in the east of Afghanistan, in an attempt to create a *cordon sanitaire,* depriving the fish of water, and so making the mujahidin vulnerable when they moved supplies. This involved frequent armoured assaults on the ground, as well as bombing raids by fixed-wing planes and heavy use of Hind helicopter gunships – the Soviets' most feared weapon. But although Soviet tactics developed as the war progressed, they never had enough men or the right equipment to dominate the ground. Their strength was never more than about 100,000, one fifth of the US forces at the height of the war in Vietnam, in a country that was five times the size.

Soviet equipment was unsuited to the terrain. Tanks were not easily manoeuvrable in the mountains, and lightly armoured troop-carrying vehicles were vulnerable to attack. Infantry found their heavy flak jackets slowed them down, especially when operating at high altitude, while 1950s-style backpacks were cumbersome. Soviet field uniforms did not provide good camouflage, and were restrictive and uncomfortable to wear, while their boots were noisy and not suitable for the mountains – commanders would issue trainers when they could get hold of them. As the mujahidin became better equipped when US funding began to flow on a large scale, Russian soldiers would try to steal their sleeping bags, since Soviet-issue cotton sleeping bags became heavy and useless when wet. Soviet army food came dried, and was hard to cook hygienically, while the tins reflected sunlight and gave away their positions.

It was not surprising that morale was low, and Soviet soldiers would sell their weapons and other kit in exchange for drugs and even food. An Estonian conscript remembered, 'Often regular Afghan army soldiers exchanged their Russian arms for food and drink from peasants. So we did the same thing, because in the chaos of war to explain the loss of a weapon is easy. We used to buy all kinds of food and drink and even bread in exchange for our weapons.' The conflict was violent and brutalising both for the Afghans and the Soviet conscript army. Travellers found carrying large amounts of money at Russian checkpoints were 'sent to Kabul', meaning taken round the back and shot so they could be robbed. A Russian ex-soldier told of an incident in his unit that led to a court martial:

One night, after drinking a lot of home-brewed beer, they decided that they wanted some hash and some lamb, so they set out for a neighbouring *kishlak* [village]. They ran into an old man on the way there, and they were so drunk that they struck the old man on the head so hard that a piece of the rifle's stock fell off . . . Soon they reached the *kishlak* and entered a house. There was a woman inside. They started raping her, and she started screaming. When her sister darted out of the house, there was nothing left for the fellows to do but to stab both of them. Then they entered the house next door. There were children inside, and the soldiers opened fire on them with their AKs. They shot all of them but one who managed to escape . . . then the soldiers took a whole sack of hashish and a lamb and returned to their unit.

They were caught after the boy who escaped reported the incident and identified them. At his trial the soldier turned to his accusing officer and said

'When I was knocking off twenty people at a time on your orders, you said, "Well done! Here's a man with excellent results in combat. Put his name on the board of honour!" But when I got hungry – all right, I did get plastered, I was drunk then – and went to get a lamb because there was no food, I killed the same people that I always killed. This time, however, it wasn't on your orders. So now you've decided to try me?'

The soldier remembered his commander saying, 'Here's a case of three fools who got caught. Do whatever you want, but don't get caught.'

The Afghan army was an unreliable ally. It faced constant defections from the start as not only individuals and units but whole divisions went over to the mujahidin, taking their personal kit and rifles as well as tanks and armoured vehicles. When units were ordered to go on operations, there was always the risk that they might defect. Ordinary logistical operations like the replenishment of ammunition had to be calculated against the likelihood of defection, while units left without ammunition were obviously useless if attacked. Conscripts were often recruited by force, with the inducement of shorter military service for those who signed up voluntarily and the threat of long jail terms for desertion. Some were signed up by deception. New university students without party membership cards were told there was no place for them in Kabul, and they would have to go to college in Charikar, not far north of the capital. When they arrived they found no college, only a military training ground. They had no choice but to sign up, and in return they would be promised a degree. One student conned in this way remembered 'the next day everybody started deserting'. Officers were rushed into the front line after just three months training.

Despite this, the Afghan armed forces did much better than predicted by many Western analysts. Their commanders competed with the mujahidin for regional support and respect, and the effective ones who emerged, like General Abdul Rashid Dostam in the north, earned loyalty similar to that given to mujahidin commanders by their fighters. However, in a dynamic that would have been recognised by rulers right back to Shah Shuja, who tried and failed to hold onto his throne in 1809, commanders waited to see which way the wind was blowing. Units would defect to the mujahidin and then sometimes return to the Afghan army, as a classic Afghan struggle for power developed under the surface of the Soviet war.

Both the Soviet army and its Afghan allies were assisted by tactical weakness and division among the mujahidin. The downside of the regional loyalty that gave the mujahidin much of their strength was the unwillingness of fighters to move out of their area, or cooperate with other commanders. Mohammed Yousaf, who led the Afghan desk of Pakistan's ISI for much of the war, became increasingly frustrated by the tendency of the mujahidin to wage heroic and preferably noisy warfare, rather than utilising the advantages of stealth and subterfuge. Gains would frequently be squandered as the mujahidin did not consolidate their victories, but grabbed what they could before running for the hills, tactics condemned by the Pakistani spy chief as 'typical tribal fighting for immediate tangible gains, localised in area, and with no higher strategic objective'.

In one incident in 1984, Yousaf, aiming to destroy the Soviet oil pipeline which ran south from the Hindu Kush delivering fuel to Bagram airbase, suggested a silent night raid to set explosive charges, and even proved it could be done on an exercise in Pakistan. But the mujahidin insisted instead that they should carry out a full-scale assault, capturing guard posts, and of course seizing what booty they could find, before finally laying a charge on the pipeline. A Pakistani plan to drive trucks loaded with explosives into the Salang tunnel, the crucial Soviet supply route through the Hindu Kush, was rejected as not being heroic enough. Worst of all from the ISI point of view, the mujahidin in the east refused to ferry supplies in to Ahmed Shah Massud during the most determined Soviet attempt to take the Panjshir valley in 1984 – their seventh. It was a bloody encounter for both sides, with one Soviet battalion losing half its troops.

What Yousaf missed in his frustration was that the success of the mujahidin against the Soviet occupation was partly explained by their disunity. They had fierce local loyalty, were achieving significant successes in a guerrilla war, and, unusually for such a conflict, inflicting more casualties than they were taking. Even if conventional forces lose guerrilla wars, as they usually do, they tend to inflict far higher casualties than they suffer themselves.

By 1985, when Mikhail Gorbachev took over in the Kremlin, none of the three forces at play in Afghanistan looked as if it had the potential to be militarily decisive. The Soviet army was big enough to take the punishment; the Afghan communist forces were improving but believed not to be strong enough to fight alone; and the mujahidin had made the country ungovernable without having the capacity to take it for themselves. The deaths of two Soviet leaders in quick succession, Andropov and Chernenko, after the long illness and death of

Brezhnev, meant that the USSR's Afghan policy had been drifting for several years. Gorbachev ordered an increase in troop numbers, and intensified the conflict with the aim of winning or pulling out if the surge failed. But 1985 was also the year that the military balance changed against the Soviet Union, as the mujahidin took delivery of their first Stinger missiles.

Ever since becoming involved in the Afghan cause, Charlie Wilson had been looking for a weapon to bring down Soviet helicopters. As early as November 1982, on a trip to Israel, he tried to commission a design for an anti-aircraft weapon that could be carried on the backs of mules. The pursuit of the weapon was such an obsession for him that the CIA code word for this project was *Charlie Horse*. Wilson went ahead with the trip to Israel although news that he was facing charges of taking cocaine in a jacuzzi in Las Vegas full of showgirls had just broken in the US press. (Wilson would later say, 'The Feds spent a million bucks trying to figure out whether, when those fingernails passed under my nose, did I inhale or exhale – and I ain't telling.') His escort in Israel, and then on to Egypt, was an American girl who specialised in belly dancing. She put on a private performance for the Egyptian defence minister, but it did not result in the anti-aircraft weapon Wilson sought.

The following year, Wilson almost missed a flight he had arranged to take key members of the House of Representatives appropriations committee to Pakistan. The police believed he had been drinking and driving, and had left the scene of a car crash. He succeeded in escaping the cordon around his apartment, hungover and unshaven, only when an official government car arrived to take him to the airport. But the Texas-trash lifestyle did not damage his ability to make the money flow into Afghanistan – in 1984 it topped $100 million a year, the following year it was three times that figure, and it kept rising until it was around three quarters of the CIA's budget. Total US spending on the mujahidin by the end was three billion dollars; $600 million of that went to Hekmatyar. And the US funds were matched dollar for dollar by Saudi Arabia.

More than a third of the money went to China to buy AK-47 assault rifles, now the standard weapon of the mujahidin, and the CIA were introducing new weapons into the battlefield every three months, including two-way radios, an early GPS system and booby-traps, like a vacuum flask that exploded if you poured water into it. Moving all this materiel across the frontier was a huge job in itself, and the increasing intensity of the war led to a problem that had been familiar to the British army in Afghanistan in the nineteenth century – a shortage of pack animals. Mules imported from Brazil could not take the climate, while Egyptian mules were ensnared by vaccination and health issues. In the end Tennessee mules proved the best option, although donors were shocked by the stories that filtered back of the mujahidin eating and having sex with them.

By 1986, the CIA operation in Peshawar was headed by a larger-than-life character called Milt Bearden. There was little pretence at cover. Bearden was happy to meet journalists in the American Club in Peshawar and talk about 'my war'. And it felt as if the tide was turning when a lucky rocket destroyed the Soviet ammunition dump in Kabul. The mujahidin were making better use of booby traps and had improved their training, and their morale went up when a certain Engineer Ghaffar shot down three Hinds on his first outing with the lightweight shoulder-launched Stinger missile. The weapon Wilson had sought for so long was finally available: Charlie Horse had ridden into the war. Two hundred Soviet aircraft would be lost to Stingers in its first year of use. Soviet ground troops began to refer to Hind helicopter pilots contemptuously as 'cosmonauts', as they took to flying high to keep out of range.

Soviet forces did make some significant advances, taking back Khost on the Pakistani border with major mujahidin casualties. Elite Spetznaz troops were employed as ordinary infantry for this operation, but this was fighting of an intensity that Gorbachev knew he could not sustain against an enemy that was well motivated, and now well funded, armed and trained as well. If the Soviets had retained air supremacy,

Gorbachev's troop surge might have been decisive, but he now had other priorities. He believed that his project to reconstruct the Soviet state, perestroika, was threatened by Afghanistan.

Gorbachev wanted new leadership in Kabul, and in May 1986 Karmal was replaced by Najibullah, the head of the feared KHAD secret police, nicknamed 'the bull'. He was a former boxer who had personally killed political prisoners by stamping on them – not an obvious appointment if Gorbachev wanted a peacemaker. At his first attempt to reach out, launching a national reconciliation commission, he appealed for talks with the mujahidin as instructed by the Kremlin. But his invitation was hardly compelling as he called them 'traitors and filthy vultures . . . in the service of sworn enemies of our people; reactionary imperialists and neo-colonialists'.

Najibullah tried to court popularity and change his ways. He had previously used the shortened version of his name, Najib, in public, but now preferred the full version as it sounded more Islamic. And to try and pretend Afghanistan was not a one-party state, he carried out a kind of reverse rigging of the polls in elections for a new parliament to ensure that the opposition won seats. But they would not take up the seats allocated to them. The pretence that his own party was a functioning organisation did not deceive Moscow, now that Marxist rhetoric had been replaced by the honesty of the Gorbachev years. A political analyst reported to the Soviet politburo that the Afghan communist party was not a party of members, but of membership cards: 'a circulatory system without blood'.

At a politburo meeting in 1987 Gorbachev laid out the stark choices available to the Soviet Union. He said that the only way to win the war would be to double the number of Soviet troops in Afghanistan, but that would wreck the rest of the reform programme he had introduced. His foreign minister Eduard Shevardnadze took the US secretary of state George Schultz aside during a session of the Afghan peace process that was rumbling on in Geneva, and said that the Soviet Union wanted a way out. The mujahidin continued to argue, refusing to talk to each other or present a united position at the peace talks, but the Soviet signal was heard in Washington, and by February 1988 agreement had been reached for Soviet troops to leave Afghanistan within twelve months.

The last Soviet soldier to leave Afghanistan was General Boris Gromov, the commander of the 40th Army. He was a stout short man, of Napoleonic demeanour with light-coloured eyes, who smoked long Astor cigarettes, with a gold band round the filter, 'more the kind that women liked', according to a Soviet journalist, Artyom Borovik. In an unusually frank discussion with Borovik, days before the end, Gromov criticised the Soviet high command for the defeat. The overall commander of the region, General V.I. Varennikov, was a living link with another kind of war. He had been an infantry officer at Stalingrad, and had gone onto the liberation of Berlin in 1945. But Gromov said the old man had not been flexible enough for Afghanistan, and had never known how to confront the mujahidin. 'If it hadn't been for him our troops would have caused five times more trouble than they have.'

The war had a savage end in late January 1989, just as the snow began to melt. To clear a route for the retreat from Kabul north through the Hindu Kush, a whole Soviet division fired a concentrated barrage onto the mountain paths on either side of the road, using mortars to try and start avalanches and block tracks. Fighters and bombers streaked overhead. Borovik said, 'The ground was torn up and shaking. The cliffs were crumbling.' Thousands of men, women and children streamed onto the main road in terror. Massud later said it was one of the war's most brutal operations. Borovik could not report the story at the time as he was working under censorship. His political supervisor in Kabul asked him what he knew, and even before he could answer he was told, 'Even if you do know something, you have forgotten it already. Right?'

Soviet control of Afghanistan was not all about military

power. In its early years Afghanistan's industrial capacity went up by 50 per cent, as new factories were opened and gas fields exploited. There was a new textile mill in Kandahar, a new bridge across the Oxus, and work had begun on a tramline in Kabul. Trade with other countries, including those outside the Soviet bloc, increased. The military effort was accompanied by a major aid push too, with volunteer teachers working across the country.

But the war devastated the countryside. Between them, the mujahidin and Soviet forces destroyed 1814 schools, 31 hospitals, 11 health centres, and tore up 14,000 kilometres of phone cable. Afghanistan began its descent into pre-industrial squalor. Around 1.5 million people died. Atrocities against civilians were committed not only by the Soviet side. The mujahidin left car bombs in Kabul that killed civilians and burnt down schools a decade before the Taliban came on the scene.

US funding of the Afghan jihad was aimed at the heart of Soviet communism but had an unintended effect that analysts later came to call Islamic blowback – creating Islamic warriors who turned on the society that had trained and financed them. American analysts were robust in defending their priorities. The former national security adviser Zbigniew Brzezinski said 'What was more important in the world view of history? . . . A few stirred-up Muslims or the liberation of Central Europe and the end of the Cold War?'

After the defeat of Soviet forces in Afghanistan the 'few stirred-up Muslims' had nowhere else to go – a network of jihadis without a jihad. The international appeal of the Afghan war for Islamists began in 1984, with a book by a warrior priest, Sheikh Abdullah Azzam, called *In Defence of Muslim lands*. Although of Palestinian origin, Azzam maintained that Afghanistan was *the* principal Islamist cause in the world, even more important than Palestine, and fighting in the jihad there was obligatory for every Muslim. He travelled constantly, telling tales of an heroic dream world, where the bodies of dead mujahidin did not decay but smelt sweetly where they fell.

It was after reading this book that Osama bin Laden was inspired to move to Peshawar, and offer travel and living expenses for every jihadi. Reporters travelling in Afghanistan learnt to be wary of 'Arab-Afghans', as the new jihadis came to be called, although many were not Arabs but Chechens, Chinese or Indonesian; and some were European. They would break cameras or attempt forcible conversions. This was the beginning of the network that became al-Qaeda.

Islamist radicalisation went both ways – out into the world and deep into Afghan society. But like an ocean liner the US sailed serenely on, not hearing the distant muffled warning bell of an Islamist threat sounding in the darkness. There was no attempt to factor the corrupting effect of the dollars that sloshed their way through the North-West Frontier, nor the politics of those who had been financed and trained, although the mujahidin made no secret of the kind of society they would like to see. Many were fighting to uphold a feudal way of life and all wanted to re-establish the traditional subservient status of Afghan women. Their leaders had formed an Islamist underground in Afghanistan ten years before the arrival of the Soviet army; and insurgents like Massud, later darling of the foreign press corps, had fought, beginning with that first failed uprising in 1975, against the 'godless communism' of the mild Western-leaning reforms of President Daoud, which included some political representation for women. Western foreign policy, nudged along by the righteous fervour of men like Charlie Wilson, had ignored all this, because Afghanistan was 'the only place in the world where the forces of freedom are actually fighting and killing Russians'.

By the late 1980s it looked as if it had worked. A generation of politicians brought up in the certainties of the cold war was mesmerised as the Berlin Wall came down, Gorbachev transformed the landscape, and after half a century of preparing for war with Russia over Europe, it looked as if it was not going to happen. Reports by the few Afghan and Islamic experts in Western foreign ministries about what this might mean for Afghanistan lay unread.

By now CIA Director William Casey was playing a tape code-named 'Mohammed the conqueror' on his car radio on the way to work. It recorded three hits against Soviet helicopters by a lone mujahidin fighter on a mountaintop; the third had been full of elite *Spetznaz* troops sent specifically to deal with him. And that was even before Stinger missiles: he had been armed with a DshK anti-aircraft gun carried up the mountain on the back of a mule. When people asked how the war was being won, the Pakistani leader General Zia would say, 'Charlie did it.'

After years of travelling to the region with different girls, Charlie Wilson had decided that one of them, a former Miss World contestant he called 'Sweetums', was his one true love, and he planned an extravagant wedding in the Khyber Pass, accompanied by mujahidin commanders, the Egyptian defence minister, and even his best Israeli contact, to be seated anonymously in the VIP stand. But shortly before the nuptials were due to take place, Wilson visited California as guest of honour at the annual Mule Day parade, to honour the role of Tennessee mules in the liberation of Afghanistan. When Sweetums called Charlie's hotel room early in the morning, it was Snowflake who picked up the phone. The wedding plans were cancelled.

'Fighting to the last Afghan'

'We prefer involvement in internal war rather than occupation by foreigners and foreign troops.'

Gulbuddin Hekmatyar

The torture and murder of thirty of Ahmed Shah Massud's commanders in July 1989, ambushed on their way from a meeting with Hekmatyar, shocked even seasoned Afghan observers. The way the freelance cameraman Rory Peck, who was travelling through the region, heard the story was that as the men were overwhelmed, only one was killed instantly. The others were cut up while still alive by their captors, who 'indulged in an orgy of blood letting, gouging the eyes out of one, slitting the nostrils of another, cutting the ears, lips, and tongue off a third, before riddling the lot of them with bullets'. Peck noted in his diary, 'Afghans can be extraordinarily cruel.' The victims were not expecting an attack in a mujahidin-controlled area, where they had been invited to discuss tactics for a planned joint assault on the Afghan communists in the northern town of Kunduz.

The killers must have been sent by Hekmatyar, who had called the meeting. It was an outrage that broke every rule of behaviour in any theatre of war, particularly in Afghanistan where the code of conduct for safe passage and hospitality was of such importance. In revenge, Massud seized a couple of local commanders associated with Hekmatyar and hanged them in public – not giving them the dignity of a soldier's death by firing squad.

This incident, six months after the last Soviet soldier left Afghanistan, showed in stark terms the main reason why the mujahidin had not yet marched in triumph into Kabul. If anything, they were now in a worse military position than they had been when Soviet forces were in the country. Predictions that Najibullah's communist-backed Kabul regime would collapse had proved wide of the mark. He still held the key airports and towns, and his supply routes were intact. The disunity of the mujahidin had boosted the morale of his forces, and in March, only a month after the Soviet forces left, the mujahidin suffered a catastrophic reversal when they failed to take the eastern town of Jalalabad.

The Jalalabad campaign had posed the hardest question for any guerrilla force – when to move onto the offensive and hold ground. If it was a tough call for a single commander, it was impossible for the Afghan mujahidin, who were not only disunited but fighting each other. The cautious approach – continuing to harass supply routes, grinding down the will of the Kabul government – was preferred by many commanders, but as so often in Afghanistan, the decision was taken outside the country.

Pakistan had a new prime minister, Benazir Bhutto. Later she would be assassinated, running for office again, but in 1989, her government financed and backed the largest single offensive by the fundamentalist mujahidin during the 13-year campaign against Soviet-backed government in Afghanistan: the assault on Jalalabad. The new head of the ISI, General Hamid Gul, believed it would deliver the swift collapse of the Kabul government expected by the world. The plans for the Jalalabad assault were made by Gul with US support, but there was little input from mujahidin leaders.

The spring is the most beautiful time of year in the wedge of land in the east, that lies lower than the high Kabul plain, like a footstep into Afghanistan. From the north the Kunar River, flanked by mountains rising in impossible folds, brings its waters down to join those of the Kabul River with all the urgency of a journey that has begun almost in the Himalayas. Despite years of intense Soviet bombardment, the mujahidin retained control here, mainly because Pakistan held the strategic high ground. The Pakistani spymaster Mohammed Yousaf saw why the border ran where it did. 'All the dominating heights belonged to Pakistan, and we had good reason to thank the colonial administrator, Durand, who had so long ago drawn his line with such tactical insight.'

To the south of Jalalabad on the far side of a plain noted as 'beautiful flat fighting ground' by Durand himself as he passed this way almost 100 years before, lies the barrier of the Safed Koh – the White Mountain range. Nearer Jalalabad are low hills, just beginning to show the new green fuzz of spring in March 1989. By the time the battle for the city was over, four months later, the scattered red of wild poppies among the green growth had come and gone.

The mujahidin assault began in waves down the Kunar valley, and along the straight road from the border at the Khyber Pass. Within a day, they controlled the airport to the east of the city. It was to be their only significant advance during the long weeks of fighting to come; they had signalled their intentions too clearly to the forces defending Jalalabad, who were well dug in. Eight different mujahidin leaders commanded separate parts of the assault, and they refused to obey Pakistan's orders to control all the access roads and mount diversionary tactics elsewhere in the country, so Najibullah was able to re-supply the defenders throughout.

A Russian journalist who spent a few days there said it was 'like Stalingrad', with very high civilian casualties from the frequent rocket attacks by both sides, and close-quarters fighting. With no overall mujahidin tactical direction, it soon became a lethal daily slog. Thousands of mujahidin died, and some units lost more men in this one engagement than in the whole of the war up to then, defeated by a determined conventional force on the only occasion they attempted an all-out assault using conventional tactics. Retreating, the mujahidin lost an important garrison at Samarkhel.

Jalalabad was the biggest set-piece battle since the Soviet invasion, and the only significant battle involving tanks on both sides. It was also the only time that Osama bin Laden is known to have led his Arab fighters directly into battle in Afghanistan, other than in skirmishes around the cave complex at Tora Bora, on the other side of that 'beautiful flat fighting ground', the plain to the south of Jalalabad. Eighty Arab-Afghans died, and bin Laden had a narrow escape, fleeing just ahead of a government assault, after the location of his field headquarters was revealed by an informer. Bin Laden was then based at Haddah, the location of one of the most effective of the mullahs who had incited the uprising against British control of the frontier in 1897.

By now the Afghan mujahidin had learnt to be cautious of the Arab-Afghans, who were dangerous travelling companions as they invited martyrdom, sleeping in white tents with lights on at night, to make it more likely that they would be bombed. In another similarity with the *ghazis* who emerged in the nineteenth century, they would write elaborate letters to the families of comrades who were killed, celebrating the news. The Afghan mujahidin also learnt to hide prisoners, because the Arab-Afghans would kill them immediately.

Victory at Jalalabad strengthened Najibullah's hand: he had governed with a measure of consent, particularly in the cities, where the prospect of mujahidin rule brought fear to many people. A woman in Kabul said, 'All I knew of the Russians in those days was that we had a lot of nice, cheap things in the shops which came from Russia. I could not help thinking at that time that a people who made useful things which were so inexpensive for us must be nice too.' Najibullah's troops were more confident and better organised, and they knew they were fighting for their lives now that Soviet forces had gone. Hundreds of weapons were handed out to Kabul residents to defend themselves, and the government even recruited a women's militia, giving training, arms and uniforms to the first thousand who answered the call.

Among them was a bank clerk called Ramia, who had no doubts about the cause as she excitedly donned military uniform, 'The Muslim rebels slit my husband's throat with a knife and they kidnapped my 17-year-old son. Now at last I have found a way to take my revenge.' Another woman swapping her civilian clothes for the brown woollen Soviet-made uniform, spoke, as if the incident had been yesterday, of the example of Malalai, the heroine killed in the Afghan victory against Britain at the battle of Maiwand, 110 years before. To her the mujahidin were just another alien force, as much a foreign invader as the British or Russians, to be combated by all patriotic Afghans.

The presence of thousands of Soviet women, who had done many different jobs during the years of occupation, had had a profound impact. Kabul women had seen them working alongside men as helicopter pilots, doctors, engineers, and other trades. And as well as job opportunities, some women now had expectations about cosmetics and clothing that they were prepared to die to defend. Many of the women joining up to fight feared the mujahidin would impose a strict clothing code if they came to power, including the burqa, and would limit their freedom in other ways. Repression of women in Afghanistan did not begin with the Taliban. Women's freedoms were already being curtailed in areas taken from Soviet-backed forces by the mujahidin.

There was simmering discontent too about women's rights across the border in the refugee camps around Peshawar, and against the same threat – Islamic fundamentalism. For most people the aim of the war against the communists had been to restore freedom to Afghanistan, not to empower the fundamentalists. But the way the war had been financed and run had empowered the mujahidin view of Afghan society, and discouraged political thought outside narrow Islamism. Despite the defeat at Jalalabad, mujahidin leaders believed that they would now win. They had seen off the Red Army, and as victory felt closer, the brutal influence of fundamentalists became tighter in the refugee camps, the crucible of the new Afghanistan.

Women in the camps had been warned for several years about wearing cosmetics, tight-fitting clothes, or going out without being escorted by a male member of their family – Pashtun village values imposed on all refugees. Now there were stricter orders, instructing women not to 'walk down the middle of the road', or even 'walk with pride'.

Tajwar Kakar, a schoolteacher who had been tortured and held in a Soviet jail in Kabul for a year, received regular death threats for teaching girls in the camps that it was not compulsory to wear the burqa. 'We women have fought hard for the freedom of our people and our nation. We have been imprisoned and tortured. Some of us have been killed. And we have been the shield for the men who carried on the jihad. The women helped fight the jihad, and now they don't care about us.'

Mujahidin threats against those who promoted women's rights were real. In 1987 Hekmatyar's Islamist gunmen had shot dead Meena Keshwar Kamal, the founder of the women's group RAWA. Other activists were beaten and jailed in the refugee camps. And Hekmatyar did not only target women. One of the main spokesmen of the mujahidin movement, Professor Bahauddin Majrooh, was shot as he came to the door of his house expecting to greet the British fund-raiser Viscount Cranborne, who was due to see him. Cranborne survived because he had been kept waiting by General Zia at an earlier meeting and when he arrived he found the urbane intellectual Majrooh, 'a whisky-loving Afghan with a good line in obscene and very unfunny anti-mullah jokes', lying dead in the street. Majrooh had organised a survey of refugees that found almost three-quarters of them wanted the king back – enough of a crime to have cost him his life. Hekmatyar's men were also blamed for the deaths of several foreign journalists.

Only a week after the ambush of Massud's commanders in

the north, Hekmatyar turned his attentions to the south, poisoning Abdul Latif, an effective mujahidin leader known as the 'lion of Kandahar'. Hekmatyar's bid for control of the opium trade spilled over into Peshawar as well, where he murdered a commander and five of his lieutenants. He helped to train Osama bin Laden's fighters, and assisted Omar Abdel-Rahman, the blind sheikh indicted for the 1993 bombing of the World Trade Center. Hekmatyar's contempt for the US was apparent as early as 1985, when he refused to shake President Reagan's hand, while 'duty' mujahidin leader in Washington – the seven leaders took it in turns, in order to keep up lobbying pressure. He went on to support Saddam Hussein in both Gulf Wars.

Yet Hekmatyar continued to receive the lion's share of US funding, despite being more of a revolutionary than the Taliban who came later. He was certainly no friend of the traditional clan-based rural hierarchy of Afghanistan. The most widely respected mujahidin leader, Sibghatullah Mujaddidi, called Hekmatyar 'a true monster and enemy of Afghanistan . . . a man no self-respecting nation should support'.

Human rights groups in the US, as well as some members of Congress, began to single out Hekmatyar as a growing problem after the Soviet pull-out. The chair of the House intelligence committee Anthony Beilenson said, 'Supplying military aid to the Afghan rebels is no longer in our interest now that the Soviets have withdrawn.' But these reservations could not overturn the effect of a decade of rhetoric that it was in the Hindu Kush that the Soviet system would be destroyed by force. It was easier for the US to keep the funds flowing than to stop them, especially as a Soviet-backed leader was still in power in Afghanistan and still getting Soviet arms and money.

Proof of continuing Soviet support came in the battle for Jalalabad, when Najibullah brought a new weapon into play with terrifying effect – the medium-range Scud missile. Four hundred were fired from Kabul onto mujahidin positions, and several fell across the line into Pakistani territory. The Soviet

Union may have withdrawn its forces, but the military establishment was powerful enough to ensure that its friends would not be let down. Soviet military aid to Afghanistan now increased to $1.5 billion dollars a year.

This funding was not consistent with the political rhetoric of Gorbachev's reformist government. At the Geneva peace talks, there were personal appeals from the Soviet foreign minister Eduard Shevardnadze to his US opposite number George Schultz for a mutual end to the funding of clients in Afghanistan. But the appearance of Soviet-financed Scud missiles on the battlefield made it easy for the US to reject Shevardnadze's appeals. The US administration would continue the conflict as long as Najibullah remained in power. When a reporter said that continuing to fund the conflict amounted to fighting to the last Afghan, he was told by a senior US intelligence official, 'The Afghans love to fight.' The official went on, 'Afghanistan is gone, but we will make the Russians pay.'

This brutal logic meant a fight to the finish, ignoring the reality on the ground that there was less effective fighting against the Kabul government during this period than there had been at any time for several years. Peter Tomsen, who arrived as the new US 'envoy to the mujahidin' six months after the Soviet withdrawal, surprised reporters with his analysis. He seemed to be unaware of the scale of the defeat at Jalalabad: 'I am confident of a military victory. The pressure is growing on Kabul, the regime's control is receding, the lines of communication are under increasing pressure and they cannot recruit troops. Time is on the resistance's side.'

The new US envoy also appeared unaware of disunity among the mujahidin, although it was now having a serious effect on the progress of the war. Conflict within mujahidin ranks led to the main commander on the crucial Kandahar front in the south even instructing his forces to hold back, leaving government forces in control, as he believed there would be chaos and clashes between rival mujahidin if they took the town.

The disjunction between reality in Afghanistan and policy in Washington meant the war would come to a much messier end than portrayed in the movie *Charlie Wilson's War,* where Tom Hanks as Wilson is shown failing to raise small amounts to build schools in Afghanistan after the Soviet pull-out. The truth is that, like a drug pusher, the system itself seemed to be addicted to sending weapons into Afghanistan. In real life Charlie Wilson's last $400 million appropriation for his free-dom fighters came as late as 1991 – a larger figure for one year after the Soviets had gone than the US had paid out in total during the first five years of the war against the Soviet invasion.

The payments continued even after Wilson went to Russia, and was impressed by talk of democracy as the country began to shake off its Soviet baggage. Andrei Kozyrev, soon to be the first foreign minister of the new non-Soviet Russia, tried to persuade Wilson to join Russia in a new common front against radical Islam. This was a similar pitch for Afghanistan against the same supposed enemy – Islamism – as the one made to Britain by General Kauffman, Russia's commander on their southern frontier in 1875. On his return from Moscow, Wilson did a softer press interview than normal, and soon found a CIA agent in his office, asking him if had traded his 'hound dog for a poodle'.

By 1991, there was no excuse for not knowing what was going on. It was clear to anyone with their eyes open that the mujahidin were not going to introduce US-style freedom to Afghanistan, but instead were increasingly fighting each other. There were hundreds of US doctors, nurses and other aid workers in the frontier region. Their convoys were regularly attacked, the contents looted, and women's programmes threatened. Disquiet grew even among those who had been the most fervent backers of funds for the mujahidin. One of Wilson's key aides, Charlie Schnabel, went on a fact-finding mission into Afghanistan after the mujahidin recaptured Khost, just south of Tora Bora in the east. He reported back that it was a ghost town, destroyed by indiscriminate attacks by the mujahidin.

In Pakistan there had been disagreements for some years. General Zia had been willing to leave Najibullah in power once the Russians pulled out. But Pakistani intelligence chiefs wanted a fight to the finish as much as the CIA. One said contemptuously of Zia's approach that 'the smell of political expediency and compromise was in the air'. Their influence was such that Zia followed their line, ignoring a commitment he had made in the Geneva peace deal to stop arms supplies. Shortly before Zia died in a mysterious plane crash in 1988, he told President Reagan that he would continue to lie about Pakistan's role in Afghanistan: 'We've been denying our activities there for eight years. Muslims have the right to lie in a good cause.'

In Afghanistan itself, commanders who had fought the war on the ground, and not from the safety of Peshawar, had been demanding more say in the post-war settlement even before the Soviet withdrawal. As early as July 1987 Ismail Khan had convened a conference in the west of 1200 commanders. Khan was a legendary figure in the mujahidin since, as an Afghan army captain, he had played a part in the uprising against Soviet influence in Herat in 1979, nine months before the Soviet invasion. The commanders he convened in 1987 easily agreed a stirring declaration that the future of the country could be sorted out only by the 'heirs of the martyrs as well as the Muslims of the trenches who are struggling on all war fronts and ready to be martyred'. But delivering this on the political stage was harder to do.

After the Soviets left, Massud called two similar meetings in the east, and then travelled from the Panjshir valley to Pakistan for the first time since the war started, to hold a high-level meeting with Pakistani officials at the ISI. He agreed to their request that he should patch up his differences with Hekmatyar. But nothing came of this either.

The concern of Pakistani intelligence, puppet-masters pulling the strings of the mujahidin for so long, was that 'their' commanders would be distracted from the business of winning the war by the power games beginning in Peshawar for jobs after the war was won. Afghans who had fled further abroad also wanted a say in the future of their homeland. There were meetings and conferences in California, Canada and Europe, the three main areas of Afghan settlement. But these initiatives were stifled at birth; the way the US and Pakistan were running the war left no role for the return of those who had gone away.

Three windows of opportunity to recover Afghanistan from the hands of Islamic fundamentalism were squandered before the attacks of 9/11, and this was the first. Long-term friends of the country, such as the British fund-raiser Viscount Cranborne, watched in dismay as money continued to be 'shovelled into the ideological pockets' of men like Hekmatyar, while more pragmatic commanders were ignored, and there was no serious attempt made to widen the political base for a new government.

Shuras, councils of Afghan leaders, had been meeting inter-mittently in Peshawar to plan the future since the late 1980s, amid fierce and sometimes violent disagreements. The influence of Pakistan and the US over the process meant that by the time the *shura* met in earnest to appoint a government that might actually take over, in early 1992, it empowered only the seven leaders, to the exclusion of royalists, returning exiles, commanders in the field, and other groups, such as Shias.

At the end of 1991, in an agreement between Moscow and Washington, both sides finally stopped arms sales. The Russian government that took over after the failed coup against Gorbachev in August took a much more determined line over ending involvement in Afghanistan, with a new foreign minister, Boris Pankin, who went as far as to condemn the invasion and Soviet behaviour during the war in Afghanistan. It was almost the last act of the USSR, dissolved 11 days after the final official delivery of Soviet guns south across the Oxus River. Afghanistan had played its part in bringing down the curtain on the 70-year political experiment of Russian communism.

In Kabul, Najibullah still clung to power. He changed the

name of his governing party to *Watan* – Homeland – and admitted that communism was not for Afghanistan. But time had run out for him. The US might have now signed its last arms cheque, but Pakistani and Saudi weapons continued to flow to the mujahidin. They had made no deal and, as if throwing petrol onto a fire, carried on giving the largest share of funding to the more fundamentalist commanders, in particular Hekmatyar, who rejected a peace plan brought back by other mujahidin leaders in their first visit to Moscow.

Kabul was comfortably within rocket range of Hekmatyar's positions to the south and east of the city, and he was now killing thousands of people a year in indiscriminate attacks. In April 1992, when the Russian president Boris Yeltsin discovered that the Russian military had managed to keep 200 advisers working in Kabul, he pulled them out, further destabilising Najibullah, who belatedly agreed to a UN plan to stand down in favour of an interim government and fresh elections. It was too late.

Among the vultures circling for a share in the spoils of Kabul was the northern leader Abdul Rashid Dostam, one of the most astute and ruthless players of the dark, dense violent Afghan game – an amiable Machiavellian thug. He generously rewarded loyalty and brutally punished failure. When a reporter noticed some blood and flesh on the ground outside Dostam's headquarters, and asked if an animal had been killed, he was told that these were the remains of a soldier who had been tied to the tracks of a tank and crushed to death that morning.

Dostam's Turkic features marked him as a descendant of the nomads from the high steppes that roll from the Black Sea across central Asia all the way down to the Hindu Kush. In Afghan tribal terms he was an Uzbek, sharing a cultural history with the newly independent Uzbekistan, across the Oxus River from his region in the north. Like many other successful mujahidin commanders, he had come up through the ranks of Soviet-backed Afghan forces, and owed nothing to the traditional clan structure of the country. But uniquely among those warlords who emerged as leaders from the wreckage of Soviet control, he remained part of the Soviet-backed Kabul government until almost the end. He was not a mujahid, but a supreme pragmatist.

Dostam had first been recruited into a militia formed to defend the oilfields in Shebargan in the north-west of Afghanistan in the late 1970s. He trained as a paratrooper, and quickly rose through the ranks of the militias that became increasingly important to the survival of the Kabul regime, particularly after Najibullah took over in 1985. Dostam's *Jowzjani* fought alongside Afghan army forces, and were the only militia in the country to be routinely deployed out of their own area, holding ground against the mujahidin in Kandahar and Helmand as Soviet forces withdrew from the south in 1988. They developed a reputation for fighting, and for looting. Their nickname *kilim jam* – the carpet is gathered up – referred to their habit of leaving nothing behind if they came to call.

As Soviet control drained away, Dostam manoeuvred himself into a position where he was more than just the Afghan military commander in the north: he was the undisputed leader of a region where he knew how to work the traditional levers of power. That first British envoy, Mountstuart Elphinstone, 200 years previously, had noticed the particular strength of elders among the Uzbeks. 'They are assembled in tribes under powerful chiefs. This peculiarity is probably occasioned by their being separated by mountains from the kingdom of Caubul, to which they belong . . . which circumstances have prevented any encroachment by their own sovereign on the rights of the local chiefs.'

Dostam did not encroach on the rights of the local chiefs, and secured their support by keeping the war away from the north as much as possible, arranging private peace deals where he could with mujahidin leaders including Massud, while at the same time staying on the right side of Kabul by making his *Jowzjani* available until the end of the Soviet-backed regime. And when Soviet arms supplies stopped at the end of 1991, he was ready to play a different game, with his eye on securing a major arms dump south of the Hindu Kush.

Dostam's defection ended any hopes that Najibullah may have had. By the spring of 1992 the mujahidin already held Bagram airbase, always vulnerable as it lay in a valley just too far from Kabul to be protected by troops in the city. Now Najibullah's deputy defence minister defected and sent planes to the north to ferry back 600 of Dostam's troops to take Kabul airport in the capital itself. This proved decisive and the city fell without a fight. Ex-President Najibullah was prevented from boarding a UN plane to India, and took refuge in the UN compound in town. On 18th April, a tank that had been stood outside the former royal palace for almost exactly 14 years, as a memorial to the revolution that had ousted President Daoud, was taken away and replaced by pots containing pink geraniums. But the symbolic gesture was misplaced. The fighting was not over, not by a long way.

Massud negotiated the defection of much of the Afghan air force and the army garrisons that lay between his stronghold in the Panjshir and Kabul. For the first time he could leave the fastness of his valley safely and make the journey out along its best defence, the narrow track next to the river as it wound a complex path along the gorge below high cliffs out to the flat dusty plain beyond. A BBC reporter, Mark Urban, watched as squadrons of ex-government helicopters landed on the wide plain flanked by the high curtain of the Hindu Kush: 'a most theatrical scene developed. Columns of mechanised troops snaked down from the mountains and came down to the parade ground. Massud walked along the line of vehicles and raised huge cheers. It was very much like Caesar reviewing his troops.'

The newly acquired helicopters took Massud's advance guard into the city, while dozens of trucks with other troops followed by road. The scale of this armoured movement, regular soldiers alongside Massud's best mujahidin, forced Hekmatyar to abandon the presidential palace and the other central locations he had occupied in the confusion of the handover. He withdrew from Kabul to positions to the east and on the Charasiab ridge to the south.

Competing mujahidin forces, armed with Soviet, Saudi and US-financed weapons, now confronted each other across Kabul, and the world stood back. Just as they had abandoned the country to its fate after Soviet forces left in 1989, in 1992 the US lost a second opportunity to bring Afghanistan back from the brink of being a failed state and the refuge of those who would destroy the World Trade Center.

There was a kind of government: 'President' Rabbani was nominated to take over from 'President' Mujaddidi later in the year. The two men were both ex-teachers in Islamic studies at Kabul University who had become mujahidin leaders. Hekmatyar, the fundamentalist who had once been their student, was offered the post of prime minister, but turned it down, and when he refused to give a guarantee that he would not shoot down the plane carrying the other leaders in from Pakistan, they had to come by road instead.

In some parts of Kabul, rival mujahidin occupied opposite sides of the same street, and when reporters asked why they were not shooting, they replied, 'We have not had the order yet.' The same clan and tribal loyalties were in play that had made the country ungovernable when Britain had tried in the nineteenth century, but this time the centrifugal forces ripping at the centre came with vastly increased firepower.

When the fighting did start, it was of an intensity unlike anything in the war in Afghanistan so far. There had been rocketing of the capital before, but not for as long nor with so little discrimination. And there had been rape before, but not used as it was now, as a weapon of war, to dominate an ethnic opposition. Massud's forces took over Afghan army positions and their heavy weapons, including tanks, armoured vehicles and artillery. Between 1992 and 1995, weapons designed for total war between armies were used against people in their homes; grand avenues and whole suburbs were reduced to sand.

News footage from those terrible years has a nightmare quality. The violence had its own momentum – men shot, looted, raped, died, because that was what they did. Rationality deserted them, as they locked horns in motiveless violence, driven as if in a nightmare summoned up from the deep sludge of the subconscious. As the rockets and bullets came without warning, some survivors lost the ability to cope. A woman said 'One of these rockets hit our house. Thank God nobody was injured, but my daughter became disabled because of the terrible sound of the rocket. Once she could speak fluently, but she cannot speak now and she cannot walk either. It is as if she is five or six years less than her real age.'

In an incident that became famous, a girl called Nahid, who was 15 years old, jumped to her death from the sixth-floor window of an apartment block, fearing rape. It was 7th February 1993, the night of Eid, the festival at the end of the Ramadan month of fasting. The family had recently returned from a refugee camp in Pakistan, and had chosen to live on an upper floor in the bleak, Soviet-era housing complex at Microroyan because they thought their daughters would be safer. A boy and his grandfather tried to fight off mujahidin gunmen who broke in, but both were shot and wounded. After the incident, neighbours thought that a rug had fallen out of the window in the chaos, but when they looked more closely they saw it was not a rug, but Nahid's red dress, spread out around her where she had hit the ground. Her sister said Nahid 'was really beautiful. She also had a good character. During that time when we first came back, she was always worrying about *kilim jams* abducting us. During the night we were very afraid and she asked another sister to tell us stories so that we'd stay awake in case anyone came in. It seemed she was aware of her coming death.'

It turned out that it was not Dostam's feared *kilim jams* who had broken in, but Massud's fighters. The family and their friends staged a protest rally the next day, carrying Nahid's body, and tried to march to the presidential palace, although according to a neighbour, 'the fighting was bad that day, with rockets and bullets flying'. Fighters allied with Massud fired at the mourners, and they were forced to turn back.

Nahid was only one of around 25,000 people to die in Kabul during those years. In August 1992 a carpenter came home to find his son dead: 'Mohammad Ismael, who was eight years old, was killed in a very nasty way – his body was left full of holes. Other members of my family who were in other rooms were injured so badly that it took a long, long time for them to heal.' On 30th December 1992, 12-year-old Baqi was killed playing in the street, by a rocket fired indiscriminately. A mother of four children was at home when another rocket hit: 'The bodies could not be recognized. Their feet and hands were thrown everywhere.' Another witness, Mohammed, said 'It was about four o'clock in the afternoon when a rocket hit our house near the door of the yard. My brother and eight or nine youths were standing in the lane and these eight or nine people except two of them got killed in a very bad way that you could not recognise them. My brother was injured seriously in his stomach and a piece of the rocket is still in his body. People collected body parts with shovels.'

During the first phase of the fighting, in 1992, the battle set Dostam, Massud and allied mujahidin against Hekmatyar's fundamentalists. A major new Iranian-backed force also came into play in the battle for Kabul. While there had been seven mujahidin groups under Pakistan, eight further guerrilla groups, centred around the Hazara region in the west, had competed for Iranian money. They now came together in one party, the Hezb-i-Wahadat.

Historians will never agree on whether the Hazaras, who have a distinctive Mongol look, really are the descendants of Genghis Khan's cavalry, but there is enough evidence to keep this romantic notion alive. They live amid a mass of bewitching red and green mountains that appear to have fallen off the western end of the Hindu Kush, where they hear the roar of a dragon in the echo of a river thundering down one ravine, and tell a local version of the old myth about the boy who saved a maiden by slaying the dragon.

Hazara literally means 'a thousand', and was historically used for a unit of horsemen; so it can also be translated as 'regiment' or 'battalion'. And the local names for their villages and hamlets appear to correspond to the names of Mongol commanders. Whatever the truth of their origins, the Hazaras certainly need a warrior tradition. In the centuries since they were left beached in western Afghanistan, as the Mongol tide receded across Asia, they have become a put-upon minority, squeezed between the Pashtun tribes of the south, and the Uzbeks and Tajiks of the north – finding themselves servants at best, and slaves at worst. In Afghanistan they are also set apart by their adherence to the Shia strand of Islam, as practised in Iran.

Hekmatyar was a Sunni extremist, and at any other time might have persecuted Hazaras, but without other support, he entered a cynical alliance with them at the end of 1992. This was the signal for Massud to sanction an all-out assault on the Hazara community in Kabul, notorious even by the standards of the time. The attack on the tightly packed streets of mud houses clinging to the side of the Afshar hill in the west of the city, involving the mass killing of civilians and systematic rape of women, left the area uninhabitable.

Massud and his allies did have a military motive to move into Afshar – to neutralise hostile artillery positions and capture the headquarters of the Hezb-i-Wahadat, now that the Hazara grouping had allied with Hekmatyar. But an investigation by a human rights group, the Afghanistan Justice Project, concluded that the Hezb-i-Wahadat headquarters in a former college building was not even hit. 'This was not a raid or skirmish but a full-scale battle, in which the Islamic State deployed the combined military resources from the old Soviet-era army and the mujahidin against targets within the capital city, all of them located in areas that were primarily residential, with the civilian population intact.'

After an intensive artillery bombardment on 10th February 1993, fighters moved in before dawn the following day. The force defending the area withdrew, leaving thousands of Hazara civilians defenceless. The mujahidin who carried out the worst abuses were from a well-financed but small group led by Abdul Rasul Sayyaf, a Wahhabi fundamentalist for now allied with Massud. Sayyaf's militia had been set up specifically to channel Saudi funds into the war. His men had been involved in frequent skirmishes with Hazara forces, where both sides claimed to have suffered significant abuses, including the rape and murder of its civilians.

The attackers moved from house to house in Afshar, raping, killing and looting. They mutilated bodies and mounted decapitated heads in windows. There is no agreement over how many were killed, but witnesses interviewed later said they saw bodies piled in the streets. Survivors were herded into shipping containers, and told to dig their own graves. Some paid huge bribes to secure their release while some escaped with harrowing accounts of what had happened: 'At night I was kept in a container; during the day I and other 10 to 20 men were made to dig trenches. There were lots of containers. At night some men would be taken out and not come back. We could hear shots and we assumed the men had been killed. I think some were buried in the trenches. I finally escaped by hiding in the river under a bridge.' Another witness was sure the attackers were a joint force of Massud's and Sayyaf's men. Before he was taken away, he heard a commander over the radio ordering the killers not to fight each other for the loot: 'I had left the door open hoping the militias would think the house empty. They came in and beat me and took me to Qargha River where I was put into a container with about 60 to 65 men. It was very crowded.'

A woman described how her husband was taken away, and then later the same day another group of soldiers came. 'My son was 11 years old. They held him and asked where his father was. They aimed their guns at him and I threw myself over him. I was shot in the hand and leg but he was shot five times. He died.' Still bleeding, she was taken down to the basement of her house and raped, along with two other women who had fled to the house for refuge and two teenage girls. One of the girls was stabbed with a bayonet when she tried to resist. The soldiers then looted everything in the house.

The Afshar massacre cast a long shadow over Afghanistan. After the Hazaras army expelled the Taliban from Bamiyan with US support in 2001, their first priority was to get to Kabul when they heard it had fallen, because they remembered what had happened to Hazaras in 1993. Securing immunity from prosecution for the killings in Kabul during those years remains one of the key preoccupations of the old mujahidin warlords to this day.

Frustrated at the inability of the mujahidin to make peace, the Saudi government invited the leaders to Mecca, the holiest place in the Islamic world, where they agreed to work together. Hekmatyar came, signed up, and went back to rocket Kabul again. Still Pakistan's favoured leader, Hekmatyar had also secured the support of a number of key ex-communist leaders from a faction of the party who remembered his support when they had tried to oust Najibullah in a coup in 1990. But even when Hekmatyar persuaded Dostam, the Uzbek leader from the north, to change sides and join him in 1994, it did not break the stalemate. Neither side could deliver the killer punch, although Dostam brought a significant number of warplanes with him; so for the first time in the civil war, both sides could carry out air attacks.

The killing dragged on into another year while the world continued to look the other way. The days of journalists packing the American Club in Peshawar, growing beards and donning *salwar kameez*, waiting to be escorted across the frontier, were long gone. The reporters who had competed for superlatives in describing the legendary guerrilla leadership qualities of Ahmed Shah Massud were nowhere to be seen as his gunmen raped and looted their way across Kabul, fuelled now by opium-processing workshops in the Panjshir, and the proceeds of extortion at roadside checkpoints.

It was a very dangerous war to cover. Apart from random attacks, there were targeted killings, such as the death of the BBC reporter Mirwais Jalil, murdered on Hekmatyar's orders. A few journalists continued to chronicle the vortex of violence with dedication and bravery, but despite their efforts editors lost interest. With no superpower involvement, Afghans killing each other was not a story – Bosnia was the new international preoccupation. There were no debates in the UN Security Council on Afghanistan between 1990 and the arrival of the Taliban in 1996.

Forgotten by the world, Kabul suffered far more damage in the struggle between rival mujahidin than during the previous Soviet occupation. Below the ancient remnants of the city wall, winding along the hill of the Bala Hissar, Kabul's grandest streets were reduced to ruins, flattened into the dust, building by building. The southern suburbs around the zoo and the university became uninhabitable as those houses not destroyed were surrounded by unexploded munitions. Remarkably a few moth-eaten animals survived the whole war in the zoo. Hekmatyar kept the lion alive by occasionally tossing in his enemies after maiming them with a knife.

The violent stalemate in Kabul also meant there was now no check on disorder and criminality across the rest of the country. Reconstruction was at a standstill. For mile after mile, mud-walled villages had been reduced to what looked like termite mounds. The main roads were bombed into dust tracks, making it quicker to cycle than drive from city to city. And every few miles travellers would be confronted by a chain marking the control of another petty warlord, who would claim a toll to provide protection. Kandahar, the capital of the Pashtun heartland, slid into a brutal decadence, culminating in a tank battle on the streets between two commanders who both wanted sex with the same boy.

Part Five

The Taliban and the US-led invasion
1994–2008

12

Virtue and Vice

'Women you should not step outside your residence. . . . If women are going outside with fashionable, ornamental, tight and charming clothes to show themselves, they will be cursed by the Islamic Sharia, and should never expect to go to heaven.'

Taliban decree. Kabul 1996

It would be hard to replicate the circumstances that led to the creation of the Taliban. They were not just another Afghan guerrilla group, fighting a civil war. They emerged like a collapsed star, sucking the war into a black hole, then governing with the force of antimatter – of Afghan creation, but as if seen through a dark mirror distorted by a generation of warfare. Nothing was as it had been in the past, nor as it seemed in the present.

The men who formed the Taliban in the mid-1990s, all from the Pashtun south, had not been connected with the most fundamentalist parties during the war with Russia, but they developed a creed that tried to go back to the seventh century. They said they revered women, and wanted them educated when the war was over, but in fact enslaved them with restrictions worse than anywhere other than Saudi Arabia; they opposed the use and trading of heroin, but were financed by it; and they cultivated an insular and remote world-view, looking inwards to Afghanistan, but ended up hosting Osama bin Laden, who had quite a different vision for Islam's place in the world.

The Taliban leader, Mullah Mohammed Omar, was a figure of dark singularity, unlike any other from his country's past. Before him, Afghan leaders had always needed to engage with the outside world; Afghanistan's position on the crossroads of Asia demanded no less. Omar viewed the world beyond his borders not with hostility, but indifference, engaging with it on his own terms, which meant not at all. He did not see the need for a foreign policy. I am one of only a handful of people from Europe or North America who has even seen the Taliban leader, and I would hardly describe our meeting as a meaningful conversation.

It was in Kandahar in 1997, a year after the Taliban took Kabul. I was travelling with Rahimullah Yusufzai, the only journalist Omar would take a phone call from. Rahimullah was well known in Afghanistan for his broadcasts on the BBC's Pashtu service, but this would be only their second meeting, and word came from Omar that it would not be 'helpful' to the movement if I came too. Waiting outside, I saw him emerge afterwards, tall, with a fair complexion for an Afghan and a Grecian nose, prominent above his unkempt black beard. There was not much to mark him out among a group of similarly dressed Taliban, their heads covered with large black turbans, and wearing cheap European-style polyester jackets over their traditional black *salwar kameez*. Omar acknowledged me with his one good eye and a simple greeting, before climbing into the back of a Toyota Land Cruiser and racing away, almost running over a man who threw himself in front of the vehicle in pursuit of some local grievance.

The man who controlled more of Afghanistan than anyone since the 1970s travelled to Kabul only once during the five years the Taliban held the capital. He ruled instead from an iron bedstead in Kandahar, in a room shut off not by a door, but just a dirty torn curtain, surrounded by Taliban who came and went with an easy familiarity. Rahimullah sat on the carpet among the Taliban, watching as Omar chatted, joked, signed letters and at one point unlocked the padlock on a box to give some money to two fighters who had arrived in town with nowhere to stay.

He said the Taliban had no territorial ambitions beyond Afghanistan, denying Russian claims that it wanted to export its Islamic revolution north across the Oxus River to the central Asian republics of Uzbekistan and Tajikistan. Against the evidence, he denied that the movement had been backed by Pakistan. 'It is a purely religious movement which has received no support from outside,' he said. He maintained the West was wrong to believe that the Taliban oppressed women; rather they revered them. In what became a standard response on the issue of girls' schools, he said there were 'priorities in war', and girls could be educated in an Islamic way once the war was won.

Despite his humble appearance, this successor to the amirs of Afghanistan had a strong sense of destiny and a taste for the theatrical gesture. He was creating the world's first pure Islamic state since the time of the Prophet Mohammed, and he did not need to go to the royal palace in Kabul to be crowned. He had already gone one better, taking the cloak believed to have belonged to the Prophet himself from its case in a mosque in Kandahar, revealing it to the crowd, and declaring himself not amir of Afghanistan, but *Amir al-Mu'minin*, leader of all the faithful. The last man to claim the title was Dost Mohammed in the 1830s.

The decade of war against the Soviet invasion had tightened the grip of Islamic fundamentalism across Afghanistan and Pakistan. President Zia encouraged these moves towards Islamicisation, particularly in education and Sharia law. The ratchet moved in only one direction, closing down avenues of independent thought, while the world looked the other way.

The men who emerged as Taliban leaders took it further, developing their own system which was quite unlike that of the

Kabul-educated mujahidin. They were not political revolutionaries – and in fact had little interest in politics or
government. Their revolution was focused instead on
controlling morality and personal behaviour.

The Taliban wanted to work with the deep social grain of
rural conservatism, not interfering with the power of tribal
elders or landowners, as long as people followed Taliban
religious practices. They viewed as superstition some of the
more colourful rural religious traditions, opposing them with
the same zeal as seventeenth-century Puritans in England did
the practices of the Catholic Church.

Under the Taliban, religious authority would rest, not with
the layers of *syeds*, *pirs* and *alims*, guardians of the Afghan Sufi
tradition, but with mullahs, who qualified through the
discipline of long years of strict religious education, centred
around constant repetition of the Koran in Arabic, a language
many of them did not even speak. Mullahs of this kind had
been present in the region for a long time, but now had
political power for the first time. Ten years of internationally
licensed holy war, followed by seven years of criminality, left a
vacuum they could fill.

At the core of the new antimatter soul being forged for
Afghanistan was 'anti-education', in which boys were taught
not about culture or the natural world, and certainly not to
think for themselves – the bedrock of education in the
developed world – but to believe that this was all taken care of
for them by Islam. An enthusiastic talib told me of the benefits
of this soon after they took Kabul. 'Islam teaches when to
wake and when to sleep, how to walk, how to talk, how to
relate to the people. It is everything.'

Taliban theology had an unbroken thread that stretched
back, through the Hindustani fanatics and *ghazis* who had
fought the British, and the Deobandi school in India, to the
deserts of Saudi Arabia where Mohammed Ibn Abd al-
Wahhab had refined his view of Islam in the eighteenth
century.

Thousands of madrassas had sprung up not just along the

frontier, but elsewhere in Pakistan during the war; several of the more important were close to the capital Islamabad itself. They ignored not just the standard curriculum of a non-Islamic school, but also centuries of Islamic intellectual achievement in astronomy, maths, philosophy and design. Not all madrassas, even those in the Deobandi tradition, were this rigid, but the open tap of funding from the Wahhabi kingdom of Saudi Arabia went to those with the most austere, exclusive and intolerant form of Islam.

The madrassas became factories turning out Taliban fighters, many of them war orphans who knew no other life. 'Talib' simply means 'student', although the word came to mean specifically 'religious student', and the madrassa system provided a formidable old-boy network, giving a sinuous strength and flexibility to the Taliban army, which otherwise lacked a formal command structure.

During major offensives those running the big madrassas would close them to send their teenage students off as cannon fodder, with the same callous zeal as the 'Mad Mullah' who had pushed boys in front of British guns a century before, witnessed by Churchill. And the madrassas provided another important support service to the Taliban campaign: fighters came straight from the front line for R&R during the wars against the mujahidin and later the US-led forces in Afghanistan.

The origins of the Taliban lie in the dust of the southern desert, perhaps the most unforgiving landscape in Afghanistan, known in the local language as *Dasht-i-Mango,* the Desert of Death. The war here in the 1980s was quite different to the guerrilla campaigns further north. Soviet conventional forces had a significant advantage in the wide flat areas between low hills with no cover for the mujahidin, who were restricted to hit-and-run raids, often using motorbikes.

To those fighting in the south it felt like a forgotten corner of a forgotten war: they received far less funding than the mujahidin elsewhere, and took higher casualties. One of the more effective commanders was a former Afghan army officer who went under the *nom de guerre* of Mullah Borjan. He said that of the 90 men he had started fighting with, only eight were left alive by the late 1980s – 'I cannot describe the suffering.' He and a small group of other Pashtun commanders became so disillusioned with the Peshawar system of funding, that they had formed their own militia, the Mullahs' Front, initially led by Mullah Abdul Razzaq, and Mullah Mohammed Rabbani (no relation to the Rabbani who became president). These three men, Borjan, Razzaq and Rabbani, were among the key founders of the Taliban.

Six years before they emerged as the Taliban, the Mullahs' Front already had some of the characteristics of the movement. They lived simple lives and needed little funding. This gave them enormous power, since they owed nothing to any patron, and were remote from Pakistani control. They also appeared honest and conscientious to the villagers they lived among, caring about civilian casualties in a way that other mujahidin conspicuously did not.

Omar had not been in the Mullahs' Front, but had fought further north, sustaining four injuries, including the loss of his eye. By the time the Russian-backed leader Najibullah was finally pushed out of office in Kabul in the spring of 1992, Omar was living a quiet life running a small madrassa in the village near Maiwand where he had lived for all of his adult life. But as criminality and corruption flourished after the collapse of central authority, he began to meet like-minded friends, who were concerned that the victory over Soviet control had been squandered. Nowhere was Pashtun nationalist feeling stronger than here. They remember the battle of Maiwand against Britain in 1880 as if it were yesterday, and like to tell visitors that it was they who first rose up against the Soviet invasion.

In 1994, when two teenage girls from his village were seized by a local commander, and repeatedly raped, after having their heads shaved, Omar led a group of 30 volunteers, only half of them armed with rifles, in an assault on the place the girls were being held. They released the girls, seized the commander, and hanged him from a tank barrel. What happened next has taken on the aura of a legend – the founding myth of a movement. In delving through the dark mirror to the antimatter beyond, *how* the tale is remembered now perhaps matters more than the narrative 'truth'.

Omar's successful operation to release the girls attracted considerable attention. He cemented his reputation by freeing the boy being held in Kandahar after the tank battle. He took no money and claimed no position after these exploits, spreading his Robin Hood reputation. He would say later, 'How could we remain quiet when we could see crimes being committed against women and the poor?' Then, at a *shura* in Omar's village, a former commander nicknamed Mullah Torak – the 'Black Mullah' – announced the formation of the Taliban. The Black Mullah later said that although he had been the main speaker, there was no dispute over who should lead the movement: 'Omar was a very brave mujahid. He was widely respected, and people knew how he had lived his life. There was no debate or confusion.' There were 24 founding shura members, but no fixed constitution or jobs. 'If somebody was pious then he could come into the shura.'

The Black Mullah had called the meeting because of concern about checkpoints along the main road. Trade was paralysed, as every few miles there was another checkpoint, and another mujahidin group demanding money. Shortly after their founding shura, the Taliban took two Japanese-made Hino trucks from Kandahar all the way east to the Pakistan border, with 90 fighters concealed under tarpaulins in the back. Omar was in the cab of one; Borjan, the commander from the Mullahs' Front, was in the other. They paid off 42 illegal checkpoints along the way, claiming that they had sheep in the back; nobody bothered to search the trucks. Arriving at Spin Boldak, the border crossing point, they took it after a brief battle, then seized an arms dump and the district headquarters.

Leaving another commander hanging from a tank barrel – already a trademark that spread their no-nonsense reputation –

they fought their way back west, opening the road checkpoint by checkpoint, until they held Kandahar itself – the most decisive military shift in Afghanistan since the withdrawal of Soviet forces five years previously. In the Afghan way, many commanders came over to them without a fight, and Taliban control of the border meant that they now had unlimited access to their main recruiting base in the madrassas.

The exact sequence of events, and the depth of Pakistan's involvement, is disputed. Within only a few months, once the Taliban had taken Kandahar, there was clearly considerable funding and support coming from Pakistan, to the extent that Kandahar had an internal Pakistani phone code, and Pakistani troops were openly giving the Taliban technical assistance. Saudi Arabia took a close interest too; this was after all a movement of ex-students from schools they had funded. The Taliban leadership insist that external support came after they had seized power for themselves, and that they were not the creation of Pakistan.

But whatever its role up to now, Pakistan, frustrated by the inability of its protégé Hekmatyar to take power, quickly switched to the Taliban, providing them with fuel for the warplanes they took at Kandahar airport, and other crucial support. The Taliban also received donations from trucking companies for re-opening the lucrative route from Iran to Pakistan that crossed the south.

In Kandahar and elsewhere in the Pashtun heartlands of the south, their victories initially came as a relief. They disarmed bandits, and imposed law and order. But their move on the more cosmopolitan western town of Herat in 1995 set alarm bells ringing worldwide.

Herat's control of trade from Iran, taking tariffs on second-hand Japanese vehicles that flowed through to Pakistan, made it the richest town in the country. Toyotas were only the latest business opportunity for this marketplace on the crossroads of Asia, which had seen trade come and go in rugs, blue glass, silks, spices and precious stones for centuries.

Herat contains some of the world's oldest and finest

mosques, and the remains of what the godfather of travel writers Robert Byron called 'the most beautiful example in colour in architecture ever devised by man to the glory of his God and himself'. He could write this even after much of it was destroyed by British forces preparing the defences of Herat against a Russian attack in 1885 that never came. Tamerlane and Genghis Khan had fought for control of a town from a different world like the Silk Road towns – Balkh, Samarkand and Bokhara – further to the north. Imprinted on the DNA of Herat were long memories of civilisation and cosmopolitan cultural values.

Before the arrival of the Taliban in Herat in 1995, girls were educated alongside boys, and women able to work in a limited range of jobs. The west and north of Afghanistan, Persian-speaking and outward-looking, was like a foreign country to the Pashtu-speaking hordes of the Taliban, with their two-dimensional Islamist world-view.

The Taliban had perfected a highly mobile form of warfare, using fleets of Toyota Hilux pickups, and living more lightly than other forces. The austerity of their background and education, their ruthless unity of purpose, allied with the speed of their approach in Hiluxes, brought a new kind of deter-mination to the Afghan conflict. The long-term mujahidin leader in Herat, Ismail Khan, spread his front line too wide, was drawn out too far, and was overwhelmed by the Pashtun blitzkrieg. He fled for safety across the nearby border to Iran.

The new governor of Herat was Mullah Razzaq, who had been leader of the Mullahs' Front in the late 1980s. He displayed a paranoid obsession about the distraction of women, going much further than demanding that they shroud themselves in the all-enveloping burqa, a garment that came to symbolise the Taliban more than anything else. Razzaq issued orders that women were not even to pass the window of his office, in case he heard the sound of their voices or the distinctive tap of their feet.

It was perhaps only an army of orphans who could have imposed this madness on Afghanistan with such enthusiasm.

Many of the fighters were still in their teens, some as young as 14, and had grown up without the company of mothers or sisters. They accepted without question that women should be banished into darkness, and whipped if they were not fully covered up, or appeared outside without a male relative. The young zealots of the Taliban had no other contact with women at all, in mosques, restaurants, shops or travelling on the road. All of their conversations were with men or boys. They dreamt of virgins in paradise, making no connection between these beings and the shapeless tents who shuffled along the gutter, or were carried like animals, squatting in the open boots of cars, while men sat in the front.

Although the Taliban seemed extreme, what they imposed were no more than normal conservative countryside Pashtun values. In some villages, women do not even have a name outside their own family. I once succeeded in asking some questions of a woman in a Pashtun village near Kabul – a bizarre four-way interview, with her husband shouting my questions through a curtain. The answers were recorded by a woman camera operator, and then relayed to my translator by the husband, since he would not allow his wife to be questioned directly. As we were leaving, I asked my translator to check her name. He pointed to the recently skinned carcass of a sheep, hanging glistening from a tree. 'That is how I would end up,' he said, 'if I tried to ask.' The interview, recorded during the Taliban years, revealed the frightening isolation of women's lives. The nameless, shapeless figure mumbling answers from under her burqa, had lost three sons in the war, two fighting for the mujahidin against the Soviet occupation, and one fighting for the Taliban. But she hardly appeared to know that the Soviet army had left, let alone who was now in power, or whether it mattered.

The long war and decades of poverty meant that there was no impetus for progress in the Afghan countryside. The Taliban were a consequence of Pashtun conservatism, not the original cause of women's repression, but in the black hole that Afghanistan had become, they enforced the toughest of regimes against women with a ferocious energy. At the same time the clan and tribal structure that had sustained Pashtun life for centuries, and might have provided a brake on extremism, had broken down. In the 1980s the mujahidin who first took up arms against the Soviet invasion knew where they came from, and could recite ancient legends as well as their family lineage, but an upbringing in a madrassa was a break with that past. At the height of Taliban power, a village elder I was staying with in Helmand Province expressed fond exasperation for their excesses: to him they were 'just boys'. He admired their zeal and honesty, while wishing they had a more rounded view of human nature.

In the cities, even in their natural power base Kandahar where they had been welcomed, Taliban restrictions quickly began to grate. They had brought law and order, but with a fanaticism that made normal life impossible. The cinema, a highly popular attraction in a country in thrall to the Bollywood dream machine, was flattened, and the ground cleared to build a mosque. In the spring of 1996 a new ministry for 'the promotion of virtue and the suppression of vice', based exactly on the model of administration from the paymasters of the Taliban in Saudi Arabia, began to impose rules that included no music, TV or non-Islamic books. Clean-shaven men were arrested and held until their beards were the approved shaggy length, and market traders stopped from displaying women's garments – or even shampoo bottles if they showed the picture of a woman.

Squatting on the floor of what looked like a stable amid ruins, the main office of the new ministry, the virtue and vice minister cheerily said that they had realised how corrupt and decadent British civilisation had become when Charles and Diana both had extramarital affairs. That kind of thing would not be allowed to happen in Afghanistan. They also clamped down hard on homosexuality, although it was commonplace, indeed routine, across Pashtun areas.

From some source, not the Koran, the Taliban learnt that the appropriate punishment for homosexuals was to have a wall pushed onto them. They were preoccupied for months with a debate on how to achieve this – whether the guilty should be buried first, or actually crushed by the wall, and whether it should be made with cement or loose stones. Imposing sharia law was not easy. A rural judge told me, in the tone of a man considering a fine legal point, that he was not sure where a hand should be cut off, at the wrist joint, or across the bone further up the forearm.

By the summer of 1996, with half of Afghanistan under Taliban control, they had Kabul in their sights. They had dislodged Hekmatyar from his headquarters on the Charasiab ridge to the south of the capital, bringing the city within range of Taliban rockets. As Britain had discovered in the Second Anglo-Afghan War, the ridge was the key to the city. The Taliban did rocket Kabul, but they also lifted the blockade imposed by Hekmatyar, allowing trade to cross the front lines, a payoff to the trucking companies that had continued to fund the Taliban since their first operation to open the road in the south.

For the beleaguered capital, the arrival of fresh food supplies in early September 1996 led some to believe that rule by the Taliban would not be all bad. Nothing could be worse than the squalor and terror of the last four years. Only foreign aid kept people alive amid the rubble. But the war had left 30,000 women without a husband to look after them, and as the days shortened, a collective shiver seemed to paralyse a city where none knew what the Islamist student revolutionaries would do once they had taken the capital.

With unbelievable cynicism, Hekmatyar now accepted the post of prime minister offered to him four years before, proposing a grand alliance with Massud. But the days of shifting alliances between rival mujahidin were over. Hekmatyar's fundamentalist Pashtun fighters were natural Taliban recruits, and after he had attempted to impose Islamist austerity on Kabul, closing the cinema and imposing restrictions on women, he fled abroad, and was reputed for a while to be the third largest investor on the Italian stock exchange. His forces defected en masse to the Taliban.

The main Taliban advance on Kabul did not come along the old British invasion route from the south, but from the east, after Jalalabad fell without a fight in September. The story the Taliban like to tell relates how Jalalabad was taken by a handful of their fighters in two Hilux pickups. Borjan, now the overall military commander of the movement, arrived in the third. Victory was lubricated by a payment of millions of dollars to the governor to persuade him to leave. It almost certainly came from Saudi Arabia – now backing a Taliban takeover.

In late September, on the night before he died in the final assault on Kabul, Borjan did his only TV interview as a Taliban commander. He was a slight man with a refined and thoughtful air, who picked his way towards us through a room crammed with fighters in a house commandeered from the departing governor. Most of the Taliban leadership opposed television, but he was different – undogmatic and willing to talk on camera. Spotting a talib he had sent to command the forces at Jalalabad airport, he ordered him back to his post. There was always a chaotic informality in this protean force. He was then handed a two-way radio to be given a report on a successful attack on a convoy carrying a local leader who opposed the Taliban.

Borjan calculated the effect of this news without smiling, as he sat down on the floor, resting an arm on one knee, with the other knee bent flat to the large Mauri-pattern rug that covered the floor of the room, its light-coloured lozenges woven on a deep blood-red sea. He put the palm of his hand flat down on the rug, and said Hekmatyar now controlled 'no more than that space'. The long, rather feminine fingers of his other hand, draped over the end of his knee, played around a ring of beads as he talked of the policies of the Taliban.

Unlike some other Taliban leaders, for Borjan the movement appeared to be a means to an end. He went through the ritual answers about girls' schools – 'when the time was right' – and wanting an Islamic system of government. But the important things for him were peace and law and order. He was old enough to remember another Afghanistan that he wanted to see again. If he had lived, perhaps he might have moderated some of the excesses of the movement.

Leaving Borjan to plan the attack, we picked our way out through the obstacle course of tightly packed warriors, breathing the same sweet feral air as men who thought they were on the eve of victory. One man caught my arm. He was older than most, with a white beard that seemed to merge with matching folds of elaborate white cotton clothing under a brocade jacket. When he opened his mouth to smile, there was the flash of a gold tooth. In his hands he held a gleaming British cavalry sword. 'My grandfather used it to cut off the head of an Englishman,' he said. 'Now I will use it to kill Massud.' Outside, the governor's large collection of ornamental birds made an enormous racket. Nobody seemed to be feeding them. Borjan left before first light.

Not all of the regional commanders had come over to the Taliban, some helping Massud's regular troops to defend the Silk Gorge, the gateway to Sarobi, the last town before Kabul. The Kabul River plunged down almost as a waterfall here, several hundred feet, before jinking to another pass and dropping another hundred feet. It was thought to be impossible to break through the gorge, as the road was narrow and covered from above by hundreds of firing points, with tanks in elevated fixed positions built by Soviet forces.

Unlike at Herat, where the Taliban success depended on speed across a wide front, here victory would involve a far larger sacrifice. The Taliban advanced after dawn prayers on 25th September, but faltered under a withering rain of fire, and fell back. Borjan had been inside his Hilux, but now climbed out, and shouted, 'What's the worst thing that can happen? If you die you will become martyrs.' The Taliban advanced again, but then halted as the fire intensified, asking for their own tanks to go ahead first. Borjan grabbed a Kalashnikov and ran forward shouting, 'I am in front. Why are you behind me?' This was the defining moment of the battle that would decide the future of Afghanistan. Following the example of their commander, the Taliban force advanced at a run, and cries of *Allah hu Akbar* were heard amid the deafening sound of gunfire, and the clatter of bullets impacting on the rocks of the gorge. Borjan was hit. His driver, a streetwise 18-year-old called Naqeeb, grabbed the dying commander and pulled him into his Hilux, where his identity was concealed by smoked glass. Other fighters crowded round, and asked who was inside, but Naqeeb told them it was just a wounded talib; Borjan was up ahead.

'If we had mentioned to the other Taliban that Mullah Borjan had been killed, they would have lost their courage to fight. And if we had not captured Sarobi, we would not have captured Kabul,' Naqeeb said. And he quoted with pleasure the taunting words of the commander defending the gorge, who had bragged, on the two-way radio listened to by both armies, that the Taliban would never get through, since 'only men who could fight' would be able to do it.

The pace of the advance, and the ability of the Taliban to take enormous losses, broke the will of the enemy, who retreated in disarray from positions they had believed impregnable. In the Afghan way, some local commanders switched sides quickly to guarantee their own survival, turning a surprise defeat into a rout. Driving just behind the Taliban advance, we saw the remains of swiftly abandoned campsites, catering vehicles and ambulances – rear echelon kit that was not moved back in time. Only then did the Taliban launch an assault from the Charasiab ridge to the south, and, in a further pincer attack, from the south-east. Massud had not expected this because that area was heavily mined, but the Taliban pushed prisoners ahead of them at gunpoint to clear the mines.

As at Herat, speed and ruthlessness ensured victory. One seasoned observer of the Afghan scene wrote, 'No Afghan force, either government or opposition, had ever carried out such a swift and complex series of operations over such a wide operation area. This was mobile warfare at its most effective.' Amid the chaos of retreating forces pouring into the capital,

Massud withdrew to the north towards his Panjshir fastness, along the same road he had come down in such hope four years previously. The road was clogged with heavy traffic made up of those who feared that life under Taliban rule might be even worse than they had suffered during the mujahidin civil war.

As the city fell, we drove into Kabul on 27th September, the only camera crew to witness the Taliban takeover, past abandoned trucks and tanks – a new accretion, adding another layer to the military archaeology of the road to Kabul, alongside rusting Russian hulks and, not far beneath the surface, the bones of the British, pushed into the mud above the remains of the soldiers of the Moghul emperors, Genghis Khan, Tamerlane and Alexander the Great, who had all marched this way, and fought over Afghanistan.

At the presidential palace a tank had broken down the gates, and now stood guard, festooned in tinsel decorations. Inside we found a white-tiled room, drenched in blood from floor to ceiling, a scene from a horror film. This was where the former communist president Najibullah and his brother had been tortured, after being dragged from their sanctuary at the UN. From the amount of blood it seemed that they were already dead when they were hanged unceremoniously from a traffic police post, both bodies mutilated and mocked with cigarettes and banknotes pushed between their fingers. They were left to swing for several days; a new kind of regime had taken power.

A statement by Mullah Omar was read on Kabul Radio. He said they had no quarrel with the outside world; they wanted good relations with other countries and recognition.

> We represent Afghanistan. After 14 years of jihad against the communists, the victors betrayed the nation and took up arms. Now there is order, there will be *kassas*, which means murderers will be executed. Twelve *kassas* punishments have already been carried out, and eight amputations. All stolen property must be returned, and thieves will be severely punished. Adulterers will be

stoned to death or lashed. All government employees should come to work as normal, except for women and teachers, who should stay at home.

The darkness began. The Taliban were stricter in the capital than they had been in Kandahar, where they were among their own. Religious police carried short lengths of rubber hose to whip people into the mosques during the compulsory five prayer times a day. Fighters slapped people with the sides of bayonets fixed to their AK-47s to make the point. Women did not just have to cover up, but told they had to have a reason to go out. Bilquis, a teacher in what had been a mixed school, said she had never worn a burqa before. 'In the worst days of the war we went out. Now there's peace and we can't.' Many bakeries had been staffed by women in a food-for-work scheme before the Taliban came. International donors were now told to deliver the flour and let the Taliban deal with it. Even a woman's aid programme making dolls' clothing for a Western mail-order firm was banned.

Zohra, an 11-year old girl, who had an artificial foot to replace one lost in a rocket attack, complained about the 'artificial mullahs' who had taken over. We interviewed her in silhouette, disguising her identity, and also did a number of Taliban interviews anonymously, because of their prohibition against the display of faces. Within days the image of Afghanistan had slipped into the shadows – the realm of antimatter.

Letters were sent to hospitals, specifying which organs could be worked on in women, while male obstetricians were banned from working with women patients at all. A group of women health workers called me over to talk, whispering their complaints through a mosquito screen. The number of women patients had gone down to a quarter of those they had seen before the Taliban takeover. They worried about what was happening to the others. A midwife said it was worse than being rocketed.

In a public display the Taliban did want filmed, 1400 cases

of beer and 400 bottles of Afghan brandy were crushed under the tracks of a tank, then covered with earth, in case anyone licked the ground. This was a routine Islamic prohibition, but the Taliban went further. They ripped reels of film out of their cases and burnt them on a bonfire in front of the city's cinema, while edicts from the new rulers straying into more bizarre areas now came thick and fast. As well as the expected bans on cinema, music and TV, people were ordered to paint their windows white, in case women were seen from outside. Normal Kabul pastimes, pigeon racing and kite flying, were now banned. The Minister for virtue and vice said this was about orderliness, in order to keep boys off roofs where they might look into the women's quarters of another house. But it was really about control.

In a police station that controlled a large section of the city, 30-year-old Mohammed Ayub, who had been a witness of the founding shura of the Taliban near Maiwand, was now the police chief. He said he had been in a madrassa for ten years, but was still not a mullah. He sat cross-legged on a couch, in flowing white *salwar kameez*, his eyes beautifully lined with kohl, alongside another young man similarly turned out, both giggling about the powers they had. The former police chief, now appointed their deputy, sat rather self-consciously on a chair, in his Soviet-era uniform, a few days growth of beard on his face, waiting for orders.

The Taliban pursued Massud's forces north to the mouth of the Panjshir valley, but neither side was strong enough for a decisive breakthrough. The Taliban had no more luck than Soviet forces taking the twisting natural defences at the entrance to Massud's lair, although they lost thousands of men trying. A damaged tank with Taliban insignia marked the northernmost point of their advance, not far up the narrow gorge.

But Massud would never threaten Kabul again, although he broke out of the Panjshir. For the next five years the front line was fluid, with both sides carrying out brutal reprisals against the villagers caught between them on the Shomali plain. This had been the most fertile part of Afghanistan, until the Taliban destroyed the complex irrigation system which brought melting snow down from the Hindu Kush into an intricate tracery of channels crossing vineyards and fruit orchards. It had also been one of the main battlegrounds in the war against the Soviet Union, as mujahidin used the cover of mud walls and dykes to disrupt the Soviet supply route to the north. Many farmers had remained throughout. The ground could not support them now though, as the remnants of vines crumbled into decay, and their fields dried to a fine talcum-powder dust.

The Taliban were now operating openly with Pakistani artillery support, but the Information Minister, Mullah Amir Mutaqqi, denied reports of this as a 'baseless allegation' although he did then explain, with no sense of irony, 'It is true to say that a large number of Taliban have come from Pakistan to congratulate their classmates on their victory.'

Pakistan had tried to play the old game and draw the Taliban into a new anti-Massud alliance, including all the other main players, Hekmatyar, Dostam and the Hazara alliance. But despite significant pressure from the Pakistani interior minister, as well as their backers on the frontier, the Taliban did not even turn up to the meeting in Pakistan, preferring to continue the war, and take power on their own. This meant that when they did take Kabul, they had few friends, and never secured the international recognition they craved. Pakistan did agree to recognise the government of their difficult client; Saudi Arabia and the United Arab Emirates were the only others that did.

The UN made an effort to engage with the new administration, taking a copy of the UN Charter translated into Pashtu to Kandahar to show the Taliban what it meant to be a country. An envoy went through it page by page, sitting cross-legged on the ground, as he was asked what it meant when it talked of 'human rights and fundamental freedoms for all, without distinction as to race, sex, language or religion'. But Mullah Omar refused to meet the UN envoy then or at any other time. And the Taliban had a particular problem with Britain, where Massud's brother continued as ambassador in London, even though Massud's control was now limited to a narrow wedge of land in the north-east.

US policy was thrown into confusion by the emergence of the Taliban, whose success had not been predicted. Afghanistan had fallen off the radar since Charlie Wilson's final huge arms procurement in 1991. The head of the south Asia desk at the State Department, Robin Raphel, was a lone voice trying to raise the issue, and as late as April 1996, only five months before the fall of Kabul, she said the Taliban appeared to 'have reached the limit of its expansion'.

When the Taliban became stronger, Raphel backed calls for an arms embargo, but argued that relations should not be completely cut off: 'The real source of their success has been the willingness of many Afghans, particularly Pashtuns, to tacitly trade unending fighting and chaos for a measure of peace and security, even with severe social restrictions . . . It is not in the interest of Afghanistan or any of us here that the Taliban be isolated.' This analysis, appearing to leave the door open to a policy of constructive engagement, explains an odd incident in the first hours after Kabul was taken, when US officials came close to recognition of the new regime – a State Department spokesman finding 'nothing objectionable' in the way the Taliban imposed Islamic law. The statement was subsequently buried, but US enthusiasm for stability in Afghanistan, no matter who was in government, was more than just the pragmatism of a superpower. It derived from Afghanistan's strategic importance in a new Great Game – not this time over empire but energy.

Wanting to contain Russian ambitions, and secure new energy supplies, the US sought new friendships in the 'Stans'. One of these desperately poor and dysfunctional countries, Turkmenistan, sits on a huge natural gas field. In an effort to cut out Iran, the US was backing a plan for gas and oil pipelines from Turkmenistan to cross Afghanistan towards markets in Pakistan, and beyond.

The Turkmen leader, Saparmurat Niyazov, was an unreconstructed Stalinist, with a personality cult of North Korean
proportions. His slowly revolving golden statue dominated the
capital Ashgabat. He banned dogs from the capital, beards,
make-up on newsreaders, and public libraries, since 'Turkmen
people do not read books.' He renamed the days of the week
and the months of the year – using his mother's name for what
had been April. If the US was prepared to work with the
megalomaniac with the revolving statue, then friendship with
the Taliban should not present major obstacles. The Taliban
professed a similar faith to Saudi Arabia, the US's largest oil
supplier and largest arms buyer. Perhaps Aghanistan might
develop along the same lines as Saudi Arabia had, with
'pipelines, an Amir, no parliament, and lots of sharia law' in the
cynical but frank admission of one US diplomat, adding, 'We
can live with that.'

Even before the Taliban took Kabul, officials from the
favoured US bidder for the pipeline, Unocal, were offering
humanitarian aid as 'bonuses' to Afghan groups who could
unite behind the project – effectively bribes for warlords. And
when the capital did fall to the Taliban, a Unocal official said it
would make the pipeline project 'easier to implement'. The
impact of the Taliban takeover on human rights seemed of
secondary interest to the pipeline deal, according to one
concerned UN official, who said the outside world appeared to
be 'just renting the Taliban for their own purposes'.

Mullah Omar was no fool, and allowed Unocal to set up an
office in Kandahar, sending Taliban officials to the US to
negotiate, but without control of more of the country the deal
was a non-starter. North of the Hindu Kush, General Dostam
was still in power. The battle for the north, as it changed hands
twice in 1997 and '98, would turn out to be the most violent of
the Taliban years, with savage consequences for civilians
caught in the middle.

At the last *buzkashi* game played in the north before it fell to
the Taliban, Dostam was unwilling to talk about their threat.
He was off duty, enjoying this traditional Afghan game played

on horseback, a mad fight without rules for possession of the carcass of a calf, and he even mounted up and rode for a time, although his rather solid barrel-like horse was not ideal for the fierce scrums and fast chases that characterised the game. He said the Taliban could never take the north, because 'they do not play *buzkashi*'.

At his over-large house in his stronghold, Shebargan, west of Mazar-i-Sharif, he was happier talking about horses than conflict. He had never heard before of the British adventurer and horse-breeder William Moorcroft, whose obsession with new bloodstock had brought him to the north, where he had died and been buried in 1825 somewhere near where we were sitting. Dostam immediately offered to arrange a search party to search for the grave.

He said he hated being called a warlord, although it is hard to think of anyone better suited to the description, and gave us the ridiculously expensive 'Blue Label' Johnnie Walker, affordable only by dictators, oil sheikhs and footballers, as fairy lights lit up plaster deer nestling in the plastic undergrowth fringing his pool. The air hostesses he used to import from Essex to sit around the pool when he briefly ran his own airline had gone now, but a few days spent with Dostam in the north were a glimpse of another Afghanistan – outward looking and central Asian; islamic but not enclosed. He took us on a tour of a medical school, walking purposefully through the girls' dormitory to shrieks of consternation, and arranged a meeting of the Shebargan 'women's committee'.

One morning he called out his praetorian guard for our inspection, a couple of hundred men with well-maintained armoured fighting vehicles. He told the stories of men he had recruited as children when they came to wipe the mud from his windscreen, who were now his senior sergeants. These were the feared *kilim jams,* who left nothing behind when they came to call. They had remained loyal to him as communist militia-men, an independent northern army, allies of Massud and enemies of Massud.

Dostam's authority was strengthened by his ability to play

his war games on away ground. His men may have been brutal in fighting south of the Hindu Kush, but hardly a shell had fallen on the capital of the north Mazar-i-Sharif, as he took money at different times from Turkey, Russia, Iran and the US. But it was all coming to an end. Soon after we met, Dostam became caught up in a local feud, and implicated in the death of a popular commander, who was shot at a funeral, his body falling, by macabre chance, into an open grave. The brother of the dead commander did a deal with the Taliban to let them into the north.

This sudden reversal of fortunes led to Dostam fleeing north across the Oxus River to Uzbekistan, rather than attempting to rally his forces. He had seen what had happened to the former communist president Najibullah and his brother. The city fell with hardly a shot fired, but Taliban rule in the north was as alien as it had been in the western town of Herat. There was a significant Pashtun minority, mostly descendants of those forcibly resettled there 100 years before as a piece of social engineering to try to unite the country by the 'iron amir', Abdur Rahman. But the majority were Uzbeks, Hazaras or Tajiks. Women did not routinely cover their heads in the streets, and they expected to be able to work. External influences had affected Mazar more than anywhere else in Afghanistan, guaranteeing more rights for women, while cinemas and video shops did a roaring trade in the latest Bollywood offerings of gory violence and stylised love.

Alongside the liberal Sunni majority, Shia customs were strong. The town was dominated by the beautiful shimmering dome of the Blue Mosque, built where Afghan legend says that Hazrat Ali, the son-in-law of the Prophet Mohammed, and revered by Shias, is buried. It is surrounded by swerving clouds of white doves, and if a black bird enters, they tell you it will turn white.

With their customary lack of nuance, the Taliban imposed their baleful rules on Mazar as they had everywhere else. It was not their restrictions on women, but their attempt to disarm the local population, that led to their downfall. Three days after the Taliban takeover, Hazaras in the north-west of the city began an insurrection, and when the shooting started, every man in the city with a rifle joined in – a lethal cacophony. As we scurried to safety along mud-walled alleys that offered no protection, we saw the real power in the town, a man they called *pahlawan* – strong man – the father of the commander whose fallout with Dostam had let the Taliban in. He was controlling events, unconcerned about the bullets whipping through the air, sitting incongruously in a striped deckchair, wearing soft bright-blue slippers. After two days of vicious hand-to-hand fighting, thousands of Taliban were killed, and thousands more taken prisoner and killed later, some sealed in shipping containers and left to suffocate.

When the Taliban returned to power in the north some months later, again after a deal with disaffected leaders, they carried out indiscriminate revenge killings of men, women and children across Mazar. A witness said, 'I could see smoke coming from the west . . . It was chaos. People were running and being hit by cars trying to leave, market stalls were overturned. I heard one man say, "It's hailing," because of the bullets.' After the initial frenzy, the Taliban specifically targeted Hazaras, going into schools, business, shops and hospitals, and killing thousands. The new Taliban governor made speeches urging them to convert to Sunni Islam, and said that Hazara Shias were not Muslims at all. Once again shipping containers were used for the wholesale murder of prisoners.

13

Sons of Dost

'Do you want to be remembered as a son of Dost
Mohammed or a son of Shah Shuja?'

Taliban recruiting slogan 2005

Sajjad, nicknamed 'the Afghan', sat warily in the middle of a
room in a prison in Kashmir surrounded by Indian soldiers.
His captors were pleased with themselves. He was their prime
exhibit in a display of prisoners that included a Lebanese
bomb-maker, another unidentified Arab and half a dozen
young Kashmiris. 'The Afghan' had fair skin, green eyes and a
wispy beard. He was from the eastern mountains of
Afghanistan, not the deserts of the Pashtun south.

It was February 1994, towards the end of winter in the
foothills of the Himalayas, and he was dressed in a single-piece
long woollen cape that pulled on over the head, a *ferung*,
standard wear for Kashmiris. 'The Afghan' would not say
much, and did not need to, for the Indian security forces had
made their point that there were increasing numbers of
foreigners coming across the mountains to fight against Indian
control of the Kashmir valley. This was a very significant catch
indeed. 'The Afghan' was the military commander of a new
force, backed by Pakistan to defeat India in Kashmir, using

weapons originally supplied to the Afghan mujahidin, principally by the US and Saudi Arabia. India did not know then, could not know, that it was at the receiving end of something more than a fight for control of Kashmir. This was the first front line in a new kind of conflict – a global jihad – war without borders, progressing towards the attacks on 9/11.

The roots of the Kashmir conflict go back 200 years. When that first British envoy, Mountstuart Elphinstone, met the 'unlucky amir', Shah Shuja, in 1809, the whole of the region, arching north from Kabul to the Kashmir Valley, including the world's second highest mountain K2, was controlled by Afghanistan. But as Britain extended its reach through the nineteenth century, 'the roof of the world' came under its influence, governed from Kashmir.

During partition between Pakistan and India in 1947, to force the issue of Kashmir's future status, Pakistan launched an invasion force of frontier tribesmen, descendants of the *ghazis* who had fought British forces for so long in the same region. They came close to taking 'The Valley' itself, a magical honeymooners' paradise of lakes with houseboats, woods of willow and giant plane trees, fringed by peaks topped with white snow like cake icing. That savage little war left Pakistan with one third of the territory of the original princely state, but not the Valley, when the UN intervened to stop the fighting. The two sides had been kept apart since by a 'line of control' that neither recognised as a border, locking them into what one governor of the Indian-controlled region graphically called 'frozen turbulence'.

Pakistan inspired a new armed struggle against Indian control of the Kashmir Valley in the late 1980s. With the US blessing Islamic holy warriors heading into Afghanistan, this seemed the best chance yet to unfreeze the turbulence. Pakistan set up training camps on its side of the line of control, concealed in the forests and hills of the Black Mountain region that had once been the stronghold of the Hindustani fanatics, the nineteenth-century forerunners of al-Qaeda.

But by 1993, the pro-Indian lobby in Congress had

persuaded the new Clinton administration to put Pakistan on its watch list as a 'State sponsor of International Terrorism'. The reluctance of Pakistani intelligence, the ISI, to secure the safe return of hundreds of Stinger missiles missing since being issued to the mujahidin, was the crucial concern for the US administration, but the issue of the worsening insurgency in Kashmir was also raised. Pakistan came off the terrorist list after dismissing several leading intelligence officials, and agreeing to close the training camps for Kashmiri guerrillas on its territory. Conveniently since the fall of the communist-backed government in Kabul in 1992, they had the perfect place to put them – eastern Afghanistan.

Not for the first time, Afghanistan was a pawn in someone else's game. The military leadership in Pakistan had as great an obsession with Afghanistan as the most Forward of British analysts in the nineteenth century, wanting to control the land beyond the Suleiman Mountains, to give them 'strategic depth', so they would not be left with their backs against the wall if India were to invade. Pakistan's funding of training camps in Afghanistan for Kashmiri guerrillas killed two birds with one stone – taking the camps off Pakistani soil to satisfy the US, and giving them a stake in eastern Afghanistan.

Pakistanis and Kashmiris trained alongside 'Arab-Afghans', among them veterans of the Soviet war in Afghanistan. Those who answered the call had a much wider agenda than a new border for Kashmir: their horizon extended beyond all borders to a misty distant dream of a reformed caliphate in a pan-Islamic world. Sajjad, 'the Afghan', was the first military commander of the new force that emerged from the Afghan camps, the *Harkat ul-Ansar*. Before 1993 most Kashmiri guerrillas reflected a more innocent age: wearing berets and face scarves, they modelled themselves on Che Guevara, and wanted no more than independence for their Valley. But by the mid-1990s, the locals were finding themselves demoted to porters and guides by the foreign fighters, whose aim was not just control of the Valley, but control of hearts, minds and souls everywhere.

The name of the new militia spoke volumes about the new mood. The main local insurgency had used an English name, the 'Jammu and Kashmir Liberation Front', and the long Afghan war had not introduced more imaginative names either: factions could for example be translated as 'Party of Holy Warriors', or 'Grouping of Islam'. *Harkat ul-Ansar* was different, reaching back to the earliest days of the faith – the Prophet Mohammed's flight from Mecca to exile in Medina. The Ansar were those who had welcomed the Prophet and his followers into their homes, and the word came to be used to describe well-armed and highly mobile horsemen, a class of warriors that more than any other were responsible for the spread of the Islamic faith in its first two centuries.

Along with the new name came a new ferocity. Several kidnappings of Western tourists in Kashmir were attributed to the Harkat ul-Ansar: some were released, some killed. It also became harder for reporters to travel in the North-West Frontier region, to secure permission to film in the madrassas, or at political rallies. There was something in the air – a new seriousness of intent, and hostility to the West.

On 18th May 1996, four months before the Taliban took Kabul, Osama bin Laden arrived back in Afghanistan after a break of six years, his fortunes at their lowest ebb. After his days as the bank manager to the mujahidin in the war against the Soviet Union, he had briefly returned home in 1990 to Saudi Arabia as a hero, and made what appears to have been a serious offer to mobilise his Arab-Afghan fighters against Saddam Hussein's invasion of Kuwait. He could not understand the Saudi government's decision to accept the US offer of six aircraft carrier battle groups, 23 army brigades and nine Marine regiments, at the head of a million-strong multinational invasion force instead.

The idea of foreign forces coming onto the sacred soil of Saudi Arabia drove bin Laden to make a decisive break with the ruling family, and in 1992 he took refuge in Sudan, where his followers said he lost hundreds of millions of dollars in useless investments, although the State Department believed he was now 'one of the most significant financial sponsors of Islamic extremist activities in the world'. He survived an assassination attempt, and fell out with the government in Sudan, who even offered to hand him over to the US – an offer that was declined. By early 1996, he was running out of places to go.

It was not the Taliban who had invited bin Laden to Afghanistan. He had no links with them, and did not fly into the area in the south they then held, but to Jalalabad, not yet under Taliban control, where he was remembered by mujahidin contacts from the Soviet war. When he arrived he was given a house, and Pakistan put some of the training camps they had set up for Kashmiri guerrillas under his control. Whatever the state of his own finances, bin Laden still had some backers to call on, and was developing a bigger project than the struggle for Kashmir. For this he needed publicity, and he did several TV interviews, and also a press conference for Pakistani journalists at a training camp, where jihadi fighters raced around in trucks, shooting in the air. A cameraman who met bin Laden said he had almost no charisma; shaking his hand was like holding a 'wet, cold fish'.

Bin Laden talked in elliptical rhetoric, but buried within the looping swirls of his speeches and interviews evoking the past of Islam, came his first significant statement since his return, in August 1996, issued from the Tora Bora cave complex that his construction company had extended a decade before, burrowing into the Suleiman Mountains. The 'Declaration of War Against the Americans Occupying the Land of the Two Holy Sites' broke with his former paymasters, both in Saudi Arabia and the US. But his detailed threats, including a demand for Arab women to boycott American goods (since presumably they do the shopping), were not taken seriously at levels that matter in Washington.

A month after this statement, the Taliban swept in to take the east of Afghanistan, and then moved on to take Kabul. They took over the training camps, ordered bin Laden to stop threatening attacks abroad, and sent him south to Kandahar, where they thought he would have a lower profile. His international agenda was a distraction from the Taliban campaign to bring law and order to Afghanistan. He moved to the south, but ignored their other orders, settling into an abandoned farmhouse with his three wives and children, to plot the downfall of the US.

Before any attack, bin Laden always chose a deliberate symbol. In an interview in early 1998 there was a map of Africa behind him. Not long afterwards, on a Friday morning, a time when all good Muslims should have been at prayer, two trucks loaded with bombs headed for US embassy buildings in Africa, one in Kenya, the other Tanzania. The bomb in Tanzania was designed to have more impact, as gas canisters had been placed around a central core of 2000 pounds of TNT, but a water tanker in front of the embassy took most of the blast. Eleven died there, none of them Americans. In Kenya though, the bomb took off the front of the embassy, killing 213 people and injuring many more.

The US at the time was in thrall to the Lewinsky affair. Military judgements about the scale and pace of retaliation demanded after the African attacks were weighed up in Washington while, across town, 'that woman' was giving oral evidence to a Grand Jury about oral sex in the White House. In the Arab world they believed that military action would be taken to save Bill Clinton, and in street demonstrations they held up placards: 'No war for Monica'.

More than sixty cruise missiles were launched, mostly from ships stationed in the Gulf, with their GPS navigation systems set for the training camps around Khost in the east of Afghanistan, where there was little physical infrastructure to destroy. Fewer than 30 people were killed, none of them an al-Qaeda leader, most of them Afghans training to fight in Kashmir.

The incident defined the world's new battlefield with precision. A defence budget that would soon top half a trillion dollars a year, designed to fight a continental war, was useless against an enemy with little to blow up. As British forces had found in the region in the nineteenth century, destroying a Fanatic camp did not destroy the movement. The offensive weapons of a superpower were worse than useless against al-Qaeda. This was the reverse side of asymmetric warfare – a phenomenon usually seen from the point of view of attempts by insurgents to develop their own weapons, like suicide bombing, in the face of overwhelming tactical superiority by conventional forces. The Khost attacks may have satisfied an understandable US desire for revenge, but were a public relations disaster: an Islamist propaganda coup.

TV pictures from Khost showed the pages of a partly burnt Koran flapping in the wind, damage to a mosque, and unexploded cruise missiles (subsequently sold abroad by bin Laden). Another dozen or so cruise missiles killed a night watchman and destroyed a factory in Sudan. US evidence that the plant was developing chemical weapons has never been proved. Later investigations suggested it was a pharmaceutical factory, as Sudan said it was.

That was the year Osama first became a popular name for boys born in the North-West Frontier; printers could not turn out T-shirts and posters showing his face quickly enough to meet the demand and disaffected young Muslim men worldwide had a cause. The US administration played its part in creating the bin Laden brand, blaming him for involvement in a long list of attacks going back to the deaths of 18 servicemen in Mogadishu in 1993, although some officials would admit that there was little evidence for much of this. The US had defined its enemy, drawing the battle lines that would develop into the Global War on Terror.

Bin Laden retreated into his cave, physically, spiritually and mentally detached from the normal world. Among the dreams of his followers was an Islamic Stealth bomber, that could fly anywhere without being detected. They drew up the plans, reasoning that their labour was given free, so they would not need the billions of dollars it cost the US to build such a plane. But amid this childish madness, a plan was developing that involved undetected planes of quite a different sort, and had asymmetric military brilliance – bringing down skyscrapers for the price of just a few pilots' licences.

The 1998 attacks in Africa, and the US response, had one clear result for Afghanistan: the fate of al-Qaeda was linked with the Taliban for ever. Only a few weeks earlier, the Saudi spymaster Prince Turki, a frequent traveller to Afghanistan at that time, believed he had succeeded in persuading the Taliban to hand bin Laden over to him. He had offered 400 of the Hilux pickups that were their preferred war chariot in return. The vehicles had been delivered, but when he arrived to collect bin Laden, Turki found that the US missile attack had changed the situation. The Taliban leader Mullah Omar insulted the Saudi royal family saying 'We may be very poor, we Afghans, and you are very rich and powerful. But we are not someone like you. You have no honour.' It was the kind of answer that would win Omar respect from Muslims worldwide, especially after the Prince insulted his hosts by leaving without eating the meal prepared for him. The US did no better: officials sent a secure satphone to Omar and had several long but fruitless conversations to try to persuade him to hand bin Laden over.

The one thing the Taliban craved was recognition as the legitimate government of Afghanistan, but that the US was not prepared to offer. Thus the third opportunity to bring Afghanistan back from the brink was squandered. Each time the country had been ignored before, when the Soviet army pulled out in 1989, and when the mujahidin took over in 1992, the suffering had been terrible inside Afghanistan. This time, the world's failure to engage constructively in Afghanistan would have more far-reaching consequences.

By now, even if recognition of the Taliban had been on the table, it might not have broken through the Pashtun honour code that gave bin Laden protection as a guest. After the Saudi attempt to arrest him, the Taliban held a shura that went on for several days to decide what to do. The decision was taken that bin Laden should be asked to try to find somewhere else to live, but as Mullah Omar made the phone call to his trouble-some guest he knew there was nowhere else. This stubborn adherence to the ancient Pashtun hospitality code looks incomprehensible from outside, but those who knew the Taliban high command well deny that Mullah Omar and bin Laden were ever close friends, despite rumours, enthusiastically retold by US officials, that they went fishing together. Omar's family has also rejected the most persistent rumour – that they were related by marriage. The Taliban did not share bin Laden's desire to change the world – they did not look beyond their own Afghan horizon. He was going to cause the movement trouble, and ultimately bring the sky crashing down on their heads, but he was a fellow Wahhabi and a guest, and that was that.

Afghan hospitality for bin Laden ended any further attempts by the US State Department to take a pragmatic line on the Taliban in order to secure the pipeline deal. And the Clinton administration's room for manoeuvre in Afghanistan became more limited because of the Lewinsky affair. When Hillary Clinton stood by her man, female voters gave him the benefit of the doubt, and anyone wanting a more nuanced approach on the Taliban was silenced. The US moved in a few months from a position of having no policy about Afghanistan to one that focused only on one aspect of the Taliban – their treat-ment of women. The cause became fashionable in Hollywood. As the *Washington Post* excitedly reported, 'Tibet is out. Afghanistan is in.'

In Kabul, a Taliban minister asked me around this time, 'Why are you so interested in *our* women?' He was perplexed by what appeared to him to be an obsession. The Taliban thought they were being respectful by sticking to the letter of the Islamic injunction that the women's world was a private space, *purdah*. The view of much of the outside world that this amounted to harsh treatment and an abuse of human rights made their cause hopeless.

Western opinion was informed by stunts that the Taliban could not combat even if they had known how to try. A major

US network anchorwoman threw off her head-covering in the middle of an interview with a Taliban minister, daring him to be shocked by the sight of her hair, while the EU humanitarian affairs commissioner, Emma Bonino, never shy of publicity, managed to engineer a situation where she and 19 Western journalists and aid officials were arrested and held for a few hours for taking photos of women patients in a hospital. Bonino described her treatment as 'an example of how people live here in a state of terror'.

In this atmosphere there was nothing the Taliban could do that was right. It was only after some years in power that they successfully banned the growing of opium poppies. The move was greeted with some cynicism internationally, and the view expressed that the move had been taken to push up prices. Financial compensation to the Taliban was minimal. This grudging and small-minded response directly caused the destruction of the giant Buddhas, that had stood like sentinels in the wall of the Hindu Kush for more than 1000 years. When Western donors appeared to care more about the Buddhas than a looming humanitarian crisis threatened by drought, the extremist wing of the Taliban, which had been arguing for their destruction for years, had their way and blew them up.

In 2001, among all of the consequences of 9/11, US retaliation against Afghanistan was the one that was most predictable, and indeed understandable, after such trauma. The Taliban's hold on Afghanistan already looked vulnerable. Isolated internationally, and coping with the worst drought seen for many years, they were facing far more determined opposition than for some years. The former northern commander, General Dostam, had dropped by helicopter into the country at the western end of the Hindu Kush several months before the attacks of 9/11, and was rallying his forces for a cavalry assault riding *buzkashi* horses against the Taliban in Mazar-i-Sharif. Iran too, outraged by a Taliban massacre of Hazaras in the spring of 2001, was stepping up aid to enemies of the Taliban.

There had been no movement though on the crucial Kabul

front, where Massud's forces had failed to break through Taliban lines. Just days before 9/11, an Arab TV crew that had been waiting for some time to secure an interview with Massud killed him with a bomb planted in their camera. The US quickly assembled a coalition of nations against the Taliban, working on the ground with what was now called the Northern Alliance, uniting those anti-Taliban forces whose disunity since the fall of the Soviet government had made space for the rise of the Taliban in the first place.

The Taliban were defenceless against the relentless aerial bombardment that went on day and night, degrading their ability to fight, and disrupting their supply lines, so that the ground offensive was short and the Taliban were ousted from power. A separate US force mounted an assault on the Tora Bora caves in a search for bin Laden. Despite an intensive bombing campaign he escaped, probably across the frontier to Pakistan. But a quick war was not followed by the expected quick peace, as another foreign force tripped up on the other side of the Suleiman Mountains.

The simple narrative of heroes and demons – 'mujahidin good', 'Taliban bad'– imposed on Afghanistan was another externally drawn picture: an Afghanistan of the Western mind just as much as the one drawn by Lieutenant Macartney, when he imagined the land beyond the mountains two centuries before. The mismatch between the simplistic analysis imposed from outside and the complex reality on the ground would have a profound impact on political and military planning.

The common TV image of Afghanistan during the Taliban years – a woman in a powder-blue burqa, trudging past ruins – told only part of the story, and did not prepare Western public opinion for the reaction to the US-led takeover of Afghanistan after 9/11. The first surprise was that women did not come out on the streets and 'throw off their burqas' as required in the script: Afghan society did not suddenly become Western.

The explanation for this, according to a teacher in Herat, filmed making up her face, before covering herself with a burqa to go out, was that the towns were full of peasants. Her face could appear on international television, but not in her own high street. The former mujahidin, who became the so-called Northern Alliance forces, that drove out the Taliban with the assistance of an international force led by the US, had brought their simple rural ways with them, and that meant women needed still to cover up. Afghan society had been fundamentally transformed during a quarter of a century of conflict, more by the Western-funded mujahidin than the Taliban. The complex and subtle tapestry of civil society had been overwhelmed by the needs of a holy war, and it was hard to stitch it back together again.

The Taliban were harsh and repressive, but only an extreme version of what was now the Afghan norm. Women's clothing did not disappear from public display in shops outside the main cities on Taliban orders. The cover-up began, even in Massud's kingdom, the Panjshir valley, much earlier, as the ratchet of Islamicisation moved in only one direction. The cheap, Russian-made, waxy-yellow plastic dummies, with their moulded blonde hair, and a slightly unsettling stare, were removed from dress-shop windows when the communists fell from power, long before the Taliban emerged.

And the more extreme punishments demanded by sharia law, including amputation for theft, were imposed a long time before the Taliban emerged, in some areas under the control of the forces that became US allies in the Northern Alliance. The communists had destroyed the old courts, and left nothing behind, so the mujahidin empowered Muslim clerics to administer justice. In 1985, a full ten years before the Taliban, the French Afghan expert Olivier Roy wrote, 'The resistance movement has brought with it a strengthening of Islam's role in shaping the social order.' Sharia made sense of chaos.

An Islamic cleric in Kabul claimed that the mujahidin government in power before the Taliban had themselves wanted a Saudi-style 'virtue and vice' ministry and religious police, and held back only because they were concerned about the international reaction.

Brutal, conservative and repressive the Taliban may have been, but the West ignored their significant popularity in parts of Afghanistan; the fact that they kept honest accounts, and raised more customs revenues in their last year than in the first year of US-sponsored democracy in 2002; that under their rule it was possible for the first time in a generation to travel safely by day or night across most of the country (as it has not been since they fell); or that once they had taken full control of the south they successfully stopped the growing of opium poppies – a tough challenge given the scale of the profits involved, particularly in Helmand, and something the international community has failed to do since.

The US did not see how their Northern Alliance allies were perceived, or how they would behave, until it was too late, because they had been portrayed as heroes of the mujahidin. The Taliban regime did collapse like sand, but just as the Soviet Union had had to reconfigure its 'limited contingent' within months, when it realised the kind of war it was fighting, so the US-led invasion force found itself in a security situation that became worse rather than better. This deterioration was not inevitable. The simple-minded repression of the Taliban in power made it hard for them to win new recruits in the early years after they were forced out. But a unique window of opportunity, when there was goodwill for the international community to succeed, closed quickly.

Afghanistan was a unique crucible where all three recent Big Ideas about political organisation were tried out. Communism and Islamism had clearly failed, now Democracy had its turn, bringing the benefits of the free market. But what came next confounded the hopes of those whose thinking had been infused by ideas about democracy's inevitable victory in a 'clash of civilisations'.

The countries backing the US-led intervention in 2001 exhibited a lack of curiosity about Afghanistan, believing in the power of a one-size-fits-all democratic model to deliver stability. In a remarkable admission later, the EU representative in Kabul, Francesc Vendrell, said they did not bother to find out what was really happening. 'People knew that there were various tribes within the Pashtun. But because there was a feeling that things were still going to become normal, it was not thought necessary for us to understand the tribal system.'

If the West forgot history, the Afghans certainly did not. It was not long before the Taliban were asking young men, 'Do you want to be remembered as a son of Dost Mohammed or a son of Shah Shuja?', reminding recruits that Mullah Omar was the first leader since Dost who had displayed the holy cloak and declared himself *Amir al-Mu'minin* against the invaders. To them, the modern 'Shah Shuja', the puppet of the foreign invader, was of course President Hamid Karzai.

Karzai emerged as the only credible presidential candidate in the early heady months after the fall of the Taliban: a fastidious man, who had learnt his English in the kind of boarding school in India left over from the empire, where boys are still taught to play up and play the game. Karzai's obvious good nature and his dress sense brought international attention of quite a new kind to Afghanistan. For a season, fashion magazines were full of pieces on lambskin hats, and how to wear those sleeveless robes. But even in the early days there were big questions being asked about whether he was the right man for a tough job.

Karzai was not Washington's first choice: they turned to him after disaster followed the return of the highly competent and popular mujahidin leader Abdul Haq, dropped by US forces into the south of Afghanistan before the Taliban fell. The Taliban discovered where he was and killed him as he tried to make his escape on horseback.

When the Taliban fell, Karzai was appointed by the US and then anointed by the *loya jirga*, a meeting of elders that approved Afghanistan's first democratic constitution. To guarantee that the *loya jirga* would not trail on for months in the Afghan way, a deadline was imposed on the availability of a temporary purpose-built air-conditioned meeting space. Afghanistan was being kicked into a new century. Perhaps it would have been better if the elders had been allowed to sit and talk for a while longer.

Tens of thousands of refugees flooded home now their homeland was under new rulers. Most came from refugee camps in the North-West Frontier, and in Iran, but others returned from the US, Canada and Europe, with goodwill to rebuild their country, many with degrees and foreign bank accounts. Abandoned shops in Kabul were taken over and filled with kitchen and bathroom equipment as a building boom began. In a yard behind the national bank, brick kilns 20 feet high burnt night and day, fuelled by bales of old bank-notes, as a new currency was quickly imposed. Karzai was duly elected in the country's first presidential election in 2004. But the US discovered, as Britain and Russia had before, that taking Afghanistan was the easy bit. This time, efforts to build a nation were defeated from within, by the very tools sent for reconstruction. The billions of dollars that flowed from abroad for development might have been better used as fuel for the kilns behind the central bank as corruption set in: the new Afghanistan was rotten to the core.

During the early years after the Taliban's fall from power returning refugees set a new more progressive tone in Afghan life; the purist austerity of the Taliban had little appeal. Ironically, it was Hekmatyar, the US's old ally against the communists, who seemed more of a threat in a NATO military analysis in 2003: 'The Taliban and al-Qaeda are no longer capable of acting in a military sense, but Hekmatyar obviously has the money, influence, political will, and power to reorganise the elements under his leadership.'

But in 2006, a generation after he was first trained as a guerrilla by Pakistan, Hekmatyar announced that he would now fight under the al-Qaeda banner. They and the Taliban had re-emerged as serious forces in Afghanistan. The Taliban fightback started in their traditional heartland in the south, and spread north, until they controlled as much as 54 per cent of Afghanistan, according to one estimate. Even a more cautious analysis by the World Bank gave them 30 per cent of

Afghanistan in 2007. The re-emergence of the Taliban five years after their fall from power owed much to the failure of foreign forces to tackle corruption.

A drive around Kabul with the head of the capital's serious crimes squad in 2006 was an instructive experience. General Paktiawal was a large engaging man who wore a wide-lapelled chalk-stripe suit and carried a revolver. He led always from the front, in a locally-armoured Land Cruiser with a metal cover built into the bullet-proof windscreen for him to lift up and shoot through. As he drove he pointed out the vast tracts of land seized by various warlords since 2001, now held by force and covered in bulbous concrete mansions painted in bright colours and built, with no thought of planning controls, in that unlovely vulgar style that infects the whole region from the Mediterranean to Delhi – 'Dubai Kitsch'.

North-east of the capital in Sherpur, where the British army had been besieged in 1879, most of the cantonment had been built over some years previously to create the upmarket district of Wazir Akbar Khan – named after Dost Mohammed's son, who led the revolt against British rule in 1841. But the last remaining corner of the former garrison area, still government-owned when the Northern Alliance swept into Kabul in 2001, had been seized by some of those appointed to the first post-Taliban administration, and parcelled out between them.

The tracks across the land were not paved, so our four-wheel-drive vehicles made slow progress as they wallowed through the fine dust, past the overlarge villas some of which went on to change hands for two million dollars each. With no public services, the area rumbled with the permanent thunder of giant generators, each the size of a ship's engine, with the carbon footprint of an African town; conflict is bad for climate change.

General Paktiawal then took us north on the trail of an illegal arms sale. The road went across the Shomali plain, beneath the tall curtain of the Hindu Kush. Several years after the fall of the Taliban the fields are still not productive. Plenty of consultants had been to visit the giant Chinese-built irrigation pumping system to the north, damaged in the war, but it was still not operational. A pure white Land Cruiser with a bunch of plastic flowers on the dashboard passed at high speed, at the head of a convoy coming in the other direction. General Paktiawal recognised it as belonging to the warlord in control of the area, and, sure enough, a few seconds later, the warlord was on the phone, demanding to know what the police chief was doing on his patch. Paktiawal reassured him with a story that he was just on his way to visit a friend at Charikar police station.

Paktiawal had not told anyone at police headquarters where he was going; he trusted nobody except his own men. We were on our own, as the trail led up a mountain track. The pursuit ended with the arrest of two men, who carried a book containing names and dates of arms deals, and some counterfeit banknotes. Only a few weeks after this incident, Paktiawal was held and beaten up in the same area.

One aspirant police chief of a northern province was told that the price was '150,000'. He turned up at the ministry of interior with his bribe, and was at first received well, but then realised his mistake: the price was to be paid *in dollars*, not the far smaller amount in the local currency. He was contemptuously thrown out.

The failure of the Karzai government and its international supporters to deliver justice or fair policing was the most significant factor in the return of the Taliban. Much of rural Afghanistan reverted to the Taliban and sharia law, for the same reason they had turned to the mujahidin after the Soviet invasion – to provide order and justice in the face of foreign failure. In Wardak Province, not in the Pashtun south, but easily accessible from Kabul, on a good road only an hour's drive west, a farmer, Nur Rahman, said 'There is no government to deal with cases. The judges, even the lowest civil servants, are corrupt and they want bribes. People go to the Taliban and tribal elders instead to sort out their problems.' The Taliban government was remembered for success in basic projects such as the delivery of fertiliser and seeds, as well as providing electricity. The hydroelectric scheme there broke down after the Taliban fell from power. 'We cannot even get an engineer from the ministry to come and look at it,' he complained.

By 2007 villagers in Wardak spoke as if the Karzai government had already fallen: 'During the time they had control here until this year, there were road blocks, and lots of thieves around. There was oppression and abuse of power,' grumbled a farmer, Mohammed Nazir. 'Since the Taliban came back, the robbers and thieves have all vanished. Security is good. And now the Taliban are solving disputes that the Karzai government did not solve.'

After taking effective control of much of Wardak, the Taliban intervened in an armed conflict between two villages, and even took a French woman journalist to see a school operating in the area under their control. Their chief spokesman admitted, in perhaps the understatement of the century, that they had got their 'public relations image wrong' when they had been in power before. Increasingly the Taliban called themselves mujahidin to extend their appeal, operating an underground network of provincial administrators, parallel to the state. The Taliban military commander in Wardak, Mullah Rashid Akhond, said, 'The Afghan people are helping the mujahidin a lot. All of the weapons stores from the jihad time have been given to the Taliban, who are now hand in hand with the former mujahidin. The nation, the Taliban and the mujahidin are united in fighting a jihad against the forces of the invaders.'

When things did not go according to plan in Afghanistan, it became fashionable for foreign analysts to say that the problem was about 'high expectations' – if only Afghan people realised that rebuilding the country would take a long time, they would be more patient and turn away from the Taliban. But this analysis ignored the negative impact of corruption in the delivery of justice, and the wholesale theft of property by warlords. The perception grew in many corners of Afghanistan that the Karzai government allowed this to happen.

One minister who fell out with President Karzai in the early years over the issue of corruption, Ramazan Bashardost, had spent his years as a refugee as a philosophy professor in France. After he left the government, he held a weekly public 'surgery' in a tent in a public park in Kabul in protest. One afternoon, a group of men arrived from the far north bearing a long list of grievances, mostly about property that had been taken from them during the years of the Karzai government.

By the light of a paraffin lamp in the gathering gloom of a Kabul winter evening, they came forward one by one, pulling ancient title deeds from beneath elaborate robes and telling their stories. One had been in charge of collecting customs revenues in his town, and although a Pashtun he was not a Taliban sympathiser, so when they took over there in 1997, he offered his resignation, since he imagined they would want their own appointee. But they told him they needed trustworthy officials and kept him in post. Following the defeat of the Taliban, when the official refused to hand over the 20 per cent of revenues demanded by President Karzai's new appointee, he was thrown out of his job and lost his house and car as well. After he had made his complaint in the tent, I asked him if he would now support the Taliban. It was a dangerous question. There were police present, craning their heads forward in the group around us to listen. He nodded a quick assent.

The main engine of corruption is the world's most lucrative illegal narcotics trade, worth more than two billion dollars annually, and fuelling both the insurgency and officials at all levels in the government, in effect blurring the distinction between the two. In this amoral world, violence against civilians was not the monopoly of the insurgency. The Taliban, ruthless and destructive though they were, denied responsibility for some of the attacks on schools. As one international development worker in Helmand said, 'To slip through the water unseen, the fish must first muddy the pool.' Disorder suited a number of different elements; 60 per cent of the police in Helmand Province were heroin addicts, and the Governor of the Province, Sher Mohammad Akhundzada, was removed from office by President Karzai at British insistence, after allegations that he too was implicated in the narcotics trade. Amid worsening tension between Karzai and the West, the President regretted agreeing to move the Governor, and nominated him to the upper house of the Afghan parliament.

International efforts to tackle the drugs trade were largely ineffective. The Provinces where they successfully stopped the growing of opium poppies have mostly turned to marijuana instead. Officials at the counter-narcotics ministry complained that international donors spent millions of dollars abroad on a public relations contract, and on planes that they did not need, while bureaucratic obstacles made it impossible to spend any of the funds earmarked for farmers to find alternatives to poppy growing.

Meanwhile middle-ranking officials trying to stop the drugs trade were picked off. Some lost their lives, others only their jobs. General Aminullah Amerkhel was removed from his post in charge of customs at Kabul airport as he was on the brink of exposing what he believed to be a major international smuggling operation. Before he was forced out, there was a remarkable insight into the power that could be exerted by the drugs trade, when a woman was arrested with several kilograms of heroin strapped to her body.

She was filmed openly threatening customs officials, and asking why she had been arrested; she clearly believed she had an arrangement to walk through freely. She claimed she had formerly worked in intelligence, and made specific threats against the customs officials: 'I am warning you. I will come to your house and you will disappear. Use your brain. Don't you understand? I can make six men like you disappear in a day.'

Later that night she was released, and only rearrested after Amerkhel went to the minister's office to complain. A few months later he was forced out of his post, and went into hiding after receiving death threats. Amerkhel had also complained about the standard of work on a renovation project for the building used by customs officials at the airport. He believed that maybe 10 per cent of the million dollars allocated was spent on the project, the rest going on payments to officials.

The biggest international failure, leading to worsening insecurity after 2001, was in the delivery of aid. Despite President Bush's talk of a 'new Marshall Plan', matching the rebuilding of Europe after the Second World War, aid flows to Afghanistan were far lower than implied by that promise – just $75 a head in the first year, compared to an average of $250 a head for other recent post-conflict countries. There were some successes: provision for women's health became possible, and infant mortality rates improved a little – from the catastrophic to the merely dreadful. But continuing problems not only affect the poor: President Karzai's helicopter pilot died in childbirth, a modern woman in a terrible medieval world.

Some schools were built, although not as many as were claimed, and to a very low standard. One of Kabul's oldest and most famous girls' schools put a plaque on its wall, proudly announcing that it was reopened with US support, but there was nothing there to boast about. When I visited it, not long after the money had been spent, it reminded me of a temporary camp erected after a major disaster, such as an earthquake. Most of the girls were still being taught in tents, hot and dusty in summer, cold and muddy in the winter, and where there were classrooms, paint was peeling and the roof was leaking. The headteacher was reluctant to complain, since she told me she knew this was one of the best schools in Kabul; most were far worse.

Several years after the fall of the Taliban, health clinics, even those within easy reach of the capital, had only the most basic treatments available, and no contraceptives, at a time when foreign consultants working for Afghan government ministries could earn $25,000 a month. The failures in development went back to 2001. A unique opportunity was lost at the beginning when civil servants shaved off the beards that had been compulsory in the Taliban years, brought out their Western-style suits from under the mattress and reported to their old ministries, only to be told to go home while an internationally approved plan was put in place.

It would be another three years before USAID, one of the biggest donors, finalised its strategy for Afghanistan, losing vital momentum, and leaving a vacuum that was filled by the Taliban. Along with corruption, the failure to rebuild the country was the other powerful driver of the worsening insurgency. The finance minister in the early years under Karzai, Ashraf Ghani, was bitter about the delay. 'We had a strategy in three months. Why is it that one has to go to parallel strategies?' He calculated that a school built by Afghans would cost only one fifth of the amount needed by an international agency working in Afghanistan. Most of the aid was spent outside the state, not building its capacity, so a weak state could not even spend the funds it was given. The effect was another kind of corruption as a parallel international system, living like a cuckoo on top of Kabul, sucked some of the best resources out of the state for itself.

Several years after the Taliban fell, I started a conversation with the security officer patting down my pockets at the entrance to one of the UN offices that had taken over large parts of the centre of the city. He was in his mid-30s, and had returned home, with his wife and two children and a degree in his pocket gained in a refugee camp – just the kind of man any new nation needed on its side. Once the consultants had agreed the initial plan for the country, he had worked for a while in the higher education ministry, planning the future for Afghan universities, but the job as a doorman for an inter-national agency paid him twice the salary.

As insecurity increased when the Taliban re-emerged, redevelopment was further hampered: security requirements absorbed more money, and aid workers could travel less. The International Committee of the Red Cross, which had long experience in Afghanistan, said the security situation was worse than at any time during nearly three decades of conflict.

1863. The Indus at
Attock was spanned
by a road built onto
boats lashed together.
The first bridge was
built when the
railway came in 1883.

1919. Air power
came to Afghanistan
for the first time.

Queen Soraya, wife of the reforming Amir Amanullah. This photograph, taken during a European tour in 1928, was used by mullahs in the revolution the following year to show how decadent the country had become.

The Amir Habibullah, pictured with his harem dressed in European clothes, c.1905

The Soviet invasion at the end of 1979 was designed only to provide temporary assistance. By the time this picture was taken in March 1980, the plans had changed and troops did not leave until 1989.

Male and female students being taught together in a computer class under Soviet control in Kabul in 1981

Gulbuddin Hekmatyar

Ahmed Shah Massud,
the 'lion of Panjshir'

Charlie Wilson wearing local
dress and riding a horse on his
only trip across the frontier into
Soviet-occupied Afghanistan

An Afghan horseman against the blue backdrop of the mountains – the landscape that
has had such an impact on the character of the people

As early as 1981 the mujahidin were successfully shooting down Soviet helicopters.

Going home: Soviet forces began their pullout after an agreement made
in Geneva in February 1988.

Mullah Omar declared himself 'leader of all the faithful', in 1996, draped in the cloak of the Prophet. This extraordinary image was taken clandestinely through a gap in the curtain in a minibus, with a TV camera resting on Peter Jouvenal's knee.

Taliban fighters in 2007 in Musa Qala, a town they occupied in breach of a controversial deal allowing British forces to leave. They were forced out in heavy fighting in December that year.

March 2002. In the early years after the fall of the Taliban, US forces focused nearly all of their effort in tracking down al-Qaeda suspects, not stabilising the country. This action in a remote mountain region was jointly conducted with Canadian forces.

President Bush with President Karzai in Kabul. In 2004, he said, 'The Taliban no longer exists in Afghanistan. And America and the world are safer for it.'

Royal Marine commandos in action in Helmand Province in early 2007, as British forces faced their most intense fighting for many years

November 2006: Tony Blair visits British troops at Camp Bastion. He told them: 'Here in this extraordinary piece of desert is where the future of world security in the early 21st century is going to be played out.'

The head of their delegation in Kabul, Reto Stocker, stated 'The conflict has not only intensified but it has also spread over the last few years. Prolonged human suffering is causing real concern in ever larger areas. There is little capacity to address it. We've never had so little access.' Across the country once again there were thousands of displaced people fleeing fighting, and complex development initiatives had to be shelved while direct humanitarian assistance – basic food and shelter – took up far more of aid budgets.

I visited a literacy project in Kandahar, where women were given a sack of grain and a litre of cooking oil a month in return for attending lessons. They discarded their burqas like muddy boots in a pile by the entrance and left their children in separate classrooms in the basement while they learnt how to read and count and sew. Inevitably most were refugees and widows from the north. But a few were local Pashtun women who had persuaded their husbands to let them go to this subversive place in return for food. It would be hard to think of any better way of spending money in Afghanistan than on women's literacy in Kandahar, the heartland of the Taliban. But at the time I was there in 2006, the World Food Programme had been forced to stop the supplies to the school because there were so many hungry mouths descending on Kandahar, displaced by the war – clever aid pushed aside for the needs of an emergency.

As they went home without the food that had been promised by the world, the women asked me what they should tell their husbands.

14

The Cheaper Man

A scrimmage in a Border Station
A canter down some dark defile
Two thousand pounds of education
Drops to a ten-rupee jezail
. . .
Strike hard who cares, shoot straight who can
The odds are on the cheaper man.

Rudyard Kipling – 'Arithmetic on the Frontier'

In February 2009 pro-Taliban militant leaders from the frontier region in Pakistan held a meeting in Quetta with Mullah Omar. They came from Swat, Mohmand, Buner, Bajaur and Waziristan – a roll-call of troublesome areas that would have been very familiar to British colonial officials trying to tackle insurgency in the same region a century before. Since he had fled across the frontier from Afghanistan when his government fell in 2001, Omar had retained overall leadership of the movement, and wanted all of its effort focussed on fighting against foreign forces in Afghanistan. But there was now a home-grown Pakistani Taliban whose main enemy was the government of Pakistan. They were increasingly confident, driving around in US military Humvees looted from supply convoys. The leaders of the Pakistani Taliban told Omar that they would still provide a haven for al-Qaeda and Afghan Taliban fighters, and allow Pashtun boys from the madrassas of the frontier to go and fight in Afghanistan, but their own military priority was now building an Islamist state in Pakistan.

The strength of this movement shook the US, and became the biggest foreign policy priority of the new Obama administration. A Pakistani deal to end fighting in the Swat valley in the spring of 2009, handing effective control to the Taliban in return for peace, was strongly opposed in Washington, where on 23rd April Secretary of State Hillary Clinton said that the world faced a 'mortal threat' if this nuclear-armed country fell into the hands of Islamist extremists. President Obama appointed Richard Holbrooke, a veteran diplomat who had been instrumental in bringing peace to the Balkans in the 1990s to conduct what was now called the 'Afpak' policy – consciously linking strategy across the frontier for the first time. Aid flows to Pakistan increased – with the British aid budget for Pakistan now larger than for Afghanistan. Much of this money was focussed on education, to counter the influence of Saudi Arabian funding that had provided the seed-bed of militancy in Wahhabi madrassas.

At the same time, General David Petraeus was promoted from heading US forces in Iraq to take overall control of the region that includes Afghanistan. The Taliban greeted his first arrival in his new command in December 2008 by rocketing Peshawar airport. Petraeus was highly intelligent, with a reputation for surrounding himself with similarly thoughtful analysts – generals with PhDs. He had written a new counterinsurgency doctrine for US forces in 2006, the first for a generation, taking account of lessons learnt in Afghanistan and Iraq – a changed military landscape in which America found itself fighting not big conventional battles against uniformed armies, but long bruising engagements against enemies motivated to die as martyrs. An influential book by a British general called the new environment 'war amongst the people', where victory depended not on superior weapons systems and the exercise of raw force, but on a far more complex set of factors. Winning 'hearts and minds' was not a soft option or an add-on to the use of force; rather it was the centrepiece of the strategic jigsaw.

Petraeus refused to use the word 'victory' at all, knowing that stabilising these troubled nations needed a new approach and new language. By 2009 he was supported by a new administration that was willing to listen. One of the few foreign policy commitments made by Barack Obama in his campaign for the presidency was to take a more active interest in Kashmir – a glimpse of a more coherent strategy emerging for the region. After all, it was in Kashmir that the radicalisation had begun in the early 1990s that had now spread worldwide.

It was very late in the day to be building a coherent policy. Since the warlord economy had been allowed to re-establish itself in Afghanistan under the nose of US forces after 2001, it had become easier for the Taliban to regroup in reaction to it. But the mistakes went back before 9/11. US involvement in the region did not begin with the war in 2001 but in 1979. Responses to the Russian invasion of Afghanistan and the seizure of US embassy staff in Iran – pursued then with the best of motives – had unintended consequences, and then worsened with the corrupting effect of Charlie Wilson's funding, particularly in the two years after the Russians left Afghanistan in 1989. The legacy was not just in military materiel but in minds. In 1979 there were some 700 madrassas, religious schools, in the frontier region. After thirty years of conflict, much of it inspired by US funding, there were more than 7000. And they had spread from the frontier to the plains of Punjab – taking their narrow world view and call to jihad across Pakistan east of the Indus.

As fighting intensified on the Pakistani side of the frontier, erupting into a full-scale war in 2009, the most pressing military challenge was the same as ever: how to deal with the formidable barrier of the Suleiman Mountains. When it was drawn in 1893, the Durand Line had protected insurgents fleeing to Afghanistan. After 2001, the military geography of the region was turned inside out, the border now giving a safe haven to guerrillas on the Pakistani side. Waziristan, the place a weary British official had called 'the plague spot of the frontier' in 1910, played its part again in the twenty-first century as the focal point of the new militancy and a place of refuge for al-Qaeda fighters.

Pakistan had retained the division of territory on the frontier established by Lord Curzon in 1904, between the settled areas in the plains, and the tribal areas in the mountains, where democracy had still not reached and traditional systems remained intact. As militancy spread after 9/11 Pakistani forces did make some attempts to tackle it, sustaining very high casualties. But the crackdown was no more successful in delivering stability than the frontier campaigns of the British empire had been. Around a quarter of the Pakistani army is of Pashtun origin, and on several occasions, large groups of soldiers were 'captured' by insurgents in the frontier region, and deprived of their weapons before being released. Even before the deal handing over the Swat valley to the Taliban in return for a short-lived peace in 2009, there were several earlier deals in which Pakistani forces withdrew, allowing local villages to police themselves – effectively handing them over to the militants. The deals incensed international forces in Afghanistan, who were themselves forbidden from pursuing insurgents across the frontier.

The increasing use of US air strikes against suspected al-Qaeda leaders from unmanned drones sent across the frontier raised anti-US sentiment in Pakistan as the inevitable civilian death toll grew. The Pakistani Taliban successfully exploited this anger to gain support among tribal elders as they promoted themselves as defenders against US attacks. They found willing recruits among those alienated by the modern world.

The radicalisation of significant elements of Pakistani society that gathered pace in the 1990s had become even more pronounced since the US-led invasion of Iraq in 2003. President Bush's rhetoric – 'if you are not with us you are against us'– left little room for manoeuvre, drawing battle lines here as elsewhere in the Islamic world.

An Italian reporter, Tiziano Terzani, witnessed a rally in Pakistan in 2002 of more than a million *tablighi*, a mass movement of men who had each agreed to give four months a year to the cause of travelling from village to village spreading a purer form of Islam. One told him, 'We don't want to be like you. We don't want to watch your television or your films. We don't want your freedom. We want our society to be governed by the *sharia*.' These men were not all political allies of the Taliban and al-Qaeda, but underground they were watering the soil in which the roots of the violence were growing.

The barefoot missionaries, whose vision of jihad had up to now been a spiritual quest following an internal personal path, were left with no option but to back the outward jihad, the insurgency against secular rule on the frontier, and against US-led forces in Afghanistan. Even if theirs was only silent acquiescence and not open support, it was enough.

'War is not a profession for bin Laden and his people,' Terzani wrote. 'It's a mission. Its roots lie in the faith they acquired in the closed-minded Koranic schools, and above all in their deep feelings of defeat and impotence, in the humiliation of a civilisation, Islam, which was once great and feared but which now increasingly finds itself marginalised and offended by the overwhelming power and arrogance of the West.'

Like the emergence of the Taliban out of the dusts of the Desert of Death in the mid-90s, something was stirring on the frontier again after 2001, fuelled by an ancient prophecy that would sweep all before it and end the humiliation of Islam.

A saying of the Prophet Mohammed in the Hadith speaks of a new army and a new leader rising from Khorassan, an old name for Afghanistan. As the prophecy is interpreted by those telling and retelling it now on the frontier, the army will carry black flags, and be led by the Imam Mahdi, whose coming will signal the battles before the end of the world. At this point, believers say, normal technology will cease to work, so armouries of swords are being assembled in Afghanistan and on the frontier, and youths are learning traditional martial arts for the war that is to come when planes and guns will not function. Osama bin Laden was still somewhere in a cave in the region, but those who believed the events on the frontier were leading to the end of the world did not think it would necessarily be him who would lead the revolt.

The prophecy of the warrior-priest Sheikh Abdullah Azzam, which brought bin Laden into the war against the Soviet Union in the 1980s, had been proved right – the Islamists had defeated one superpower. For that conflict they had had funding and support from Muslim governments all the way from Saudi Arabia to Pakistan. Now, as they were taking on the last superpower, those same governments were seen as enemies as much as the United States itself. In the new conflicts of the twenty-first century, al-Qaeda and the Taliban did not need to rely on governments; they collected money from individuals across the world, especially in the Islamic countries of the Gulf, where the resurgence of the Taliban was seen as fulfilling the prophecy. Could this at last be the emergence of the army of the Mahdi, the black-flagged fighters from Khorassan, after many false sightings during the centuries?

The Taliban's move into the use of suicide bombers fitted the prophecy, as it said there would be killing in 'ways that have not been seen before'. In this fevered atmosphere, the North-West Frontier in the first decade of the twenty-first century became a wartime society no less than it had been in the days of the mujahidin campaign against the Soviet Union. Every Friday in mosques, and not just those in the Wahhabi tradition, preachers ranted against the United States, before raising money for the armed struggle. And spreading person to person through the bazaars, on DVDs, and through the Internet, were speeches demanding total sacrifice. In one made at a wedding, a mullah condemned the use of music for weddings, telling the groom that he should not paint the traditional henna on his hands.

> Allah loves blood not henna now. Blood is a beautiful colour and Allah wants this blood. You should encourage each other to get married without henna, at a young age. If you don't get married then the Americans will take your young girls from you. The reason for Americans to come here is not to make us prosperous, they are lying, I swear by Allah. They are your enemies. Do not sit with them. They are here to dishonour you and enter your houses. They look at your women with dishonour.

It was an appealing message to some Islamic youth, and did not even need to be backed by a majority to fuel worsening violence in Pakistan as well as in Afghanistan. 'In order for a guerrilla war to succeed, a *portion* of the local populace must support or acquiesce to the presence of the indigenous guerrillas in their midst,' wrote US General Theodore Mataxis, whose credentials as a counterinsurgency expert went back to Vietnam. 'There must be a willingness to accept significant casualties – combatant and non-combatant. Guerrillas must have a safe haven and a source of supplies.' The Taliban and al-Qaeda could tick every box – significant local support, a safe haven and source of supplies.

And given the failure of the Pakistani state to provide even basic services in the tribal areas, support for militancy was not surprising. Pakistan's leader at the time of 9/11, General Pervez Musharraf, who had taken power in 1999 in a military coup, was one of the first to sign up for President Bush's 'War on Terror' and received ten billion dollars in aid in return, but little of that money found its way to develop the frontier. By the time President Obama came to office, public spending per head in these tribal areas was one third of the Pakistani average; electricity, water supplies, and health services hardly existed; male literacy was 17 per cent, female literacy a pitiable 3 per cent. The Pakistani legal system was slow and corrupt, while the *sharia* system promised by the Taliban delivered swift justice. An opinion poll in the frontier tribal areas in 2008 showed there was still considerable support for *swara*, the practice of handing over girls to be forcibly married in order to resolve clan disputes.

Amid this poverty and ignorance, the inaccessible mountain terrain and deep clan loyalties in the tribal areas made a perfect base for the Islamist ideological struggle, which had been carefully nurtured by Pakistan for thirty years, boosted with big US financing for the war against the Soviet Union in Afghanistan. The Pakistani Intelligence Service, the ISI, had deep roots with Islamic militancy, having backed it for so long. By the time Pakistan realised the dangers at US insistence after 9/11, it was too late. One former official from Pakistani Intelligence, the ISI, said, 'We indoctrinated them and told them, "You will go to heaven." You cannot turn it around so quickly.' Some agents continued to fund and train fighters that others in the same service were trying to kill.

The fact was that the ISI had lost control of the monster it had created, suffering an 'Islamic blowback' of the most extreme kind as the fundamentalists targeted their own society. The turning point in the history of Pakistan, defining the new battle lines, came when the government stormed the Red Mosque in the heart of Islamabad in 2007, killing around one hundred people and riddling the site with bullets and shells.

The assault on the Red Mosque was a decisive moment, since until that point the fundamentalist mullah who ran it, Abdul Rashid Ghazi, had preached his virulent message with government support and funding. Mullah Ghazi had attracted significant support from students, including a brigade of young women activists, who campaigned for a more restrictive dress code and took direct action against video shops, beauticians, and massage parlours, kidnapping women working there. They had the same ardour for paradise as their male counterparts. Hameeda Sarfraz, the nineteen-year-old daughter of a bus driver, said, 'In heaven, if a martyr feels hungry, food appears, the best quality food, and you won't even know where it came from.' There were many women and some hostages among the dead at the Red Mosque, killed after President Musharraf could no longer ignore the arsenal of weapons being gathered in the heart of the capital.

Before the Red Mosque was stormed, there had been several attempts on the life of Musharraf, seen by many as too pro-American. After it was left a smoking ruin, the number of suicide attacks increased dramatically, including against the very Pakistani intelligence establishment that had such a long history of support for violent fundamentalist groups. The most ominous sign of change was the first suicide attack against buses carrying ISI employees. The insurgency went underground, with messages passed in secret meetings and on the Internet. Previously the ISI had always been able to look into the kaleidoscope and interpret the changing patterns. After the destruction of the Red Mosque, the glass was broken; they could not have controlled the militancy even if they had wanted to. Islamism had slipped its leash.

The Pakistani political establishment took heart from the defeat of fundamentalists in elections in early 2008, but missed the most significant feature of the elections – the low voter turnout in the North-West Frontier, a repudiation by many of democracy itself.

The elections did seem also to offer a glimpse of another Pakistan: a significant and growing part of society that had high hopes for democracy and opposed militancy, in the North-West Frontier as everywhere else. A new middle class was plugged into a vision of a globalised world different from the pan-Islamic caliphate of the jihadis. Private TV channels were a window into another life, where the young looked outwards to the world wearing jeans and not traditional *salwar kameez*, and women did not cover their heads with scarves.

Western policymakers liked the look of this, and backed leaders they could understand – 'people like us'– who spoke the same language, and might even have been to the same university as themselves, rather than searching out other power-brokers with different clothes, customs, and speech.

The high hopes for Pakistan placed on Benazir Bhutto in late 2007 in London and Washington read just like British dispatches about Shah Shuja in the 1830s. Shuja persuaded his British hosts, during his years in exile living on a British salary, that he was the answer for Afghanistan, and was disastrously imposed by force on the country.

Bhutto's assassination during the Pakistan election campaign on 27 December 2007 deprived the world of seeing whether she would fulfil her promise. She knew what the West wanted to hear, writing a book that warned of the perils of Islamic fundamentalism – although in her earlier time in office her government had backed the mujahidin and then armed and financed the Taliban when they first emerged in Afghanistan. Her husband Asif Ali Zardari became president after the election and did change the tone of Pakistani diplomacy, offering concessions to India on nuclear weapons, and forging a better relationship with President Karzai in Afghanistan. But real power still lay with the army and the ISI, a state within a state, controlling much of the national economy. The US had always understood this well. In the six decades after Pakistani independence, US presidents visited the country *only* at times of military dictatorship, never when there was democracy. President Bush continued this dismal record when he visited Pakistan while it was still under military rule after the fall of the Taliban in Afghanistan, but not after its later democratic election. To the Bush White House, democracy was something to be imposed on countries that were defeated – Afghanistan and Iraq – but it was not essential for allies such as Pakistan.

There are uncanny parallels between the time after 9/11 and the early 1980s, after the Soviet invasion of Afghanistan, when President Reagan befriended the Pakistani military dictator General Zia, who had not only ousted a democratic government but also hanged the former president. Both times the United States wanted to make war in Afghanistan – the 1980s and 2001 – a military government in power in Pakistan was facing the threat of sanctions for trying to build nuclear weapons. In supporting President Musharraf after 9/11, the

United States even had to ignore the fact that Pakistan had recently exploded a trial nuclear weapon.

Pakistan's nuclear test in 1998 was performed under conditions of elaborate secrecy – duplicity might be a better word. The test site was camouflaged to look like shepherds' huts while US spy satellites passed overhead. Any movement above ground happened only when the satellites were on the other side of the world. When it came, the explosion deep underground shook the dust from the mountains of Baluchistan, turning them white in an instant. But in the same way as there had been no US criticism of Israel for its nuclear weapons programme, so there would be only the mildest of sanctions against Pakistan, and even those were lifted when Pakistan promised help after 9/11.

Afghanistan's western neighbour, Iran, was treated in quite a different way. US hostility to Iran had been set in stone since the 1979 Islamic revolution that brought the ayatollahs to power. Any Iranian attempt to secure nuclear weapons technology was faced by sanctions backed with an implicit threat of force. In 2001 there was an opportunity for a fresh start in relations after the Taliban fell, but it was not taken up by Washington. Kabul and Tehran had mutual regional interests, including Afghanistan's most important trade route, the repatriation of hundreds of thousands of Afghan refugees who had fled to Iran during the conflict, and a desire to stop illegal drugs smuggling. Iran cannot fail to be involved in the future of Afghanistan, given the length of their shared border – a line on a map of the desert. However many foreign invaders come and go from Afghanistan, Iran will still be on the other side of that border.

Once the Taliban had gone, Iran quickly moved to exert its influence in Herat, the town nearest their border with Afghanistan, building mosques, schools, and a road, and arming Afghan police, while Iranian secret police could be seen driving about, not very secretly. But Iran's inclusion as part of the 'axis of evil' in President Bush's first State of the Union speech after 9/11 complicated the potential for the new

Afghanistan as it tried to form its own relationship with Iran. Local Afghan politicians were at a loss as to how to respond, given their deep links with Iran and their desire to form good contacts with the United States, the new power in the land.

The 'axis of evil' speech in 2002 marked a time between 9/11 and the 2003 invasion of Iraq when international diplomacy appeared to be adrift of its moorings. Classic statecraft, employing the principle that 'My enemy's enemy is my friend', should have ensured at least some US contact with Iran – an appeal for neutrality if not an alliance – before embarking on an invasion of Afghanistan. But instead the United States took an evangelical stand, a realignment of the world between good and evil. It led to an invasion of not one but *both* of Iran's neighbours – Iraq and Afghanistan – as if Iran were not there, with the somewhat inevitable consequences of a multifaceted conflict developing across the region. Feeling encircled, Iran unsurprisingly turned up the heat and did what it could to undermine US attempts to stabilise Afghanistan and Iraq.

This was not taken into account by US political leaders at the time, confident above all of the capacity of superior military technology to deliver results. The awesome scale of US military spending and the competence and professionalism of its forces led to a suspension of normal critical faculties in that strange time after 9/11. The idea that Iran, or any other complicating factor, might affect the restoration of stability in Afghanistan counted as nothing.

But Afghanistan's ancient ability to confound invaders re-emerged in a twenty-first century disguise. When the United States built the first decent road network since the Soviet invasion, Taliban attacks made it too dangerous to use. They switched to classic guerrilla warfare – inflicting damage without seeking to hold ground. Their military commander in 2005, Mullah Dadullah, explained, 'Taking cities is not our present tactic . . . We have attacked and occupied certain locations for a short period of time, to achieve the objectives of the operation. But we will always retreat to our safe bases.' Dadullah was known among his troops as *the lame Englishman* –

'lame' because of a war wound, and 'Englishman' because of his devious ways. With some fanfare, British forces successfully moved a giant turbine at slow speed across Taliban-held ground, fighting all the way, to try to repair power-generating capacity at the Kajaki dam, which had formerly generated power for the south of the country. But once power was restored the Taliban could still disrupt supplies any time by taking down pylons at night.

As British forces had discovered in the nineteenth century, victory was an illusion. Gradually the realisation dawned that the Karzai government did not really exist across much of the country; top-down democracy had not worked. Even where aid programmes had been attempted, most were stalled by the worsening conflict, and military and civilian casualties were rising.

Only Britain, Canada, and the Netherlands were initially willing to put troops alongside US forces on the ground in the south after the Taliban resurgence began in 2005, with the British force being the biggest of these by far. But the politicians who took the decision to send more troops did not anticipate the scale of the task.

The Defence Secretary at the time, John Reid, said, 'We would be perfectly happy to leave in three years and without firing one shot.' But even before the end of the first year British forces had fired more than a million bullets in Helmand in fierce fighting, and had had to withdraw from four towns where they had originally set up positions. The aim of the so-called 'ink spot' strategy had been to spread security in widening areas, like ink seeping through blotting paper, until they all joined up, but the troops came under fierce attack from the day they arrived. They were able to withdraw with their vehicles intact from one of the towns, Musa Qala, only after a controversial deal with tribal elders who brokered a Taliban ceasefire during the withdrawal. The deal was publicly criticised by US officers in Afghanistan, who saw it as a sign of weakness, and Musa Qala was not retaken for another year.

Privately, some senior British officers expressed surprise at the conditions they found in Helmand. They had come to provide support for an aid programme but there did not seem to be much to support, as strict health and safety rules prevented aid workers from going out on the ground.

The army had read General Petraeus's new US counterinsurgency manual, repeating as it did an old lesson warning against trying to fight guerrillas with the single club of military force. They knew that without effective development and a capable, non-corrupt local administration, fighting would never achieve a positive result – especially as the insurgency was fuelled by drug money in an area with an open back door to a ready supply of fresh fighters across the frontier. The politicians may have taken a while to catch up, but British soldiers could see quickly that they would not be leaving 'without firing one shot', as they deployed onto ground where their ancestors had once fought.

Sangin, one of the four towns taken and then surrendered in Helmand, was the place where British forces had first faced the determined opposition of those forerunners of the Taliban, *ghazis*, in the south in 1878. And it had been a fierce uprising across Helmand in the winter of 1840 that was the initial spark igniting the fire that engulfed British forces during that war.

A Guards officer who served in Sangin in the first deployment in the summer of 2006, Captain Leo Docherty, said that much of the military effort appeared to be just for show. There was no coherent plan for the operation in Helmand, but instead just a series of 'disjointed ill-considered directives from headquarters. Everything else, all the well-meaning reconstruction stuff, is an illusion. . . . the time spent there now seems to have been an egotistical folly.' Military adventurism for no good end – it sounded like the campaigns waged on the frontier at the beginning of the twentieth century, mocked then as 'General Willcocks's weekend wars'.

Beyond the obvious deficiencies in development, what led to Docherty and others speaking out was the weakness and duplicity of Britain's allies, including the police, who they saw beating people and keeping confiscated drugs for their own use. 'Violence will surely breed more violence, until the whole thing is beyond our control.' Docherty thought the campaign was lost before it began – a 'tragic replay of Soviet clumsiness'. Their allies were worse than useless: 60 per cent of Helmand's police were heroin addicts. As the fighting intensified and Afghan commanders changed sides, it became difficult to know who to trust. An uneasy feeling grew among senior British commanders that rather than fighting for a government against an insurgency, they were being drawn in on one side of a drug turf war.

In October 2006, after several months of negotiations, I spent a few days with the Taliban opposing British forces near Musa Qala in northern Helmand. The failure of the international community to improve the lives of Afghans since the fall of the Taliban was the first issue raised by a local commander, Mahmud Khan, to explain why the Taliban were making a comeback. 'We gained our freedom from Britain 160 years ago, and should remain free. We don't accept the claim that they are here to rebuild our country. They have done nothing for us.'

Driving around the region with the commander was a little like visiting villages in Britain with a popular local politician. He knew everybody, and stopped often to chat. He made a virtue of the fact that he could walk around unarmed, although he carried a discreet 9mm pistol in a belt slung over the driving seat of the car. He had gathered together a display of captured weapons to show off, including two US heavy machine guns – one mounted on a wheelbarrow – that the Taliban were using against British forces in Helmand.

My security was the Pashtun honour code; I was an invited guest and would be protected. I had a dramatic opportunity to see this in practice when a group of fighters heard I was there and came to kill me. My host, Mullah Abdul Manan, the overall military commander of the Taliban, told them if they wanted to kill me they would have to kill him first, and after a fierce argument he persuaded them to let me live.

He was a thoughtful man with a neat beard and soft, city

hands, quite unlike the stereotype of a Taliban fighter. 'You destroyed our government for just one guest – Osama,' he said. He admitted that mistakes had been made during Taliban rule, and if they returned to power they would not want to impose themselves so harshly on people. But hosting Osama bin Laden was not a mistake in his eyes. We talked until late into the night, in what must have been the women's side of a house commandeered for just that night, as he had to stay on the move all the time. The family were not there, of course, but their presence was everywhere. A Chinese-made sewing machine had been pushed aside and small scraps of cloth littered the floor, soon mingling with the rinds and pith of pomegranates thrown down by the Taliban fighters who filled the room, eating as we talked.

We sat cross-legged on thin felt mattresses lining the wall, with the commander propped up on a cushion in the corner. He spat his pips into a small bowl, breaking off our conversation frequently to listen to a two-way radio, receiving news at one point that a British military vehicle had detonated a landmine.

He denied that the Taliban supported the growing of opium poppies, claiming that they were trying to persuade people to stop because it is against Islam. Since their attempt to return to power, the Taliban have been funded by the opium trade, but the commander said it was the British presence that allowed warlords and bandits to flourish.

The following day I was taken on a hair-raising patrol at high speed for several hours across the desert of northern Helmand, wedged between ten men sitting on the open back of a new Toyota Hilux, their legs over the side. On the way we passed the burnt-out remains of a Spartan armoured personnel carrier, destroyed in August 2006 with the loss of three British lives.

I did not see a single woman while I was with the Taliban, and when we stopped in a village one evening to break the Ramadan fast, kept zealously by the Taliban fighters through the daylight hours, I was ordered to finish eating quickly so we would not lay eyes on the women who would sit where we had sat, with only the scraps from half-eaten communal bowls of food to eat. These remote villages, scattered across the huge expanse of the northern Helmand desert, were very poor, and made poorer by several years of drought. The Taliban arrived and insisted on being fed, although all the villagers had to offer was a little rice, a stew made only of okra, and flat, roughly ground country bread.

Poppy growing has not brought prosperity to many of the people of Helmand caught between the Taliban, drug barons, and the increased pace of the war since 2006. The Taliban did not develop Helmand when they were in power either, but it is now easy for them to promote themselves as protectors of the people, especially as civilian casualties increase. The Taliban took me to a village called Regan, damaged in an SAS night attack a few days earlier.

Two bombs were dropped during the raid. One hit a house, killing six members of a family, including three young girls. Two boys from the family, Sher Ahmad and Nur Ahmed, survived the attack, although both were injured. The other bomb partially demolished a mosque. Then villagers saw four helicopters land. Haji Mullah Sadeq ran out of his house. 'I was carrying two children, one on my shoulders, and one in my arms, when the helicopters landed and they started shooting at me. God saved me and I escaped.' Some of the villagers were too angry to talk to me because I was British. One merely pointed to the torn and bloody women's clothing left in the ruins of the house and said bitterly, 'Are these the kind of houses they have come to build – the kind where clothing is cut to pieces?' NATO sources said the village was strongly defended by the Taliban, who fired on the British soldiers throughout the operation.

While British soldiers were being drawn into this quagmire, the political context could not have been worse. Illegal checkpoints returned to the main road crossing the south, extorting money at gunpoint from every driver. It was to stop just this kind of casual theft by petty warlords in the disorder of the mujahidin years that the Taliban was first formed in 1994. In the new Afghanistan after 2001, those manning the illegal checkpoints were Afghan police and soldiers – the most powerful symbol of how the institutions of the state were just another part of the warlord economy. The checkpoints were a public relations gift to the resurgent Taliban after 2006. They even began to receive payments from their former donors in the trucking companies to fight against the Afghan army and police and their British backers. The Taliban could portray themselves as protectors of the local people and British soldiers as predators.

My trip caused a minor stir at the time, leading to questions in Parliament and attacks by opposition politicians on that more influential cockpit of public opinion – the BBC's *Question Time*. There were even demands that I be tried for treason. A defence minister said, 'We don't need David Loyn to tell us what the Taliban think, we know what they think'– a questionable assertion given that the entire political and military plan had needed to be radically rewritten during 2006 to take account of the situation in Helmand, which was far from what had been at first expected.

A more substantial response to my report came in a letter from the British military commander in the south, pointing out that the Taliban were 'tactically defeated' every time they encountered British forces. It would be remarkable if they were not, given the overwhelming superiority of British technology, training, and firepower. But at what cost? A rough back-of-an-envelope guess by an officer who knew about this kind of thing revealed that to attack a target – for example, a Taliban sniper in a tree – might cost about two million dollars, taking air cover and bombs into account.

It was a new version of Kipling's poem 'Arithmetic on the Frontier', in which an officer with 'Two thousand pounds of education/Drops to a Ten Rupee jezail'. Kipling believed the 'cheaper man' would prevail. A more modern caution against the deceptive lure of tactical superiority came in Petraeus's 2006 counterinsurgency manual, which includes this warning:

'As important as they are in achieving security, military actions by themselves cannot achieve success in counterinsurgency. Insurgents that never defeat counterinsurgents in combat still may achieve their strategic objectives.' In other words, the Taliban have time on their side. Facing forces that could always beat them in a head-to-head confrontation, the Taliban adapted their tactics using hit-and-run raids, roadside bombs, and suicide bombers. They saw that suicide bombers had had a significant impact on morale in Iraq, and although the tactic had not been part of recent Afghan conflicts, it was not unknown in the past, as seen in the assassins who faced inevitable death for an attack on a British officer in the nineteenth century. The senior Taliban commander I spent a few days with in 2006, Abdul Manan, said the tactic of suicide bombing would be employed far more extensively in the future. He was trying to keep control of it. 'There are thousands waiting at the border. We are trying to stop them because they would cause chaos if they all came at once.' He was killed in a targeted air attack a few months after our interview.

NATO spokesmen have characterised suicide attacks as evidence of weakness or desperation from a force with no better options against vastly superior NATO weapons, training, and tactics. This is a dangerous misreading of the tactical thinking behind suicide bombing, a weapon with an impact far more widespread than the immediate casualties – damaging morale and threatening every contact the international force has with the local population. Far from being a weapon of indiscriminate terror, suicide bombers began to be deployed by the Taliban with tactical precision. Using a new strategy on 13th June 2008, an assault on a jail to release more than 400 Taliban prisoners in Kandahar deployed suicide bombers like artillery. After the suicide bombers blew open the gate, Taliban fighters on motorbikes assaulted the prison and released their comrades, who rode away on the backs of the motorbikes.

The attack was yet another reminder that superior military technology is not crucial for success in war in Afghanistan.

After watching the south go from bad to worse, the US sent in more troops. But there were still far fewer troops in the US-led NATO coalition in 2009 than in the Russian force defeated in the 1980s.

There were 100,000 Soviet troops in Afghanistan, double the size of the NATO force; they could be deployed anywhere, and absorb huge casualties, while NATO planners found themselves restricted by the conditions that kept the soldiers of most countries out of the front line. Soviet forces were backed up by more than half a million Afghan soldiers and uniformed militias, strong enough to hold off the mujahidin for three years after the Soviet withdrawal. In contrast, even the most optimistic supporters of the NATO-trained Afghan National Army would not expect them to hold off the Taliban and al-Qaeda for long on their own.

Soviet forces had other advantages too during their long war: they had no scruples about causing civilian casualties; they had a ruthless secret police; they used anti-personnel mines, reducing the number of troops required to defend their bases; they deployed hundreds more planes and tanks than NATO; they had access across a land border they could reinforce easily; and they could bring in fuel through fixed pipelines. And still they lost.

A *Pravda* correspondent was asked to report to the Soviet government on his experiences in the field. Comrade Shchedorov's letter, from 1981, contains lessons for those fighting in Afghanistan more recently, particularly in Helmand. 'Upon completing an operation, the Afghan-Soviet troops as a rule return to their bases and the regions fall back under the control of the rebels . . . In the course of those operations, housing and the agricultural fields are often destroyed, the civilian population is killed, and in the end everything remains the same.' Soviet forces found, as British forces would later in Helmand, that they were fighting over the same ground again and again.

A Russian military analysis after their war concluded that they should have remembered the more distant past:

'Alexander the Great took five years to break the resistance of the Pashtun tribes. Ten centuries later, Arab conquerors met the desperate resistance of the Afghan tribes. Six times they launched an offensive against Kabul and the area of the central plateau. Each time, they were forced to withdraw, having suffered heavy casualties.'

Six years into the Soviet war, a new leader in the Kremlin, Mikhail Gorbachev, signalled a new policy. He would have one last major attempt to control Afghanistan and then pull out if it did not work. In the same time frame in 2007, six years after the US-led invasion, the mood in public statements changed, as the awareness grew that securing Afghanistan would be a marathon and not a sprint.

In London the breezy triumphalism of the Blair years was replaced by a far more realistic assessment demanded by Gordon Brown. Diplomats in the field no longer had to hide their view of how bad things had become, but for the first time could be honest to London about the shallow roots of democracy, the depth of corruption, the weakness of the aid effort, and the growing violence. The new tone echoed the gritty new realism of the early Gorbachev years, that heralded the last desperate attempt by Soviet forces to hold Afghanistan. It ended in defeat and the last Soviet soldier to leave, General Gromov, said that before Gorbachev they had suffered from the 'disease of the stagnation period: to inform the central offices only of what would be well received, rather than what was actually taking place'.

Gorbachev's new direction came in a politburo meeting where he read out letters from the mothers of soldiers serving in Afghanistan, demanding they should be brought home, a remarkable example of grassroots direct action having an effect at the highest level. His orders were clear: 'You'll have to revive Islam, respect traditions, and show the people some tangible benefits from the revolution.'

Substitute 'democracy' for 'the revolution' and Gorbachev's policy could have been written in London in 2007, as a push began to seek Afghan solutions to Afghan problems. An awareness emerged that something different needed to be tried. The social advances boasted about with the arrival of democracy after the fall of the Taliban, such as a higher proportion of women MPs than in many Western countries, rang hollow if it was too dangerous for the MPs to walk the streets of their own constituencies. In late 2008 one of those women members of Parliament, Malalai Joya, even said that for women in Afghanistan seven years after the US-led invasion the 'situation was as catastrophic as it had been under the Taliban'.

Western policymakers, particularly in Europe, began to listen for the first time to those officials who had been patiently proposing that they needed to work with the warp and weft of tribal and religious life, the real Afghanistan behind the illusion. When they looked they found a tribal structure degraded by war – doing deals in the shadows could be an ugly and complex business. But without a dramatic shift in policy of this sort, American, British, Canadian, Dutch, and other soldiers may eventually prove to have fought and died in vain, and the US-led invasion may end up as another foreign failure during the two centuries since the modern world tried to engage with Afghanistan.

The new mood of engagement with Afghanistan was consistent with one of the most important messages in the Petraeus counterinsurgency doctrine – each word headed with a capital letter so the impact could not be missed – 'The Host Nation Doing Something Tolerably Is Normally Better Than Us Doing It Well.' But the problem was that the host nation was becoming increasingly difficult to deal with.

On Christmas Day 2007, representatives of two of the big new international players in Kabul, the EU and the UN, were called to the presidential palace to hear unwelcome news: two of their most senior people were being ordered to leave on the next available flight. It was an extraordinary diplomatic request, the kind of demand made by a pariah regime – for example, the Soviet Union at the height of the cold war – not by a country liberated at no little cost.

Afghanistan was asserting itself, exactly 170 years after the first Russian and British envoys to Kabul, Alexander Burnes and Ivan Vitkevitch, had sat down to a civilised Christmas dinner during their attempts to carve up the country.

President Karzai knew that the international life support system would not be turned off. Although just 5 per cent of government needs could be raised from locally raised revenue, a figure comparable with that of the poorest country in Africa, he was confident that the international community would not use the significant leverage this gave them. He was flexing his muscles after successfully blocking the appointment of the ex-high representative to Bosnia, the British politician Paddy Ashdown, as coordinator of the international programme in Afghanistan. As relations with Western countries, in particular Britain, became increasingly strained, Karzai grew impatient with the West's obsession with women's rights. He told a visiting minister, 'The last king of Afghanistan who tried to give rights to women ended up dead.'

The offence of the two men expelled, Michael Semple and Mervyn Patterson, who were working closely with British intelligence, was to attempt to talk to the Taliban in Helmand. According to Assadullah Khalid, the governor of neighbouring Kandahar Province, the reason the two had to leave was because they were offering money: 'It was like a business deal.' He said that talking to the Taliban was the right of Afghanistan alone; Britain should not interfere.

The problem was that the Karzai government had no strategy for talking to the Taliban. The victors in 2001 had deliberately kept the Taliban out, and although Karzai talked vaguely at press conferences about ex-Taliban figures coming over, he had no interest in bringing the movement into the political mainstream – quite the opposite. His was not an inclusive process. Instead he was playing the game of a nineteenth-century Durrani nobleman, refined by the warlord ethics of the late twentieth century: power was about all or nothing. When a former Taliban minister, living openly in Kabul, tried to hold a meeting of sympathetic mullahs in

Jalalabad to open channels to the Taliban, Karzai put him under house arrest to prevent him from going.

By 2008, when policy changed and Afghan government officials themselves began to open channels with the Taliban in a meeting in Saudi Arabia, it was too late. Western ministers had begun to say openly that there would be no settlement for Afghanistan that did not include the Taliban in some way. But the intensity of the fighting, with around 3000 bombs dropped from the air every year, as infantry and particularly US Special Forces called in air strikes, had radicalised the population. The Taliban were now far less interested in negotiating peace than they had been in 2001.

The failure of the West to distinguish the Taliban from their al-Qaeda allies at the beginning had the perverse effect of fusing the two organisations more closely together. The Taliban had never shared the internationalist dream of Islamist world domination of al-Qaeda, but instead had identifiable nationalist aims; like the IRA in Northern Ireland they had grievances that could have formed the starting point of negotiations. But US and British foreign policy analysts did not make this distinction. Instead policy makers talked of a hard inner core of Taliban that was 'irreconcilable' and a wider circle of 'Ten-dollar-a-day' Taliban who they believed could be split off from the movement. This was a dangerous misreading. The Taliban foot soldiers were, if anything, more extreme than some of their commanders. Like the bearers of the ten-rupee *jezail* a century before, they had a stubborn loyalty to their cause. Even as the organisation became corrupted by banditry and the interests of the opium trade, it remained a coherent force with a clear nationalist agenda. But Western failure to address this reality encouraged a more hard-line stance and a stronger alliance with the global jihadi martyrs of al-Qaeda.

The US forces with the hardest task were those based in the harsh and remote regions on the frontier. They learned quickly and adapted to a new way of fighting that delivered some results: living among the people, spending far longer in the field than other foreign forces – more than a year at a time –

and returning after a break to the same villages they had patrolled previously. It gave them a significant advantage in intelligence gathering. One of the main commanders who developed this strategy was related to John Nicholson, still remembered as 'Nikal Seyn', the maverick but most effective of the British frontier political officers who began the effort to tame the frontier in the 1850s.

But once again the appearance of Afghanistan as seen by the outside world was an illusion, concealing a darker reality. Temporary successes in mountain villages were of no long-term value while there was an open door to Waziristan and an Afghan political system that did not punish corruption.

Soldiers and aid workers worked hard, but too much of the money allocated for reconstruction went straight back to the West in the pockets of security firms and contractors. The aid was a sideshow, given the scale of theft and corruption in the country. The real invasion was the return of warlords, who carved up the country in a 'victor's peace', in the graphic words of a report by the International Crisis Group: 'In many ways the conflict today is a continuation of almost three decades of war involving nearly all the same players . . . Commanders raced to establish their own authority, creating a patchwork of predatory, competing fiefdoms. A culture of impunity was allowed to take root in the name of 'stability', with abusers free to return to their old ways as long as they mouthed allegiance to the central government.'

The jails filled with people who had had their land seized and could not afford to bribe the courts. Afghanistan did not need aid workers, it needed property surveyors and clean justice. But there was no appetite for that in the kleptocracy that emerged as drug barons, warlords, and former mujahidin competed for influence in a classic Afghan power struggle. A World Bank report in 2007 said that it could be argued that the 'prominent foreign presence undermines the very objective of building a credible and legitimate Afghan state'.

As the understanding of this problem grew, Gordon Brown signalled a new direction in policy in April 2009, proposing to focus spending on building a functioning Afghan state, rather than on conventional aid projects such as schools and hospitals. The West had tried everything else. Neither development spending nor democracy had delivered results, putting even more pressure on military forces as they fought a worsening insurgency. Three of the seven parties set up by Pakistan and the United States to fight the Soviet Union in the 1980s were back in the field by 2007, fighting alongside the Taliban against the Karzai government and its foreign backers on ground that favours guerrilla warfare.

Two hundred years after Elphinstone was the first envoy to encounter the country, his caution about war there still held true. He concluded that even if a Western power succeeded in taking the country and putting its choice of leader in power, 'maintaining him in a poor, cold, strong and remote country, among a turbulent people like the Afghans, I own it seems to me to be hopeless'.

Modern tactics may have moved on from the frontier raids derided as 'butcher and bolt', but as the military activity intensified, the effect on an Afghan farmer must have felt exactly the same as the war ebbed and flowed across his fields with no sign of an end. Too many Afghans have experienced a deterioration in the basics of life – food, shelter, access to electricity, employment opportunities, and security. Polio, an unknown disease in most of the world and easily preventable, increased in southern Afghanistan after 2001: a litmus test of neglect – the mark of failure. Older people remember a time before the Soviet invasion in 1979 when there was wealth not generated by poppies – a thriving agricultural economy, roads, electricity, and schools, at least in the cities. Afghanistan considered itself civilised in those far-off pre-war days.

But the thirty-year nightmare that began in the late 1970s meant there was no golden age to look back to for younger Afghans, easily persuaded by preachers of the value of looking forward to martyrdom. The Taliban promoted themselves as the defenders of Afghanistan against another wave of foreign invaders, with a permanent supply of new recruits in the madrassas on the Pakistani side of the frontier. And instability worsened there as more than a million people were displaced from their homes in fighting for the Swat valley in 2009.

The land remained as unyielding as when it was described by George Forster in the 1780s: 'a chain of rocky mountains, whose scanty slips of valley afford but the coarsest provision for human wants', inhabited still by people who 'have made so slow a progress in civilisation'.

And the recourse to political Islam in the region at a time of crisis had not changed either. There were 1.5 million students in madrassas in the frontier area. Some followed the traditional path of inward jihad, but in schools that had become Taliban factories, many more were drawn to war.

The lesson of history was clear: this would be a difficult kind of force to defeat. The US counterinsurgency expert General Theodore Mataxis wrote, 'The guerrillas remained when the French left Algeria and Indochina, the United States left South Vietnam, and the Soviets left Afghanistan. The side with the greater moral commitment, be it patriotic, religious, or ideological, eventually won because of higher morale, greater obstinacy, stronger national will, and the determination to survive.'

The descendants of fighters in the Frontier Corps, first set up under British rule in 1907, fought again in the Swat valley, against militants inspired by the descendants of the political mullahs who had stirred up the frontier tribes against Britain a century ago, and were backed by the United States to defeat the Soviet Union in the 1980s. And now there was a new line of Millennialist thinking, alongside the uncompromising Wahhabi faith, that meant some recruits for the front line believed they were fighting the battles that would bring on the end of the world.

Notes and Sources

One constant theme across two centuries of foreign intervention in Afghanistan has been short-termism. The aspirations of invaders and nation builders alike have never matched the challenges of this magnificent, sometimes harsh country and its complex and courteous, warlike but always gracious people. I owe a particular debt to the insights of a number of journalists and historians in telling the story: Charles Allen, who has done the hard work researching the connections shared by Wahhabi warriors on the frontier of the past and present; Christina Lamb, for her account of motorbike journeys with the young warriors who later led the Taliban; the late George Crile for chasing down that larger-than-life character Charlie Wilson; and Ahmed Rashid, who understood better than anyone the importance of oil and the bigger strategic questions around the Taliban, working more as a detective than a journalist. The politics around the First Anglo-Afghan War have been researched by J.A. Norris, and no one told the military story of that war better than Patrick Macrory. I have drawn most of the narrative for Chapter 3, 'Retreat', from Lady Sale's extraordinary diary.

I am grateful for the assistance of retired Brigadier Bill Woodburn, who was generous and hospitable while sharing his impressions of how Kabul felt in the nineteenth century.

As well as understanding the importance of the Bala Hissar itself, Bill has brought his military engineer's mind to the layout of the cantonments set apart from the rest of the city that were to play such a key role for British forces. The house the BBC has rented for many years, where I usually stay in Kabul, is inside what were the walls of the large cantonment at Sherpur built by Shir Ali for his army, and held by the British force led by General Roberts during the desperate days of the siege of December 1879. It is so big that Bill believes it must have been originally conceived as a new fortified town.

I commend the work of the archivists of the nineteenth century who collected diaries, notes and reports from the frontier and the battlefield for the Political and Secret Department and for Parliament, and their successors in the India Office section of the British Library who preserve this collection with such dedication.

I am grateful to Alex Maxwell for her skill in drawing maps that show what the country feels like, and illustrating them with such beauty. And I pay tribute to my agent Annabel Merullo for constant support.

Other than those already named in the introduction, during the years I have been reporting on Afghanistan I have shared useful conversations with Fisnik Abrashi, Robert Adams, Ashraf Ghani, Amir Shah, Nicholas Barrington, Baqer Moin, Roderic Braithwaite, John Burns, Kate Clark, Tom Coghlan, Daud Qarizadah, Tony Davis, Lyse Doucet, Farah Durrani, James Fergusson, Dick Fyjis-Walker, Phil Goodwin, Adam Holloway, Ismael Saadat, John Jennings, Clare Lockhart, Anthony Loyd, Dominic Medley, Mostapha Zahir, David Page, Colin Peck, the late Juliet Peck, William Reeve, John Simpson, Rory Stewart, Mark Tully, Mark Urban, and Elizabeth Winter. Vaughan Smith was brave and resourceful during several long trips when we travelled light in the months after 9/11, dropping by helicopter behind Taliban lines. He made TV history by transmitting the first news pictures to be sent to the BBC from a laptop through a lightweight satphone link – technology that is now commonplace. And I want to make special mention of some other crews I have travelled with, in particular Fred Scott, Andrew 'Sarge' Herbert, and Vladimir Lozinski, who shared the risks, shooting and editing pictures during the turbulent years between 1995 and 1997 on both sides of Taliban lines as the country fell to this strange new force. Vlad carried the first pictures of the seizure of the Afghan capital by the Taliban on an epic drive from Kabul to Islamabad, bribing guards to let him through the Khyber Pass, in time for the evening news on the day the city fell.

There is no right or wrong way to spell many of the terms used in this book that are transliterations from other scripts. I have tried to steer a course between clarity and authenticity, wanting to retain archaic usage where appropriate – Caubul, Affghanistan, Mahometan – but not where it would obscure meaning. For consistency I have used 'British' when writing about armed forces from the Raj, although the term was hardly used in the earlier period when the word English was far more widespread, and forces were distinguished between those who were native or Queen's army. Similarly I have used 'US-led' for the fluctuating coalitions of foreign forces that have been in Afghanistan since 2001, since the US military contribution has been by far the largest, although under varying leadership as the needs of the intervention have evolved.

I have used Pashtun as the term for Afghanistan's largest tribe, although Pakhtun tends to be used on the Pakistani side of the frontier. The old term Pathan, which long pre-dates the British presence in the region, is now considered derogatory.

Chapter 1   *Wild and Strange*

Page

3   **Elphinstone was dazzled . . .**
     Mountstuart Elphinstone, *An Account of the Kingdom of Caubul*

4   **'events seem rapidly approaching . . .**
     John Crokatt, *Thoughts on the Defence of India*, 28th January 1808

5   **An early British traveller . . .**
     George Forster, *A Journal from Bengal to England*

6   **Personally charismatic, as a teenager** . . .

Sir Edward Colebrooke, *Memoir of the Honourable Mountstuart Elphinstone*

14   **Britain had responded to the threat . . .**
This extraordinary tale of diplomatic incompetence was put together
by Sir John Kaye in *History of the War in Afghanistan.*

19   **One of the early travellers . . .**
Alexander Burnes, *Cabool*

22   **When the British horse-breeder . . .**
William Moorcroft and George Trebeck, *Travels in the Himalayan
Provinces*

24   **A few months later Burnes set out . . .**
Mohan Lal, *Travels in the Punjab, Afghanistan and Turkistan*

25   **These accounts only confirm . . .**
Ellenborough, *Diary*

Chapter 2 *A War of Robbery*

28   **'Russia alone threatens . . .**
John McNeill, *Progress and Present Position of Russia in the East*
'In lieu of distributing . . .
All Kamran Khan quotes are from Mohan Lal, *Travels in the Punjab.*

29   **the best rampart India could have . . .**
J.A. Norris, *The First Anglo-Afghan War 1838–1842*
females, both of high and low family . . .
Mohan Lal, *Travels in the Punjab*

32   **tall stature and haughty . . .**
Mohan Lal, *Life of Dost Mohammed of Kabul.* (This account was written
from memory; his first interviews were seized by Akbar Khan, who
refused to return them, in the chaos in Kabul in 1842.)
Of later years, by all accounts he had been ambitious . . .
Arthur Connolly, *Overland Journey to the North of India*

34   **Vitkevitch had a colourful past . . .**
Russian Expedition to Khiva Under General Perofski in 1839

35   **The English, who are not soldiers . . .**
All of this colourful detail comes from Mohan Lal's *Life of Dost.*

36   **ex-king at Loodiana . . .**
Norris, *The First Anglo-Afghan War*

38   **'a riddle, wrapped in a mystery, inside an enigma . . .**
Coined by Churchill in a broadcast in October 1939

41   **The Russian fiend . . .**
Peter Hopkirk, *The Great Game*

42   **The magnitude of the measures . . .**

Norris, *The First Anglo-Afghan War*

42 **a picture of military splendour** . . .
J.H. Stocqueler, *Memorials of Afghanistan*
an unseemly display of dancing girls . . .
This was Henry Havelock, later the hero of the siege of Lucknow,
quoted in Norris. His statue stands in Trafalgar Square.

43 **You have brought an army into** . . .
Lal, *Life of Dost*

45 **'The only objection is that of expense** . . .
Norris, *The First Anglo-Afghan War*

46 **forlorn hope** . . .
Term used since the sixteenth century for raiding parties sent out
ahead of a main force in face of overwhelming odds
'If Shah Shuja is really a king . . .
Norris, *The First Anglo-Afghan War*

47 **A chief who had come across** . . .
The story of how Outram was foiled in pursuit of Dost is in
Stocqueler, *Memorials.*
'not more than three hundred effective men . . .
Outram quoted in Stocqueler, *Memorials*

48 **respectful, decorous, even cold reception** . . .
Norris, *The First Anglo-Afghan War*

49 **'I cannot but congratulate you on quitting this country** . . .
Patrick Macrory, *Signal Catastrophe*

51 **'The cession by the Sikhs of all the countries west of the Indus** . . .
Macnaghten letters
'most firm friends and most steadfast allies . . .
Letter, September 1837. British Library D 1165/5
'the most unhappy step taken during the campaign . . .
Lal, *Life of Dost*

52 **'I am far from able to decide** . . .
Lal, *Life of Dost*
drive these ferengee Kafirs out of the country . . .
Stocqueler, *Memorials*

53 **'Why is it that Englishmen everywhere are rough** . . .
Macrory, *Signal Catastrophe*
'The Iron is hot . . .
Norris, *The First Anglo-Afghan War*

54 **Shuja's agents went ahead to spread the word** . . .
Lal, *Life of Dost*

55 **they heard the unearthly clang** . . .

Thomas Seaton, *From Cadet to Colonel.* Seaton has a wonderful and warm eye for detail.

Chapter 3   *Retreat*

56 **'a rampart and ditch an Afghan could run over . . .**
Lady Sale, *Diary*
'as great a scoundrel as ever lived . . .
Norris, *The First Anglo-Afghan War*

57 **'a season of such profound tranquillity . . .**
Norris, *The First Anglo-Afghan War*
'The drama that played out on the night . . .
Lal, *Life of Dost*

60 **'death to dishonour . . .**
Lady Sale, *Diary*

61 **'Dangerous it is, but if it succeeds, it is worth all risks . . .**
Lal, *Life of Dost*

63 **'All was confusion from before daylight . . .**
Lady Sale, *Diary*

64 **'An immense number of poor wounded wretches . . .**
Vincent Eyre, *The Military Operations at Cabul etc.*

65 **a persistent Afghan legend . . .**
Louis Dupree walked through the route in 1963 at the same time of year as the retreat, and uncovered strong folk memories of the events. *Journal of the Indiana Folklore Institute*

67 **'The confusion became terrible, all discipline was at an end . . .**
Quoted in Dupree, *Afghanistan*

68 **Captain Arthur Connolly, without fear of retribution . . .**
It was a bad time for the Connolly family: Arthur's brother John died in captivity in Kabul, and another brother had been killed two years before by a sniper.

69 **When he had set out to 'thrash' the rebel tribes . . .**
Seaton, *From Cadet to Colonel*

70 **'most conspicuous from the city . . .**
Stocqueler, *Memorials*

71 **'Returning to Istalif the morning after its sack . . .**
Charles Allen, *Soldier Sahibs*
'I'm sorry; it's the fashion in earthquakes' . . .
When Shelton died in Dublin after falling from his horse in 1845, his regiment went out onto the parade ground to raise three cheers.

72 **The retreat from Kabul, with Lady Sale waving a sword . . .**

Macrory, *Signal Catastrophe*
73 **But the Select Committee of the East India Company ...**
Dupree, *Afghanistan*
As the blame game began ...
Norris, *The First Anglo-Afghan War*
74 **We could prevail upon our dear Friend ...**
Norris, *The First Anglo-Afghan War*

Chapter 4   *The Great Game*

79 **In 1836 an old man arrived in the Russian ...**
Russian expedition to Khiva under General Perofski in 1839
81 **'The position of Russia in central Asia is that ...**
Sir William Fraser-Tytler, *Afghanistan*
82 **'I never heard a word uttered of doubt as to our success ...**
Parliamentary papers, L Parl 2 182
83 **'Yours is an army of tents and camels ...**
John Lawrence, *Lawrence of Lucknow*
'a good, honest, useful piece of rascality' ...
Fraser-Tytler, *Afghanistan*
84 **'You will never be able to get the Afghans to make a treaty ...**
Fraser-Tytler, *Afghanistan*
86 **Fifteen years previously, in his first campaign ...**
Charles Allen, *Soldier Sahibs*
87 **'There is an air of masculine independence about him ...**
Paget and Mason, *Record of the Expeditions Against the North-West Frontier Tribes 1873 and 1884*
'between the eyes, and there they found – a man ...
Olav Caroe, *The Pathans*
89 **Hardly a year passed between 1849 ...**
Parliamentary papers, L Parl 2 284
90 **And now something else was stirring on the frontier ...**
Much of this narrative is drawn from Charles Allen, *God's Terrorists*.
92 **'the inhabitants, a semi-civilised race, are fanatical Mahometans ...**
Edward Thornton, *A Gazetteer of the Countries Adjacent to India*
The American adventurer General Josiah Harlan ...
The model for Kipling's *Man Who Would be King*
93 **mobilised by the akhund of Swat ...**
a name gently mocked in the Edward Lear poem of 1862:
Who or Why, or Which or What, is the Akhund of Swat?
Is he tall or short, or dark, or fair,

Does he sit on a stool or sofa, or chair or squat
The Akhund of Swat?

94 **'the only danger to British rule in India . . .**
Abdur Rahman, *Life*

95 **Tolstoy may be best remembered . . .**
Tolstoy's image of the tough daisy is echoed in the description of the mountain tribes by Badshah Khan, known as the Frontier Gandhi for his efforts to unite and liberate the Pashtun people in the 1930s. 'The courage of our tribal brothers is described as wildness, passion for freedom as lawlessness, their proverbial hospitality as an irrepressible urge [for] begging, borrowing and pillaging . . . Like untended, wild daisies they bloom and fade away in mountain ridges.' Quoted in Rajmohan Gandhi, *Ghaffar Khan*. The Frontier Gandhi's grandson was elected chief minister of the North-West Frontier Province in 2007 with a mandate to change its colonial name.

98 **'savage with a touch of insanity . . .**
Fraser-Tytler, *Afghanistan*

Chapter 5 *'Afghanistan as a whole could no longer exist'*

99 **'A non-recognition of their failures . . .**
General Soboleff was the former chief of the Asiatic Dept of the Russian General staff, and wrote this highly critical account of British military prowess in Afghanistan in order to make the case for an invasion of India. It was translated in Calcutta and widely distributed by Forward policy advocates.
'Afghanistan as a whole could no longer exist' . . .
Fraser-Tytler, *Afghanistan*

101 **the immense importance to us of the triangle . . .**
Parliamentary papers, L Parl 2 284

102 **'affectation to apply the nice distinctions . . .**
Political and Secret Department papers, 1/ps/20/memo3
offered the same as before, 87,000 rupees . . .
Official Account of The Second Afghan War

103 **The first shots in the Second Anglo-Afghan War . . .**
Official Account of The Second Afghan War

107 **'Some of the cavalry I have dismissed . . .**
Parliamentary papers, L Parl 2 182

109 **'only by those who know the coldness of the nights . . .**
Official Account of The Second Afghan War
'act of retributive justice' . . .

Roberts, *Forty-one Years in India*
'Towards the afternoons the main bazaars . . .
Nancy Dupree, *Kabul*

110 **'The prolonged occupation by foreign troops . . .**
Official Account of The Second Afghan War

111 **This was an enormous site with low walls . . .**
I owe this and much other intelligence about the forts of Kabul to retired Brigadier Bill Woodburn.

115 **'rights of the savage'**
Roland Quinault, *Afghanistan and Gladstone's Moral Foreign Policy*

120 **'Total defeat and dispersion of General Burrows's force . . .**
Leigh Maxwell, *My God – Maiwand!*

121 **'Everything which belonged to the state . . .**
Political and Secret Department papers, 1/ps/20/memo3
In the words of an anonymous diary . . .
Political and Secret Department papers, 1/ps/20/memo3

Chapter 6   *The Oasis war and the Durand line*

This chapter is drawn almost wholly from three sources – the beautifully observed narrative by Colonel Holdich, *The Indian Borderland*, and the accounts left by the two negotiators who locked horns over the frontier, the Amir Abdur Rahman, and Sir Henry Mortimer Durand.

130 **'did not know a Pathan from a Poobah' . . .**
The reference is to Gilbert and Sullivan's opera *The Mikado*.

Chapter 7   *'Tribes generally are rising'*

145 **On 3rd November 1895, before first light . . .**
Parliamentary papers, L Parl 2 284

146 **'liberate Afghanistan for Islam from the English' . . .**
Abdur Rahman, *Life*
His book on jihad, passed from hand to hand on the frontier . . .
Abdur Rahman, *Jihad* (translated by Najibullah Razaq 2008)

148 **'The priesthood, knowing that their authority . . .**
Winston Churchill, *The Malakand Field Force*

149 **'Any attempt to subjugate the Waziris . . .**
Parliamentary papers, L Parl 2 284

150 **'had no wish to conquer or dominate the country . . .**
Notes for Parliament on 1897 conflict

'Waziris kill sheep, distribute food and hold meetings . . .
Parliamentary papers, L Parl 2 284

154 **Lieutenant Harry Rattray, the commander of the detachment . . .**
Son of the founder of his regiment – 'Ratrray's Sikhs'

155 **'a boy aged thirteen or fourteen on whose head he bound a turban' . . .**
Parliamentary papers, L Parl 2 284
Bands of *ghazis*, worked up by their religious enthusiasm . . .
Quoted in Charles Allen, *Soldier Sahibs*

158 **'most open and audacious violation . . .**
Notes for Parliament on 1897 conflict
'the unprovoked aggression on Khyber pass gravely affects . . .
Parliamentary papers, L Parl 2 284

159 **'the gateway to the Khyber Pass, was under Subedar . . .**
Colonel H.C. Wylly, *From the Black Mountain to Waziristan*

160 **'Burning houses and destroying crops unless followed up . . .**
In 1900, when he was made Commander-in-Chief in South Africa
during the Boer war, Lord Roberts did not sanction the clearing of
villages. It was only after he returned to Britain that Boer settlements
were systematically burnt and the controversial policy begun of
bringing families into camps where many died from disease.

161 **'The Commander-in-Chief dissents' . . .**
Parliamentary papers, L Parl 2 284

162 **'deal with the hearts and minds of the people' . . .**
Commons debate in 1898, the year after the conflict, Parliamentary
papers, L Parl 2 284. One Liberal MP said in the debate that Britain
was now facing 'patriotism inflamed by fanaticism, and this was a very
much more formidable force than patriotism independent of
fanaticism'.
The Marquess of Salisbury, prime minister . . .
Parliamentary papers, L Parl 2 284

Chapter 8 *Bolt from the Blue*

163 **'His Highness asked me about his marital duties' . . .**
Bird's diary is in Dane family papers.

166 **'infatuated nonsense' of the Forward policy . . .**
David Gilmour, *Curzon*. Curzon had travelled in the region as a young
man, meeting Abdur Rahman, and had won the Gold Medal of the
Royal Geographical Society, credited as the first European to reach

the source of the Oxus River.

166 **'The sudden alarm, the long dust-choked ride . . .**
William Fraser-Tytler, *Afghanistan*. Fraser-Tytler later served on the Frontier in several leading roles, and never forgot the pointless excursions he had undertaken as a young officer.

167 **'None had any substantial experience of the frontier' . . .**
Parliamentary papers, L Parl 2 284
'young British officers have gone in and out among the tribes . . .
Parliamentary papers, L Parl 2 284
'I do not advocate the crushing and disarming of the tribes . . .
Lt Col Sir George Roos-Keppel, *Papers*

168 **Germany has the distinction of being . . .**
Britain was exploiting jihad at that time in Arabia of course.

172 **Since 1911 a highly influential fortnightly . . .**
L.B. Poullada, *Reform and Rebellion in Afghanistan 1919–1929*

174 **'a French municipal office . . .**
Robert Byron, *The Road to Oxiana*

Chapter 9   *'Muslim Reactionaries'*

179 **Congressman Charlie Wilson from Texas . . .**
George Crile, *Charlie Wilson's War*
one of the richest, and certainly the most influential . . .
Ishtiaq Ahmad, *Gulbuddin Hekmatyar*

180 **As a student leader in Kabul in the late 1960s . . .**
Olivier Roy, *Islam and Resistance in Afghanistan*
Development meant that Afghanistan exported . . .
Louis Dupree, *Afghanistan*

181 **The travel writer Bruce Chatwin . . .**
Introduction to Robert Byron's *The Road to Oxiana*
In Kabul student elections in 1970 . . .
Olivier Roy, *Islam and Resistance in Afghanistan*
Daoud rejected offers from the Saudi government . . .
Author interview with ex-student

182 **Pakistan quickly recognised the potential . . .**
Ishtiaq Ahmad, *Gulbuddin Hekmatyar*

183 **Massud was released . . .**
Michael Griffin, *Reaping the Whirlwind*, quoting Jane's Defence Weekly
The Panjshir uprising gave the President . . .
Olivier Roy, *Islam and Resistance in Afghanistan*

Chapter 10   *Charlie Horse*

203 'typical tribal fighting for immediate tangible gains . . .
Mohammad Yousaf and Mark Adkin, *Afghanistan The Bear Trap*
204 'The Feds spent a million bucks trying to figure out . . .
George Crile, *Charlie Wilson's War*
206 'traitors and filthy vultures . . .
Henry Bradsher, *Afghan Communism and Soviet Intervention*
'a circulatory system without blood' . . .
Letter by Colonel K. Tsagolov, translated for NSA archive
207 'more the kind that women liked' . . .
Artyom Borovik, *The Hidden War*
208 Around 1.5 million people died . . .
Estimate by Human Rights Watch: hrw.org
Between them, the mujahidin and Soviet forces . . .
Document in NSA archive

Chapter 11   *'Fighting to the last Afghan'*

211 'The way the freelance cameraman Rory Peck . . .
With thanks to Colin Peck for access to the diary of his late brother
213 'All the dominating heights belonged to Pakistan . . .
Mohammad Yousaf and Mark Adkin, *Afghanistan The Bear Trap*
A Russian journalist who spent a few days . . .
Author interview with Vladimir Snegirev, who was then a Pravda correspondent
214 dangerous travelling companions as they invited martyrdom . . .
Author interview with Rahimullah Yusufzai
A woman in Kabul said . . .
John Fullerton, *The Soviet Occupation of Afghanistan*
215 Among them was a bank clerk called Ramia . . .
Christopher Walker, *The Times*, 28th Feb 1989
216 walk down the middle of the road . . .
Afghanistan Justice Project: *War Crimes and Crimes Against Humanity 1978–2001*
Tajwar Kakar, a schoolteacher who had been tortured . . .
Mark Fineman, *Los Angeles Times*, 12th Feb 1989
Cranborne survived because he had been . . .
Author interview
217 Hekmatyar turned his attentions to the south . . .
Ishtiaq Ahmad, *Gulbuddin Hekmatyar*
'a true monster and enemy of Afghanistan . . .
Ishtiaq Ahmad, *Gulbuddin Hekmatyar*

'Supplying military aid to the Afghan rebels . . .
George Crile, *Charlie Wilson's War*

218 'The Afghans love to fight . . .
Selig Harrison, *Washington Post*
'I am confident of a military victory . . .
Christina Lamb, *Financial Times*, 28th July 1989

220 'the smell of political expediency and compromise . . .
Mohammad Yousaf and Mark Adkin, *Afghanistan The Bear Trap*
'We've been denying our activities there . . .
Henry Bradsher, *Afghan Communism and Soviet Intervention*

221 'shovelled into the ideological pockets . . .
Author interview with the Marquess of Salisbury

222 When a reporter noticed some blood and flesh . . .
This was Ahmed Rashid, who told the story in *Taliban*.

224 'a most theatrical scene developed . . .
Author interview with Mark Urban

225 'One of these rockets hit our house . . .
The personal accounts of horrors during these years, including the
uncovering of the Afshar massacre, are taken from Afghanistan
Justice Project: *War Crimes and Crimes Against Humanity*.

230 After the Hazara army expelled the Taliban . . .
Witnessed by author

Chapter 12   *Virtue and Vice*

239 The origins of the Taliban lie in the dust . . .
Christina Lamb, *The Sewing Circles of Herat*. Among her companions on
her travels in the south in the 1980s was a young Hamid Karzai.

240 'I cannot describe the suffering . . .
Lamb interview with Borjan
In 1994, when two teenage girls from his village . . .
Author interviews in Kandahar

241 'How could we remain quiet . . .
Rahimullah Yusufzai interview with Omar
'Omar was a very brave mujahid . . .
Rahimullah Yusufzai interview with the Black Mullah

243 'the most beautiful example in colour . . .
Byron, *The Road to Oxiana*

247 reputed for a while to be the third largest investor . . .
Ishtiaq Ahmad, *Gulbuddin Hekmatyar*
It almost certainly came from Saudi Arabia . . .

Rashid, *Taliban.* The Saudi ex-spy chief, Prince Turki, has denied that he personally handed over this money.

248 **'What's the worst thing that can happen . . .**
Author interview with driver Naqeeb

249 **One seasoned observer of the Afghan scene . . .**
Tony Davis, *How the Taliban Became a Military Force* – from *Fundamentalism Reborn*

251 **'In the worst days of the war we went out . . .**
Author interview

253 **'It is true to say that a large number of Taliban . . .**
Author interview

254 **The head of the south Asia desk at the State Department . . .**
Raphel had a curious personal connection with the region. Her former husband Arnold, divorced at the time of his death, was the US Ambassador to Pakistan killed in the plane crash that killed General Zia in 1988. All Raphel quotes here are from Ahmed Rashid, *Taliban.*

255 **'pipelines, an Amir, no parliament, and lots of sharia law . . .**
Rashid, *Taliban*
At the last *buzkashi* game . . .
Author interviews

258 **'I could see smoke coming from the west . . .**
Afghanistan Justice Project: *War Crimes and Crimes Against Humanity*

Chapter 13   *Sons of Dost*

259 **Sajjad, nicknamed 'the Afghan' . . .**
Witnessed by the author

260 **'frozen turbulence' . . .**
Title of book by Jagmohan, governor of Jammu & Kashmir 1983–1987
Pakistan inspired a new armed struggle . . .
Sati Sahni, *Kashmir Underground* (Har-Anand Publications 1999)

261 **Pakistan's funding of training camps in Afghanistan . . .**
Benjamin & Simon, *The Age of Sacred Terror*, and US intelligence documents in the online archive at George Washington University

262 **attributed to the Harkat ul-Ansar . . .**
Or its affiliates; the names of organisations changed often.
Osama bin Laden arrived back . . .
Lawrence Wright, *The Looming Tower*

263 **shaking his hand was like . . .**
This was Peter Jouvenal; the story is told in my earlier book *Frontline*.

265 **TV pictures from Khost showed the pages** . . .
These exclusive pictures were taken by Rahimullah Yusufzai.
Among the dreams of his followers . . .
Documents found by Peter Jouvenal and Anthony Loyd in Osama bin
Laden's house in Kabul after the fall of the Taliban revealed this and
other far-fetched plans.
266 **The vehicles had been delivered** . . .
Rashid, *Taliban*
Turki found that the US missile attack . . .
Wright, *The Looming Tower*
'We may be very poor, we Afghans . . .
Author interview with Rahimullah Yusufzai who spoke to several
people at the meeting
US officials sent a secure satphone to Omar and talked . . .
Rashid, *Taliban*
267 **'Tibet is out** . . .
Quoted in Rashid, *Taliban*
270 **The cover-up began, even in Massud's kingdom** . . .
Witnessed by Rory Peck in 1989
An Islamic cleric in Kabul . . .
Author interview
271 **raised more customs revenues in their last** . . .
Author interview with Clare Lockhart, adviser to the Afghan finance
ministry
272 **'People knew that there were various tribes** . . .
Interview with Alastair Leithead for BBC *Newsnight*, December 2007
273 **'The Taliban and al-Qaeda are no longer capable** . . .
Spokesman for the International Security Assistance Force, 31st
March 2003; quoted on AFP
Hekmatyar announced that he would now fight . . .
Interview with al Jazeera quoted in International Crisis Group report:
Countering Afghanistan's Insurgency, 2nd November 2006. See
crisisgroup.org
controlled as much as 54 per cent . . .
Estimate by Senlis Council 2007
274 **seized by some of those appointed** . . .
ICG report: *Countering Afghanistan's Insurgency*
275 **One appointee for police chief** . . .
Anthony Loyd, *The Times*, 24th November 2007
'There is no government to deal with cases . . .
BBC interview, December 2007

276 **Their chief spokesman admitted . . .**
Author interview
it became fashionable for foreign analysts . . .
For example, the deputy head of the UN mission, Ameerah Haq, interviewed for the ICG report: *Countering Afghanistan's Insurgency*
278 **The Provinces where they successfully . . .**
Author interview
General Aminullah Amerkhel was removed . . .
Author report for BBC *Newsnight*, 2006 (this report was part of a portfolio that won the first Orwell prize for TV news)
279 **just $75 a head in the first year . . .**
Report by Care. See www.care.org/newsroom/specialreports/afghanistan/09302002 policybrief.pdf
President Karzai's helicopter pilot died in childbirth . . .
There's a poignant photo of her at the controls of a helicopter in *Women of Courage – Intimate Stories from Afghanistan* by Katherine Kiviat and Scott Heidler.
280 **'We had a strategy in three months . . .**
Author interview
281 **'The conflict has not only intensified . . .**
Richard Norton-Taylor, *Guardian*, 13th February 2008

Chapter 14   *The Cheaper Man*

282 **In February 2009...**
Sources close to the Taliban speaking to the author
283 **Aid flows to Pakistan increased...**
In April 2009 UK aid to Pakistan was set at £665 million for the next 4 years, and £510 million for Afghanistan.
He had written a new counterinsurgency doctrine...
http://www.fas.org/irp/doddir/army/fm3-24.pdf
An influential book by a British general...
Sir Rupert Smith, *The Utility of Force*, Allen Lane 2005
284 **In 1979 there were some 700 madrassas...**
Ahmed Rashid, *Descent into Chaos*, Allen Lane 2008
285 **'the plague spot of the frontier'**
Lt Col Sir George Roos-Keppel, *Papers,* Mss Eur D613
286 **An Italian reporter...**
Tiziano Terzani, *Letters Against the War*, India Research Press 2002
288 **'Allah loves blood not henna now...**
DVD found in Peshawar and translated by Najibullah Razaq

'In order for a guerrilla war to succeed...
General Theodore Mataxis, quoted in introduction to version of the Russian General staff analysis of the Soviet war in Afghanistan, translated by Lester W. Grau and Michael A. Gress. Mataxis was an adviser to the mujahidin in Afghanistan during the Soviet war.
and received ten billion dollars in aid in return...
Husain Haqqani of Boston University calculates that the overt and traceable U.S. aid to General Musharraf's Pakistan amounted to $9.8 billion – of which 1 per cent went for children's survival and health, and just one-half of 1 per cent for democracy promotion (and even that went partly to a commission controlled by General Musharraf) *New York Times*, 10th April 2007

289 **An opinion poll in the frontier...**
Understanding FATA, www.camp.org.pk
'We indoctrinated them and told them...
Carlotta Gall & David Rohde, *New York Times*, 15th January 2008
'In heaven, if a martyr feels hungry...
Somini Sengupta, *New York Times*, 23rd July 2007

291 **writing a book that warned of the perils...**
Benazir Bhutto, *Daughter of the East*
but hanged the former president...
And by a horrible ironic symmetry, that president was Zulfikar Ali Bhutto, Benazir Bhutto's father.

292 **Pakistan's nuclear test in 1998...**
Author report for BBC News
US hostility to Iran...
There is good evidence that the crucial part of the jigsaw, tipping the Soviet Union to invade Afghanistan in 1979, was the belief that the USA would invade Iran, threatening to change 'the military-strategic situation in the region to the detriment of the interests of the Soviet Union'. Georgy Kornienko, *The Cold War: Testimony of a Participant*, online archive at George Washington University
Iran quickly moved to exert its influence in Herat...
Author report for BBC *Newsnight*, January 2002

293 **'Taking cities is not our present tactic...**
Interview for Al Jazeera, 2006; Dadullah was targeted and killed in May 2007.

294 **'We would be perfectly happy to leave in three years...**
BBC interview, 24th April 2006
British forces had fired more than a million bullets in Helmand...
This figure was divulged in a parliamentary answer and became the

title of James Fergusson's book on the first phase of the Helmand campaign: *A Million Bullets*, Bantam Press, 2008.

only after a controversial deal with tribal elders...

Author interview with the Taliban who did the deal; this aspect remained strongly disputed by British commanders on the ground.

295 **'disjointed ill-considered directives from headquarters...**

Leo Docherty, *Desert of Death*

299 **A defence minister said...**

Adam Ingram on *Newsnight*, 26th October 2006

the British military commander in the south...

Brigadier Ed Butler in a letter to the *Independent*

300 **suicide bombers were deployed almost as artillery**

Tom Coghlan, *Daily Telegraph*, 15th June 2008

301 **There were 100,000 Soviet troops...**

These figures are from a military analyst with long experience in Afghanistan, who was not willing to be named.

Comrade Shchedorov's letter...

Letter to the central committee of the communist party, 12th November 1981, online archive at George Washington University

302 **'Alexander the Great took five years...**

The Russian General staff analysis edited by Grau and Gress

'disease of the stagnation period...

Artyom Borovik, *The Hidden War*

'You'll have to revive Islam...

Anatoly Chernyaev, *Notes from the Politburo*, 17th October 1985, online archive at George Washington University

303 **'situation was as catastrophic as it had been...**

Malalai Joya, acceptance speech at the Frontline Club in London after winning the Anna Politkovskaya award, 7th October 2008

304 **Although Afghanistan could raise just 5 per cent...**

UK International Development Secretary Douglas Alexander in evidence to International Development Committee of House of Commons, 17th January 2008

The last king of Afghanistan who tried...

Alexander in evidence to International Development Committee

According to Assadullah Khalid, the Governor...

Author interview 20th February 2008

When a former Taliban minister, living openly in Kabul...

Author interview on condition of anonymity, December 2007

306 **'victor's peace', in the graphic words of a report...**

International Crisis Group, *Countering Afghanistan's Insurgency: No Quick Fixes*, 2006

The jails filled with people who had had their land seized...
Author interview with Sibghatullah Mujaddidi, Speaker of the upper
house of the Afghan Parliament, 2006
prominent foreign presence undermines...
Service Delivery and Governance at the Sub-National Level in Afghanistan,
World Bank, July 2007

307 **'maintaining him in a poor, cold, strong...**
Mounstuart Elphinstone, *An Account of the Kingdom of Caubul,* 1815

308 **'a chain of rocky mountains...**
George Forster, *A Journey from Bengal to England,* 1790
There were 1.5 million students in madrassas
Estimate by Hanif Atma, Afghan Education Minister, in author
interview, November 2007
General Theodore Mataxis wrote...
Quoted in introduction to the Russian General staff analysis of the
Soviet war in Afghanistan, translated by Grau and Michael

Bibliography

Books

Ahmad, Ishtiaq, *Gulbuddin Hekmatyar* (Pangraphics Pvt)

Allen, Charles, *Soldier Sahibs* (John Murray 2000)

Allen, Charles, *God's Terrorists* (Little, Brown 2006)

Benjamin, Daniel & Stephen Simon, *The Age of Sacred Terror* (Random House 2002)

Bergen, Peter, *Holy War, Inc – Inside the Secret World of Osama bin Laden* (Weidenfeld & Nicolson 2001)

Bhutto, Benazir, *Daughter of the East* (Simon & Schuster 2007)

Binyon, T.J., *Pushkin* (Harper Collins 2002)

Borovik, Artyom, *The Hidden War – A Russian Journalist's Account of the Soviet War in Afghanistan* (Faber and Faber 1991)

Bradsher, Henry, *Afghan Communism and Soviet Intervention* (OUP 1999)

Burnes, Lieut Col Sir Alexander, *Cabool – A Personal Narrative of a Journey to, and Residence in That City* (1841, reprinted Indus Publications 1986)

Byron, Robert, *The Road to Oxiana* (reprint Pimlico 2004)

Campbell, Alastair, *The Blair Years* (Hutchinson 2007)

Caroe, Sir Olaf, *Soviet Empire – The Turks of Central Asia and Stalinism* (Macmillan 1953)

Caroe, Sir Olaf, *The Pathans* (OUP 1958)

Churchill, Winston S., *The Story of the Malakand Field Force: An*

Episode of Frontier War (Longmans 1898)

Coll, Steve, *Ghost Wars* (Penguin 2004)

Connolly, Arthur, *Overland Journey to the North of India* (1829)

Crile, George, *Charlie Wilson's War* (Thorndike 2003)

Curzon, George Nathaniel, *The Pamirs and the Source of the Oxus* (1896, reprinted Elibron Classics 2005)

David, Saul, *Victoria's Wars – the Rise of Empire* (Viking Penguin 2006)

Dey, Kally Prosono, *Life of Sir Louis Cavagnari* (1881 Calcutta)

Docherty, Leo, *Desert of Death* (Faber 2007)

Dupree, Louis, *Afghanistan* (Princeton University Press 1978)

Eggermont, P.H.L., *Alexander's Campaigns in Sind and Baluchistan* (Leuven University press 1975).

Elliott, Jason, *An Unexpected Light* (Picador 1999)

Dupree, Nancy Hatch, *Afghanistan* (Afghan Tourist Organisation 1978)

Dupree, Nancy Hatch, *An Historical Guide to Kabul* (Afghan Tourist Organisation 1972)

Ellenborough, Lord, *Diary 1828–1830* (published 1881)

Elphinstone, Mountstuart, *An Account of the Kingdom of Caubul* (1815, reprinted Indus publications 1992)

Eyre, Sir Vincent, *The Military Operations at Cabul, Which Ended in the Retreat and Destruction of the British Army* (John Murray 1843)

Forster, George, *A Journal from Bengal to England, Through the Northern Part of India, Kashmir, Afghanistan and Persia, and Into Russia by the Black Sea* (1790)

Fraser-Tytler, Sir William, *Afghanistan – A Study of Political Developments in Central Asia* (OUP 1950)

Fullerton, John, *The Soviet Occupation of Afghanistan* (Methuen 1984)

Gandhi, Rajmohan, *Ghaffar Khan* (Penguin India 2004)

Gilmour, David, *Curzon* (John Murray 1994)

Girardet, Edward, *Afghanistan: The Soviet War* (Croom Helm 1985)

Giustozzi, Antonio, *Koran, Kalashnikov and Laptop – The Neo-Taliban Insurgency in Afghanistan* (Hurst 2007)

Grau, Lester W., *The Bear Went Over the Mountain* (Frank Cass 1998)

Green, Col Sir Henry, *The Defence of the North-West Frontier of India, With Reference to the Advance of Russia in Central Asia* (1873)

Griffin, Michael, *Reaping the Whirlwind* (Pluto Press 2003)

Halliday, Fred, *Threat from the East* (Pelican 1982)

Hensman, Howard, *The Afghan War of 1879–80* (Allen 1881)

Herodotus, *The Histories* (translated by Aubrey de Selincourt, Penguin 2004)

Hodson, Peregrine, *Under a Sickle Moon – A Journey Through Afghanistan* (Abacus 1986)

Holdich, Sir T.J., *The Indian Borderland* (Methuen 1901)

Hopkirk, Peter, *The Great Game* (OUP 1991)

Hopkirk, Peter, *On Secret Service East of Constantinople* (Murray 1994)

Jalal, Ayesha, *Partisans of Allah – Jihad in South Asia* (Sang-e-Meel Publications 2008)

Kaye, Sir John, *History of the War in Afghanistan* (W.H. Allen 1851)

Kepel, Gilles, *Jihad – The Trail of Political Islam* (I.B. Tauris 2004)

Khalil, Jehanzeb, *Mujaheddin Movement in Malakand and Mohmand Agencies 1900–1940* (Hanns Seidel Foundation 2000)

Kipling, Rudyard, *Kim* (Macmillan 1901)

Lal, Mohan, *Life of Dost Mohammed Khan of Kabul* (Longmans 1846; reprint 2004 Asian Educational services, New Delhi)

Lal, Mohan, *Travels in the Punjab Afghanistan &c* (W.H. Allen 1846)

Lamb, Christina, *The Sewing Circles of Herat: My Afghan Years* (HarperCollins 2002)

Lawrence, John, *Lawrence of Lucknow* (Hodder 1990)

Lermontov, Mikhail, *A Hero of Our Time* (translated Paul Foote, Penguin Classics 2001)

Macrory, Patrick, *Signal Catastrophe – The Retreat from Kabul 1842* (Hodder & Stoughton 1966)

Maley, William, ed., *Fundamentalism Reborn? Afghanistan and the Taliban* (Hurst 1998)

Maxwell, Leigh, *My God – Maiwand!* (Leo Cooper 1979)

Molesworth, G.N., *Afghanistan 1919* (Asia publishing house 1962)

Moorcroft, William and George Trebeck, *Travels in the Himalayan Provinces of Hindustan and the Punjab from 1819 to 1825* (Reprinted OUP 1979)

Mortimer, Edward, *Faith and Power – the Politics of Islam* (Faber & Faber 1982)

Norris, J.A., *The First Anglo-Afghan War 1838–1842* (Cambridge 1967)

Paget and Mason, *Record of the Expeditions Against the North-West Frontier Tribes 1873 and 1884* (Whiting and Co)

Poullada, L.B., *Reform and Rebellion in Afghanistan 1919–1929* (Cornell University Press 1973)

Rahman, Abdur, *The Life of Abdur Rahman, Amir of Afghanistan* (1895)

Rahman, Abdur, *Jihad* (translated by Najibullah Razaq 2008)

Rana, Muhammad Amir, *A to Z of Jehadi Organisations in Pakistan* (Mashal 2007)

Rashid, Ahmed, *Taliban – The Story of the Afghan Warlords* (I.B. Tauris 2000)

Roberts, Lord, *Forty-one Years in India* (Richard Bentley 1897)

Robertson, Charles Gray, *Kurrum, Kabul and Kandahar – Three Campaigns Under General Roberts* (reprinted Sang-e-Meel Publications 2002)

Robertson, Sir George, *Chitral: The Story of Minor Siege* (reprint Bhavana Books 2001 New Delhi)

Roy, Olivier, *Islam and Resistance in Afghanistan* (Cambridge 1986)

Roy, Olivier, *Failure of Political Islam* (Harvard 1994)

Russian General staff, *The Soviet-Afghan War* (translated and edited by Lester W. Grau and Michael A. Gress, University Press of Kansas 2002)

Sale, Lady Florentia, *Journal of the Disasters in Afghanistan* (John Murray 1843)

Sale, Gen Sir Robert, *The Defence of Jellalabad* (1843)

Seaton, Maj Gen Sir Thomas, *From Cadet to Colonel* (Hurst and Blackett 1866)

Smith, Vincent, *Oxford History of India* (OUP 1981)

Soboleff, Maj Gen L.N., *The Anglo-Afghan Struggle* (translated and printed by the superintendent of govt printing, Calcutta 1885)

Spear, Percival, *The Oxford Modern History of India 1740–1975* (OUP 1965)

Stewart, Rory, *The Places In Between* (Picador 2004)

Stocqueler, J.H., *Memorials of Afghanistan* (Calcutta 1843)

Thornton, Edward, *A Gazetteer of the Countries Adjacent to India* (1844, reprinted Indus Publications 1996)

Tolstoy, Nikolai, *Hadji Murat* (translated by Hugh Alpin, Hesperus 2003)

Urban, Mark, *War in Afghanistan* (Macmillan 1988)

Vigne, Godfrey T. A., *Personal Narrative of a Visit to Ghazni, Kabul and Afghanistan and of a Residence at the Court of Dost Muhammad; With Notices of Ranjit Singh, Khiva and the Russian Expedition* (1840)

Wright, Lawrence, *The Looming Tower – Al-Qaeda's Road to 9/11* (Allen Lane 2006)

Wylly, Colonel H.C., *From the Black Mountain to Waziristan* (Macmillan 1912)

Younghusband, Captain F.E. and Captain G.J., *Relief of Chitral* (1895)

Yousaf, Mohammad and Mark Adkin, *Afghanistan The Bear Trap* (Pen & Sword Books 1992)

Russian Expedition to Khiva Under General Perofski in 1839 (translated by the superintendent of government printing, Calcutta 1867)

Official Account of The Second Afghan War 1878–1880 (John Murray 1908)

The Truth About Afghanistan (Novosti Press Agency Publishing House 1986)

The Russian General staff, *The Soviet-Afghan War* (translated and edited by Lester W. Grau and Michael A. Gress, University Press of Kansas 2002)

India Office records in the British Library

Crokatt, John, *Thoughts on the External Defence of India from the Projected Invasion of the French and Russians* 1808. Mss Eur D1070

Dane, Sir Louis William, *Papers.* D 659 1–11 (includes Dr Bird's diary)

Durand, Sir Henry Mortimer, *Papers.* D727/17

Keane, Baron Edward, *Papers* 1840. Mss Eur B315

Macnaghten Sir William Hay, *Letters.* D727/17

Parliamentary Reports – L Parl 2 182; L p&s 20.memo3; L parl 2 284

Masson, Charles, alias James Lewis, *Private Notes of Mr Masson as Drawn Up From Memory: 1827–1829.* Mss Eur B218

Roos-Keppel, Lt Col Sir George, *Papers.* Mss Eur D613

Articles and websites

Administration of Sir John Lawrence (Calcutta Review 1869)

Afghanistan-USSR Boundary, Office of the Geographer (US State Dept. 1983)

An 'Anglo-Indian', *Our Russian Neighbours and How to Deal with Them* (Calcutta Review 1868)

Colebrooke, Sir Edward, *Memoir of the Honourable Mountstuart Elphinstone* (Journal of the Royal Asiatic Society 1861)

Dupree, Louis, *The Retreat of the British Army from Kabul* (Journal of the Indiana Folklore Institute Vol 4, 1967)

Green, Col Sir Henry, *The Great Wall of India* (The Nineteenth Century, May 1885)

McNeill, John, *Progress and Present Position of Russia in the East* (1836)

Quinault, Roland, *Afghanistan and Gladstone's Moral Foreign Policy* (History Today, December 2002)

Trench, Captain F., *The Central Asian Question* (Royal United Services Institute lecture, 1873)

www.crisisgroup.org:

Countering Afghanistan's Insurgency: No Quick Fixes (Asia Report N°123, 2nd November 2006)

Afghanistan's Endangered Compact (Asia Briefing N°59, 29th January 2007)

Afghanistan: The Need for International Resolve (Asia Report N°145, 6th February 2008)

http://www.gwu.edu/~nsarchiv/NSAEBB/NSAEBB227/index.htm
US and USSR docs on Afghanistan

www.**afghanistan**justiceproject.org/**warcrimes**and**crimes against**humanity19782001.pdf
Afghanistan Justice project: *War Crimes and Crimes Against Humanity 1978–2001*

http://www.fas.org/irp/doddir/army/fm3-24.pdf
David Petraeus, *US counterinsurgency doctrine*

Index

Shuja, Shah
Elphinstone's meeting with, 3,
5, 11, 13
defeated by Sikhs, 21
loses power and flees, 21–2
British support claims of, 36, 37,
39, 40, 41
with British force entering
Afghanistan, 41, 44
Dost Mohammed loses throne
to, 46
orders execution of
fundamentalists, 47, 90
returns to Kabul, 48–9
difficult relationship with the
British, 54
failings become apparent, 57
mosques stop praying for, 57
and insurgency, 58, 59, 60–1
killed by mob, 68
brief references, 53, 260, 272, 291
Shuja al-Mulk, 152
Shutar Gardan Pass, 134, 140
Sikhs
British alliance with, 21
defeat Shuja, 21–2
and battle of Jamrud, 30
British policy towards, 30
Dost Mohammed aims to
confront, 31
and British negotiations with
Dost Mohammed, 32, 34
Shuja agrees to pay tribute to,
39
Britain expects support from,
39–40
Dost Mohammed accused of
unprovoked attacks on, 40
and British invasion force, 42–3
succession problems after death
of Ranjit Singh, 45

forces support the British, 47
act against British interests, 51
British ignore Macnaghten's
warnings about, 51
wars with Britain, 83
British view of, 87
mujahidin threat to, 91
brief references, 50, 57, 85, 88,
89, 112, 141
Silk Gorge, 248–9
Silk Road, 94–5, 118, 243
Simla, 100, 107, 158, 159
Simla Manifesto, 40, 74
Simonich, Count, 38
Simpson, John, xvii
Sind, 83, 112
Singh, Bow, 58
Sittana, 91
Snowflake, 179, 198, 210
Soboleff, Major General L.N.,
99
Somnath, 74
Soraya, Queen, 175
Souter, Captain, 67, 73
Soviet Union
relations with Britain in 1920s,
171
events leading up to invasion of
Afghanistan, 183–4, 185–8
decision to invade, 188–9
invasion, 189–90
international response, 190–1,
198–9
mujahidin struggle against see
mujadidin
initial response to mujahidin,
192–3
shift in military policy, 193
CIA view about battleground
against, 195–6
tactics, 199

354

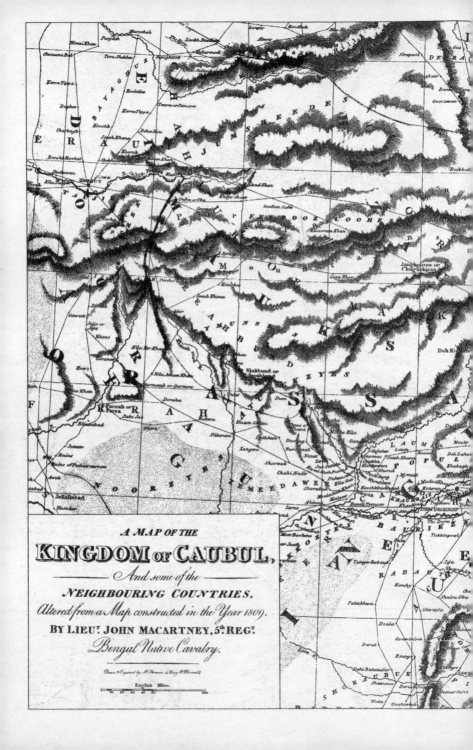

A MAP OF THE

KINGDOM OF CAUBUL,

And some of the

NEIGHBOURING COUNTRIES,

Altered from a Map constructed in the Year 1809.

BY LIEUT. JOHN MACARTNEY, 5TH. REGT.

Bengal Native Cavalry.

English Miles.

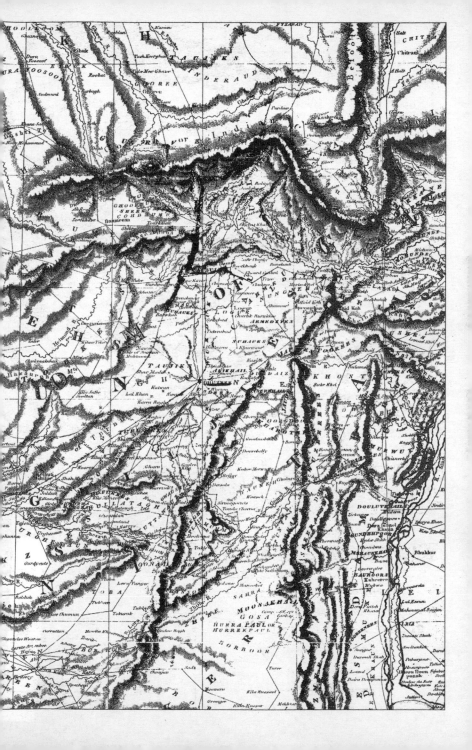